Object Relations in Psychoanalytic Theory

Object Relations in Psychoanalytic Theory

Jay R. Greenberg and Stephen A. Mitchell

Harvard University Press 1983

Cambridge, Massachusetts, and London, England

Eleventh printing, 1998

This book is printed on acid-free paper, and its binding materials
have been chosen for strength and durability.

Library of Congress Cataloging in Publication Data

Greenberg, Jay R., 1942-
    Object relations in psychoanalytic theory.

    Bibliography: p.
    Includes index.
    1. Psychoanalysis.   2. Interpersonal relations.
I. Mitchell, Stephen A., 1946-   .   II. Title.   [DNLM:
1. Object attachment.   2. Psychoanalytic theory.
WM 460.2.02 G7980]
BF173.G714   1983   150.19'5   83-8580
ISBN 0-674-62975-2

Grateful acknowledgment is made for use of material from the following:
Wallace Stevens, "Le Monocle de Mon Oncle," from *The Collected Poems
of Wallace Stevens,* 1955; copyright by Wallace Stevens. Reprinted by per-
mission of Alfred A. Knopf, Inc.;   William Butler Yeats, "Crazy Jane
Talks with the Bishop," from *The Collected Poems of W. B. Yeats;* copyright
1933 by Macmillan Publishing Company, renewed 1961 by Bertha Georgie
Yeats. Reprinted by permission of Macmillan Publishing Co., Inc., Michael
B. Yeats, Annie Yeats, and Macmillan, London Ltd.;   William Carlos
Williams, *Paterson,* copyright 1946 by William Carlos Williams. Reprinted
by permission of New Directions Publishing Corporation.

To Olga and Margaret

Preface

The idea for this book grew out of our experiences in teaching aspects of the historical development of psychoanalytic ideas. Both of us had taught courses organized along conventional lines—Freud, the American "ego psychologists," Sullivan, the "British school" of object relations, and so on. Although this way of dividing the material has merit — particularly in maintaining boundaries between systems that operate on the basis of incompatible and potentially confusing fundamental assumptions—it also has limitations. We had struggled to help students grasp something of the larger context from which various traditions of psychoanalytic theorizing have emerged and understand the common conceptual problems for which adherents of each tradition have fashioned unique solutions. This required us to venture outside the framework of a specific theory to draw comparisons with other approaches.

Many discussions of the challenge of teaching theory revealed that we were reacting to the problems in quite similar ways. On the one hand, we had concluded that it was impossible to teach Sullivan as if his approach was entirely *sui generis,* having nothing to do with his complex and often ambivalent reaction to Freud. On the other hand, the intricate theoretical emendations introduced by Freud's loyal followers could not be understood fully without realizing that they had been created at a time when the basic premises of Freud's original model were under attack by the interpersonalists, the culturalists, and the object relations theorists. A full appreciation of the evolution of Freud's thinking—a sense of *why* the theory changed *when* it changed — requires careful evaluation of the provocative role of his early adherents who eventually became opponents of Freudian psychoanalysis.

Out of these considerations came our decision to write this book. We needed an organizing principle through which the dialectic tension between competing theories could be understood, and we found it in the currently popular concept of "object relations," the general term encompassing people's relationships with others. These relationships are and always have been central to the *clinical practice* of psychoanalysis, but assigning them a theoretical role remains controversial. We believe that understanding different approaches to object relations contributes to understanding the various trends in the evolution of psychoanalytic thinking in the different schools.

The organization of the book follows naturally from its purpose. Part One explores the troublesome term "object relations" and takes up general considerations of the place and nature of theory in psychoanalysis. We then turn to the work of the two men who, more than any others, are responsible for the initiation of the two conceptual models that have dominated the field. We examine Freud's creation of psychoanalysis in terms of his early decision to build his theory on a vision of man emphasizing the internal workings of a psychic apparatus fueled by the energy of instinctual drive. We follow his later work as he moved toward integrating forces derived from relations with external reality into a psychic apparatus that is still essentially governed by the operation of the drives. We then consider the innovative significance of Sullivan's alternative framework of the interpersonal field and his study of the development of the self. We demonstrate that Sullivan's radical departure from the drive model constitutes a fundamentally different approach to the problem of object relations, with vastly different implications for theory-construction.

Part Two examines the major figures within the British tradition of object relations theory. Each of the authors included has chosen to reject significant aspects of Freud's drive theory. The seminal work of Melanie Klein, with her altered meaning of the concept of drive, serves as a transition from drive theory to subsequent approaches. Fairbairn's "object relations theory of the personality" is considered in detail, with emphasis on his divergence from both classical drive theory and the Kleinian approach, leading to a model which is quite compatible with Sullivan's. Turning to the rich and innovative writings of Winnicott, we attempt to clarify his subtle blend of language derived from the Freudian and Kleinian traditions with the object relational concepts developed from his study of mother-infant interactions. We evaluate the extent to which Guntrip's extensions of Fairbairn's theoretical system are an emendation of the latter's work or a new and radically different approach to psychopathology.

Part Three presents the work of theorists who approach object relations through the conceptual model of Freud's drive theory. Each author considered retains drive at the center of the theory but attempts to modify the theory to account for the data derived from the study of object relations. We review the work of Heinz Hartmann, the most elegant and comprehensive drive theorist after Freud himself, in terms of his attempt to make psychoanalysis a general psychology and to integrate into the theory considerations derived from man's need to adapt to and live in a world of other people. We turn next to the mutually complementary contributions of Edith Jacobson and Margaret Mahler, each of whom attempts to reconcile drive theory with data generated by the study of the early relationship between mother and child. Jacobson stresses aspects of fantasy inferred from clinical work with severely disturbed adult patients, while Mahler draws primarily on the study of very ill children and on direct observation of the behavior of normal children and their mothers. We consider the attempt of Otto Kernberg to retain his lineage with Freud by integrating the approach of Jacobson and Mahler with concepts imported from the work of Klein and Fairbairn.

Part Four is a broader consideration of strategies of psychoanalytic theory-construction. Some authors have attempted to reconcile their concern for continuity with their interest in innovation by mixing different conceptual models. We examine the various strategies of Heinz Kohut, the most important recent proponent of such an approach. His effort, like that of Joseph Sandler, who pursues the same theoretical strategy in a very different way, runs into difficulties that suggest an ultimate incompatibility between the two major models which have dominated psychoanalytic thought. In the final chapter, we explore the influence, durability, and fundamental divergence between the two models by considering them as manifestations of two alternative currents within the larger tradition of Western social philosophy.

This book has been a richly rewarding collaborative effort. It was four years ago that we discovered that we were planning to write the same book, and the ensuing development, dialogue, and integration have resulted in one that well expresses a confluence of our interests and understanding. Many people have made important contributions to our work. First among these has been Dr. Earl Witenberg, Director of the William Alanson White Institute. Dr. Witenberg was aware of our project from the outset, and his generous encouragement was largely responsible for its getting beyond the early planning stages. Even where his perspective differed from our own, he was consistently supportive and helpful.

Of those who have read all or parts of the manuscript, Drs. Merton Gill and Philip Bromberg deserve special mention. Each devoted a great deal of time to thinking through the issues we have addressed, and has offered most useful and incisive suggestion. Others who made helpful comments include Ms. Ruth Gruenthal and Drs. James Grotstein, David Halle, Jay Kwawer, Linda Marcus, James Meltzer, Richard Rubens, Robert Shapiro, and Brenda Tepper.

Arthur Rosenthal, Director of Harvard University Press, has been a tremendous source of support throughout our work. More recently, Ann Louise McLaughlin has edited the manuscript with unfailing good humor and a sharp eye for the clumsy sentence. We gratefully acknowledge their crucial role in turning an idea into a book.

In addition to these acknowledgments, which we share equally, each of us would like to mention individually those who have been closest to us personally during our work.

I would like to give special thanks to Drs. John Schmerler and Rona Bank, whose painstaking, thoughtful, and challenging reading of various drafts improved their quality considerably, and to Dr. Joseph Newirth, whose encouragement and counsel throughout the long process of producing the book has been deeply appreciated. I would also like to express my gratitude to my wife, Margaret Black, whose impact on my contribution to the book is difficult to delineate because it has been deeply pervasive. So many of my ideas have been born and shaped in dialogue with her that attribution is impossible beyond an expression of deep thankfulness for the opportunity to share with her so much of my fascination with the intricacies and richness of the psychoanalytic process and psychodynamic theorizing.   S.M.

I owe a tremendous debt to my wife, Dr. Olga Cheselka, who has contributed both personally and professionally to everything I have done here. Her critical listening to ideas as they took shape, her thoughtful and always kind comments on them, and the personal support for the often preoccupying nature of the task made my work on the book possible.   J.G.

Contents

It is just this confrontation of object and subject, their mingling and identification, the resultant insight into the mysterious unity of ego and actuality, destiny and character, doing and happening, and thus into the mystery of reality as an operation of the psyche — it is just this confrontation that is the alpha and omega of all psychoanalytical knowledge.

— THOMAS MANN, "Freud and the Future"

Introduction

For student and practitioner alike, the current state of psychoanalytic theory, with its complexity and heterogeneity, often seems overwhelming. Psychoanalytic therapy has become the treatment of choice for a far wider range of patients than had been thought possible until recently. New patients lead to new clinical data, and in turn to new theories. As a result, a broad spectrum of theoretical positions, each with a distinct line of conceptual development and its own idiosyncratic language, beckons the analyst. Communication among the various "schools" is minimal. Their adherents often attempt to bring order to conceptual complexity by declaring one position to be the only "true psychoanalysis," rendering unnecessary any attempt at integration, synthesis, or comparison with other points of view. This leads to a costly clarity.

To collapse psychoanalysis around a particular approach or a specific mode of interpreting psychodynamic content is to lose the diversity that has made it a vital if difficult discipline. The resulting confusion among theories and premature closure within them has led many clinicians to abandon formal theories altogether, concentrating instead on what they consider the uniqueness of each analytic encounter and on pragmatic technical advice for dealing with their patients. This threatens to deprive psychoanalysis of the exciting interplay between theory and practice that has sustained it over the ninety years of its history.

We believe that a less reductionistic, more synthetic approach is needed. This approach, something on the order of what Roy Schafer

(1979) has termed a "comparative psychoanalysis," will provide a conceptual framework within which the confusion among competing theories can be clarified. A comparative psychoanalysis will aid the theorist and the student of theory by illuminating significant areas of convergence and divergence obscured by the isolation of various psychoanalytic schools from each other and by the internal complexities of each. It will aid the practitioner by drawing out the implications of different theoretical perspectives for a wide range of clinical issues, thus offering a structure for the integration of theory and practice. It is to these goals that our volume is dedicated.

The current diversity of psychoanalytic schools of thought has a long history. In the fifty years following Freud's first major theoretical statements, the most important movement within the field may be described as centrifugal. Freud's theory of instinctual drive served as a focus from which spun one after another divergent movement, each in its own particular direction. These include the early theoretical departures of Jung and Adler, the attempts at revising classical technique by Rank and Ferenczi in the 1920s, and the establishment and elaboration of the major so-called neo-Freudian schools by Fromm, Sullivan, and Horney during the 1930s and 1940s. Those who retained the designation "Freudian" underwent a three-way split. Some adhered to Freud's theory as he had developed it during his own life, refusing to accept any alteration. Among those inclined toward modification, a major ideological schism developed during the 1930s between the followers of Melanie Klein and those who embraced the approach which has become known as American ego psychology (initiated in the work of Anna Freud and Heinz Hartmann). These major divergences were interspersed with innumerable additional revisions and alterations which attracted less notice and smaller followings.

In the last twenty years there has been a reversal of this centrifugal movement. Underlying the apparent diversity of contemporary psychoanalytic theory there is a convergence of basic concerns. Comparing the works of today's theorists is like looking at different paintings of the same landscape by painters from varying stylistic and aesthetic traditions. What first meets the eye are the distinctions in sensibility, palette, and tone. On closer examination, however, features of the common landscape emerge—the same village, the same mountain, the same trees. The common "landscape" of psychoanalysis today consists of an increasing focus on people's interactions with others, that is, on the problem of object relations. We refer to object relations as a common "problem" because there is no consensus within the current psychoanalytic literature concerning their origins, their meanings, or the major patterns of their transformations. Although the clinical centrality of object relations is accepted by virtually all current psychoanalytic schools, there are vast differences in the ways in which this importance is understood. In fact, the approach to the problem of object relations sets the framework for any particular theory, determines the cast of that theory, and fixes its place vis-à-vis other psychoanalytic theories.

Why does the clinical centrality of relations with others pose a problem for psychoanalytic theorizing? The early development of psychoanalytic theory was built around the concept of drive. Freud's research took him into what he regarded as the "depths" of human experience, the impulses that were manifestations of man's biological nature, demands generated by the body which provide the energy for, and the goals of, all mental activity. He did not consider relations with the external world and other people unimportant, but his investigation of drives and their vicissitudes seemed more important, more pressing. In later works, when Freud did take up the problem of the "ego" and its relations to the external world and other people, it was by no means apparent how to position, how to set those processes and issues within his theory of drives. Object relations had to be accounted for; their origins, significance, and fate were by no means automatically provided for and encompassed within the earlier drive theory.

There have been two major strategies for dealing with the problem of object relations. The first, employed originally by Freud, has been essentially preservative and consists of stretching and adapting his original conceptual model based on drive to accommodate later clinical emphases on object relations. Within Freud's drive theory all facets of personality and psychopathology are understood essentially as a function, a derivative, of drives and their transformations. Thus, to solve the problem of object relations while preserving drive theory intact requires the derivation of relations with others (and of the individual's inner representations of those relations) as vicissitudes of the drives themselves. Freud and subsequent theorists employing this first strategy understand the role of objects largely in relation to the discharge of drive: they may inhibit discharge, facilitate it, or serve as its target. The second, more radical strategy for dealing with object relations has been to replace the drive theory model with a fundamentally different conceptual framework in which relations with others constitute the fundamental building blocks of mental life. The creation, or re-creation, of specific modes of relatedness with others replaces drive discharge as the force motivating human behavior. The clearest expression of this strategy came during the 1940s in the work of Harry Stack Sullivan and W. R. D.

Fairbairn. We regard the conceptual approaches of these two theorists as fundamentally compatible and able to be integrated, and, taken together, as the major systematic alternative to drive theory.

Much of the heterogeneity and complexity of current psychoanalytic theory is clarified by an approach that takes as its starting point the dialectical tension between these competing strategies for understanding object relations, one preserving the original drive model and the other replacing it with a fundamentally different model. The contribution of any given theorist is best understood in terms of his basic stance with regard to these models; salient similarities and differences among theories become clear when approached from this perspective. Our purpose is to articulate the principles underlying each model and to place the major theorists within the history of psychoanalytic ideas with respect to the models. *Accounting for the enormous clinical significance of object relations has been the central conceptual problem within the history of psychoanalytic ideas. Every major psychoanalytic author has had to address himself to this issue, and his manner of resolving it determines the basic approach and sets the foundation for subsequent theorizing.* An understanding of the most significant strategies for dealing with this issue and the two very different conceptual models that underlie them makes it possible to position major psychoanalytic theorists vis-à-vis each other in a fashion that illuminates their basic similarities and differences, often obscured by lesser issues, psychoanalytic politics, and differences in the use of language.

The approach to the history of psychoanalytic ideas and the problem of object relations developed within this book is different in perspective and broader in scope than existing commentaries on object relations theories, which tend to operate from within one model or the other. Adherents of the drive theory model and the strategy of accommodation (Modell, 1968) tend to minimize the contributions of more radical theorists who have abandoned the drive theory; adherents of more purely innovative models and the strategy of radical departure (Guntrip, 1971) tend to minimize the contributions of those object relations theorists who have remained within the drive theory framework. Both lines of theory-construction have been significant, fruitful, and can be understood as struggling in different ways with the same problems.

In order to avoid misunderstandings of our purposes, let us clarify at the outset what we are *not* doing. We are not providing a comprehensive history of all psychoanalytic ideas or a model for understanding the nature and structure of all psychoanalytic theories; we are not considering the complex question of validity and verifiability within scientific theories in general and psychoanalytic theories in particular (see Suppe,

1977, for a discussion of the vast range of views within the philosophy of science concerning these issues). Our purposes are descriptive and analytic. We hope to provide, through critical analysis of different approaches to a common conceptual problem, a thread which can be followed through the labyrinth of psychoanalytic ideas, so that the reader may better understand their underlying structure and more easily make his way through them.

A comparative psychoanalysis is not undertaken without risk. Different schools of psychoanalytic theory have developed out of different intellectual traditions, are based on vastly divergent philosophical and methodological assumptions, and employ different languages. Each theory is an intricate network of concepts which has developed through an internal progression particular to that theory, often in isolation from other psychoanalytic schools of thought. Therefore, it has been argued, psychoanalytic theories cannot be meaningfully compared without doing violence to the integrity of each. Surely the dangers to which this line of reasoning points, of forced and misleading comparisons and of reductionistic collapsing of distinct theoretical systems, must be kept in mind.

Careful and respectful comparisons of theories are, however, not only possible but necessary. The disavowal of synthetic and integrative approaches has its own dangers, perhaps even more troublesome. Without such approaches, psychoanalysis may become a discipline fragmented into semi-isolated and insulated schools, separated not by substantive conceptual differences but by political and fraternal traditions. Such a process would transform psychoanalytic formulations from a growing set of clinical and theoretical inquiries and hypotheses into a series of cultish islands of thought.

Morever, we believe that an argument against comparing and integrating different theories ignores the facts of psychoanalytic life. Every analyst, even the most rigidly atheoretical, is at least implicity a theorist. What one hears from a patient is informed by what one knows about living; it is shaped by a theory which the analyst may or may not articulate (even to himself) and which is derived from what he has read (within and without the technical literature), seen, and lived. With the exception only of the most doctrinaire, each analyst's clinical practice rests on a theory which is already a synthesis of information derived from many sources. It is our hope that our explicit comparative psychoanalysis will aid the clinician in doing what he has in fact done all along, by sharpening his perspective on the approaches of those who have consigned their particular theory to the written word.

Part One

Origins

Every man carries within himself a world made up of all that he has seen and loved; and it is to this world that he returns, incessantly, though he may pass through, and seem to inhabit, a world quite foreign to it. —CHATEAUBRIAND, *Voyage en Italie*

1   Object Relations and Psychoanalytic Models

The daily work of the psychoanalyst is intimately bound up with his patients' relations with other people. Like everybody else, patients spend a good deal of their time talking about people. Even when their associations run toward concerns somewhat divorced from the main-stream of social intercourse—to dreams, fantasies, symptoms, and so on—the presence of others can always be inferred. Moreover, the patient in analysis is talking *to* someone; his communication is shaped by his understanding of and relation with the person he is talking to. All theories of psychoanalysis recognize this. In Freud's earliest drive theory (1905a), the object of a drive (in broad terms, the person toward whom the drive is directed) was, along with its source and aim, postulated as one of its essential characteristics. Although the object was seen as the most variable element of drive, one not inherently or originally con-nected with it, there could be no expression of drive demand without at least an implicit object. Drive, insofar as it was psychologically rather than physiologically comprehensible, became known through its derivatives, through its direction toward some object. In this sense, all psychoanalytic knowledge must begin with the individual's relations with others.

Psychoanalytic approaches to object relations are, however, infinitely complicated by the realization that the "people" about whom the patient is talking do not necessarily behave in a way that another observer of those same people would confirm. This fact appeared dramatically in the first psychoanalytic treatment ever attempted, that of Anna O (Breuer and Freud, 1895). Anna O's pseudocyesis and her belief that Breuer was acting like her lover rather than like her physician, initially led not to increased understanding of the dynamics of human interaction but to the premature termination of her therapy. It was left to Freud, with his courage in the face of conventionally unacceptable phenomena, to interpret Anna O's reaction in a way that deepened our comprehension of people's interaction with each other. The resulting theory of transference made it impossible ever again to assume that the "objects" about whom patients talk necessarily correspond in a one-to-one fashion with the "real people" of the external world. The concept of transference suggests that the "object" of the patient's experience (be it analyst, friend, lover, even parent) is at best an amended version of the actual other person involved. People react to and interact with not only an actual other but also an internal other, a psychic representation of a person which in itself has the power to influence both the individual's affective states and his overt behavioral reactions.

Examples of this are commonplace in clinical practice outside of the transference in the more technical and limited sense of the term. For instance, a patient, a man of middle age who lives alone and who in treatment has been talking about feelings of shame at having wasted many years of his life pursuing chimerical goals, reports in session that his niece and her boyfriend will be visiting him for the holidays. In preparation for this visit he has been polishing his lamps, wiping fingerprints off the walls, and, in general, preparing for the onslaught of intensely critical, parental intruders. His mood as he describes his preparation matches the story; he is apprehensive, timid, and embarrassed by the living conditions his guests will observe. In the next session, following the holiday, he says that the visit went surprisingly well, except that the "kids" who stayed with him were "bums" and "slobs," wanting only to lie around in bed all day, reveling in the freedom to do this away from their watchful parents. His affect once again matches the situation as he describes it. He is haughty and contemptuous, condescending and judgmental.

What is striking about this very ordinary example is the tangential relationship between the patient's description of his responses to his guests and any "actual" characteristics of the niece and her boyfriend. The only consistency between the two sessions lies in the relationship described, that of an angry, critical, and self-righteous parent and a misbehaving, shameful child. In the first session the guests are assigned the role of the parental figures; in the second the role is assumed by the patient. We may speculate that it was the visitors' failure to conform to the patient's expectations — their failure to *act* parental — that instigated the dramatic shift in his perception of them (and of himself). For the purpose of the present discussion, however, what matters is that this man's account of an experience with other people is decisively shaped by a pattern of relationship that includes a template of the other and, in everyday language, is "carried around in his head." The relative impact of the characteristics of actual people and of these internal images varies widely among different individuals, but their presence and activity is to some extent demonstrable in everyone.

The existence of these mental representations of others, sharing as they do some of the characteristics of "real" people as well as some of their capacity to trigger behavioral response, yet being demonstrably "different," raises critical conceptual problems for any dynamic theory of the mind. Such images go under various names in the psychoanalytic literature. In different theoretical systems they are called variously "internal objects," "illusory others," "introjects," "personifications," and the constituents of a "representational world." Their functions within the psychic economy are likewise a matter of debate. They may be understood as serving as a kind of loose anticipatory image of what is to be expected from people in the real world; as becoming closely entwined with the individual's experience of who *he* is; as persecutors, fulfilling the function of a kind of critical internal fifth column; or as a source of internal security and resource, invoked in times of stress and isolation.

What is generally agreed upon about these internal images is that they constitute a residue within the mind of relationships with important people in the individual's life. In some way crucial exchanges with others leave their mark; they are "internalized" and so come to shape subsequent attitudes, reactions, perceptions, and so on. This observation presents the psychoanalytic theorist with a range of difficult questions to which a great deal of contemporary theorizing is directed. How do the characteristics of internal objects relate to those of "real" people, past and present? Is the internal object a representation of the individual's perception of a total relationship with another person or of specific aspects and characteristics of the other? What are the circumstances in which such images become internalized, and what is the mechanism by which they are established as part of the individual's inner world? What is the connection between these internal representations and subsequent relations with real others in the external world? How do internal objects function within mental life? Are there different types of internal objects? Do different circumstances and mechanisms of internalization lead to different kinds of internal objects?

The term "object relations theory," in its broadest sense, refers to attempts within psychoanalysis to answer these questions, that is, to confront the potentially confounding observation that people live simultaneously in an external and an internal world, and that the relationship between the two ranges from the most fluid intermingling to the most rigid separation. The term thus designates theories, or aspects of theories, concerned with exploring the relationship between real, external people and internal images and residues of relations with them, and the significance of these residues for psychic functioning. Approaches to these problems constitute the major focus of psychoanalytic theorizing over the past several decades.

Discussion of theories of object relations is complicated by the fact that the term has been used in many different contexts and with any number of different connotations and denotations, resulting in considerable ambiguity and confusion. Some authors take exception to the broad usage just described, arguing that it threatens to deprive the term of all specificity of meaning and to blur significant areas of theoretical disagreement (Lichtenberg, 1979). They prefer to restrict the designation "object relations theory" to the works of a particular theorist. But in this usage a further problem develops, because the term is applied to more than one, often incompatible, theoretical stance. It is often used exclusively to describe the approach developed by Melanie Klein, and equally often with respect only to the theory of W. R. D. Fairbairn, despite the fact that the nature, origin, and content of "objects" varies dramatically in these two approaches. In more recent years, Otto Kernberg (1976) has applied the term to his own particular blend of the ego psychology of Jacobson and Mahler, influenced by terms and emphases derived from the writings of Melanie Klein.

A further difficulty with the term is that its use by many authors has tendentious and polemical overtones. Guntrip (1969) opposes the "object relations theory" of Fairbairn and Winnicott to what he considers the "mechanistic" psychology of Hartmann and the American ego psychologists, a distinction that allows him to conclude that the former is better because it is "more human." Theorists operating within the more orthodox psychoanalytic tradition use the term as one of opprobrium. It is a way of accusing another author of concentrating on the psychological superficialities (behavior with other people) at the expense of the mental depths. "Object relations theory" in the view of these authors implies a concession to behaviorism; the phenomena to which it refers are more adequately described by the concept of "drive derivative," referring to the manifestations of drive as they appear in the experience of the individual (Brenner, 1978). Another group of theorists, particularly the followers of Harry Stack Sullivan, view "object relations" as a weak term of compromise (Witenberg, 1979). Object relations, they argue, are interpersonal relations, but the term allows its user to proclaim continued allegiance to drive theory.

It might be argued that the term object relations theory is overused, too variable and hopelessly entangled with theoretical dispute to warrant retention. With so unclear a referent, this argument might run, to attempt a theoretical approach to the treatment of object relations is a project based on shifting sands. However, because the term is so widely used in psychoanalytic literature, the substitution of a set of novel, more narrowly defined terms would necessitate unfeasible translation of massive segments of the existing psychoanalytic literature into a new language. Simply dropping the term would result in more rather than less confusion, particularly in a project that centers around an exposition and comparison of different theoretical traditions. Accordingly, we will retain the term object relations in a general sense; it is important, however, that we specify *our* definition at the outset, and that we keep in focus the term's specific referents for the different theories we examine.

The concept of object relations originated as an inherent part of Freud's drive theory. The "object" in Freud's language is the *libidinal object* (in the later theory also the object of the aggressive drive). In this sense the meaning of the word "object" parallels its dual usage in everyday English, in which it refers both to a thing and to a goal or target. Freud's object *is* a thing, but it is not *any* thing; it is *the* thing which is the target of a drive. The "object" of psychoanalysis is thus not the "object" of academic psychology, that is, simply an entity existing in time and space (see Piaget, 1937). In its original usage, the concept of object was intertwined with and contingent upon the concept of drive. Despite this connection, some psychoanalytic theorists have retained the terms "object" and "object relations" although they eliminated entirely the concept of drive in the classical Freudian sense (see Fairbairn, 1952; Guntrip, 1969). Other theories which stress the role of the object and which hold that they deal with the problems of object relations *are* drive theories (see Jacobson, 1964; Kernberg, 1976). Thus, the term, although seemingly theory-bound, does not adequately discriminate between those approaches which accept Freudian libido theory and those which do not.

Because of this ambiguity we reject narrow definitions of object relations. Dispute as to whose theory constitutes a "true" object relations approach is a barren enterprise that has caused endless confusion to students of psychoanalysis. In this book the term refers to individuals' interactions with external and internal (real and imagined) other people, and to the relationship between their internal and external object worlds. We believe that the term retains utility only in this broad usage. All psychoanalytic theories contain theories of object relations; they must if they are to maintain contact with the day-to-day experience of the individual. Various approaches are differentiated by their use of observations concerning relations with others and by the extent to which these observations are integrated with classical drive theory. It follows from this that our usage explicitly dissolves any assumption of a tie between the terms "object" and "object relations" and the concept of underlying drives. Despite its origin in drive theory, we believe that the term "object," divorced from that origin, retains its theoretical utility:

1. Within the history of psychoanalysis the term has been used to describe both real people in the external world and the images of them that are established internally. This dual connotation is useful in describing the interchange between "inside" and "outside" that occurs in every analytic treatment (see Modell, 1968; Stierlin, 1970).

2. The word "object" is vague enough in ordinary usage to connote a wide range of characteristics. This accords well with the experience of patients, whose world can be populated by "objects" which are active or static, benign or malignant, alive or dead, and so on. The very generality of the term indicates the variability of one's experience with other people.

3. Although the term itself is general, the concept object suggests tangibility. Again this accords well with the experience of patients, who see exchanges with their objects as having all the experiential reality of transactions in the external world. Although in the phenomenology of the patient's experience "internal objects" are felt actually to exist, our use of the term does not imply the physical reality of such objects. These are certainly not entities, or homunculi within the mind.

4. Returning to the ordinary usage of the term, an object, despite its durability, can be manipulated and modified. It can be reshaped, repainted, cut in two, repaired, even destroyed. This connotation lends itself well to the psychoanalytic concept of intrapsychic operations that can be performed upon objects, and the experiences that many patients report corresponding to these operations.

Conceptual Models in Psychoanalytic Theory

Psychoanalysis is, by its very nature, an interpretive discipline. Psychoanalytic theorizing operates within a continual dialectic of cross-fertilization with clinical data. Freud developed his theory *from* the clinical material provided for him by his patients; the theory in turn continually shapes and illuminates the newly emerging clinical data. Although the practicing psychoanalyst attempts to suspend his formal theoretical preconceptions as he listens to his patients, to stay as close as possible to the phenomenology of the patient's experience, theory must enter at some point. The very nature of psychoanalytic practice as a collaborative inquiry into the patient's life presupposes that something is missing in the patient's experience of himself. Whether this is conceptualized as being the result of repression (Freud), inattention (Sullivan), disclaimed action (Schafer), self-deception (Fromm), or bad faith (Sartre), the assumption is that some salient aspects of the patient's reality, some crucial dimension of meaning, is absent in his account of his own experience, whether or not the patient is aware of it (Ricoeur, 1970).

Psychoanalytic theories provide interpretive possibilities aimed at supplying missing dimensions in the patient's account of himself. Each theory selects from the complexity of life certain aspects or dimensions which are understood to lie at the center of human concerns, coloring much of the seemingly diffuse and variegated aspects of the patient's experience. This dimension provides content for interpretations, a reservoir of meanings within which the clinical material can be understood. The basic concepts within each psychoanalytic theory become the warp and woof out of which the complex tapestry of human experience is woven. In the psychoanalytic process itself, if the work is proceeding in a rich and vital way, broad underlying theoretical principles are almost invisible. The analyst, once past his earliest apprenticeship, does not retain his theory in mind for active, focused use as a lexicon of meanings. He does not continuously shift back and forth between his patient's communications and his theory, deciphering piece by piece as he goes along. He listens to the patient's account of his experience, and his attention is drawn now this way, now that. Certain themes stand out, certain pieces do not fit together. Gradually his thoughts about the patient crystallize. Some underlying processes in the patient's life and his communication of his experience emerge. The analyst begins to have a sense of what has been omitted, and this awareness shapes his thoughts concerning possible interpretive interventions. How can he communicate something of his experience and understanding of the salient omissions in the patient's account in a way which will enrich the patient's understanding? Throughout this process, theoretical concepts as such may be missing from the analyst's thoughts. Nevertheless, they provide the invisible backdrop, the unseen framework, within which the analyst hears the patient's story. Thus, basic concepts within psychoanalytic theory provide interpretive possibilities for orienting the clinician toward crucial and hidden dimensions of meaning by informing his sensibilities as a listener.

Does the characterization of psychoanalysis as an interpretive discipline challenge its credibility as a scientific discipline? Not at all. Recent approaches to the philosophy and history of science have highlighted the presumptive and interpretive features of all scientific disciplines and shed considerable light on the ways in which psychoanalytic theories function.

Until the last several decades, Western philosophy of science has been dominated by an understanding of science and its theories grounded in a thoroughgoing empiricism and, in this century, elaborated by the philosophical doctrines of logical positivism. Within this understanding, termed by recent philosophers of science "The Received View," there is an assumed one-to-one correspondence between good theory and actual events and processes in the real world: facts are established irrefutably through objective observation; theories offer different explanations of these facts on the basis of which testable predictions can be made; experimentation determines the correctness or error of the theory; science proceeeds through a gradual accumulation of neutral observations and confirmed hypotheses; scientific understanding changes through the absorption of earlier, more limited theories into increasingly broader and more inclusive theories.

In the 1950s and 1960s this view of the philosophy and history of science came under increasing criticism, and a very different understanding was developed by a series of authors all employing what has been termed "weltanschauung" analyses (Suppe, 1977). In this view, science is not an unbroken line of ideas representing a closer and closer approximation to the "truth." Steeped in the current scientific climate heavily influenced by relativity theory, Heisenberg's Uncertainty Principle, and the seemingly infinite regress of particle physics, contemporary philosophers of science have reconsidered the relation between science and "objective" reality. There are no purely objective facts and observations which lie outside of theory, according to this new view. One's theory, one's understanding, one's way of thinking, *determine* what are likely to be taken as facts, determine how and what one observes. Observation itself is understood to be "theory-laden." Science, in this view, necessarily takes place within a community, employing a common language, taking for granted certain basic and ultimately untestable premises. Science thus operates within a conceptual perspective, a weltanschauung. Among the different theories developed within this approach, the contributions of Thomas Kuhn (1962) have been most influential and most widely employed. Truth, he argues, is unknowable; the concern of science is with problem solving, and the history of scientific ideas consists of a series of models, "ways of seeing the world" (p. 4) which are more or less useful in solving problems. The more comprehensive and influential of these models, or paradigms, do not necessarily presuppose or incorporate the preceding paradigms. They represent a series of alternative solutions, pictures of the universe, which are crystallized out of pieces of data and concepts. Kuhn suggests that those contributions which are to be understood as paradigms have two defining characteristics: "their achievement was sufficiently unprecedented to attract an enduring group of adherents away from competing modes of scientific activity. Simultaneously, it was sufficiently open-ended to leave all sorts of problems for the redefined group of practitioners to resolve" (p. 10). Each major paradigm forms the framework for observation and theorizing for a period of time and is eventually replaced by a new crystallization, a new picture, casting a different light on things, useful in solving different problems. The reigning paradigm at any particular time has an enormous influence on scientific activity. It determines what data are taken to be meaningful and real, what methods are to be considered valid, and where the scientist is to be positioned in relation to his object of study.

One of the most intriguing aspects of Kuhn's work is his focus on the transition between paradigms. If science consists of a series of discontinuous models, how does one move from one paradigm to the next? What are the features of such a transition? His depiction of this process highlights what might be considered to be the more "political" features of the history of scientific ideas. Paradigms, because they are models of reality taken for the "truth," inspire loyalties. During the peak period of influence of a paradigm, nearly all workers within the particular field are under its sway. There is shared agreement on the epistemological assumptions, the methodological approaches, and the observational perimeter which it provides. As that peak period is passed, new data, new ideas begin to emerge outside the boundaries legitimized by the paradigm. At that point an array of different strategic options presents itself. Some remain loyal to the old paradigm and discount the validity of new, discordant data and concepts altogether. Another strategy, which might be termed accommodation, entails attempts to stretch the concepts and boundaries of the old paradigm to encompass what is new. This may work for some time, depending on the novelty of the new data, the resiliency of the old paradigm, and the interpreter's skill at casuistic explanations. However, at some point, Kuhn suggests, "retooling" is unavoidable—a shift in paradigms is "economically" necessary and essential to further progress. Then the old paradigm fades and a new one emerges.

Kuhn and other proponents of weltanschauung analyses have come under criticism of various sorts. Kuhn's term "paradigm" has been attacked as so vague and elastic to be meaningless (Masterman [1971] catalogues twenty-two different meanings). His view of science as proceeding through successive "revolutions" has been judged applicable to certain historical periods and scientific disciplines but not to others. Proponents of weltanschauung analyses in general have been accused of giving too little weight to the place of rationality in science and to the extent to which objective, reasoned argument plays an important role in choices among different theories. Thus, while "The Received View" was based on an unquestioned belief in the objectivity of science, and weltanschauung analyses emphasized nonobjective, presumptive features, contemporary philosophers of science are struggling toward a middle course. Kuhn, in response to these criticisms and suggestions, has revised his approach. In his later work he specifies the kind of objective criteria which do play a part in theory choice, and has himself rejected the term "paradigm" as so broad and vague as to invite oversimplification and misuse.*

Scientific communities hold in common many complex kinds of beliefs and "cognitive commitments," Kuhn now suggests, and this vast array of beliefs constitutes a "disciplinary matrix." Among the various kinds of conceptual tools employed within a disciplinary matrix for explaining phenomena are many different kinds of models. Some serve as simple analogies or heuristic devices—"A behaves or can be regarded like B." Other models have a much deeper and more pervasive role within a scientific community, in which the model provides a basic framework of orientation and belief, serving as "objects of metaphysical commitment: the heat of a body *is* the kinetic energy of its constituent particles, or, more obviously metaphysical, all perceptible phenomena are due to the motion and interaction of qualitatively neutral atoms in the void" (1977, p. 298). It is precisely this sort of model which psychoanalytic theorizing organizes itself around; thus, in speaking of models within psychoanalytic theory, we are employing the term to refer to the kind of metaphysical commitment that Kuhn describes. In

*Kuhn's concept of "paradigm" has been used by various authors (Modell, 1968; Lifton, 1976; Levenson, 1972) to characterize the basic shifts in theory in the history of psychoanalytic ideas. These groupings of theories are quite different, for each author sees the basic "paradigms" of psychoanalytic thought in his own distinctive fashion. This elasticity of the term "paradigm" is exactly what led Kuhn to replace it with a set of more specific concepts like "examplars," "models," and so on.

employing his approach, we are not necessarily implying its applicability as a general account of all sciences, nor are we entering the complex philosophical tangle concerned with questions of objectivity, subjectivity, and verification of theories. We are suggesting that Kuhn's approach to the development of scientific ideas and his definition of models as metaphysical commitments are highly applicable to the history of psychoanalytic thought and constitute a useful way to approach the different strategies of theory-construction.

Psychoanalytic theories operate as models reflecting metaphysical commitments because they are based upon untestable premises concerning four fundamental issues. The first issue, the approach to which shapes many other aspects of the theory, concerns the basic unit of analysis. What is primary and what is derivative? What are the basic constitutive building blocks of experience: drives, wishes, values, goals, relations with others, identifications, choices, action, and so on? Of what are the "structures," the patterns, the "stuff" of the personality composed? Once this broad foundation has been delineated, three other more specific and overlapping dimensions of theoretical concern must be addressed. First, *motivation*: What do people want? What are the prevailing and underlying goals of human activity? Second, *development*: in the transformation from the relatively unformed infant to the relatively patterned adult, what are the crucial events? Third, *structure*: What gives an individual his or her distinctive shape, governing the regularity of behavior, events, and relationships within an individual life? What mediates between past events and present experience and behavior? Concepts in each of these areas touch on, interact with, and are contingent upon concepts in other areas. Taken together, the approaches to issues within each area form a broad framework for generating clinical hypotheses and interpretive possibilities. When different theorists reflect fundamental similarities in their approaches we consider them as working within the same model. Psychoanalytic theories which deal with these issues in a fashion which is fundamentally different from preceding solutions are considered to be operating out of an alternative model.*

    *Our use of the term "model" is very different from that employed by Gedo and Goldberg in *Models of the Mind* (1973). They distinguish "models" from "theories," using the former term in a much more limited fashion to refer to the simple "categorization of clinical data." The topographical model, the structural model, the reflex arc model, and object relations theory are all seen as devices for explaining different discrete clinical problems. They organize these "subsystems" of mental functioning into an overall developmental hierarchy according to the principles of general systems theory. This presupposes that these are simply neutral, observational categories, independent of any larger theoretical premises. We disagree with this view, and our analysis of various dimensions of psychoanalytic

The most significant tension in the history of psychoanalytic ideas has been the dialectic between the original Freudian model, which takes as its starting point the instinctual drives, and an alternative comprehensive model initiated in the work of Fairbairn and Sullivan, which evolves structure solely from the individual's relations with other people. Accordingly, we designate the original model the *drive/structure model* and the alternative perspective the *relational/structure model*. We have chosen these terms as a means of highlighting the differences between the models in their metaphysical commitments concerning the underlying content of mind. All psychoanalytic theories presuppose enduring, characteristic patterns and functions that typify the individual personality. Such patterns and functions organize experience and mediate between experience and subsequent behavioral response. Most theorists term them "psychic structure," to emphasize their consistency and temporal continuity. (Sullivan [1953], wary of the danger of reification inherent in the use of concepts like "structure," substituted "dynamism.") We retain the term structure, mindful that such usage implies a metaphor of "spatialization" that is not to be taken literally (see Schafer, 1972). We are using it in the sense suggested by Rapaport, who designates "structures" within psychoanalysis as configurations "having a slow rate of change" (1967, p. 701), and Lawrence Friedman, who characterizes structures in terms of a "reactive stability" (1978b, p. 180).

---

theorizing demonstrates its untenability. The different models that characterize psychoanalytic thought are not simply organizational devices, but reflect different visions of reality. They cannot be meaningfully combined into a single theory.

Who could remain unmoved when Freud seemed suddenly to plunge towards the origins? Suddenly he stepped out of the conscious into the unconscious, out of everywhere into nowhere, like some supreme explorer. He walks straight through the wall of sleep, and we hear him rumbling in the cavern of dreams. The impenetrable is not impenetrable, unconsciousness is not nothingness.

—D. H. LAWRENCE, *Psychoanalysis and the Unconscious*

2 Sigmund Freud: The Drive/Structure Model

Psychoanalysis is, for all intents and purposes, the creation of one man. Although he began with a method borrowed from Josef Breuer and brought to his thinking a sensibility shaped by familiarity with neurology, physiology, philosophy, psychology, and evolution theory, Sigmund Freud developed psychoanalysis by working, essentially alone, for ten years before he was joined by similarly minded colleagues. This singular course of development makes psychoanalysis unique among intellectual disciplines, for by the time Freud's work was "discovered" and he acquired coworkers, he had evolved a fully articulated (though by no means final) vision of his creation. By 1900 Freud had invented not only a field of investigation but also a method of inquiry and a psychotherapeutic modality. He had arrived at a body of findings and had advanced a comprehensive set of hypotheses to explain them.

Freud's fundamental vision of the human condition is embodied in what we have called the drive/structure model. As the term implies, the core concept of the model is the idea of drive. In Freud's most widely used definition, drive is a concept on the frontier between the psychic and the somatic, an endogenous source of stimulation which impinges on the mind by virtue of the mind's connection with the body. It is a "demand made upon the mind for work," the activator of the psychic apparatus (1905a, 1915a). Freud implied at times that drive is to be understood as a quasi-physiological quantity, which exercises force mechanistically within the mind. The express intention of the *Project for a Scientific Psychology* (1895a) was to establish psychology on the same materialistic basis as that which supported other natural sciences. Freud never fully abandoned this intention, although in his later works it became a wishful rather than a realistic goal. He often expressed the hope that his hypothesized psychic structures would someday be confirmed by anatomical findings, and his attempts to create a pictorial representation of the mental apparatus (1923a, 1933) indicate that he thought of the mind as existing in physical space.

Most drive theorists since Freud have pursued this aspect of the meaning of drive.* Hartmann and Rapaport, two of his most important interpreters, make it quite clear in their writings that they consider psychoanalysis a biological science. Its goal is the understanding of mental mechanisms, the explanation of the "how" of man's mental life. Hartmann's comment (1948) that there is no phenomenological counterpart to the psychoanalytic concept of drive illustrates this approach; for him the drives are no closer to having any experiential referent than are brain processes. Psychoanalytic metapsychology is the attempt to take apart the psychic machine, to figure out the forces and counterforces that operate within it.

This approach to Freudian theory has in recent years engendered a great deal of criticism both from theorists trained within the drive/structure model and from those whose origins are outside it. Psychoanalysis, they believe, is not a biological science, it is essentially an interpretive discipline. Thus, its constructs must address the meaning with which people endow their daily experience. Guntrip (1971), George Klein (1976), Gill (1976), Holt (1976), and Schafer (1976) have questioned whether a psychology predicated on mechanistically defined drives, and on structures derived from transformations of drive energy, can adequately fulfill this psychoanalytic goal. Drive theory, they argue, because it cannot link a psychology built on concepts of energy and structure with a psychology of meaning, cannot fully account for human motivation.

These critics read Freud very much in the mode of Hartmann and Rapaport, but they reject the biological thinking which they find implicit in Freud's theorizing. Schafer (1972, 1976) points both to Freud's tendency to attribute spatial extension to the mental apparatus and to the dangers inherent in this approach. Stressing the theory's

---

*Although in the *Standard Edition* Strachey (1966) chose to translate the German *trieb* as "instinct," in this book we generally speak of "drive." In addition to being the more literal translation, "drive" refers to what Ornston calls "a surging and rather undifferentiated 'need'" (1982, p. 416), in contrast to the more structured "instinct." In agreement with most writers we use the adjectival form "instinctual drive" and occasionally refer, again conventionally, to the "dual-instinct" theory.

biological roots, Holt (1976) criticizes the energy concept on physiological grounds. Gill (1976) argues that "metapsychology is not psychology," that Freud intended his metapsychological concepts to be taken in a biological/mechanistic sense rather than psychologically, and that these concepts lack the implication of intention and meaning that any psychology must have. In his most recent formulation, Gill (1983) states that "as presently constituted, metapsychology is in a different universe of discourse from that of meaning, namely the natural science universe of force, energy and space. As such it is incompatible with a hermeneutic science."

Freud's loyal followers and his critics both overlook a fundamental ambiguity in the theory of drive, an ambiguity highlighted and clarified by our framework for the understanding of theoretical models. Within any science a model is a comprehensive perspective designed to encompass the entire range of phenomena within its scope. No observer of human behavior can fail to notice that people act on the basis of the meaning which they attribute to their experience of themselves and of the world around them. Thus, if the drive/structure model is a model in the true sense of the word, it must contain a theory of meaning. There must be a link between Freud's language of force, counterforce, and energy transmuted into structure and his vision of human experience — between the "how" and the "why."

In constructing the drive/structure model Freud drew on biological metaphors. One would expect nothing else from a theorist trained in medicine in the intellectual climate of late-nineteenth-century Vienna. But stressing Freud's biological metaphor can obscure the acute psychological vision, the very theory of meaning, which gave rise to it. We suggest, therefore, that the distinction between psychoanalysis as a natural science and as an interpretive discipline is spurious. The very principles Freud thought explanatory in the mechanistic sense also provide an interpretive thrust; his theory of mechanism *is* a theory of meaning. The drives in this sense embody Freud's understanding of our elemental passions; they represent the fundamental human urges. Seen in this way, the drives are not only the *mechanisms* of the mind, they are also its *contents*. Because our focus is principally on these mental contents, throughout this book we stress Freud's theory of meaning. This neither invalidates nor denigrates a natural science vision of his creation; the choice is not either/or.

Although Freud often referred to his goal of creating a scientific psychology, he also underscored the importance of viewing drive theory as a theory of meaning. He states that the "power of the id expresses the true purpose of the individual organism's life," and that the activity of the drives "gives rise to the whole variegation of the phenomena of life" (1940a, pp. 148, 149). Elsewhere he says: "The theory of instincts is so to say our mythology. Instincts are mythical entities, magnificent in their indefiniteness" (1933, p. 95). Freud refers to the theory of mental to- pography as "a fiction," and he stresses the metaphorical nature of the structural model by giving everyday names to the three mental agen- cies — *das Ich* (I), *das Es* (it), and *das Uber-Ich* (above-I), instead of "giv- ing them orotund Greek names" (1926b, pp. 194-195). (This metaphor- ical translation is lost in the *Standard Edition*'s translation into ego, id, and superego — a point recently addressed by Bettelheim [1982] and by Ornston [1982].) He was well aware of the ambiguous status of the drive concept, writing that, "The concepts of 'psychical energy' and 'discharge' and the treatment of psychical energy as a quantity *have become habitual in my thoughts since I began to arrange the facts of psychopathology philosophically*" (1905c, p. 147; italics ours).

Approached from this perspective, the metapsychological formula- tions of the drive/structure model are highly determinate as to the meaning of any event — interpersonal exchange, affect, fantasy, and so on. The meaning is determined precisely by the operative drive or com- ponent drive plus the operative defenses which are derived from the conflict between the imperatives of passion and the counterpressures of civilization. In the first dual instinct theory, motivation is reducible to sexual (or sensual) meaning when governed by the libidinal drives, or to self-preservation when governed by the ego instincts. In Freud's revised view, meaning is determined by the ebbs and flows and complex in- terplay of the life and death instincts.

The drive/structure model of psychoanalysis originated in and was elaborated over the course of Freud's writings. This can obscure the fact that over time Freud made many crucial changes in the framework of his theory. We do not intend to extract from the multiplicity of his theoretical statements "a" Freudian theory, for there are many, but rather the essence of the drive/structure model. There are certain fun- damental principles which, once he arrived at them, Freud never changed, which imbue his writings throughout his career with a par- ticular view of the nature of man and of the basic constituents of human experience. Other elements of the theory (such as the concept of iden- tification and the reality principle), although fundamental to psychoanalysis as we know it, are not an intrinsic part of the drive/struc- ture model, but we will attempt to show how they fit with and sometimes modify its essential nature.

Freud's psychoanalytic theorizing can be divided into three phases.

During the first, which lasted from his adoption of Breuer's cathartic method in the late 1880s until 1905, he worked with concepts of affect and of defense in a way that shares some of the sensibilities of the relational/structure model and which at times bears a striking resemblance to contemporary perspectives (see Rapaport, 1958). The second phase begins with his public abandonment of the seduction theory (Freud, 1905a, 1906). Between 1905 and 1910 he developed and articulated many of the concepts which define the drive/structure model; by 1910, with concepts which were never to change, it was firmly in place. Freud introduced the third phase with his paper on the "Two principles of mental functioning" (1911a). From this point on, much of his work was devoted to integrating relational concepts into the established structure of the drive model. These changes were often initiated in response to dissents, particularly those of Adler and Jung. If Freud invented the drive/structure model, he also invented, within psychoanalysis, the strategy of theoretical accommodation, and the third phase of his career is best understood in terms of accommodating strategies.

The Constancy Principle, Affect Theory, and the Defense Model

The idea that Freud's model contains, simultaneously, a theory of meaning and a theory of mechanism is tested as soon as we consider one of its most fundamental postulates—the constancy principle. First articulated by Breuer (but attributed by him to Freud) in the *Studies on Hysteria* (Breuer and Freud, 1895) and restated by Freud throughout his theoretical writings, this principle states that it is the aim of the psychic apparatus to keep stimulation as close to zero as possible. Quiescence is pleasant, excitation unpleasant, and we therefore initiate whatever action (alloplastic or autoplastic) is best suited to reducing the level of stimulation.

Freud's formulation of the constancy principle reflects the influence of now outmoded neurological conceptions (the nervous system seeks to rid itself of all tension) and the influence of hydraulic metaphors (the mind is constructed like a machine driven by the flow of energic forces). It is not one of the most palatable elements of the drive model. It is a mistake, however, to argue that because it is based on biology the constancy principle is without psychological content. It is in fact a direct although incomplete statement about human intention, one which illustrates the manner in which Freud used his model to develop a psychological interpretive framework. Simply put, the constancy principle suggests that what matters most to people is to rid ourselves of stimulation. It both depends upon and reinforces the most basic assumption of the drive/structure model: that there is such a thing as a discrete individual who can be treated, both theoretically and clinically, as a closed energy system. Tensions build up within this system and must be discharged by it. If one channel is dammed up so that discharge through it is prevented, another must be found. The more "open" systems of the relational model neither require nor can support the constancy principle.

In the *Studies on Hysteria* (Breuer and Freud, 1895) and the *Project for a Scientific Psychology* (Freud, 1895a), despite their vastly different theoretical perspectives, human behavior is understood to be regulated by the constancy principle. Without it, none of the formulations in the *Studies on Hysteria* make sense. Events become pathogenic when the affect associated with them cannot be adequately discharged, because of external circumstances or because those affects are in conflict with other, highly valued states of mind, such as moral and ethical values. The treatment modality suggested in the *Studies*, which derives directly from the theoretical assumptions, is that recovery of the repressed memories will make abreaction possible. Without this full discharge of pent-up affect which was stifled at the time of the event and which, therefore, operated continuously to fuel the consequent neurotic symptoms, illness is inevitable.

The constancy principle has never been popular with psychoanalysts. It accords poorly with many of our observations, including the observation that people often seek out states of excitement and consider them pleasurable. Freud himself was not entirely comfortable with his formulation; throughout his life he reworked its place within his theory. However, it is clear that the tendency to quiescence remained as a central motivational force throughout the many transformations of his theoretical perspective.

The full development of the drive/structure model requires, in addition to the constancy principle, specificity as to the source or sources of the excitation which the psychic apparatus is designed to discharge. This specificity is a development that required fifteen years of clinical and theoretical work. Given the constancy principle alone, theorists are free to speculate as to the source of excitation which the individual seeks to discharge. The excitation may arise endogenously or exogenously, it may be active or reactive, it may be the product of transformations of fundamental drives or involve the full range of human emotions as primary sources of stimulation. Although only one element of the drive/structure model, the constancy principle, once in place, continued to inform Freud's theorizing for some forty years.

Prior to the full articulation of the drive model, the psychic quantity that the constancy principle was understood to regulate, the stimuli that required discharge, were equated with the affects. An event—for all intents and purposes an interpersonal exchange—may elicit an almost endless variety of responses. We may come out of such an exchange sexually excited, or we may be angry, or we may be frightened, or we may be pleased, or we may be vengeful, and so on. The nature of the affect evoked is determined by our own personalities and by the nature of the event itself. The particular culture in which we live, its values and standards, is crucial in determining which affects we find acceptable. This in turn determines which affects are most likely to become embroiled in conflict, which cannot be adequately discharged. The memory of the event which triggered these affects thus becomes subject to repression and can exercise a pathogenic force. The theory is not specific as to the fundamental nature of the stimuli with which the psychic apparatus must deal. In other words, at this point in Freud's thinking there were no fundamental passions, no irreducible forces determining our human nature. What mattered was simply what grew out of particular interpersonal encounters.

From the beginning Freud distinguished between the "actual neuroses" and the "psychoneuroses" (1895b, 1895c). The former, including anxiety neurosis and neuraesthenia, he attributed to dysfunction in the patient's current sexual life: their mechanism was understood to consist in the damming up and subsequent transformation of chemical sexual substances. This process was construed as physiological; the actual neuroses were not thought of as psychological disorders. The psychoneuroses, considered susceptible to psychoanalytic treatment and therefore central to Freud's theoretical interest, were caused by conflict brought about by the incompatibility of ideas and the consequent failure to discharge affect (1894, 1896a). There was no specificity as to the content of the conflicting ideas. The *Studies on Hysteria*, Freud's major work of this period, considered sexuality the area most likely to produce conflict, and thus psychoneurotic symptoms, but by no means the only one. Defining trauma, he says, "The incompatible idea, which, together with its concomitants, is later excluded and forms a separate psychical group, must originally have been in communication with the main stream of thought. Otherwise the conflict which led to their exclusion could not have taken place. *It is these moments, then, that are to be described as 'traumatic'*" (Breuer and Freud, 1895, p. 167; italics ours). Incompatibility and conflict, regardless of their sources, are considered pathogenic at this phase of the theory.

In a series of papers published soon after the *Studies* Freud introduced the concept of early seduction into the etiological framework which he had developed for the psychoneuroses (1896a, 1896b, 1898). Some early occurrence, which "must consist of an actual irritation of the genitals" occurring before puberty (1896a, p. 163), is the core repressed memory which is evoked by contemporary experience and which produces symptoms. However, although the advent of the seduction theory made sex an essential constituent of the neurotic process, it is not on that account a driving force in all human experience. Early seduction provides a traumatic experience precisely because the immature sexual apparatus is poorly equipped to handle the excitations that are stimulated, nor is the immature personality equipped to deal with their emotional concomitants. The place of sexuality in the early theory was arrived at purely on an empirical basis (although, as Freud was soon to discover, the inevitability of seduction in the psychoneuroses was a mistaken conclusion). Sexuality was far from its role in the drive/structure model: a force motivating all human behavior. The prehistory of the drive/structure model differs from the full development of the model precisely in its lack of specificity as to motivational contents.

The Wish Model

The publication of *The Interpretation of Dreams* (Freud, 1900) marked a transition point in the development of the drive/structure model. In the theoretical presentation of its chapter 7, Freud published for the first time a generalized model of the workings of the psychic apparatus. This model offers a more specific statement of the content of human motivational force, but the specificity that characterizes the fully articulated theory of drive is still missing.

Freud begins by stating the constancy principle, arguing that "at first the [psychic] apparatus's efforts were directed towards keeping itself so far as possible free from stimuli; consequently its first structure followed the plan of a reflex apparatus, so that any sensory excitation impinging on it could be promptly discharged along a motor path" (p. 565). The "exigencies of life" interfere with this function, and Freud states that the first of these are "the major somatic needs." This leads to an attempt to discharge the excitation through motor activity, which constitutes an expression of emotion. The discharge accompanying early motor activity does not work effectively over long periods of time; an "experience of satisfaction" is required if the constancy principle is to be satisfied. Part of this experience is a particular perception, the memory of which becomes associated with the excitation produced by the need. Thus, the next time the need arises, there will be an attempt on the part of the psychic apparatus to recathect (that is, reinvoke) the perception, to reestablish the original experience of satisfaction. The impulse to do this Freud terms a "wish," and the fulfillment of the wish is the reappearance of the perception. The earliest attempt to do this is through hallucinatory re-creation of the perception, the mechanism utilized later in life by the dream. In Freud's language, the fulfillment of the wish is embodied in the creation of a "perceptual identity." Perceptual identity means that the earlier gratifying *situation* is reestablished, either in reality or in fantasy. The content of the unconscious as Freud presented it in 1900 is exclusively made up of wishes. Dreams are formed by the press toward satisfaction of those wishes; the motive force of all dreams is to be found in the unconscious. This concept is extended so that wishes are found behind all psychic activity. As Freud expresses it, "nothing but a wish can set our mental apparatus at work" (p. 567).

From the perspective of mechanism, the wish of 1900 has the same status as the drive of later theory. Both create the internal tension which, experienced by a psychic apparatus which operates under the rule of the constancy principle, moves the mind to action. As the drive is the motive force of the later theory, so the wish is the motive force of this transitional phase. If forbidden drive derivatives (particular impulses) require repression in the later model, desires for forbidden experiences of satisfaction are repressed in the earlier theory. The difference between the two concepts lies in their content, that is, the difference is found at the center of the assumptions of the two models.

With the full articulation of the drive model, the content of any action is fully specified by the quality of the drive which underlies it (plus, of course, the defenses against the original impulse). Each of Freud's dual instinct theories points to independently derived and irreducible motivational contents. In the model of the *Studies on Hysteria* it is the situations which are specific, not the internal stimuli. Freud's shift in models can be conceptualized as follows: in the first view the situations are determinative, the affects contingent; in the last formulation the drives are determinative, the situations contingent.

We are now in a position to appreciate the transitional nature of the model of *The Interpretation of Dreams*. Wishes are desires to reestablish *situations*, but the situations are desirable only because they once satisfied an internally produced need. The need itself, however, is unspecific as to content: Freud is explicit in noting that only the earliest of the "exigencies of life" which require satisfaction derive from the major somatic needs. The wish model gives us great latitude of interpretive possibility; we are quite free to fill in the need which the wish is designed to satisfy. The need may be sexual, or destructive, or self-preservative, or it may be a need for security or for emotional warmth.

Unlike the later model, this formulation offers little by way of direction. It moves beyond the earlier approach, however, in hinging the importance of the wished-for situation on the fact that it *was* once satisfying relative to *some* internally arising need.

The Advent of the Drive/Structure Model

The concept of drive was introduced in the *Three Essays* where it is defined as follows:

> By an "instinct" is provisionally to be understood the psychical representative of an endosomatic, continuously flowing source of stimulation . . . The concept of instinct is thus one of those lying on the frontier between the mental and the physical . . . [They] are to be regarded as a measure of the demand made upon the mind for work. What distinguishes the instincts from one another and endows them with specific qualities is their relation to their somatic sources and to their aims. The source of an instinct is a process of excitation occurring in an organ and the immediate aim of the instinct lies in the removal of this organic stimulus. (Freud, 1905a, p. 168)

Drive is an energy source, the activator of the psychic apparatus. With the publication of the *Three Essays on the Theory of Sexuality* Freud abandoned the indeterminacy of his early wish model. The content of what is wished for is a function of forces that impinge upon the mind by virtue of the mind's connection with the body. These forces determine man's essential nature. Throughout Freud's subsequent career he emphasized the unique status of drive as a determinant of motivation. This status is variously described in the statements that drive is "a demand made upon the mind for work" (1905a, 1915a), that it is "the ultimate cause of all activity" (1940), and that "every psychical act begins as an unconscious one" (1912a).

Each of these statements has essentially the same meaning. Each requires that every human action, from the diffuse discharge of affect in the infant, to the symptoms of the neurotic, to the creations of the artist, to the evolution of a social structure that unites men into civilized groups, be traced in its origin to ultimate, irreducible, and qualitatively specifiable instinctual sources.

An answer to the question of the specific quality of the drives would complete the specification of content which characterizes the drive structure model. Freud writes:

> What instincts should we suppose there are, and how many? There is obviously a wide opportunity here for arbitrary choice. No objection can be

made to anyone's employing the concept of an instinct of play or of destruction or of gregariousness, when the subject-matter demands it and the limitations of psychological analysis allow of it. Nevertheless, we should not neglect to ask ourselves whether instinctual motives like these . . . do not admit of further dissection in accordance with the *sources* of the instinct, so that only primal instincts—those which cannot be further dissected—can lay claim to importance.

I have proposed that two groups of such primal instincts should be distinguished: the *ego*, or *self-preservative*, instincts and the *sexual* instincts. But this supposition has not the status of a necessary postulate . . . it is merely a working hypothesis, to be retained only so long as it proves useful. (1915a, p. 124; italics in original)

This statement constitutes another central postulate of the drive/structure model. On the basis of evidence derived from his clinical experience in analyzing the transference neuroses, and in accord with what he called the "popular distinction between hunger and love" (1914a, p. 78), Freud specified the content of the demands made upon the mind for work: they were held to derive from a primary, irreducible sexual drive and an equally primary, equally irreducible drive toward self-preservation. As Freud predicted later in the passage, he was to modify his dual instinct theory (in 1920) to embrace sexual and destructive drives, but from 1905 (when both the sexual and self-preservative drives first appeared) onward, the indeterminacy of the wish concept was filled with a primary, fully specified content.

In discussing the early development of sexuality in young children, Freud states that "a sexual aim . . . consists in replacing the projected sensation of stimulation in the erotogenic zone by an external stimulus which removes that sensation by producing a feeling of satisfaction" (1905a, p. 184). But what is the mechanism by which the infant can become aware of the existence of such external stimuli? Freud replies: "This satisfaction must have been previously experienced in order to have left behind a need for its repetition; and we may expect that Nature will have made safe provisions so that this experience of satisfaction shall not be left to chance" (1905a, p. 184). We recognize in this formulation a restatement of the earlier concept of the wish, with its push toward the establishment of "perceptual identity" that allows a reexperiencing of the earlier satisfaction. Here, however, the nature of what is pleasurable is strictly defined: it consists precisely in a satisfaction of the *sexual* aim achieved through stimulation of the appropriate erotogenic zone. This permits a discharge of a quantity of excitation, just as in the early model. But the nature of that quantity is now specified: it is a *libidinal* quantity, the energy of the sexual drive. From this point forward in Freud's theorizing, specificity of content is never absent from his account of the forces which lead to activation of the mental apparatus.

Freud's development of the drive/structure model both depended upon and reinforced his abandonment of the old seduction theory. He had arrived at this conclusion on empirical grounds as early as 1897 and announced it in a letter to Fliess (Freud, 1950, Letter 69). In the *Three Essays* he says that "Obviously seduction is not required in order to arouse a child's sexual life; that can also come about spontaneously and from internal causes" (1905a, pp. 190-191). Once sexuality is posited as an internally arising force underlying human activity, seduction becomes theoretically vestigial, and the importance of childhood *events* correspondingly declines. This change is of the greatest importance in understanding the drive/structure model approach to problems of object relations.

From its origins, the drive/structure model was a dual drive theory. The sexual (libidinal) drive always operated alongside of or in conflict with another, independently derived drive. However, throughout his life Freud thought of the libidinal drives as fundamentally more important than the opposing drive, particularly insofar as the unconscious and the genesis of neurosis (for the most part, the center of his theoretical interest) were concerned. Even after the introduction of the second dual instinct theory, Freud's focus remained directed toward the manifestations of the sexual drive. The aggressive drive, like the drive toward self-preservation that preceded it, is given no developmental phases comparable to those of the libido. And, parallel to the lack of vicissitudes of the ego instincts, Freud states, "we have always believed that in a neurosis it is against the demands of the libido and not against those of any other instinct that the ego is defending itself" (1926a, p. 124).

The neglected areas of drive theory, the developmental history of the self-preservative instincts (somewhat rectified by Freud later when their function was transferred to the structure ego), and the developmental history of aggression are major aspects of contemporary psychoanalytic theorizing; they play a major role in the thought of some relational/structure model theorists. Their absence from Freud's thinking, however, underscores the determinacy of the drive/structure model. The empty areas of the early model have been filled with forces derived primarily from the sexual instincts, although of course this represents only one-half of the picture of Freud's conflict theory.

Resistance and Repression

During the 1890s Freud focused on the delineation of states of conflict between sets of incompatible ideas. The conflicts gave rise to what he termed "defense" (or, its equivalent at the time, "repression"), by which he meant the intentional, although not on that account conscious, exclusion of certain ideas from awareness. The incompatible ideas were those that carried with them unpleasant affect; there was no specificity as to the nature of the ideas themselves and the unpleasure connected with them was typically situationally determined. The general thrust of Freud's early papers is on the dynamic process of defense, and on the ways in which different defense mechanisms give rise to different psychoneurotic syndromes (Freud, 1894, 1895a, 1896a, 1896b, 1896c; Breuer and Freud, 1895).

The question that arises is what might render an idea "incompatible" and what it would have to be incompatible *with* in order to give rise to defensive processes. Throughout this period Freud is somewhat vague on this point. His clearest statement comes in a discussion of the case of Miss Lucy R. in the *Studies on Hysteria*: "The basis for repression itself can only be a feeling of unpleasure, the incompatibility between the single idea that is to be repressed and the dominant mass of ideas constituting the ego" (Breuer and Freud, 1895, p. 116).

The power of the repressive force thus derives from the fact that the dominant mass of ideas is dominant, that it is a coherent and organized "structure" (in the nontechnical sense of the term) which, by virtue of its coherence and organization, has achieved a great deal of power within the psychic economy. The dominant mass of ideas is strong enough to keep any single, opposing idea from joining it and thereby from sharing access to consciousness. Banishment of the incompatible idea to the unconscious and the consequent blockage of its affective charge from the most expeditious release enables the idea to exercise its pathogenic effect.

How does the dominant mass of ideas become dominant? Freud is almost totally silent on this point during the early phase of his theorizing, yet his argument has some clear implications. What become dominant are what we might today think of as "proper" ideas, those which fit well with our view of ourselves as we would prefer to be. They are socially sanctioned ideas which fit well with our own values, standards, and morality. In a later work Freud suggests that repression "proceeds from the self-respect of the ego" (1914a, p. 93). Beyond this he has little to say on the developmental history of those standards: this was not at the center of his interest early in his career.

Although values and morality are not the only forces opposing ideas which become incompatible, most of Freud's examples are drawn from this prototype. The incompatible idea is incompatible *within a given context*, a particular social situation. A vengeful fantasy, to use an example from the *Studies*, may be incompatible if it is directed toward one's boss, and would on that account be repressed. In another context (this is contingent on the individual personality as well) the vengeful affect might be discharged immediately with a sharp verbal assault or even with a physical attack. The importance of sexuality in the etiology of the neuroses (before the articulation of seduction theory and even to some extent carrying into that theory) is stressed because of the tendency of sexual feelings to arise in socially inappropriate situations or to be directed toward people unsuited for romantic involvement. The tension between one's impulses and the social structure into which one must fit is what determines repression. Freud returned to this approach later in his career, particularly with respect to superego development, but not before he attempted an approach which is very different indeed.

The advent of the drive/structure model put Freud in an uncomfortable position vis-à-vis his early theory of repression. He was attempting to formulate a theory in which human activities were understood as deriving from man's biological nature. Unconscious impulses ruled by sexuality were seen as setting the mind at work. Freud wanted an equally innate, equally phylogenetically determined counterforce to oppose those impulses. With such parallelism he would have created a truly individual psychology drawn from the principles of evolution theory. (See Sulloway, 1979, for a discussion of this aspect of Freud's thinking.)

Describing the modification of his early views (including the abandonment of trauma theory and the altered notion of repressive processes), Freud states that "accidental influences have been replaced by constitutional factors and *'defence' in the purely psychological sense has been replaced by organic 'sexual repression'*" (1906, p. 278; italics ours). The concept of something organic playing a role in repression first appears in a letter to Fliess written in 1897 (Freud, 1950, Letter 75). Here, long before he chose to publish the concept, he linked the appearance of repressive forces—disgust, shame, repugnance, and so on—to the abandonment of infantile sexual zones. This development is particularly clear in the sequence in which pleasure in anal functioning is replaced by repulsion. Freud saw organic repression as an example of ontogeny recapitulating phylogeny: each individual repeats the process by which man, as a result of his adoption of an upright posture, repudiated old pleasurable sensations, particularly those connected with the sense of smell (1950, pp. 268–271).

With the publication of the *Three Essays on the Theory of Sexuality* the concept of organic repression was integrated into a more clinically oriented developmental framework. Speaking of sublimation and reaction formation, Freud says that abandoned impulses "would seem in themselves to be perverse — that is, to arise from erotogenic zones and to derive their activity from instincts which, in view of the direction of the subject's development, can only arouse unpleasurable feelings. They consequently evoke opposing mental forces (reacting impulses) which, in order to suppress this unpleasure effectively, build up the mental dams [of] . . . disgust, shame and morality" (1905a, p. 178).

This is a morality without society. It is, like the sexual drive itself, an endogenously arising force. In the same way that seduction has been replaced by impulse, so has social restraint been replaced by innate aversion. In another passage from the *Three Essays*, Freud writes:

> One gets an impression from civilized children that the construction of these dams is a product of education, and no doubt education has much to do with it. But in reality this development is *organically determined and fixed by heredity, and it can occasionally occur without any help at all from education.* Education will not be trespassing beyond its appropriate domain if it limits itself to following the lines which have already been laid down organically and to impressing them somewhat more clearly and deeply. (Freud, 1905a, pp. 177–178; italics ours)

With this formulation we are at the height of the purest form of the drive/structure model. There is no superego to mediate social demands, no ego to decide among competing pressures, no reality principle in whose service the psychic apparatus must function. Even the "ego instincts" which, in a later formulation (Freud, 1910a) will oppose the demands of sexuality, have not yet been introduced. The second group of instincts in the *Three Essays* does not oppose sexuality but helps it, by channeling libidinal impulses toward an external object. Conflict in this period is simply a function of sexuality and organically determined reactions to it.

Although the theory of organic repression was not important for long in Freud's thinking, along with its introduction he undertook further modification of the theory of repression which was to inform his subsequent theorizing throughout his life and which also represents a movement toward the consolidation of the drive model. He proposed a framework in which sexuality was more directly involved in the repressive process; this Freud labeled the "push-pull" theory of repression. This revised approach looks not only to current factors but to infantile amnesia as the explanation for a particular act of repression.

The push-pull theory is elaborated in a major codification of the principles of the drive model, presented in the five papers on metapsychology. Freud writes that:

We have reason to assume that there is a *primal repression*, a first phase of repression, which consists in the psychical (ideational) representative of the instinct being denied entrance into the conscious. With this a *fixation* is established; the representative in question persists unaltered from then onwards and the instinct remains attached to it . . .

The second stage of repression, *repression proper*, affects mental derivates of the repressed representative, or such trains of thought as, originating elsewhere, have come into associative connection with it. On account of this association, these ideas experience the same fate as what was primally repressed. Repression proper, therefore, is actually an after-pressure . . . Probably the trend towards repression would fail in its purpose if these two forces did not cooperate, if there were not something previously repressed ready to receive what is repelled by the conscious. (1915b, p. 148; italics in original)

In what sense does the push-pull theory of repression represent a step in the establishment of the drive model? In the defense model, repression was wholly determined by the incompatibility of an idea which emerged within a particular context. The hypothesis of a group of repressed ideas exercising an attraction on new ones generated in contemporary situations deemphasizes the importance of the new situation; simple incompatibility in the face of circumstances no longer is sufficient to explain the phenomenon. The specific affects generated by the situation are less important than they had been in the earlier model. Rather, the particular fixations which characterize an individual's personality structure have been thrust into the foreground of the explanatory system.

The ideas which undergo "primal repression" are not random; they are precisely those which constitute the individual's infantile sexuality. The amnesia for childhood is an amnesia for sexual development, and the events of this development form the "fixations" of which Freud speaks. The push-pull theory requires that behind every act of repression there must be an associative link to early sexuality, and the repressive forces are characterized by their opposition to specifically sexual impulses. This includes distant derivatives of these impulses, and it is the function of analysis to discover the forbidden sexuality behind each act of repression. In the same way that the evolution of the early affect theory into the intermediate wish model and finally into the theory of instinctual drive can be explained as a movement toward specifying the content of our motivating impulses, so the modification of the theory of repression represents increased specificity with respect to the anti-instinctual forces. The later theory of anti-cathexis (1915b, 1926a), in which the energy for defense is specifically defined as energy withdrawn from the threatening impulse itself, developed this approach.

With these considerations, we do not yet have a concept which fully replaces the "dominant mass of ideas" of the defense model, a force capable of carrying out repression. This is a point on which Freud changed his views rapidly and often. Between his introduction of the drive/structure model and the beginnings of his moves toward accommodation, little formal discussion of the nature of any counterforce is attempted, a fact to which Freud himself alludes (1913a, p. 325). However, in a rather offhand remark he does suggest that what he had earlier termed the self-preservative instincts might be thought of as "ego instincts," thus replacing the identification of the ego with the "dominant mass of ideas" with an instinctual definition. In this passage Freud spells out the idea that "every instinct tries to make itself effective by activating ideas that are in keeping with its aims" (1910a, p. 213) and suggests that the aim of the ego instincts is self-preservation, which specifically opposes the aim of the sexual instincts. With this concept Freud defined the field of conflict (impulse versus repression) totally in instinctual terms. This perspective is carried through to the metapsychological papers, with Freud arguing in "The Unconscious" that not only derivatives of the sexual drive are operative in the unconscious, "but also some of the impulses which dominate our ego—something, therefore, that forms the strongest functional antithesis to the repressed" (1915c, pp. 192–193).

Unlike the other fundamental premises of the drive/structure model—the constancy principle, and the motivational centrality of drive—Freud's view of repression underwent a decisive final change with the advent of the structural model, a change which in some ways reverts to the sensibilities which led him to postulate his earliest views. We must postpone discussion of this until we have laid the groundwork for it through consideration of Freud's late theory. For the moment, let us note that the structural model, with its emphasis on reality relations and on identifications with the caretaking figures who are also the carriers of social values, brings back into the dynamic picture a concept of repression motivated by the individual's need to renounce instinct in order to fit into society, particularly on account of the tendency of the impulses to arouse guilt. Social demands regain the role assigned in the defense model: they represent the principle force opposing the discharge of an impulse.

The Nature and Formation of the Object

In considering Freud's approach to object relations, we must distinguish between the role the object plays in people's psychological functioning and the nature of the object, including views as to how it comes into be-ing. Much confusion, including a blurring of central theoretical dif-ferences, has been caused by the failure to make or adhere to this distinction.

With the introduction of drive theory, the role of social influence in shaping personal attitudes toward one's impulses was greatly decreased vis-à-vis the earlier defense model. This implies a deemphasis on the im-portance of object relations. The theoretical status of relationships with others was at a low ebb from the introduction of the drive model until the advent of the structural model.

The structural model brought with it a new emphasis on the psychological derivatives of object relations. Freud's introduction of identification (1917a, 1923a), the evolution of the structures ego and superego out of early relationships with caretakers (1923a), the developmental unfolding of modes of relating to others (1926a), and preoedipal object ties (1920b, 1925a, 1931, 1933) each endow the ob-ject, seen as a figure in reality, with an important role in the psychic economy. It is often argued that, given this framework, the radical revi-sionism of the relational/structure model is rendered gratuitous. Cer-tainly from the perspective of the object's role Freudian theory changed dramatically over the years.

What *is* the object in Freud's theory? Is it simply an internal represen-tation of the parent or of a series of interactions with him or her? Or, is the object an externalization of endogenous sensations which have found a convenient "container" in the persons of the caretaking figures? If the latter is the case, then, regardless of the role assigned to the "ob-ject," the theory remains outside of the relational model because the evolution of the object itself is reducible to the vicissitudes of an underlying drive.

Freud's use of the object concept is inherently connected to the con-cept of drive. Thus, we would not expect that this idea had a prehistory in the early defense model in the sense that the idea of drive is preceded by that of unspecified affect (or psychic quantity). This is in fact the case; the early theory speaks of relationships with people in specific socially determined situations, a framework within which the idea of the object as it was later defined has no place. There is a critical conceptual difference between "objects" and "people," one manifestation of which is that there is no theoretical requirement in the drive/structure model that the object be a person at all.

In the evolution of Freud's thinking there is a reciprocal relationship between the specificity of the postulated motivational force and that of the object. The wish model of *The Interpretation of Dreams*, true to its transitional role, prefigures the new approach to the problem of the object. When Freud speaks of the aim of the wish being the establishment of "perceptual identity" (1900, p. 566), he is referring to the aim of reestablishing the conditions in which disturbing needs were formerly met. "Perceptual identity" points to a set of conditions in the world which the infant associates with earlier experiences of satisfaction. However, the nature of these conditions is entirely contingent upon the nature of the wish. Moreover, the original need which genetically gave rise to the wish is endogenously determined and has no necessary connection to an object at all.

The object in its full technical sense first appears in Freud's writings in the *Three Essays*. His first definition of the term is deceptively simple: "Let us call the person from whom sexual attraction proceeds the *sexual object*" (1905a, pp. 135–136; italics in original). But complexities soon develop. In the course of his discussion of homosexuality, Freud argues that we must reject "the crude explanation that everyone is born with his sexual instinct attached to a particular sexual object" and concludes that "we have been in the habit of regarding the connection between the sexual instinct and the sexual object as more intimate than it in fact is" (1905a, pp. 140–141, 147–148).

He returns to this issue in "Instincts and Their Vicissitudes," in which he states that the object "is what is most variable about an instinct and *is not originally connected with it, but becomes assigned to it only in consequence of being peculiarly fitted to make satisfaction possible . . .* It may be changed any number of times in the course of the vicissitudes which the instinct undergoes during its existence; and highly important parts are played by . . . displacement of instinct" (1915a, pp. 122–123; italics ours). This formulation echoes the earlier wish concept, with its idea that the object is determined by the conditions set down by the wish for its satisfaction. In the revised theory, however, the more highly specified nature of drive requires that *the drive itself determine the nature of the object*. The fact that drive is defined as capable of undergoing displacement (and other vicissitudes that characterize the primary process; see Freud, 1909a) indicates that the object may easily be changed at any point.

The suggestion that the object is not initially attached to the drive would indicate that objectlessness is the original developmental state of affairs. Freud, however, seems uncomfortable with any firm position on the question of whether a truly objectless state is possible. His hypothesis of an original state of autoerotism suggests that it is. In his discussion of early thumb-sucking, he says that the drive "At its origin . . . has as yet no sexual object, and is thus auto-erotic" (1905a,

p. 182). An objectless state of autoerotism appears to characterize the earliest distribution of libido, a viewpoint to which Freud returns (see 1911b).

A famous passage in the *Three Essays*, however, suggests a different point of view:

> At a time at which the first beginnings of sexual satisfaction are still linked with the taking of nourishment, the sexual instinct has a sexual object outside the infant's own body in the shape of his mother's breast. It is only later that the instinct loses that object, just at the time, perhaps, when the child is able to form a total idea of the person to whom the organ that is giving him satisfaction belongs. As a rule the sexual instinct *then becomes auto-erotic*, and not until the period of latency has been passed through is the original relation restored. There are thus good reasons why a child sucking at his mother's breast has become the prototype of every relation of love. The finding of an object is in fact a refinding of it. (1905a, p. 222; italics ours)

This passage has been used by some theoreticians in an attempt to bridge the gap between Freud's formulations and those of some relational/structure model theorists. This is not a fair interpretation. The passage contradicts Freud's other formulations about the earliest state of relatedness to the object, in the *Three Essays* and elsewhere, and stands essentially alone. In his paper on the two principles of mental functioning (1911a) Freud embraces Bleuler's (1912) concept of autism as representing the infant's original condition, and in the Schreber case (1911b) autoerotism is specifically postulated as a developmental phase preceding the choice of an external object. In "Instincts and Their Vicissitudes" autoerotism is presented as the state of affairs existing "at the very beginning of mental life" (1915a, p. 134). The thrust throughout Freud's writings indicates that a relationship to an external object is achieved developmentally.

If the object is not present from the beginning it must be either discovered or created, and Freud's thinking leads us to emphasize the latter. In his discussion of the case of Little Hans, Freud says that Hans "had obtained . . . pleasure from his erotogenic zones with the help of the person who had looked after him—his mother, in fact; and thus *the pleasure already pointed the way to object-choice*" (1909a, p. 108; italics ours). This point is reiterated in the paper on narcissism, with the comment that young children "derived their sexual objects from their experiences of satisfaction" (1914a, p. 87). It is stated in its clearest and strongest fashion much later, when Freud writes: "repeated situations of satisfaction have *created an object* out of the mother" (1926a, p. 170; italics ours).

These formulations exhibit considerable continuity with the views expressed in the wish model, in which the particular content of the wish was prescribed by the earlier experiences of satisfaction. With the postulate of a specifically sexual drive, however, those early experiences are now themselves determined by the nature of the operative drive or component drive. Object formation must always be understood in terms of this drive, and its existence is contingent on its ability to satisfy the particular active instinctual aim.

From this we can develop a good picture of Freud's view of the evolution of object relations. At the beginnings of life the sexual drive as a unified, organized motivational force has not yet come into existence; the infant is a creature of independently operating component drives. As these partial sexual drives, through their anaclitic relationship with the self-preservative drives, are carried outside of the infant's own body (as autoerotism is gradually replaced), the infant accrues a set of satisfying and frustrating experiences. These experiences, particularly the satisfying ones, lead him to form an image of what satisfaction is like. The association of these satisfactions with the conditions under which they were experienced leads to object formation.

The fact that the first object is that of component instincts (partial drives) means that it will be a part object. To the extent that the object is created out of experiences of satisfaction of the oral drive, it will be the orally satisfying part of the relevant person, for example, the mother's breast. If the operative component instinct is the exhibitionistic trend, the object will be the mother-as-looker, not the "whole" mother as she would be defined by the objective observer. Throughout his writings Freud makes it clear that the nature of the object relationship that a person is reporting is contingent upon the active drive. Visions of the mother as poisoner reflect aspects of the relationship which are colored by orality, while reports of the father as seducer are, correspondingly, a function less of his behavior in reality than of the oedipal impulses which governed the patient's relationship with him (see Freud, 1933, p. 120). The libidinal phases provide precisely the *content* of which we have spoken, which, in this case, is the content of the object relationship.

For Freud, as for most psychoanalytic theorists, the benchmark of successful development is the ability to establish consistent relationships with a whole object. Within the terms of the drive/structure model, formation of the whole object depends upon the integration of the discrete currents of childhood sexual impulses (each of which has generated its own part object) into a single current of genital sexuality which can, by its nature, cathect a whole object. Freud states in *Group Psychology* that love "is nothing more than object-cathexis on the part of the sexual instincts with a view to directly sexual satisfaction." Enduring love develops out of the initial sexual interest because "It was possible to calculate with certainty upon the revival of the need which had just expired; and this must no doubt have been the first motive for directing a lasting cathexis upon the sexual object and for 'loving it' in the passionless intervals as well" (1921, p. 111). The capacity for enduring love relates also to development of the capacity for sublimation, which allows friendly, affectionate relations to be established with the family members who were the objects of the childish drives.

For relational model theorists, the achievement of whole object relationships is generally construed in perceptual terms; the task is to overcome the forces that have led to the separation of early experiences and thus to the splitting of both object and self-representations. This allows the individual to forge a unity that is a more or less accurate image of the real person. Once this unity is formed, the direction of a variety of feelings and impulses toward the same person becomes possible, indeed, almost automatic. Genital sexuality, viewed in these terms, is a natural expression of the relationship achieved.

In the drive model this explanation is reversed. The crucial developmental achievement is the integration of the early component instincts and erotogenic zones under the primacy of the genitals. If, and only if, this is achieved will the constant object be formed, and the object itself is simply a natural consequence of the organization of the components into a unified sexual instinct.

Because within the drive model the object is the *creation* of drive, object relations remain a *function* of drive. For example, in the *Three Essays* Freud states that "If an erotogenic zone in a person who is not sexually excited (e.g. the skin of a woman's breast) is stimulated by touch, the contact produces a pleasurable feeling; [and] it is at the same time better calculated than anything to arouse a sexual excitation that demands an increase of pleasure" (1905a, p. 210).

Reading this statement today, we may be puzzled or even shocked that Freud could fail to appreciate the role of the interpersonal context in which the "stimulation" occurs. But the perspective represented in it is not a mere oversight. Compare Freud's approach to his patient Dora. Freud describes a meeting which the young girl had with her father's friend Herr K:

He then came back, and, instead of going out by the open door, suddenly clasped the girl to him and pressed a kiss upon her lips. This was surely just the situation to call up a distinct feeling of sexual excitement in a girl of fourteen who had never before been approached. But Dora had at that moment a violent feeling of disgust, tore herself free from the man, and hurried past him to the staircase and from there to the street door . . .

. . . *the behavior of this child of fourteen was already entirely and completely hysterical.* I should without question consider a person hysterical in whom an occasion for sexual excitement elicited feelings that were preponderantly or exclusively unpleasurable. (Freud, 1905b, p. 28; italics ours)

Here, in a clinical situation, we see Freud applying the principles articulated in the *Three Essays*. He believes that Dora's reaction must have been determined by the erotogenic stimulation, and that this stimulation is in itself sufficient to account for the nature of her relationship with Herr K!

Freud has frequently been criticized for mishandling the Dora case (Erikson, 1962; Muslin and Gill, 1978; Muslin, 1979). This line of criticism is important, and it is compelling on clinical grounds. However, it overlooks the extent to which Freud's understanding of Dora's reaction to Herr K is consistent with, and in fact demanded by, the premises of the drive/structure model. Although this particular example is drawn from Freud's early writings, and although it was published at what we have referred to as the height of the drive model, it is not on that account atypical, because it illustrates the way in which drives are construed as the sole determinants of an object relationship. (Compare Freud's account of rescue fantasies in 1910b.)

The drive/structure model, like other models, by positing a clearly defined hermeneutic system, directs our attention to certain aspects of a situation and away from others. Although in this respect the examples we have just cited are particularly glaring, the focus Freud maintains on the instinctual roots of object relations can often lead to valuable theoretical and therapeutic insights about the way in which relationships with others are shaped by endogenously arising needs. This approach to the nature and formation of the object is another major aspect of Freud's theory that never changed.

The Fundamental Premises of the Drive / Structure Model and Their Application

The fundamental premises of the drive/structure model never ceased to inform Freud's theoretical perspective. They enable us to understand the issues with which he was dealing at the time he formulated them and to apply the drive model approach to contemporary problems in psychoanalytic theory. Let us review the basic assumptions:

1. The unit of study of psychoanalysis is the individual, viewed as a discrete entity. Man is not, in Aristotle's terms, a "political animal"; he does not require a social organization to allow him to realize his true human potential. Society is imposed on an already complete individual for his protection, but at the cost of renunciation of many of his most important personal goals (1912–13, 1930). It is thus possible and even necessary to speak of a person divorced from his interpersonal context in a way that is not possible given the fundamental assumptions of Aristotle, Rousseau, Sullivan, or Fairbairn.

2. Because it is possible to speak of the individual in a meaningful psychological way, it is possible to speak of a "constancy principle" which regulates the distribution of energy within an organism. The constancy principle holds that it is the purpose of the psychic apparatus to keep the level of stimulation within the individual as close to zero as possible. It thus provides the earliest motivational postulate of the drive/structure model, that the essential aim of the individual is to achieve a state of quiescence, of freedom from the press of endogenously arising stimulation.

3. With the full evolution of the drive model the nature of the stimulation which presses to be discharged under the influence of the constancy principle was conceptualized in the theory of instinctual drive. The origin of every human activity can be traced ultimately to the demands of drive, although a full explanation of behavior requires that we include an analysis of the forces which oppose its pressures. From the perspective of content the drives are reducible to two independent sets of needs which arise on the basis of man's biological inheritance. Their origin is in no way influenced by the social context, and they stand in relation to society exactly as do Locke's "natural rights" of life, liberty, and property (Locke, 1690). Of the two postulated drives Freud leans on the sexual currents for the bulk of his explanatory hypotheses, and the major thrust of early drive model thinking is on the elucidation of their operations.

4. There is no inherent object, no preordained tie to the human environment. The object is "created" by the individual out of the experience of drive satisfaction and frustration. For Freud the object must suit the impulse, while for theorists of the relational model the impulse is simply one way of relating to the object.

Psychoanalytic models are broad theories that attempt to interpret a wide range of existing data. The strength of a model, however, lies in its flexibility, its expandability. The existence of a strong model leads to the generation of new information, and the success of the model depends on its ability to encompass within its fundamental premises explanations of the new phenomena. The relationship between a model and the data of a science is reciprocal, and no model can be viable if it cannot account for phenomena beyond those which led to its initial formulation.

Freud began his psychological theorizing with an investigation of phenomena derived from his study of a relatively circumscribed group of disorders: the "transference neuroses" of hysteria and the obsessive-compulsive disorders. Even within the area of psychopathology, many syndromes were considered beyond the scope of psychoanalytic inquiry; these included the "actual neuroses" (anxiety neurosis and neuraesthenia), the psychoses, and melancholia. Problems which today seem at the core of psychoanalytic thinking—character formation and its relation to difficulties in living is probably the clearest example—were not central to Freud's thinking during the period in which he evolved the drive/structure model.

Despite the limited field of investigation, from the outset Freud intended to use what he saw to create a general psychology. Not long after he devised a theory based on the transference neuroses he moved to extend it to encompass a broad range of issues in both personal and social development. Freud's scope as a thinker is infinitely greater than that of any other psychoanalyst. Eventually he wrote on virtually all areas of psychopathology, about many aspects of the normal development of the individual, and about the evolution and meaning of many important aspects of civilization. Yet in each area he remained based in the fundamental premises of the drive/structure model. This is an index of the strength of the model and of Freud's skill as a theoretician.

One of the most controversial issues in contemporary psychoanalytic thinking, bearing decisively on the problems of object relations, concerns the nature of the fundamental ties which bind people together. The work of Bowlby (1958, 1969) has engaged this question directly, and it is an implicit but pervasive leitmotif in the writings of Margaret Mahler. A particular approach to the problem is a major aspect of Hartmann's (1939a) concept of the "average expectable environment," and it deeply informs Kernberg's (1976) position on the role of object relations in early development. Perhaps the clearest expression of the relational model view of these ties is expressed in Sullivan's (1953) concept of "communal existence," which suggests that a reciprocal relationship with other people is a fundamental part of being human.

In the terms of the drive model, social ties are secondary; they are contingent upon the ability of other people to facilitate the discharge of drive-derived needs. Although people may in some way be unusually well suited to serve this function, the concept of the object within the drive model grants them no unique status in this regard. And yet no observer, certainly not Freud, can overlook the importance of the social ties which people form with each other. This issue, which transcends the domain of psychopathology, is one in which the flexibility of the model would be put to a critical test.

Freud addresses the question of social ties in a number of publications. In *Totem and Taboo* (1912–13) he applied the principles of his individual psychology to the organization of primitive societies, tracing many of their practices to efforts to control unconscious hostility, incestuous strivings, and ambivalence. In this work and in the much later *Civilization and Its Discontents* (1930) Freud argues that society itself is founded on man's need to renounce his innate instinctual tendencies. Thus, society, like the structure ego, is a secondary derivative of drive: it comes into being as a way to allow a certain amount of drive gratification and an even greater amount of control.

Freud's most comprehensive discussion of man's social relationships comes in *Group Psychology and the Analysis of the Ego* (1921). Because he addresses the nature of the ties which bind people together, the views respond to those of later relational model theorists. He begins by noting that "In the individual's mental life someone else is invariably involved, as a model, as an object, as a helper, as an opponent; and so from the very first individual psychology, in this extended but entirely justifiable sense of the words, is at the same time social psychology as well." The inevitable involvement of others does not, however, mean that individual psychology *is* group psychology; quite the reverse. Freud holds that "the social instinct may not be a primitive one and insusceptible of dissection," and that in fact social phenomena are explicable entirely within the terms of an individual psychology which "explores the paths by which [man] seeks to find satisfaction for his instinctual impulses" (pp. 69, 70). The drive model is capable of telling us all that we need to know about people's lives as members of groups.

This leads us to the question of how group members influence one another, an issue crucial to the psychological question of how people grow up to be what they are. One central aspect of the problem is the communication of affective states. Sullivan, for example, attributes the appearance of anxiety to a process of "contagion" by the anxiety of a significant other person (1953). Kohut (1977) broadens this view to include the empathic communication of a wide variety of affective states.

But, like social psychology itself, contagion is not irreducible within the framework of the drive model. Freud argues that "There is no doubt that something exists in us which, when we become aware of signs of an emotion in someone else, tends to make us fall into the same emotion; but how often do we not successfully oppose it, resist the emotion, and react in quite the opposite way? . . . [W]e should have to say that what compels us to obey this tendency is imitation, and what induces the emotion in us is . . . suggestive influence" (1921, p. 89).

Once emotional influence has been reduced to suggestion, Freud is on familiar grounds in terms of the drive model. Suggestion is a concept which had occupied his attention since the early days of his work with hypnosis, and he had long established that it is itself not an irreducible phenomenon. Rather, suggestion is completely determined and explained by the nature of the libidinal relationship between the individuals involved. Group behavior (and, therefore, many aspects of family dynamics) are thus encompassed within the explanatory framework of the drive/structure model.

At the time of the articulation of the drive/structure model the problems of group psychology and the nature of man's social ties had been addressed in philosophical and psychological investigations. Another issue of concern to psychoanalysts in recent years, but which had not been explicitly raised during the time Freud was creating his theoretical structure, has been variously conceptualized as the development from absolute dependence to mature dependence (Fairbairn, 1952), the achievement of separation and individuation (Mahler, 1968), and the evolution of a cohesive self (Kohut, 1977). Each of these developmental achievements, rooted in the movement from the earliest period of childhood dependency to more advanced stages of object relations, appears to add to psychoanalysis a dimension absent in the earlier model, a "developmental line" in Anna Freud's (1965) phrase independent of those sketched out within the drive model. Our question is whether Freud's theory addresses these issues or whether they constitute approaches to novel data which cannot be encompassed within the earlier model.

Our answer, although not entirely unambiguous, casts light on the model concept in general and on Freud's use of the drive model in particular. Fairbairn, Mahler, and Kohut emerge from their investigations with particular sensibilities about the earliest years of life, the preoedipal period, with insights about the transactions between parents and children not found in Freud.

But if the *process* of separation is depicted differently by Freud than by more recent theorists, it does not follow that the *theme* is given less weight. We are confronted by a situation similar to that dealt with in considering the existence of a social instinct. The drive model contains within it an approach to the problem, but sees it not as irreducible (that is, not as a fundamental motivational force in its own right) but as yet another manifestation of the impact of drive.

In several places Freud stresses the developmental importance of the movement from dependence to autonomy. He states that the "course of childhood development leads to an ever-increasing detachment from parents" (1924a, p. 168) and that detachment is a task facing every individual, leading to "difficulties which are inherent in all psychical . . . development" (1930, p. 103). But what are the forces that underly this developmental process? There is a clue here in Freud's account in *Beyond the Pleasure Principle* of the "*da-fort*" game played by his toddler grandson. In this game, the child, by throwing away and retrieving a small toy attached to a string, re-created, under his own control, the experience of his mother's coming and going. Freud rejects the possibility that there might be an independent drive for mastery. He interprets the game as representing "the child's great cultural achievement, *instinctual renunciation*" (1920a, p. 15). The child has renounced in part his drive-derived demand on his mother by affecting a reversal from passivity to activity; he rather than she is now in command of the leaving process. But, the activity is not an end in itself, it is merely a mechanism for dealing with the pressure of his libidinal attachment.

The concepts of activity and passivity, although they refer in Freud's writings to instinctual aims, provide alternative explanations for the same phenomena covered in later theories by the concepts of autonomy and dependence. With the advent of the drive model Freud saw this distinction as one of the most critical in determining the ebbs and flows of human experience. He writes that "the contrast between activity and passivity . . . is among the universal characteristics of sexual life" (1905a, p. 159). The meaning of this in terms of early object relations is made clear in a late formulation:

> The first sexual and sexually coloured experiences which a child has in relation to its mother are naturally of a passive character . . . A part of its libido goes on clinging to those experiences and enjoys the satisfactions bound up with them; but another part strives to turn them into activity . . . the child contents itself either with *becoming self-sufficient . . . or with repeating its passive experiences in an active form of play*; or else it actually makes its mother into the object and behaves as the active subject towards her. (1931, p. 236; italics ours)

In the same way that Mahler (1968, 1972a) or Jacobson (1964) depicts an ongoing tension between stable individuation and the pull to narcissistic re-merger with the early caretaker, Freud (1915a) talks of the polarity between active and passive sexual aims.

The early tension between active and passive aims paves the way to the ultimate disentanglement of the child from his early dependency. The crux of the detachment issue arises with the most critical developmental period of childhood, the establishment and dissolution of the Oedipus complex. For Freud, the surmounting of oedipal ties, the overcoming of incestuous fixations, is necessary for later independent functioning. Only by abandoning these fixations can the child find in the outside world (the world outside his family) appropriate and available sexual objects (1910b, 1912a, 1918a). We might argue that the formulation of the Oedipus complex relates only to the tension between early dependency and later autonomy with respect to libidinal needs, but this very perspective is characteristic of the drive/structure model. The movement from passivity to activity and the movement from embeddedness with the oedipal objects *is* the movement from dependence to autonomy, accounted for with the explanatory principles on which the model is based.

If sex were all, then every trembling hand
Could make us squeak, like dolls, the wished-for words
But note the unconscionable treachery of fate,
That makes us weep, laugh, grunt and groan, and shout
Doleful heroics, pinching gestures forth
From madness or delight, without regard
To that first, foremost law.

— WALLACE STEVENS, "Le Monocle De Mon Oncle"

3   Sigmund Freud:
The Strategy of Accommodation

The drive/structure model of psychoanalysis did not remain unchallenged for long. Within a few years of its introduction, two of its earliest adherents became dissenters. After breaking with Freud, Alfred Adler and C. G. Jung criticized the model's fundamental premises. The early writings of both Adler and Jung, before they embarked on their unique theoretical paths, strikingly resemble the contributions of recent relational/structure model theorists. Adler emphasized the role of the interactions that characterize the relationships of family members. His concepts of inferiority and the inferiority complex were rooted in the child's reality, in the fact that he is small and powerless in comparison with his parents. Adler consequently postulated a primary drive for power or mastery that reflected the child's objective interpersonal situation and the developmental tasks he realistically had to accomplish (Ansbacher and Ansbacher, 1956). Jung's original dissent was broader and more theoretically based than Adler's, whose concerns both theoretically and therapeutically always had a pragmatic cast. Jung objected to the central thesis of the drive model—that the origin and quality of libido was solely and invariably sexual. He proposed broadening the libido concept to designate an energy source without assumptions as to its content. Libido would acquire sexual aims only on the basis of the individual's developmental experience (Jung, 1913).

Freud's dispute with Adler is described most fully in the *History of the Psychoanalytic Movement* (1914b). Freud criticizes Adler for overemphasizing the ego at the expense of the libidinal drive and for suggesting that the desire for power is an irreducible motivational force. (Even before Adler's dissent Freud had argued against the irreducibility of the drive for power; see 1905c.) He challenges Adler's view that the underestimation of women is socially determined, arguing that small children are unaware of social values and that the resemblance of their opinions to those of society at large must have some other source. Each of these issues is central to the fundamental premises of the drive model. In the first, Freud charges that Adler has substituted an interpersonal motive for an instinctual one. In the second, he holds that Adler has failed to recognize that the views of children and of society derive from a common, instinctual source: the undervaluation of women follows naturally from the awareness of one's narcissistic vulnerability in the face of the "reality" of castration. This instinctually derived fear, and not the communication of parental (and therefore social) values, determines attitudes toward women, even in the early years of life. (Adler's view has been embraced by relational model theorists such as Horney [1937, 1939] and Thompson [1964]).

Freud criticizes Adler's indifference to whether or not an idea is conscious, a perspective reflecting Adler's deemphasis on the close relationship within the early drive model between the system Ucs. and drive. He takes issue with Adler's view that the manifest content of dreams reflects the dreamer's attitudes toward his current life situation rather than operating as a translation of early wishful impulses. Freud rejects Adler's idea that resistance in the psychoanalytic situation is an expression of opposition to the analyst rather than to the emergence of repressed instinctual derivatives.

Freud's critique of Jung (1914a, 1914b) focuses on his blurring of the distinction between the libidinal and self-preservative drives. By reducing the libido concept to a contentless "psychic energy," he argues, Jung has overlooked both the individual's dual, phylogenetically determined functions of self-preservation and preservation of the species as well as the evidence of the transference neuroses, which demonstrate the conflict between the two classes of instincts. As with his response to Adler, the thrust of the argument is to maintain the specifically sexual quality of libidinal energy at the center of the motivational system of psychoanalysis.

Freud's responses to Adler and Jung did not stop with his criticism of their heterodox views. Each dissent evoked a major revision in his own theory. These revisions not only preserved the fundamental premises of the original model, but actually advanced it. The modifications generated a richer, more textured view of the nature of human experience.

The period of theoretical accommodation lasted for more than half of Freud's career as a psychoanalyst. His contributions during this time are among the most important of his life; many are fundamental to what is considered "Freudian psychoanalysis." The new concepts of this period build on the fundamental premises and guide our interpretive focus to new possibilities.

From the wide range of topics which Freud touched upon after his introduction of the drive/structure model, four broad areas are most representative of his strategy of accommodation: the role in the psychic economy of reality and the reality principle; changes in the approach to the nature of drive and to the constancy principle regulating drive discharge; the corresponding change in the theory of affect; and the evolution of the structural model, with its refinements in the approach to the role of object relations in normal and pathological development.

In the early defense model reality factors were assigned a central psychodynamic role in the formation of neurotic symptoms. Although in the slightly later seduction model there is less place for *current* reality (because contemporary events are pathogenic only insofar as they establish connections with memories of a specified content), the seductions themselves were seen as actual occurrences. The wish model represents a further, but not yet decisive, movement away from reality. The aim of establishing "perceptual identity" relates back to a situation which was once perceptually present, but it is the content of the endogenously arising need rather than the external conditions that is determinative. As the fully articulated drive/structure model develops, the role of reality becomes decidedly secondary; impulses and reactions against them are construed as endogenous pressures.

Adler's charge that Freud did not pay enough attention to reality factors resulted in Freud's first theoretical accommodation: the introduction of the reality principle in the "Formulations on the Two Principles of Mental Functioning." This brief paper contains a schematic outline of what in retrospect can be seen to have occupied Freud's attention for the remainder of his life. He introduces the reality principle with the statement that:

> the state of psychical rest was originally disturbed by the peremptory demands of internal needs. When this happened, whatever was thought of (wished for) was simply presented in a hallucinatory manner, just as still happens to-day with our dream thoughts every night. It was only the

non-occurrence of the expected satisfaction, the disappointment experienced, that led to the abandonment of this attempt at satisfaction by means of hallucination. Instead of it, the psychical apparatus had to decide to form a conception of the real circumstances in the external world and to endeavor to make a real alteration in them. A new principle of mental functioning was thus introduced; what was presented in the mind was no longer what was agreeable but what was real, even if it happened to be disagreeable. This setting-up of the *reality principle* proved to be a momentous step. (1911a, p. 219)

The implications of the reality principle are vast, encompassing consciousness, attention, notation, the impartial passing of judgment (reality testing), action, and thinking. In later years all these functions will be attributed to the structure ego: they are concerned not with the generation of impulse but with the relation of impulse to the real world. They are the bridges to reality that had faded into the background with the advent of the drive model.

Throughout its history, psychoanalysis has been a conflict theory in which opposite trends within the individual struggle for a dominant role in controlling mental life. The most crucial of these pairs of polar opposites consist of the forces representing the repressed and those representing the repressive. This is true of each phase of Freud's theorymaking, from the defense model through the drive model.

Although the conflict between the repressed and the repressive is always critical, Freud's personal interest was from the beginning focused mainly on the former (thus psychoanalysis was labeled a "depth psychology"). He is vague on the details of the dominant mass of ideas in the earliest theory, and the "organic repression" of the *Three Essays* and the "ego-instincts" of later works are less thoroughly explored than the forces which they aim at controlling.

In the passage just quoted, reality enters the psychic economy on the side of the repressive forces. Adler's work, and that of relational/structure model theorists since Fairbairn and Sullivan, was aimed at integrating considerations drawn from reality into the theory of impulse itself (see Adler's "masculine protest" and "inferiority complex"). Freud does not allow reality to infiltrate the theory of instinctual drive at all; it remains on the "surface," and is seen in terms of introducing contingencies that require the control of impulse rather than as influencing the nature of impulse itself. One is reminded of the way in which the culture of India has managed to remain relatively resistant to foreign influence for many thousands of years: new ideas are assimilated into the complex structure of society, and their impact is therefore defused. Thus, when Buddhism arose to provide a formidable challenge to Hinduism, the

Hindus adjusted by acknowledging the importance of Buddha and holding that he was in fact one of the ten major incarnations of their god, Vishnu.

It would be misleading to say that reality influenced the drive model as little as Buddha did Hinduism. The changes introduced with the reality principle had far-reaching consequences in Freud's own thinking and perhaps even greater implications when they were addressed by subsequent drive model theorists. It is important, however, to keep in mind the different value which attaches to changing the theory of repressive forces as compared with that of changing the theory of the repressed; the bulk of Freud's strategy of accommodation is directed toward operations on the psychic "surface."

Even within the paper on the two principles of mental functioning Freud sets clear limits on the power of the reality principle, which develops out of disappointment and frustration. These are far more apt to arise with respect to the self-preservative drives than with the sexual drives, because the latter are capable of being gratified autoerotically and also because the period of latency interrupts sexual development while the establishment of the reality principle is being firmly consolidated. Thus, to a great extent sexual impulses remain outside the reality principle; they are more closely tied to primary process operations and to fantasy. Freud thus keeps from the grips of reality precisely that group of impulses which is most central to drive model thinking. The "Two Principles" is a masterpiece of giving with one hand and taking away with the other, although it is at the same time a framework for a far more comprehensive integration of reality considerations into the existing model.

Although with the introduction of the reality principle the external world regained some of the theoretical status lost when Freud abandoned the seduction theory, its place remains secondary. The infant turns to reality only as the result of frustration at the failure to satisfy internally arising needs. (When he can satisfy them autoerotically, reality remains of little interest.) The reality principle is at a far remove from Fairbairn's concept of a drive which is inherently directed toward an object existing in reality. It implies that channels to the external world—perception, memory, and so on—evolve solely through conflict. The approach laid down by Freud is a point of departure for Hartmann's (1950c, 1939a) concept of autonomous ego functions and of a conflict-free sphere which provides such channels independently of the frustration of drive-derived needs.

Following publication of the "Two Principles," Freud took up the role of reality in the onset of neurotic disorders, an idea at the center of the early defense model (Freud, 1912c). However, it is principally in the psychotic disorders that reality impresses itself on the psychoanalytic observer, because the most prominent symptoms that characterize them—such as delusions and hallucinations—involve the failure to discriminate internal from external events. In papers on neurosis and psychosis (1924b, 1924c) Freud suggests that the difference between the two classes of disorder can be found in the relations among id, ego, and reality. In neurosis, he argues, the ego responds to intolerable id demands by repudiating them—that is, by repression. In psychosis, the ego repudiates the reality that makes the id demands unacceptable. This defense, termed "disavowal" or, later, denial, is a defense against *perceptions*; unlike all other defenses, it is directed outward rather than inward. The first occasion for disavowal, Freud argues, arises when the little boy discovers that little girls lack a penis (1923b). This is an intolerable shock to the boy's narcissism, and he is forced to repudiate what he has noticed. Maintained within narrow limits, disavowal may lead to fetishism in the adult (Freud, 1927, 1940b); applied broadly, it is a fundamental defense mechanism employed by psychotic patients.

In his paper on "Neurosis and Psychosis" Freud argues that:

> Normally, the external world governs the ego in two ways: firstly, by current, present perceptions which are always renewable, and secondly, by the store of memories of earlier perceptions which, in the shape of an "internal world," form a possession of the ego and a constituent part of it . . . [The internal world is] a copy of the external world . . . [In psychosis] The ego creates, autocratically, a new external and internal world; . . . this new world is constructed in accordance with the id's wishful impulses [due to] some serious frustration by reality of a wish. (1924b, pp. 150–151)

The new emphasis on defenses directed against external perceptions was further developed by Anna Freud in *The Ego and the Mechanisms of Defense* (1936), in a manner stressing the critical developmental role of environmental conditions. By postulating an outward-directed defense, Freud paved the way for bringing realistic object relations more within the framework of the drive model. Even this modification, however, preserved the essential theoretical thrust: from the Schreber analysis through the papers on psychosis more than a decade later, the defensive process itself is necessitated by the incompatibility of reality with the demands of the id, which still arise independent of external influence. The modification has once again been undertaken in the theory of the repressive, not the theory of the repressed.

Freud's statement that the psychotic internal world is created "in accordance with the id's wishful impulses" bears a striking similarity to his earlier discussion of *normal* object formation. Immediately following his introduction of the structural model, Freud apparently became convinced briefly of the role of objects *in reality* as forces in psychic structure formation. He referred to the inner world of normal and neurotic people as a "copy of the external world," and said that the superego "retained essential features of the introjected persons—their strength, their severity, their inclination to supervise and to punish." Although he does mention that in the process of introjection the characteristics of these people, especially their severity, may become intensified, he concludes that they "belong to the real external world. It is from there that they were drawn; their power, behind which lie hidden all the influences of the past and of tradition, was one of the most strongly-felt manifestations of reality" (1924a, p. 167).

These comments, typical of the papers between 1923 and 1926, are quite different both from Freud's earlier formulations about object formation and from the later view of the genesis of the superego out of reintrojected aggressive energy. They represent a reemergence of his interest in reality considerations. The superego of 1924 is not unlike the "dominant mass of ideas" of 1894; it is largely a creation of authority and cultural tradition which, in the later model, is mediated by the parent and internalized by the child. In subsequent writings, however, Freud returned to the view of object formation (and, consequently, psychic structure formation) that is dictated by the fundamental premises of the drive/structure model.

The Nature of Drive and the Constancy Principle: Changing Views

We have emphasized the reciprocal relationship between the degree of qualitative specificity attributed to psychic energy and the importance attributed to external events in Freud's theory. Our view of the overall trend of his thinking leads us to expect that with the increasing attention paid to reality, drive and its vicissitudes would carry less predictive power than before. This was in fact the case. In his later contributions Freud introduced a series of important theoretical modifications aimed at decreasing the monotonic emphasis on drive processes as the sole determinants of human experience and behavior. These modifications included his new approach to the constancy and pleasure principles, his introduction of the concept of narcissism as a normal developmental stage, his recasting of the dual instinct theory, his use of the idea of

drive fusion, and his revision of the theory of sublimation. Each introduced a note of indeterminacy into his concept of the drive processes
themselves, leaving a gap which can then be filled by external circumstances.

Early in Freud's career he saw the constancy principle and the pleasure
principles as identical. Pleasure was defined in quantitative terms: it cor-
responded to a lowering to the minimum possible of the amount of
stimulation impinging on the psychic apparatus. Because man is moved
exclusively by the desire for pleasure, the direction which his behavior
will take is fully determined: he will strive to discharge any perceived
build-up of internal pressure. (The desired forepleasures of sex are only
an apparent exception to this rule; they are sought after not because
they are stimulating, but because they satisfy pregenital component instincts [1905a].)

The full specification of pleasure inherent in the original formulation
leaves no room for environmental contingencies. For example, the family members with whom a child grows up are granted no role in defining
what is going to be experienced as pleasurable by the child. The possibility that one family might see pleasure in excitement while another
might set a high store by quiescence is irrelevant in this view; the nature
of pleasure and thus the fundamental direction underlying all human
motivation is fully determined by our phylogenetic heritage.

Although Freud had expressed doubts as much as five years earlier,
the tie between the pleasure and constancy principles was firmly broken
in his paper on "The Economic Problem of Masochism." There the constancy principle is identified with the Nirvana principle, which regulates
the death instinct. With this change Freud was free to redefine the
nature of pleasure:

> Pleasure and unpleasure . . . cannot be referred to an increase or de-
> crease of a quantity (which we describe as "tension due to stimulus"), al-
> though they obviously have a great deal to do with that factor. It appears
> that they depend, not on this quantitative factor, *but on some character-*
> *istic of it which we can only describe as a qualitative one*. If we were able
> to say what this qualitative characteristic is, we should be much further
> advanced in psychology. Perhaps it is the rhythm, the temporal sequence
> of changes, rises and falls in the quantity of stimulus. We do not know.
> (1924a, p. 160; italics ours)

We encounter in this formulation just the indeterminacy that we expect.

Although the constancy principle remains in force under the name of
the Nirvana principle, the death instinct which it regulates is less central

in Freud's motivational system than are the libidinal drives (1926a). The fundamental thrust of man's actions is still toward the achievement of pleasure, but this pleasure is no longer such a simple matter as it was in the earlier theory. The element of quantity has been replaced by quality, and just what quality that might be cannot be spelled out. (Freud never seriously pursued his attempt to provide determinacy through the concept of rhythmicity.) Quality in the new model is not the kind of phylogenetic given that quantity was in the old model. In fact Freud even suggests in *Beyond the Pleasure Principle* that "it is not advisable for us analysts to go into the problem further so long as our way is not pointed by quite definite observations" (1920a, p. 8).

If pleasure is central to human motivation, and if the nature of pleasure is not spelled out in clear quantitative terms, where are we to look for this most important aspect of our mental lives? Freud's modification of his earlier theory shifts the focus from phylogeny to ontogeny. The revision of the pleasure principle opens the hermeneutics of the drive/structure model to a greater emphasis on the conditions in which pleasure was experienced during the course of each individual's development. The specificity which drive has lost, the interpersonal context has gained or, more accurately, regained.

Freud defines primary narcissism as a normal developmental phase. There is "an original libidinal cathexis of the ego, from which some is later given off to objects, but which fundamentally persists and is related to the object-cathexes much as the body of an amoeba is related to the pseudopodia which it puts out" (1914a, p. 75). Narcissism for him is not, strictly speaking, the earliest stage of development (although it is so viewed by subsequent drive/structure model theorists). Freud argues that because "a unity comparable to the ego cannot exist in the individual from the start," and since "The auto-erotic instincts . . . are there from the very first," something must be added to autoerotism to allow its transformation into narcissism (1914a, p. 77). What must be added is the development of the ego, the evolution of a consolidated "unity" to receive the libidinal cathexis. Narcissism thus constitutes an intermediate state between autoerotism and object love (1911b).

The apparent simplicity of this definition of narcissism conceals many difficulties with the concept, particularly with respect to the relationship between narcissistic libido and the established ego instincts. In a 1915 addendum to the *Three Essays on the Theory of Sexuality* Freud states that "our method of research, psycho-analysis, for the moment affords us assured information only on the transformations that take place in the object-libido, *but is unable to make any immediate distinction be-*

tween the ego-libido and the other forms of energy operating in the ego" (1905a, p. 218; italics ours). He makes a similar point in the course of his first extensive theoretical discussion of the problem in his paper "On Narcissism" (1914a, p. 76). The difficulty in making this differentiation proved so formidable that it led Freud eventually to discard his first dual instinct theory, to eliminate the ego-instincts as an independent force, and to divide their functions among the libidinal drives, the destructive drives, and the structure ego.

Part of the difficulty with the concept of narcissism can be traced to its instigation by the dissent of Jung, who argued that libido should be construed as a general kind of psychic energy distinct from its qualitative connotation and freed from its postulated relationship to specifically sexual aims (1913). Freud's response to this argument is that much of the energy which appears at first to be operating on behalf of the ego has a sexual origin: narcissism as a theoretical concept allows the ego to "capture" sexual energy; therefore, some ego aims at least can be traced genetically to sexual aims. Narcissism thus prevents the dethroning of sexuality which was the implication and intention of Jung's argument. At the same time, it introduces a hermeneutic indeterminacy of precisely the sort we have been considering. There is little *psychological* evidence for the distinction between narcissistic libido and other forms of ego energy, so a particular manifestation of ego operations cannot be clearly *interpretively* related to one or the other energy source. Freud even goes so far as to say, "I should like . . . expressly to admit that the hypothesis of separate ego-instincts and sexual instincts (that is to say, the libido theory) *rests scarcely at all upon a psychological basis, but derives its principal support from biology*" (1914a, p. 79; italics ours).

Apart from these considerations, which are internal to the theory and of which Freud himself was clearly aware, there is an ambiguity in the concept of narcissism which bears directly on the issue of motivational specificity which we have been discussing. As we have presented Freud's definition of narcissism as "an original libidinal cathexis of the ego," it is apparent that he is thinking in terms of an object relationship, with the ego in the role of the object. This is clear in his statement that "We see . . . , broadly speaking, an antithesis between ego-libido and object-libido. *The more of the one is employed, the more the other becomes depleted*" (1914a, p. 76; italics ours). Narcissism has as its metapsychological referent simply the location of libido in one "place" or another, as the analogy with the amoeba and its pseudopods suggests. The process of regression to narcissism which underlies melancholia points to the same conclusion (Freud, 1917a).

Ambiguity arises, however, from the fact that the concept of an "object" is applied very differently where the ego is concerned than it is in any other situation. In every other case the object is an entirely passive recipient of cathexis. This is true of the objects of the autoerotic instincts which are parts of the subject's own body, and it is true of the "external" objects (more accurately, of their inner representations) of later developmental phases. Neither the infant's thumb nor the oedipal mother has any role in the further disposition of libidinal energy once they are cathected; their images are merely containers into which and out of which libido may flow.

The cathexis of the ego, on the other hand, has far-reaching consequences in terms of subsequent psychic activities, because the ego can play an active role in disposing of the energy with which it is cathected. Although this implication is present from the beginnings of Freud's discussion of narcissism, it is not supported by the underlying theory at that time. Between the time Freud abandoned the theoretical equation of the ego with the dominant mass of ideas and the time when he introduced the later, structural definition, the ego's metapsychological status was shadowy. His use of the concept during this period (under the sway of the topographic model which lasted from 1900 to 1923) is generally understood as similar to ways in which Hartmann was later to use the "self," as a *representation* of something like the "whole person." This would accord well with Freud's explicit definition of narcissism, since the concept would refer to a movement of libido from one representation (the external or autoerotic object) to another (the ego, or self).

It is a central premise of Freud's thinking that a representation cannot function in an active role vis-à-vis psychic energy; it cannot use or dispose of it. Yet it is clear from his earliest use of the concept that the ego *is* capable of using the energy with which it is originally invested or which it is able to capture from other objects. The ego can use the energy to pursue its own aims, which may be congruent with or opposed to the aims determined by object libido. Thus, both the withholding or release of feces during the anal period (1917c) and the castration complex (1923b) are viewed as embodying conflicts between narcissism and object love.

Perhaps the clearest example of this use of the idea of narcissism is the concept of "narcissistic object choice" (Freud, 1914a, 1917a, 1921). Phenomenologically, this refers to two aspects of object choice: first, choosing an object on the basis of similarity to oneself or to what one would like to be (in this sense it is both opposite and inferior to anaclitic object choice, which proceeds on the basis of the object's similarity to the early caretakers); second, choosing an object not because of the love one feels for it but because of the love one feels coming from it. Meta-psychologically, given the topographic definition of narcissism, the term itself is oxymoronic. Libido is invested in one place or another; if it is invested in an external object, it cannot be narcissistic libido, and vice versa. The concept makes sense only if we assume that once the ego is able to capture libido, it can make use of that energy for its own aims, aims *imposed* on the energy secondarily and by virtue of its association with the ego.

This argument suggests that along with the introduction of narcissism Freud was moving toward a more active conceptualization of the ego, which was not fully announced until the publication of *The Ego and the Id*. The focus on narcissism can be understood as an important early stage in the evolution of the structural model. Even more important, this argument suggests that the concept of narcissism represents another step in the diminishing specificity attributed to drive. In the model as it was originally proposed in the *Three Essays* (and even as it was elaborated in "Instincts and Their Vicissitudes," which is contemporary with the papers being discussed) the instinctual aim is completely specified by the nature of the instinct. This aim may be opposed by the forces of repression (disgust and shame, or the ego-instincts), and behavior represents a compromise among the various forces involved, but the nature of the aim itself can never be fundamentally changed. Aim-inhibition (Freud, 1915a) in these terms is the result of a conflict, something imposed upon an unyielding drive.

With the idea that the ego can deploy libido for its own purposes, the original libidinal aim recedes in importance. It is still relevant genetically, but not dynamically, because it is subject entirely to the ego's intentions (retaining the penis, being loved, and so on). But where does the ego *get* its "intentions"? With the concept of narcissism we have a set of aims that have a life of their own, free of the quality of the drives, which can use the energy of the drives to pursue these independent goals. Once again we have encountered the indeterminacy inherent in the strategy of accommodation. We are left, as we were with the revision of the pleasure and constancy principles, to seek the origin of these aims outside of the nature and operation of the drives themselves. As with the other modification, much of the indeterminacy will be filled with considerations drawn from reality relations. At the same time as he was developing the theory of narcissism, Freud was working toward a more sophisticated approach to problems of ego development, an approach in which early object relations play a highly significant role and which reached its culmination in the set of hypotheses that constitute the structural model. However, even with this revision, the ego's aims require instinctual energy as their driving force.

The problem of narcissism is closely connected with the change in the dual-instinct theory and the concepts of instinctual sublimation and fusion. The introduction of libidinal drives operating on behalf of the ego's aims had made the first dual-instinct theory problematic because it implied a differentiation which could not be maintained by psychoanalytic investigations. With the publication in 1920 of *Beyond the Pleasure Principle* Freud abandoned the hypothesis of an independent self-preservative drive, dividing its functions between the sexual instincts (Eros) and the newly proposed death instinct. Later, with the postulate of a structural ego, important aspects of self-preservation were held to operate under the ego's control.

Freud assumed that the death instinct operated quietly within the individual, that, unlike the sexual drives, it was not obvious even to psychoanalytic inquiry. Some of its manifestations, destructive impulses and certain types of masochism, were construed as its most accessible results. The death instinct was not assumed to be of the same etiological importance in the neuroses as libido and its vicissitudes.* Therefore, even after his revision of the theory of drive, Freud never paid quite as much attention to the death instinct as to the libido.

The second instinct theory broadened Freud's thinking about the energy sources assumed to be at work in the mind. Libido, destructiveness, and self-preservation, each with its own sources and histories, competed for expression. Which is going to be the strongest drive, how is its strength going to express itself, and to what extent is it going to be compromised in its aims by other considerations? As we increase the number of forces that affect the mind, we are going to have to look beyond them for the resultant, the vector, that will represent their expression. In structural terms, this leads to the postulate of a stronger ego with powerful executive functions. In interpretive terms, it will lead us to an appreciation of the context within which the forces operate: it will lead us back to reality.

Similar considerations emerge with regard to the problem of sublimation. Sublimation was always a critical issue within the drive/structure model because, along with other instinctual vicissitudes and especially

*The balance has changed in recent years. Drive theorists such as Hartmann, Jacobson, and Kernberg attribute to the aggressive drive—the modern version of the death instinct—a critical role in the etiology of more severe psychopathology. As such pathology has moved to the forefront of psychoanalytic interest, aggression has become a correspondingly more important theoretical force.

reaction formation, it provided the crucial bridge between the antisocial nature of the drives and the exquisitely social behavior motivated by the drives. In his early use of the concept in the *Three Essays*, Freud makes it clear that he is referring to the diversion of the instinctual aim from its original purpose to one which is socially more acceptable. He states that sublimation "enables excessively strong excitations arising from particular sources of sexuality to find an outlet and use in other fields, so that a not inconsiderable increase in psychical efficiency results from a disposition which in itself is perilous" (1905a, p. 238). The drive itself remains unchanged; the process of sublimation is a process of opening up certain channels for discharge while damming up others (see also Freud, 1910c).

Freud modified this view considerably after the introduction of the concept of narcissism. In *The Ego and the Id* he writes:

> The transformation of object-libido into narcissistic libido . . . obviously implies an abandonment of sexual aims, a desexualization—a kind of sublimation, therefore. Indeed, the question arises . . . whether this is not the universal road to sublimation, whether all sublimation does not take place through the mediation of the ego, which begins by changing sexual object-libido into narcissistic libido and then, perhaps, goes on to give it another aim. (1923a, p. 30)

This formulation implies not just a rechanneling but a modification in the nature of drive energy carried out through the transformations between object and narcissistic libido. Sublimation becomes possible because once the ego captures a quantity of libidinal energy it is able to impose its own aims upon it. The late view of sublimation is thus both a product of and a cause of the new indeterminacy with respect to drive.

Once he had postulated the revised theory of instinct, Freud turned to the idea that the two instincts might be joined together. He states that "the two classes of instincts are fused, blended, and alloyed with each other; . . . that this takes place regularly and very extensively is an assumption indispensable to our conception" (1923a, p. 41). This concept takes, in the second theory, the place that had been occupied in the first by the anaclitic relationship between the libidinal and self-preservative drives. The change parallels that in the construction of sublimation. In the same way that sublimation was originally construed as a rechanneling without changing the essential nature of what was being channeled, so the anaclitic relationship suggested that the self-preservative drive and the sexual drive might travel together, so to speak, without essentially modifying each other. In the later view, both sublimation and fusion suggest that the nature of the drives themselves may be fundamentally altered.

With these theoretical emendations, the trend that characterized the evolution of the drive/structure model from the early defense and wish models—the trend toward increasing specificity with respect to the sources of energy activating the psychic apparatus—has been reversed. Where we once had libido, with self-preservation in a secondary role, we now have libido, aggression, grades of fusion and defusion of the two, libido that is sublimated in varying degrees, self-preservative aspects of both drives, and aims imposed on libido by the ego's ability to affect a transformation from object-choice to narcissism. Although the essential assumption that motivation is derived ultimately from endogenously arising, biologically determined drive is maintained, the specificity as to the content of those drives has been considerably weakened. In place of this specificity, our attention is directed to the early relationships within which the multiple demands of drive are organized and actualized.

The Role of Anxiety and the Late Affect Theory

In Freud's early defense model, repression was instigated because an idea was threatening to break through into consciousness which, as a result of incompatability with the dominant mass of ideas, would bring with it an unpleasurable affect. The quality of the affect, its value with relation to pleasurable or unpleasurable feelings, was seen as determined both by the personality of the individual and by the situation in which he found himself. Affect was thus the primary motivating factor in conflict, repression, and the genesis of neurotic symptoms.

With the advent of the drive/structure model, affect was relegated to a theoretically secondary position. In the metapsychological papers, it is presented as a derivative of drive. In his paper "Repression" Freud holds that "the term *quota of affect* . . . corresponds to the instinct in so far as the latter has become detached from the idea and finds expression . . . in processes which are sensed as affects." Again, discussing the fate of the quantitative (libidinal) factor of a repressed instinctual representative, "it appears as an affect which is in some way or other qualitatively coloured" (1915b, pp. 152, 153). The emergence of affect was seen as evidence that repression was at least partially failing, and the qualitative coloring that the discharged quantity took on was considered relatively serendipitous, and in any case inconsequential from the dynamic point of view.

Whatever the nature of a given affect, at the height of the drive/structure model its analysis required that we uncover the libidinal force which has led to its appearance. This represented a major change from the early model of the papers on the neuropsychoses of defense and the *Studies on Hysteria*, in which intolerable affects set the processes of repression, and thereby of symptom formation, in motion. The specific quality of affect, determined by a range of factors including the nature of the situation, the values of the individual involved, and the standards of society, was the primary determinant of the future course of events. With the establishment of the primacy of drive, the specific qualities of affects were disregarded, except as they reflect the nature of the repressed instinctual impulse.

Among the affects, anxiety has played a particularly important role in psychoanalytic thinking because it is an almost universal symptom of neurotic disorders. In Freud's early view of the actual neuroses he saw anxiety as the product of dammed-up libido which had become "toxic"; because there were no opportunities for discharge, the libido had become (physiologically) transformed. The theory of anxiety in the psychoneuroses, and the theory of affect generally, was imported from this approach to the actual neuroses. Anxiety was seen as the result of a damming-up, not in this case because of inadequate sexual opportunity, but because of repression.

The decreasing specificity in Freud's drive theory might be expected to lead to a recasting of affect theory to bring it more to the center of his theoretical system. This was in fact the case, although, as in other situations, the defection of a former adherent was the immediate impetus to Freud's theoretical revision. In this instance the defector was Otto Rank (1929), who suggested that the birth trauma was the core cause of neurotic development. Freud responded by arguing that, although the experience of birth gave shape to the experience of anxiety (a point which he had argued many years before; see Freud, 1910b), it was not on that account the cause of all anxiety.

In *Inhibitions, Symptoms and Anxiety* Freud undertook one of his most far-reaching revisions of his earlier theory. He reversed the relationship between anxiety and repression. Anxiety was the revival of remembered feelings that had occurred in a range of dangerous situations the first of which was birth. The situations were dangerous because they warned of an approaching trauma, and trauma was defined as the helplessness of the organism in the face of an overwhelming build-up of instinctual need.

The ability to recall and reexperience these feelings was attributed to the ego for use at its discretion. When the ego senses that a dangerous instinctual impulse is on the verge of breaking through to consciousness, it can summon up a small dose of the relevant mnemic image and, by doing so, calls to its aid the pleasure principle. With the pleasure principle on its side, the ego has the strength to instigate the repression of the threatening impulse. Anxiety is thus used by the ego as a signal to initiate defensive activity.

The idea that repression is initiated as a result of the anxiety signal turns our attention to the circumstances in which the ego senses that an impulse could be dangerous, which is reminiscent of Freud's earliest defense model. The revised anxiety theory places unpleasant affect and its situational aspects back at the center of the dynamic point of view. Here, however, the danger relates, finally, back to the demands of drive. The ego defends itself against the experience of nonsatisfaction, of a "growing tension due to need," and of helplessness in the face of instinctual pressure (1926a, p. 137). The contextual emphasis of the early theory has been retrieved, but it has been filled by a content which is determined by the nature of drive, and especially of the libidinal drive.

Freud's clinical application of the new anxiety theory illustrates the implications of this particular aspect of theoretical accommodation. In his *New Introductory Lectures on Psycho-Analysis* he describes the origin of an animal phobia in the conflict of the oedipal period:

> It is true that the boy felt anxiety in the face of a demand by his libido — in this instance, anxiety at being in love with his mother . . . But this being in love only appeared to him as an internal danger, which he must avoid by renouncing that object, *because it conjured up an external situation of danger* . . . The danger is the punishment of being castrated, of losing his genital organ. You will of course object that after all that is not a real danger . . . But the matter cannot be dismissed so simply. Above all, it is not a question of whether castration is really carried out; what is decisive is that *the danger is one that threatens from outside and that the child believes in it*. (1933, p. 86; italics ours)

Castration is thus not merely a reactive fantasy of the child. Freud suggests that such threats are frequently made, and that castration as a punishment for incestuous wishes has a long history in the phylogeny of the human race. Although the fear is based on a distorted perception of reality, it is nonetheless experienced by the child as originating in reality (unlike, for example, the feelings which are at the root of "organic repression" in the *Three Essays*), and this is the critical dynamic factor in the generation of anxiety and, consequently, of repression.

Freud has stopped short here of attributing to reality circumstances all that he might have, although the formulation does direct our attention to environmental conditions. What he has not done is to develop the implication that in different circumstances, that is, in different families, the castration threat might be experienced more or less intensely. The emphasis on phylogeny turns us away from the idea that different parents react with different levels of hostility to the child's impulses and, in fact, to the child himself.* This strategy of theoretical preservation parallels that which we have seen with respect to the regulatory principles and which we will encounter again in our discussion of the Oedipus complex.

An instructive comparison can be drawn between the definition of trauma at the time of the defense model and that of the late anxiety theory. In the former, trauma was defined as the moment in which the incompatible idea had forced its way into consciousness (Breuer and Freud, 1895). There is no specificity as to the nature of the incompatible idea, or even as to the nature of the opposing dominant mass of ideas. In the late perspective, the notion of something forcing itself on something else returns, but here the intruding idea is specifically instinctual in nature. Trauma in the late theory refers to helplessness in the face of drive demand. As Freud puts it, "the loved person would not cease to love us nor should we be threatened with castration *if we did not entertain certain feelings and intentions within us*" (1926a, p. 145; italics ours). And of course the intentions are always the derivatives of fully specified instinctual drives.

The late anxiety model, in summary, gives the impression of the sort of drawings used by Gestalt psychologists to illustrate the ambiguity of figure-ground relationships. The primacy now of external circumstances, now of drive demands comes to the foreground as we examine clinical material. Although Freud himself, true to the fundamental premises of the drive/structure model, continued to maintain drive at the center of the theoretical structure, the late model moved others to a more focused consideration of the role of reality factors, especially of the realistic aspect of object relations.

Developmental History, the Structural Model, and Object Relations Theory

From the perspective of the practicing psychoanalyst, the role of realistic object relations in patients' lives can at times be obscure. People in analysis talk about repetitive, self-defeating patterns in their lives, patterns that emerge consistently in situations which are, realistically, very

*Within the drive model it was almost twenty years before Hartmann, Kris, and Loewenstein (1949) suggested that the intensity of the child's castration anxiety reflected the intensity of the parent's aggression toward him, aggression which might be veiled and which would have begun long before the oedipal period. This perspective restored the importance of reality factors to its place in the defense model.

different. In the adult, the analyst is confronted with a set of channeled, structured aims that operate consistently with a range of apparently indifferent objects. With the emergence of the transference the analyst becomes aware that he has, for the time being at least, become a part of the patient's problem; the same patterns are being repeated with himself as the object, despite "objective" differences between himself and other people in the patient's life. Transference as Freud conceived it is a clear index of the resistance of the adult patient's internally determined motivations to influence by different external conditions, a fact he considered the most conclusive evidence for his drive theory (1914b).

If the study of adults leads us to emphasize structured aims, the observation of children and of child development underscores the importance of interactions between the individual and his environment in bringing about this structuralization. Winnicott's statement (in Guntrip, 1975) that "There is no such thing as a baby" is not only an expression of his theoretical bias but also of his observational position as a pediatrician and child analyst. Even clinicians steeped in the premises of the drive/structure model, if they work extensively with children, cannot fail to be impressed with the constant interaction between instinctual aims and parental response. It is these observations that underlie the important theoretical emendations of Anna Freud and Margaret Mahler.

Freud's observational base during his evolution toward the drive/structure model consisted entirely of clinical experience with adults, and for his first twenty years as a psychoanalyst he had hardly any developmental theory at all. His first attempt to trace the genesis of neurosis beyond the initial appearance of symptoms led him to postulate the seduction theory, which bears only on pathogenic events and which Freud himself quickly abandoned. The first edition of the *Three Essays on the Theory of Sexuality* does have a rudimentary approach to early development in the ideas that independently operating component instincts must come together into a unity if the child is to be adequately prepared for mature object relations and that the finding of a sexual object depends on the anaclitic relationship between the sexual drives and those serving self-preservation. This approach, however, is sketched only vaguely.

Even the developmental history of the libido, a concept often considered the center of Freud's theory, was in fact a late arrival. The original version of the *Three Essays* mentions only the autoerotic phase. The narcissistic phase was added in Freud's analysis of the Schreber case (1911b), the analsadistic phase in his paper on "The Disposition to Obsessional Neurosis" (1913), the oral phase in an addendum to the *Three Essays* in 1915, and the phallic phase not until 1923 in the paper on the infantile genital organization (1923b). The development of repressive forces received even less attention in the early years; the first detailed account comes in the "Two Principles of Mental Functioning."

The theory of the developmental phases of libido evolved under the influence of Freud's earliest purely psychological model of the mind, the topographic model introduced in *The Interpretation of Dreams* (1900, 1915c). The three psychic systems delineated in this model—the unconscious (Ucs.), preconscious (Pcs.), and conscious (Cs.)—were defined both in terms of the accessibility of their contents (ideas) to consciousness and in terms of their basic principles of operation (the primary and secondary processes). From the outset Freud suggested that the mind of the infant at birth consisted virtually entirely of primary process operations, that is, the system Ucs; the Pcs. and Cs. were understood to appear during the course of development. There was no articulated concept of what would influence this course or of how the growing child's experience would affect his acquisition of the more advanced capacities beyond the suggestion that hallucinatory gratification of need must eventually give way to a solution more in tune with realistic considerations. Freud's depiction of the preconscious and conscious strata of the mind was far less elaborated than his vision of the Ucs.; the early phase of the topographic model leaves us in considerable doubt about just what mechanisms the Pcs. and Cs. might need or use.

In the paper on the two principles of mental functioning Freud (1911a) proposes the reality principle as a developmentally achieved modification of the original pleasure principle; he also suggests that various mental functions—perception, cognition, memory, reality testing, and so on—emerge to guarantee the effectiveness of this modification. These new functions make possible the postponement of drive discharge until a time when an appropriate object is realistically available: they are the nuclear functions of what in the later theory will be the structure ego. The ideas of the "Two Principles" provide a framework for bringing an originally autistic infant into some kind of relationship with the outside world.

The developmental theory of 1911 is organized around the infant's reality experiences in that the institution of the reality principle and of its attendant functional capacities is made necessary by repeated situations of drive frustration. It is, however, a reality still without an important role granted to the infant's objects; the frustrations are inevitable, regardless of who is responsible for meeting the infant's needs. There is no framework for embracing differences among caretakers. The "rejecting" mother influences the establishment of the reality principle and the cognitive capacities no differently than does the "smothering" mother.

In fact, there is no place in the theory at all for different sorts of mothers.

With his introduction of the concept of narcissism Freud began to modify his views on the role of the object in the psychic economy and to embrace a more articulated view of development. The idea that libido captured by the ego can be used for its own narcissistic aims supplements the explanatory framework of the topographic model by ascribing activity and therefore structural influence to the ego. In addition, Freud attributes a crucial developmental vicissitude to the ego's original store of libido: it is used in the formation of the ego ideal, a differentiated part of the ego which, as Freud puts it, "finds itself possessed of every perfection that is of value" (1914a, p. 94). Like the ego once the theory of narcissism evolved, the ego ideal from the outset has an important structural role; it is "the conditioning factor of repression" (1914a, p. 94). Tension between the ego ideal and the actual ego, mediated by the agency of the "conscience," determines which impulses can be allowed expression, which must be defended against. The ego ideal thus plays the role of the "dominant mass of ideas" in the early defense model.

The ideas that the ego is divided into different structural units, one of which instigates repression, and that the ego ideal has genetic roots in early childhood clearly indicate the beginnings of Freud's shift toward the structural model and its developmental implications. There is, however, a major gap between the 1914 approach and the later emphasis on object relations: the movement from narcissism to ego ideal development is here construed as a libidinal vicissitude. The content of the ego ideal is determined essentially by the content of the drive. Where the "dominant mass of ideas" had important social constituents, the ego ideal as originally postulated does not. Freud has proposed a structure, a container, to be filled; in the earliest formulation, the libido determines its contents.

This approach did not, however, dominate Freud's thinking for long. In "Mourning and Melancholia" (1917a) he turned to analytic experience with depressed patients, noting the relationship between the loss of an object in reality (or the loss of especially valued characteristics of the object, such as its love) and a perceived ego loss (that is, loss of self-esteem). He suggests that when libido is withdrawn from an object following its loss, under certain circumstances it is not employed in the establishment of new object cathexes but is rather withdrawn into the ego (that is, secondary narcissism is established). When this occurs, the libido "served to establish an *identification* of the ego with the abandoned object. Thus the shadow of the object fell upon the ego, and the latter could henceforth be judged by a special agency, as though it were an object, the forsaken object. In this way an object-loss was transformed into an ego-loss and the conflict between the ego and the loved person into a cleavage between the critical activity of the ego and the ego as altered by identification" (1917a, p. 249; italics in original). Here, in the concept of identification, we encounter for the first time the ability of the object to influence the nature of psychic structure.

In "Mourning and Melancholia" Freud sketched out some of the most important aspects of the structural model. But in 1917 identification was limited to pathological cases; it was presumed to occur on the basis of the regression to narcissism of an originally narcissistic type of object relationship. Identification appears as a normal mechanism in *Group Psychology and the Analysis of the Ego* (1921), in which the close ties between the nature of the ego ideal and relationships with important objects is also discussed. The structural model in *The Ego and the Id* moved Freud's theory to final acceptance of the developmental approach to object relations.

With the concepts of narcissism, identification, and the ego ideal, the topographic model was bursting at its seams. The division of the mental apparatus into the systems Ucs., Pcs., and Cs. was, under the old theory, considered to exhaust the functional regions of the mind. Yet the new insights pointed the way to an ego with a differentiated "special agency" that had an important role to play. The situation was somewhat analogous to that which exists today with respect to the concept of the self: how can it be fit into a presumably inclusive psychological map? Can it be subordinated (or supraordinated) to existing structures or must the present model be completely overhauled to make room for the new concept?

Two clinical issues determined Freud's approach to the problem in 1923. First, he observed that resistances in psychoanalytic treatment generally operated as far from consciousness as did the repressed forces themselves. This was unsupportable within the topographic model, in which resistance was attributed to the system Pcs. Furthermore, the frequently occurring "negative therapeutic reaction" pointed to unconscious feelings of guilt, and feelings could not be unconscious within the terms of the older theory. These observations, added to the theoretical pressures generated by Freud's work from 1914 on, caused him to abandon the topographic model.

In *The Ego and the Id* he proposed a new tripartite structure of the mind. The model organized around the phenomenon of accessibility to consciousness was abandoned; the terms referring to this lost their systematic connotations and were used to refer only to qualities of ideas. (This represents a return to the original defense model, before the pub-

lication of *The Interpretation of Dreams*.) Each of the three hypothesized structures—the id, ego, and superego—had unconscious aspects,
although only the latter two had any access to consciousness at all. The
id of the structural model, in terms of its contents and its mode of functioning, is virtually identical to the system Ucs. of the earlier theory.
This central feature of Freud's strategy of theoretical accommodation
represents once again his tendency to modify the theory of the repressive
forces while leaving the theory of the repressed intact.

With the ego and the superego Freud's theory had formally defined
structural components of the psychic apparatus for which he had already
begun to sketch a developmental history. All that was needed was to
generalize the process described in "Mourning and Melancholia" and
elaborated in *Group Psychology*. The emergence of identification, an alteration of the ego on the basis of an earlier object relationship following
object loss, was now viewed as a normal and inevitable developmental
process: the universal road to ego and superego formation. The loss of
the early object, more accurately the series of losses which occur so frequently in the course of growing up, played somewhat the same role as
frustration in the model of the "Two Principles." They were seen as inevitable and crucial to the development of mature psychic structure.
Now, as Freud puts it, "the character of the ego is a precipitate of abandoned object-cathexes and . . . it contains the history of those object-
choices" (1923a, p. 29).

By far the most important object loss the child experiences is the loss
of the oedipal object, or, more accurately, of his fantasies about it. It is
this loss which gives the major impetus to ego and especially to superego
formation; thus, the Oedipus complex constitutes the cornerstone of
both healthy and neurotic development. The dissolution of the Oedipus
complex leads to the identifications that constitute the superego and to
the capacities for sublimation that allow the ego to operate most effectively. The Oedipus complex also gives rise to the reactive guilt which is
the most important source of neurotic conflict in later life.

The Oedipus complex is part of an object relations theory because it
involves interaction among three people, each of whom brings his own
aims to it. Because its outcome determines the nature of the ego and the
superego, in stressing the Oedipus complex Freud could be altering
some of his fundamental theoretical premises. There is some discrepancy
here between Freud's clinical observations and his theoretical formulations. In his analysis of Leonardo da Vinci (1910c) and in his case history
of the Wolf Man (1918b) he makes it quite clear that the conscious and
unconscious attitudes of the parents shape the nature of an individual's
particular oedipal experience. In a general statement he notes that,

when turning to the incestuous object, the child "usually follows some indication from its parents, whose affection bears the clearest characteristics of a sexual activity . . . As a rule a father prefers his daughter and a mother her son; *the child reacts to this* by wishing, if he is a son, to take his father's place, and, if she is a daughter, her mother's" (1910d, p. 47; italics ours).

The full theoretical exposition of the Oedipus complex downplays these interpersonal observations in favor of constitutional factors. Freud states that its establishment and dissolution are "determined and laid down by heredity" and that, regardless of the actual interpersonal transactions that characterize the period for a given individual, it will pass "when the next pre-ordained phase of development sets in" (1924d, p. 174). As far as the result of the phase itself, he holds that "in both sexes the relative strength of the masculine and feminine sexual dispositions is what determines whether the outcome of the Oedipus situation shall be an identification with the father or with the mother" (1923a, p. 33).

By postulating a psychic apparatus that includes the ego and the superego, structures with a developmental history, and by underlining this history with the exposition of the Oedipus complex, Freud enormously increased the role of the object in the mental economy. The new model, however, still abides fully by the fundamental premises of the drive/structure model. The formation of the object, even as the object itself is identified with and influences character formation, is still determined by the nature of the underlying drive. Moreover, the balance of forces at work in the mind strongly favors the id. The ego, endowed with no energy source of its own, is dependent entirely on the id in this respect. This is the meaning behind Freud's famous comment that the ego "in its relation to the id is like a man on horseback, who has to hold in check the superior strength of the horse; with this difference, that the rider tries to do so with his own strength while the ego uses borrowed forces . . . Often a rider, if he is not to be parted from his horse, is obliged to guide it where it wants to go; so in the same way the ego is in the habit of transforming the id's will into action as if it were its own" (1923a, p. 25). And the source of energy in the id is precisely that of the Ucs. dating back to the formulation of the *Three Essays*.

Despite their clearly articulated relation to reality figures, the ego and the superego are genetically tied to the id. The id, like the system Ucs., comprises the whole of the psychic apparatus at birth. The ego differentiates out of the id as a result of its exposure to reality. The superego, although its history begins later and its emergence represents a further differentiation within the ego, is fueled by the id's cathexes which have been withdrawn from lost objects. Thus, the superego often acts *like* the id while it is acting *in opposition* to it; its functioning is often characterized by the same harshness and peremptoriness as the id's demands. In emphasizing the ties of these structures to their instinctual roots, Freud remains within the framework of the drive model. The enhancement of the role of the object in the structural model is crucial theoretical change, but it is also theoretical accommodation.

The extent to which Freud remained faithful to his fundamental assumptions becomes clear in some late statements concerning superego formation. He argues that the fact that psychic structure results from early identifications does not imply that that great influence comes from the actual person identified with. He states that "the original severity of the super-ego does not—or does not so much—represent the severity which one has experienced from it [the object], or which one attributes to it; it represents rather one's own aggressiveness towards it" (1930, pp. 129–130; brackets in original). He returns to a similar point later in the statement that "There is no doubt that, when the super-ego was first instituted, in equipping that agency use was made of the piece of the child's aggressiveness towards his parents for which he was unable to effect a discharge outwards on account of his erotic fixation as well as of external difficulties; and for that reason the severity of the super-ego need not simply correspond to the strictness of the upbringing" (1933, p. 109). The particular tie between object formation and libidinal phase is underscored in the very late comment that the superego's "excessive severity does not follow a real model but corresponds to the strength of the defence used against the temptation of the Oedipus complex" (1940, p. 206).

If the Oedipus complex is easily treated by the drive/structure model analyst as a fantasy—as an external playing out of endogenous impulses—the matter is different when it comes to preoedipal issues. During the oedipal period we are confronted with a fairly well-developed personality, with an apparently consistent motivational structure and correspondingly channeled methods of achieving aims. The situation is somewhat analogous to that pertaining to the analysis of adults: there is a stability and direction behind the individual's psychic operations that appears to function quite independently of environmental response. In the case of very young children, however, our observations lead us in a different direction. What is clearest is the child's vulnerability, his need for other people. His instinctual aims are difficult to discern; they are fragmented, inchoate. We focus, then, less on those aims than on the child's vulnerability and security needs, and these force on our attention an awareness of the exquisite interaction between the child and his care-takers.

It is not surprising that the theoretical appreciation of object relations *in reality* is enhanced by observational attentiveness to the earliest years of life. This Freud was slow to do, especially since he relied for his data on the verbal reports of adult patients, reports of memories that tend not to be capable of coherent expression before the age of four or five years. The structural model, however, pointed to the need for a theory of preoedipal object relations, especially as they bear on ego development. Moreover, with the postulated relationship between object loss, identification, and psychic structure formation, the model had at least a rudimentary framework for such a theory.

In the same year that he published *The Ego and the Id*, Freud discussed a sequence of narcissistic losses that precede and pave the way to castration fears. These include the loss of the mother's breast after sucking, the loss of feces in the act of moving his bowels, and the separation from his mother at the time of birth (1923b, p. 144). This sequence prefigures the famous list of early danger situations in *Inhibitions, Symptoms and Anxiety* and is notable for both its similarity to and difference from the developmental sequence of libidinal stages. The crucial difference here is that for the first time object relations are given an ego (narcissistic) as well as a libidinal determinant. In the later formulation the ego aspect is stressed even more clearly. The danger situations include, in chronological order: birth, the loss of the mother, the loss of the mother's love, castration, and the loss of the superego's love (Freud, 1926a). These situations refer not only to the cause of the danger, but also to a progressively differentiated concept of the object. The child first fears loss of the mother as an environment (birth), the loss of a state in which there is genuinely no distinction between self and object. Next, with at least the relative awareness of the mother as separate and caretaking, he fears separation from her. In the third stage he is aware that not only the mother's presence is crucial, but that a particular aspect of her as a person — her attachment to him — is necessary. The fourth stage tokens the emergence of the tie between child and mother into a highly specified, channeled aim. It is the loss of the ability to relate to the mother as an object of the sexual drives expressed through phallic impulses that is feared. Finally, in the fear of the loss of the superego's love, the object has been internalized and continues to operate effectively even when not present. Independence from the need for the object to be present makes self-regulation possible, and the early danger situations give way to fear of the loss of the benign presence of the object transformed into structure.

The theory of a sequence of narcissistic losses and of early danger situations never led Freud to a fully articulated vision of early object relations. He felt that each of the danger situations was ultimately based upon the ego's inability to master an increase of instinctual pressure (1926a), so that the reality implications of the new model were subordinated in explanatory power to instinctual determinants. It was left to his followers to build upon the framework to which he had been led by the structural model.

Freud's most penetrating discussions of preoedipal object relations appear in a series of papers on female sexuality. His most widely noted, and criticized, idea on this subject is that in the transition from preoedipal to genital sexuality women must abandon their leading sexual organ, the clitoris, in favor of vaginal pleasure. All Freud's discussions of the issue make this point, and it lends them a somewhat anachronistic flavor. However, the overall impression that one gets from the series of papers is that Freud believed that the major problem for women was not the change of sexual zone, but the change of sexual object. Unlike the boy, who can carry his original attachment to his mother into the oedipal years, the girl, if she is to achieve heterosexuality, must make the switch from her mother to the oedipal father. This focuses Freud immediately on the problem of what it is about the girl's preoedipal tie to her mother that makes possible this renunciation.

Freud's first discussion of the issue occurs in his description of a case of female homosexuality (1920b), in which a fixation to the mother has made the necessary change impossible. Shortly thereafter he talks of girls' experience of disappointment with the mother, which gives rise to the need to switch objects and to the possibility of doing so (1925a). Disappointment is a relational concept that points to the actual characteristics of the object, who may be more or less disappointing in reality. Freud does not develop this aspect of the problem in his first approach to it. Rather, he emphasized the girl's disappointment at not being given a penis, which he sees as sufficient cause for her rejection of the earliest love relationship. The onset of the Oedipus complex, with the wish to be given a child by the father, is seen as compensation for the earlier failure.

In Freud's later works, although the failure to receive a penis remains a crucial undercurrent, disappointment, hostility, and fear are traced to a broad spectrum of transactions characterizing the early mother-daughter relationship. They are the result of what Freud considers the boundless demands of childhood, which can never be fully gratified, and of the mother's role in the prohibition of early masturbation. Moreover, he says of the girl's fear of the mother, "It is impossible to say how often this . . . is supported by an unconscious hostility on the mother's part which is sensed by the girl" (1931, p. 237).

This last comment points, perhaps more decisively than anything else in the body of Freud's writings, to the importance of reality in preoedipal object relations. It reemerges in a fascinating discussion of girls' reports of oedipal seductions. In his *New Introductory Lectures* Freud reiterates his belief that these seductions are fantasies, but he takes a different view of earlier relationships. He writes that when it comes to preoedipal situations, "the phantasy touches the ground of reality, for it was really the mother who by her activities over the child's bodily hygiene inevitably stimulated, and perhaps even roused for the first time, pleasurable sensations in her genitals" (1933, p. 120). The mother thus *realistically* both seduces the child and punishes her for her later masturbatory transgressions; the ambivalence inherent in this position vis-à-vis the child's early impulses paves the way for the eventual object shift.

While his discussions of preoedipal object relations occur specifically within the context of female sexuality, Freud (1931) accepts Lampl-de Groot's (1928) view that the situation is the same for both sexes. However, he never developed the issue in any detail with respect to the little boy, perhaps because the clarity with which he had articulated the male Oedipus complex would have been disturbed. In fact, with his view of the early situation introduced quite late in his life, Freud was never able fully to integrate the realistic aspects of object relations into his developmental theory. It might follow, for example, that the view of the mother as a realistic early seducer could be carried forward into the theory of the establishment and the dissolution of the Oedipus complex, but it never was. Nor was the idea that the mother's unconscious hostility might parallel an unconscious sexual aim, or that both of these might be important aspects of the father's response to the child. It should be clear, however, that Freud in the 1930s was moving toward a more thorough appreciation of these issues.

Discussing the impact of new approaches to the preoedipal period on his existing theory of female sexuality, Freud writes: "Since this phase allows room for all the fixations and repressions from which we trace the origin of the neuroses, it would seem as though we must retract the universality of the thesis that the Oedipus complex is the nucleus of the neuroses . . . [But] we can extend the content of the Oedipus complex to include all the child's relations to both parents" (1931, p. 226). With this statement, which suggests the possibility of an extension that Freud never actually introduced, he touches the heart of the issue we have been stressing. The statement implies that the Oedipus complex itself is a theoretical structure, a container which, to be useful, must be filled with assumptions drawn from a particular model. The container was once filled with constitutionally determined drives and their vicissitudes; these in and of themselves had the specificity to imbue it with interpretive possibilities, with meaning. With the discovery of new data that meaning is no longer adequate, and the container must be filled with something new. Here Freud turns to the multitextured interplay of various relations among the members of a family. Further clinical experience may be integrated into the structure, which will expand to accommodate new information. Keeping in mind that drive lends its distinctive cast to the contents of the theoretical container, we may appreciate the power, elegance, and flexibility of the model which Freud created.

*One might say of Apollo what Schopenhauer says . . . of man
caught in the veil of Maya: "Even as on an immense, raging sea,
assailed by huge wave crests, a man sits in a little rowboat trusting
his frail craft, so, amidst the furious torments of this world, the individual sits tranquilly, supported by the* principium individuationis
*and relying on it." . . . Apollo himself may be regarded as the
marvelous divine image of the* principium individuationis, *whose
looks and gestures radiate the full delight, wisdom, and beauty of
"illusion."*
—NIETZSCHE, The Birth of Tragedy

4 Interpersonal Psychoanalysis

For the first forty years of its history psychoanalysis was relatively homo-
genous, constituting a broad transition evolving from Freud's work,
from which several splinter movements had broken off from time to
time. Jung and Adler, subsequent to their defections in the early 1900s,
developed theories in very different directions. Jung elaborated a complex and esoteric system of universal, spiritually grounded archetypes,
and Adler extended psychodynamic thinking into social and educational
areas. During the 1920s Rank and Ferenczi introduced some important
criticisms and alternative approaches specifically concerning analytic
technique, but they did not develop their work into a fully elaborated
theoretical position or attract broad followings. It was not until the late
1930s that a broad, alternative tradition began to emerge, deriving in
part from the earlier defections, explicitly breaking with the basic premises of Freud's drive/structure model. The comprehensive framework
developed within this alternative tradition has come to be designated as
Interpersonal Psychoanalysis.

Interpersonal Psychoanalysis does not constitute a unified, integral
theory, as does classical Freudian drive theory. It is instead a set of
different approaches to theory and clinical practice held together by
shared underlying assumptions and premises, drawing in common on
what we have characterized as the relational/structure model. The key
figures in this movement—Harry Stack Sullivan, Erich Fromm, Karen
Horney, Clara Thompson, and Frieda Fromm-Reichmann—knew each

other and worked together, and their individual contributions reflect considerable cross-fertilization. They began at a common starting point: a conviction that classical drive theory was fundamentally wrong in its basic premises concerning human motivation, the nature of experience, and difficulties in living and, therefore, that drive theory provides an inadequate and essentially misleading foundation for psychoanalytic theorizing and clinical technique. They also shared a common belief that classical Freudian theory underemphasized the larger social and cultural context which must figure prominently in any theory attempting to account for the origins, development, and warpings of personality. This emphasis on cultural contributions to personality sets them apart from the other major source of the relational/structure model—the British school of object relations theory.

The interpersonal tradition has been classified as "culturalist" and represented, particularly by its critics, as essentially "sociological," viewing the individual as a passive vehicle for cultural values, a blank slate on which social norms are written (Sugarman, 1977; Guntrip, 1961). This charge is common among defenders of the drive/structure model, for whom the spatial metaphor of a psyche filled with energy derived from drives, pushing from underneath, is presumed. Within the drive/structure model, social reality constitutes an overlay, a veneer superimposed upon the deeper, more "natural" fundaments of the psyche constituted by the drives. Any theory omitting or replacing the drives as the underlying motivational principle and, in addition, emphasizing the importance of personal and social relations with others is, from this point of view, superficial by definition, concerned with the "surface" areas of the personality, lacking "depth." The interpersonal tradition has been accused of failing to do justice to human passions, the deepest individual motivations and conflicts, viewing the individual as merely a cultural product. This constitutes a serious misreading. Sullivan, Fromm, and Horney all portray the human experience as fraught with deep, intense passions. The *content* of these passions and conflicts, however, is not understood to derive from drive pressure and regulation, but from shifting and competing configurations composed of relations between the self and others, real and imagined.

Sullivan has been one of the most influential, most ambitiously radical, and most frequently misread figures in the history of psychoanalytic ideas. His role has been elusive and paradoxical. His work, although rarely studied comprehensively and in the original, has had enormous influence on modern American psychiatry and contemporary psychoanalytic thinking. It has been suggested that Sullivan "secretly dominates" much of modern clinical psychiatry in the United States (Havens and

Frank, 1971), and that he has been "America's most important and unique contributor to dynamic psychiatry" (Michels, quoted in Havens, 1976). Sullivan's concerns and formulations, derided by classical authors during his lifetime (Jacobson, 1955) or ignored, have resurfaced, at times in strikingly unaltered form, within the most important and popular Freudian authors of the past decade. Yet he is rarely credited with originating these approaches and ideas.

These paradoxes derive from the political consequences of Sullivan's radical break with Freudian orthodoxy as well as from the demands posed by the substance and style of his approach. He was greatly interested in the misuse of language by patients, by therapists, and by theorists. He was deeply concerned by what he considered the prevalent use of words to obscure rather than to deepen experience, to conceal rather than to communicate, and to impart an illusory sense of control, knowledge, or power. Sullivan demands more of his readers than most analytic authors; he tries to startle them, to jar them from habitual and unwittingly obfuscatory thinking and communicating. He wants his audience to realize that the manner in which they usually view human experience and difficulties is fundamentally misconceived, based on erroneous yet comforting illusions. Sullivan's goals are extraordinarily ambitious, and he was well aware of the paltry tools language provides. He never systematized his concepts into anything approaching a formal unity; most of the books published under his name are compilations of transcripts and notes from his lectures and talks. This failure to integrate and formalize his contributions seems to have been a product both of Sullivan's great wariness concerning the misuse of theory as dogma and overcautiousness, a deep fear of being misunderstood. Thus, the body of work which he left is difficult and challenging and, ironically, easily misunderstood. Reading Sullivan is an acquired taste that requires an extremely active and critical engagement with the flow of his ideas.

The greatest influences on Sullivan's vision and urgent sense that psychiatry and psychoanalysis required a radically different approach were the intellectual milieu characterizing American thought in the early twentieth century, dominated by the philosophy of pragmatism, and his experience with schizophrenics, who constituted almost exclusively his patient population in the early years of his career. Sullivan studied medicine during the 1920s in Chicago, hub of the tremendous fervor which characterized American intellectual life at that time. Pragmatism, with its distinctly American roots and character, dominated philosophy and served as the foundation for the great activity taking place within what Sullivan's biographer, H. S. Perry, characterized as the "mosaic of Chicago social science" (1964, p. xix). Sullivan's theories developed in the same medium as, and were greatly influenced by, the work of George Herbert Mead, Charles H. Cooley, Robert E. Park, Jane Addams, W. I. Thomas, and Edward Sapir. Pragmatism, in its broadest terms, was a reaction to the lofty, immaterial abstractions characteristic of nineteenth-century European metaphysics. The pragmatists argue that philosophy should concern itself with lived experience, practical reality, life as it is sensed and felt. The various social sciences infused with the spirit of pragmatism were characterized by an orientation toward the practical, social reality, and what can be seen and measured and away from unseen abstractions. The psychiatrists who most influenced young Sullivan (Edward J. Kempf, Adolf Meyer, and William Alanson White) were adherents of this point of view, putting great emphasis on the social reality of the patient's life, the concrete circumstances in which he lives, and the importance of, as White put it, making an effort to "determine what the patient is trying to do" (quoted in Sullivan, 1940, p. 177). Sullivan's reaction to the intricate and elegant edifice of classical Freudian psychoanalysis, newly introduced onto the American continent, was very much informed by this pragmatic sensibility.

The area of psychopathology to which Sullivan applied this approach was schizophrenia, a field dominated at the time not by the work of Freud, but by the formulations of Emil Kraepelin. Between 1923 and 1930 Sullivan ran, with great personal care to detail and staffing, a small ward for male schizophrenics at the Sheppard and Enoch Pratt Hospital in Towson, Maryland. This experimental ward was the first example of what is now called a "therapeutic community" and greatly influenced the attention to the social and interpersonal setting which characterizes most progressive psychiatric hospitals today. It was in this context that Sullivan honed his considerable clinical skills and fashioned the basic elements of his interpersonal theory. Many of his principles and emphases can be fully understood only in the context of their origins as reactions against Kraepelinian psychiatry in his struggle to understand schizophrenic phenomena.

Sullivan and Kraepelin: The Early Use of Freud
The world in which Sullivan began his clinical work with schizophrenics differed markedly from the broad range of approaches, theories, and treatments which characterize the current psychiatric and psychoanalytic community. Psychiatric thought in the first several decades of the twentieth century was dominated by the work of Kraepelin, "father of modern psychiatry," whose textbook, continually revised and updated, was considered the most reliable and "scientific" guide through the

murky and disconcerting realm of psychotic disorders. Kraepelin had organized disorders such as catatonia, delusions, hallucinations, and hebephrenia, which had previously been understood to represent different pathologies, under the more general disease entity he termed dementia praecox. These "subtypes," he argued, all reflect a similar underlying, irreversible deterioration, leading to a total disintegration of mental and emotional functioning. Unfortunate victims of the disease could be usefully studied and contained within custodial care, but any attempt at ameliorative treatment was useless.

Freud's early psychodynamic formulations concerning schizophrenia were very different from Kraepelin's biological approach, but in terms of their treatment implications they were consistent with his point of view. Freud had distinguished between the "transference neuroses," in which libido remains attached to object images, making transference and analytic treatment possible, and "narcissistic neuroses" (including schizophrenia) in which libido has been directed exclusively toward the self, making transference and analytic treatment impossible. Sullivan began his early researches amid this deeply rooted consensus concerning the untreatability of schizophrenia, and his reaction to Kraepelinian thought concerning schizophrenia set the basic themes, principles, and emphases that dominated his subsequent contributions.

Sullivan was struck by the disparity between *his* patients (whose pathology seemed to reflect an adaptation to circumstances, whose utterances often seemed comprehensible, and who seemed accessible to therapeutic intervention) and the convictions, based on Kraepelin's views, held by the majority of the psychiatric community. How was this disparity possible? He became intrigued by the way in which scientists like Kraepelin develop erroneous concepts and misleading labels and adhere to their beliefs despite evidence to the contrary. Kraepelin's authority on schizophrenia was bolstered by post hoc tautological diagnoses; if the patient recovered, it was argued, he did not really suffer from dementia praecox, since the latter constitutes an irreversible deterioration.

Kraepelin would demonstrate his views by public interviews of patients hospitalized for years. Sullivan questioned his interpretation of this data, suggesting that what Kraepelin was demonstrating had less to do with schizophrenia than with the phenomenon which has come to be known as "hospitalism." He argued that Kraepelin's theory rested on the "compilation of observational data on the developed disorders, illustrated with specimens (occasionally of the 'side-show' variety) collected after the abnormal reactions had become habitual and relatively immutable adjustments to reality" (1925a, 32n). Sullivan argued that such an approach reflected more about the theorist's own "diagnosing zeal and taxonomic enthusiasm" than about the patient (1925a, p. 26); he decried the "mysticism and cant," (p. 30) prophesy, and "diagnosis by outcome" (1962, p. 159) that pervaded these popular views of schizophrenia. His early papers on schizophrenia call for a new methodology which would force the researcher's attention onto the person suffering the pathology rather than on the researcher's own preconceived formulations and explanations, whose major function, Sullivan began to feel, is to impart an illusory sense of power, knowledge, and "objectivity." He called for the "intimate personal observation of schizophrenic content and behavior" rather than "neurological explanations, dualist bugbears and anthropomorphic reifications" (1924, p. 9). "Anything of value in our work," he argued, "comes from the intimate and detailed study of particular individuals" (1925a, p. 28).

In mounting an attack on the conventional wisdom of his day, in his early papers Sullivan drew on a wide amalgam of terms and concepts from Bleuler's study of schizophrenia, Jungian theory, mechanical physics, philosophical pragmatism, and academic psychology. His most important intellectual source, however, was Freud. Sullivan attempted to demonstrate that schizophrenic phenonema were not random products of neurological deterioration, but conveyed *meaning*, in the same way that Freud had demonstrated the meaning of neurotic symptoms twenty years earlier. Sullivan's dense early mixture of theory and concepts accompanies detailed accounts of the history, treatment, and outcome of cases of schizophrenia, striking in their sensitivity to and respect for the patient. This early work resulted in several deep and pervasive convictions which constitute the foundation for his later expansion of his theory to nonschizophrenic areas of human experience.

Schizophrenia is not a process emerging from within the individual organism: it is a reaction to processes and events taking place between the individual and his environment, the latter consisting of both the significant persons with whom the patient interacts and the larger social and cultural values which they transmit. It is now a commonplace experience of most beginning practitioners within the mental health field to be powerfully struck by the meaningfulness of seemingly incomprehensible aspects of schizophrenic psychopathology when viewed within the context of the patient's family setting and parents' personalities (see Laing and Esterson [1964] for perhaps the most dramatic portrayal of this phenomenon). Sullivan's study of schizophrenics and their families opened up this area for the first time. It became clear to him that the salient dimension of schizophrenic pathology, underlying its exotic and bizarre surface, was a severe disturbance in the capacity to relate to other people, and that this disturbance was a product not of an irreversible biological process, but of the history of the patient's interactions with significant others. Schizophrenic phenomena, he argued, are difficult to comprehend only when they are examined apart from the interpersonal context from which they derive and take their meaning. Actual relations with others, past and present, are the ground from which schizophrenia arises. And Sullivan came increasingly to feel that all milder maladjustments as well were the result of disorder in the patient's relationship with one or more members of the family group.

Schizophrenia reflects a fundamental disorder or "warp" in the basic organization of the personality, constituting a "disaster to self-esteem." Recovery from it, Sullivan emphasized, is contingent not upon insight alone but on the fundamental reorganization of the personality, entailing the incorporation of previously unintegrated experiences into the self.

The personal relationship between patient and therapist is the most important determining factor, positively or negatively, in the fate of the patient. Sullivan was as impressed by the magical use of language by the psychiatric "scientist" to support an illusory sense of knowledge and control as he was with the autistic use of language by the patient. "There is no difficulty in psychological inquiries in arriving at erroneous but gratifying conclusions" (1929, p. 206).

These three observations led Sullivan repeatedly to voice strong opposition to the presumption of "objectivity" and "detachment" in work with schizophrenic patients — a concern that had considerable importance in his later approach to psychoanalytic technique. Within the context of the disturbing and disconcerting pressures created in the presence of schizophrenic patients, he came to feel, "far more than any single action of the physician, it is his general attitude towards the patient that determines his value" (1924, p. 20).

The basic principles and emphases of Sullivan's interpersonal theory were forged by his efforts to disentangle the psychiatry of his day from its history of biologisms and pseudo-objective nosological preoccupations, and to move it in the direction of a more truly psychodynamic point of view. Throughout these efforts his attitude toward Freudian psychoanalysis was characterized by a marked ambivalence. On the one hand, Freud's depiction of psychic conflict, repression, and unconscious mental processes provided Sullivan with the key conceptual tools he needed to challenge Kraepelin's fatalistic, biologically based view of schizophrenia as irreversible neurological deterioration. Sullivan's early papers were written in what he himself characterized as a "strict conformity to the delineation of Professor Freud" (1925b). He utilized many concepts drawn from classical libido theory, although often in a highly idiosyncratic fashion. He anticipates later contributions of Klein, Fairbairn, and others by pointing out the frequency with which sexual wishes and conflicts are the vehicle for other, often earlier, infantile thoughts and impulses involving dependency longings (1925a, pp. 92–93); he suggests that dreams express not only "latent" content but the character structure of the dreamer; he adds to the technique of "free association" the "careful use of questions," which would become the hallmark of his later contributions to analytic technique; he anticipates Fairbairn by redefining the Oedipus complex as a product of a "segregation" of bad impressions onto one parent and good ones onto the other (1972, p. 144). Sullivan also emphasized the importance to him of his own personal analysis; "There is nothing else," he says admiringly, "in the activity of man that approximates the complexity and subtlety of the psychoanalytic situation" (1934, p. 314).

On the other hand, like his senior colleagues Meyer and White, Sullivan was concerned about the growing dogma generated by Freud's theories and what he felt were the limitations of that approach when applied to lower-class American patients, particularly those suffering from more severe disorders. He never addressed Freudian theory head-on; his criticisms are made in short passing references, often in footnotes. Perry (1964) suggests that Sullivan was very concerned with not undermining the tenuous reception Freudian psychoanalysis had received within the American psychiatric community and that this caution limited his criticism of Freud and was a major reason for his refusal to publish the volume *Personal Psychopathology* (1972) which contains the most critical references to Freud to be found in Sullivan's work. Sullivan and his collaborators existed in a state of relatively peaceful coexistence with Freudian psychoanalysis until the 1930s, when, following the influx of European analysts as emigrés, political lines and rigidity created complex schisms among the institutes.

Despite Sullivan's avoidance of a fully developed critique of Freud, by piecing together scattered references we can reconstruct the four major lines of his increasing reservations concerning Freudian thought. First, in formulating the concept of "narcissistic neurosis," Freud had taken too pessimistic a view of the therapeutic possibilities of work with schizophrenic patients. Second, Freud was too free in postulating universal principles like castration anxiety from a minimal amount of data (1972, p. 222n); like Kraepelin, he assumes a license for speaking of processes, like the death instinct, in no way accessible to observation (1972, p. 223n). Third, Freud had underemphasized the importance of relations with others, both on an immediate, interpersonal level and also in terms of the broad impact of culture on individual functioning. At one point or another throughout his writings and lectures, Sullivan suggests that every major tenet of Freud's drive theory can better be understood in terms of interpersonal and social processes. The Oedipus complex, he suggests, is an artifact of the prominence in our society of competitiveness, jealousy, prolonged dependency, and sexual hypocrisy (1925a, p. 94). Oral dynamics are "generally tendencies of a social rather than hedonistic nature"; orality concerns not pleasure per se, but the taking in of "substance" (1927, p. 168). The predominance of sexual conflicts in many patients is not a product of the clash between polymorphously perverse sexuality and a universal incest taboo, but of cultural institutions requiring late marriage, a taboo against premarital sex, and a constriction with respect to sexual pleasure in general, making Western men and women "the most sex-ridden people of whom I have any knowledge" (1940, p. 59). Sullivan accuses Freud of cultural myopia: he mistakes his own cultural context for the universal human condition and assumes, as did Kraepelin, a misleading and impossible "objectivity," leaving out the "social and cultural aspects of the thinker's opinion-formation" (1931, p. 276). Fourth, Sullivan repeatedly expresses concerns about the dangers not of Freud's work per se but of what might be termed Freudianism—the establishment of his views as dogma, demanding devotional fealty and claiming comprehensive answers to all issues. He decries the "scholasticism of certain psychoanalytically inclined psychiatrists" (1931, p. 274), the "quest for certainty" in the use of psychoanalytic formulations, the cultish snobbery of the appeal to esoteric knowledge among psychoanalysts aspiring to the "society of the faithful" (1948, p. 261), and the "rabid disciple of the New Knowledge" (1972, p. 350). Nowhere is Sullivan's ambivalence toward the contributions of Freudian psychoanalysis in understanding schizophrenia expressed more clearly than in his warnings against those unsuited for psychotherapy with schizophrenics.

> The unanalyzed psychiatrist and the psychiatrist filled with the holy light of his recent analysis are in general not to be considered for this work. The former have generally a rigid system of taboos and compromises which are rather obvious to the schizophrenic intuition, so that the patient comes early to be treating the physician, and to be fearing him. The analytic zealot knows so many things that are not so that the patient never makes a beginning. (1931, p. 289)

Sullivan's Methodology

Sullivan's contributions to psychoanalytic thought fall into two broad categories which blend and intermingle in the development of his ideas:

a sweeping critique of existing psychiatric and psychoanalytic language and methodology based on the principle of operationalism (borrowed from the physicist Bridgeman); and the generation of a set of new theoretical principles, a new interpretive framework for understanding human experience and difficulties in living. Some of Sullivan's interpreters have minimized the importance of the latter dimension, the theory, arguing that he simply provides a methodology, a pragmatic, data-based way of looking, along with a series of discrete observations. These dismiss his work as a "point of view" rather than a "substitute" theory (Modell, 1968, p. 4). Other, more positive readings minimize the theory as such while glorifying the methodology, claiming that Sullivan has developed a way of observing clinical data which is free from theoretical presuppositions and philosophical presumptions. We believe that Sullivan *does* provide a theory, and that the theory has been at least as important within the development of psychoanalytic ideas as the methodology. He provides not only a critique of traditional methodology and a different *way* of seeing the data but also a markedly and pervasively different *vision* of human experience. What Sullivan *sees* is different, organized differently, understood differently. The principles upon which his new vision is based are not inherent or observable in the data per se; they are brought to the data, as are Freud's drive model concepts, in an effort to make the data meaningful and understandable.

Sullivan's stress on operationalism is directly derivative of the intellectual concerns and sensibilities informed by Pragmatism as well as of his own early work with schizophrenic patients. The sharp contrast between the actuality of his schizophrenic patients and the abstract and undemonstrable biologistic formulations which presumably explained them made a lasting impression on Sullivan. A useful theory, he resolved, is one whose terms are clearly understood and whose data consist of that which is publicly available. The patient's behavior, the content and manner of the patient's speech, information supplied by others about the patient, the feelings and actions of the therapist in the presence of the patient—these are data subject to consensual validation, data in the "public" realm. Because of Sullivan's methodological emphasis on data that are clearly observable and accessible he is sometimes misread as a "behaviorist" or "sociologist," suggesting that only *behavior*, only *social interaction,* constitute legitimate data, eliminating the experiential—fantasy, wishes, the "depths" of human experience. This is incorrect. What Sullivan is arguing is that we can only meaningfully study what we can observe, and that we can only observe what we can see and hear. Clinical phenomena are "phenomena that go on between the observer and the observed in the situation created by the observer participating with the observed" (1940, p. 12). This specifically includes the patient's "verbal report of subjective appearances (phenomena)" (1938a, p. 34) as well as wishes, fantasies, all of the most private and personal of experiences, as long as they can be expressed in language or conveyed nonverbally.

Two areas *are* specifically excluded: events or feelings which take place within the patient's experience but are ineffable, unable to be communicated, "immutably private"; and processes *presumed* to be taking place inside the patient's experience to which neither the patient nor the therapist have direct access. Sullivan's use of the concept of the unconscious is instructive here. Clearly there is much in human experience that is discontinuous, characterized by gaps, suggesting the workings of covert or unconscious mental processes. In speaking of covert processes, hypotheses are necessary and these are often not wholly demonstrable. In that sense operationalism functions more as an ideal than as an always practical standard (1953, p. 15). It is precisely for this reason that Sullivan warns against the assumption of a license to fill in these gaps in a specific and elaborate fashion.

> The unconscious, from the way I have actually presented the thing, is quite clearly that which cannot be experienced directly, which fills all the gaps in the mental life. In that rather broad sense, the postulate of the unconscious has, so far as I know, nothing in the world the matter with it. As soon as you begin to arrange the furniture in something that cannot be directly experienced, you are engaged in a work that requires more than parlor magic and you are apt to be embarrassed by some skeptic. (1950a, p. 204)

Language, he insists, is very dangerous; it is possible to speak of all sorts of places and processes, objects, structures, and drives, presumably inside the patient's head or mind. The sharpest differences between Sullivan's version of the relational model and those developed with the British school of object relations concerns precisely the use of language suggesting "internal" objects, structures, and processes with presumed phenomenological referrents. Kleinian theory, in its elaboration of an entire world of unconscious phantasy, represents the fullest development of the kind of theorizing Sullivan was extremely wary of.

Paralleling Sullivan's cautiousness in the use of theory is a deep respect for the intricacy and uniqueness of individual experience. "There is an essential inaccessibility about any personality other than one's own . . . There is always an ample residuum that escapes analysis and communication . . . No one can hope fully to *understand* another. One is very fortunate if he approaches an understanding of himself" (1972, p. 5). One must not take one's theory, one's diagnostic concepts, one's explanations, too seriously, he emphasizes over and over. In the end, the actuality of the living person always eludes the theory and is more complex than the diagnostic formulations (1972, p. 306). As scientists, we are limited to consensually valid information and hypotheses; yet, there is always a gap between the consensually valid and the personally valid (1972, pp. 24, 27). This deep sense of finitude and humility with respect to theory construction pervades Sullivan's theorizing as well as his approach to therapy; the latter is portrayed as a perpetual and necessarily incomplete inquiry, resulting in a "closer and closer approximation" to the ultimately unknowable lived reality of the patient's life. Sullivan's respect for the uniqueness of the individual and the limits of theory is often overlooked by critics who focus on his inveighing against the "illusion of unique individuality."

Basic Concepts
"The field of Psychiatry is the field of interpersonal relations — a personality can never be isolated from the complex of interpersonal relations in which the person lives and has his being" (1940, p. 10). This deceptively simple statement is the basis for Sullivan's approach and contains important epistemological, metaphysical, and methodological implications. All knowledge of another person, he suggests, is mediated through interaction: we come to know another by observing what he does, by observing ourselves in interaction with him, and by listening to his reports of his interactions and experiences. In that sense, the data-gatherer is never simply an objective reporter, but always a "participant-observer." "Personality is made manifest in interpersonal situations, and not otherwise" (1938a, p. 32). Personality, Sullivan argues, is not an entity, a concrete structure that can be perceived, known, and measured. Personality is by definition a temporal phenomenon, a patterning of experiences and interactions over time, and the only way in which personality can be known is through the medium of interpersonal interactions.

Sullivan's placing the study of personality within the interpersonal field presumes a larger metaphysical vision, drawn from Whitehead and based on the principle that life is process and flux, a never-static, continual series of energy transformations. Sullivan suggests that "the ultimate reality in the universe is energy" (1953, p. 102). Thus, on metaphysical as well as on methodological grounds, he objected to the metaphor and language of structure in psychoanalytic theorizing, the generation of concepts presumed to reflect intrapsychic "quasi-entities" such as the superego, ego-structures, introjects, and so on. There are no "structures," he argued, only patterns of energy transformations — *structure is energy*.

Sullivan's concept of energy differs from Freud's as contemporary physics differs from Newtonian physics. For Newton, whose weltanschauung informed the vision of Freud and all other nineteenth-century scientists, the world is constituted by matter and force; energy acts upon matter, moving preexisting structures. Thus, for Freud the psychic apparatus is distinguishable from the energy (the drives) which propels it into motion. Within contemporary physics, on the other hand, matter and force are interchangeable; matter *is* energy. For Sullivan, as for Whitehead, the mind is a temporal phenomenon, energy transforming itself through time. The only meaningful referent for the term "structure" is a pattern of activity; the only meaningful referent for the concept of a psychic "energy" is the entire stuff of mental life, not separable quantities that propel mental life. (Fairbairn also argued this point of view, more explicitly and fully, in his critique of drive theory metapsychology.)

Sullivan substitutes the term "dynamism," defined as the "relatively enduring pattern of energy transformations" (1953, p. 103), for the classical term "mechanism," to "avoid too close an ideational association of known function to unknown structure" (1972, pp. 17–18n). Human experience consists of patterns of processes, not "concrete, substantial mechanisms" (1950a, p. 324). Likewise, Sullivan views psychopathology not in terms of disease "entities," but in terms of "syndromes," characteristic patterns of integrating relations with others, "processes of living." A person *is* what he *does*, and everything he does which is knowable is done within the interpersonal field.

Persons are motivated by "needs," separable, in Sullivan's system, into two broad categories: needs for satisfactions, and needs for security. The relative balance between these needs is the key factor in determining emotional richness and health versus constrictive difficulties in living. Both sets of needs operate in the interpersonal field and are intrinsically concerned with relations between the self and others.

Needs for satisfactions include a broad range of physical and emotional tensions and desires. Many of these, such as needs for food, warmth, and oxygen, pertain to the chemical regulation of the interaction between the organism and the environment, and thus concern the survival of the organism. Other needs for satisfaction pertain to the necessity for emotional contact with other human beings, beginning with a simple "need for contact" in the infant and proceeding, through the various developmental epochs, to needs for more and more complex and intimate relations with others. Needs for satisfaction also include the simple and joyful exercise of capacities and functions, beginning with the pleasure which infants find in "playing with their abilities" and extending to more adult forms of play and self-expression (1950a, p. 211).

Because the infant cannot satisfy his own needs, the satisfaction of the infant's needs requires another person. Sullivan stresses repeatedly that the infant is inconceivable outside of an infant-mother dyad: "There has to be a mothering one . . . [since] . . . the infant is not himself adequately equipped" (1953, p. 37). He devised what he calls his "tenderness theorem" to explain the manner in which the infant's expression of needs induces the integration of an interaction with the mother leading to the satisfaction of that need. "The observed activity of the infant arising from the tension of needs induces tension in the mothering one . . . experienced as tenderness and as an impulsion to activities toward the relief of the infant's needs" (1953, p. 39). Thus, the expression by the infant of his need calls out a reciprocal and complementary need impelling the caretaker to care for the infant's needs. The cry of the hungry baby arouses a tender feeling in the mother, accompanying the physical engorgement of the breasts with milk. The baby needs to be fed; the mother needs to nurse. A successful integration is achieved. All other needs for satisfaction operate similarly: their expression calls out complementary needs in others. Needs for satisfaction generally operate as "integrating tendencies"; thus each of the needs of the infant is "ingrained from the very beginning of things as an interpersonal need" (1953, p. 40).

The satisfaction of needs requires an exchange between the organism and the environment, and these exchanges are localized at what Sullivan calls "zones of interaction," which operate as the "end station in the necessary varieties of communal existence" (1953, p. 64). The primary zones in the infant include: oral, retinal, auditory, tactile, vestibular, kinaesthetic, genital, and anal. The zones of interaction function not as a source for the generation of their own energy and motives but as a channel for the more general needs for satisfaction. "Excess" energy within the zones of interaction not used in the service of other needs can be experienced as a desire for the exercise of those zones, the need to manifest various capabilities as they mature. There is often a need for sucking, for example, apart from the need for nourishment and contact. Only these purely zonal needs, according to Sullivan, can be gratified self-sufficiently, apart from interaction with others. Thumb-sucking, for example, can provide a satisfactory discharge of excess energy within the oral zone. The primary function of the zones of interaction, however, is to provide a channel to the other, to facilitate the interpersonal integrations necessary for the satisfaction of needs, operating as integrating tendencies.

Only some of the infant's needs for satisfaction are present at birth—others, emotional needs in particular, emerge over the course of development. Sullivan groups emotional needs under the generic heading of the "need for tenderness," which undergoes various transformations over the course of development, beginning with the infant's earliest requirement of bodily contact, a "need for contact with the living" (1953, p. 290). Sullivan then delineates various developmental epochs defined in terms of the prevalent kind of relatedness which is sought: the child (age one to four) seeks participation of adults as an "audience" for his play and efforts; the juvenile (four to eight) seeks competition, cooperation, and compromise with other juveniles; the preadolescent (eight to puberty) seeks an intimate, collaborative, and loving relationship with someone of the same sex, the "chum"; and the late adolescent (postpuberty) seeks an intimate, collaborative, loving, and sexual relationship with someone of the opposite sex. Each developmental threshold is introduced by the emergence of a need for a new, more intimate form of relatedness. The failure to satisfy these interpersonal needs results in loneliness, which, according to Sullivan, is the most painful of human experiences.

If living concerned only the emergence of various needs for satisfactions, life would, according to Sullivan, proceed simply and sweetly. Various needs develop and draw one into contact with others in whom complementary needs are evoked, resulting in successful interpersonal integrations. The fly in the ointment, the hidden menace that interferes with simple living and successful integration of situations, is anxiety. The power anxiety wields over our lives, Sullivan suggests, derives from the circumstances characterizing its appearance within the infant's experience.

The infant's experience of anxiety is identical to "fear." Fear is caused either by violent disturbances in perceptions (such as loud noises or cold) or by dangers posed to the existence or biological integrity of the organism (hunger or pain); anxiety, in the highly specific manner in which Sullivan uses this term, is "caught" from caretakers. He suggests that anxiety in those around the infant is picked up, even if the anxiety has nothing to do with the infant per se. The process through which anxiety is conveyed he terms "empathic linkage." Because of its origin, the state of anxiety is unique within the infant's experience and comes to dominate his life. All other tensions experienced, created by needs for satisfactions, are ameliorable and constructive. As the infant expresses other needs, tenderness is evoked in the caretakers leading to a successful integration with the infant in which the original tensions are resolved. No so with anxiety. The anxious infant expresses his discomfort. The caretaker likewise feels tenderness and attempts to minister to the infant's needs. But with anxiety, the caretaker only makes things worse. He is the *cause* of the infant's anxiety in the first place; his attentions, although well-meaning, bring him in his anxious state closer and make the infant *more* anxious. The infant becomes more distressed, creating more anxiety in the caretaker, which in turn creates more anxiety in the child.

This cataclysmic snowballing of distress constitutes the most intense experience in living in the early months of life. In fact, Sullivan suggests, the first distinction the child learns, the first discrimination in living he or she achieves, is between nonanxious states (including relaxed, tensionless times as well as the emergence and resolution of various needs for satisfaction) and anxious states. All other tensions are manageable and operate as integrating tendencies; anxiety cannot be controlled or resolved; it is a disintegrating tendency that interferes with other possible integrations involving satisfaction. When intensely anxious, the infant, like the adult, cannot successfully eat, exchange tenderness, play, and so on. The earliest anxiety is an experience that torments the infant mercilessly and from which there is no exit.

The infant possesses few cognitive or organizational skills; thus, the earliest experiences with caretakers are "nebulously cosmic in proportions, vested with the most extreme 'felt' aspects of comfort and discomfort and essentially without relationships other than temporal coincidence and succession" (1950a, p. 310). Others are experienced in global and nondistinct terms. Because the presence or absence of anxiety in the mother is *the* factor determining the presence or absence of anxiety in the infant, Sullivan terms this earliest discrimination in the infant's experience between nonanxious and anxious states "good mother" and "bad mother" respectively. The term "mother" is in no way to be confused with the actual mother. From the infant's point of view, the distinction between anxious and nonanxious people takes precedence over any other distinctions someone else might care to make. "Good mother" and "bad mother" are composite personifications, the former composed of nonanxious, tender experiences with all the significant others the infant comes into contact with, and the latter of all the anxious experiences with those same others.

We have suggested that in Freud's drive/structure theory the infant creates the object as an extrapolation and realization of features inherent in the demands of component drives themselves. In Sullivan's relational/structure theory the infant discovers the object or, rather, discovers himself in relation to his objects. According to Sullivan's account of the phenomenology of the infant's experience, the dawning of self-consciousness is precipitated by the first discrimination of two global states: a rhythmic oscillation between tensions and euphoria ("good mother"), and recurring, terrifying bouts of anxiety ("bad mother"). These terms refer not to a distinct "other," differentiated from the self, but to two diffuse and undifferentiated states of being in which images of self and images of others are fused. Thus, the infant begins to become aware of himself by discovering two types of interactions he finds himself immersed in. Sometimes he participates in interpersonal integrations triggered by some felt need, which provokes a complementary need in the caretaker, leading to a successful integration and resolution. Other times he participates in interpersonal disintegrations, triggered by anxiety in the caretaker.

Only gradually do the various components of these global states — the respective characteristics and contributions of the caretakers and the infant — become teased apart and perceived somewhat separately. In Sullivan's view, the actual features of the caretakers as people have an enormous impact on the child, both before and after they are apprehended and articulated. Parental character is the medium within which the child's personality is structured. The distribution of anxiety-free and anxiety-filled areas of functioning in the caretakers sets the context within which the child comes to experience him- or herself, and the subtleties of parental responsiveness interfuse all aspects of the child's self-awareness. The infant in Sullivan's system has no psychological existence prior to his or her embeddedness in interactions with the caretakers and discovers him- or herself as well as the "object" through a complex developmental process.

Sullivan felt it would be incorrect to classify the residues of the early experiences as perceptions; they are too indistinct, too vague, too inaccessible to awareness. He characterizes these early images and sensations, as well as aspects of later experiences which are retained although not clearly understood or formulated, as "prehensions." The infant's prehension of the "bad mother," filled with and spewing anxiety, is in marked contrast to the experience of the "good mother," filled with tenderness and responsive to every need.

Sullivan defines security as freedom from anxiety.* Because of the

---

*This definition of security is drawn from Sullivan's latest lectures (1953). In earlier formulations (1940) he links the need for security with a need for "power," as an antidote to the helplessness caused by early parental disapproval. In later formulations he drops the notion of an independent power motive (reminiscent of Adler) and portrays the pursuit of security in negative terms — the avoidance of anxiety — which may or may not entail a search for power.

noxious and inescapable quality of early anxiety, the need for security becomes the dominant concern in the infant's developing capabilities and continues to be so throughout life. How can the infant escape anxiety? Sullivan delineates a sequence of steps in which the infant first learns to discriminate "signs" connected with the anxious as opposed to the nonanxious mother—wrinkled brow, postural tensions, and so on. These earliest prehensions are registered because they are *useful*. The infant learns to anticipate whether anxious or nonanxious mother will appear. The infant gradually realizes that good mother and bad mother are a single person and prehends that some of his behavior makes mother more anxious and some of his behavior makes mother less anxious. With this discovery, which peaks at the age of about one year and is facilitated by the inception of language, the infant begins the development of a complex set of processes to control the mother's anxiety and thereby, through the empathic linkage, his own anxiety. These processes entail the constrictive patterning of the infant's experiences and the blocking of certain dimensions of this experience from access to awareness. This brings us to Sullivan's concept of the self and a brief digression concerning his use of it.

Sullivan uses the term "self" in a highly specific and idiosyncratic fashion differing from the connotations found in other authors. His formulations concerning the self fall into three major phases. In his early papers on schizophrenia, he employs the phrase "sentiment of self-regard," borrowed from academic psychology, in a general sense to refer to the abysmally low sense of self-worth that characterizes pre-schizophrenic and schizophrenic persons.

During the 1930s Sullivan's formulations concerning the self became more specific, and he began to distinguish between the self and the personality. Personality refers to the entire functioning of the person, and is describable in terms of the predominant patterns of behavior and experience. Self refers to a particular organization of experience *within* the personality, constituted by images and ideas concerning the person's experience of himself. One's personality is what one *is*; one's self is what one *takes oneself to be*. What one takes oneself to be, Sullivan theorized, drawing heavily on the social psychology of G. H. Mead, is largely a product of what others take one to be; "each of us constructs from the perceived reactions of others to us a body of beliefs as to our personality, this going to make up the self" (1972, p. 64). "The self may be said to be made up of reflected appraisals" (1940, p. 22). Thus, the personality has a "dichotomous character"; experiences consistent with appraisals of significant others are organized into the "self"; other experiences, incongruent with the appraisals of significant others, remain the "extra-self," functional within the personality but unrecognized and unacknowledged. The self is perpetuated and protected within the personality by a complex set of rationalizations, self-deceptions, and denigrations of others (entailing transfer of unwanted features of the personality onto them).*

In his late lectures Sullivan's portrayal of the development of the self changes becomes more subtle and moves beyond Mead's work; the self is no longer simply a collection of reflected appraisals. The self now is considered a complex organization of experience, derived from but not lifted out of, the child's interactions with significant others: "the self-system, far from being anything like a function of or an identity with the mothering one, is an organization of experience for avoiding increasing degrees of anxiety" (1953, p. 166).

The infant's earliest organization of experience is based on the distinction between anxious states (bad mother) and nonanxious states (good mother). As the child's cognitive capacities mature, he begins to anticipate and to link his behaviors with the mother's affective state. Some areas of experience and behavior meet with mother's approval, evoking more tenderness and less anxiety; therefore, through the empathic linkage, they make the child less anxious. These areas of the personality Sullivan designates "good-me." Some areas of experience and behavior make mother more anxious and therefore, through the empathic linkage, make the child more anxious. These areas are "bad-me." Some areas of the personality evoke *intense* anxiety in the mother and thus create intense anxiety in the infant. This experience is dreadful for the infant and produces an amnesia for the events leading up to the precipitation of the intense anxiety. Such experiences remain completely unknown and unintegrated. This area of the personality Sullivan designates as "not-me." All of the infant's characteristic experiences

---

*Sullivan uses the term "self" with two distinct kinds of referents. Sometimes it refers to *content*, the beliefs, images, and ideas generally derived from reflected appraisals which the person retains concerning himself. Other times "self" refers to the set of processes which establish and protect that content, "a selecting and organizing factor" actively determining which experiences will be incorporated into the self (1938, p. 36). Until his last lectures, Sullivan's use of terminology in referring to these two aspects of the self (which Barnett [1980] calls its "representational" and "operational" qualities respectively) is inconsistent; he uses the same words (self-system, the self, the self-dynamism) variably to cover both meanings. It is not until the lectures delivered in the last five years of his life that he provides a more systematic terminological separation of these two dimensions of experience. He employs "self-system" only in reference to the functional, operational aspects of the self. It is a vast system of processes, mental states, symbols, and signs of warning, operating to minimize anxiety. Sullivan introduced a new term in the late lectures — the "personification of the self" — to refer to the representational aspects, or content, of the self.

become colored by the affective response they generate in the mother and, through the empathic linkage, in the infant. Eventually the intervening stage of the mother's response is no longer necessary: experiences within good-me are accompanied by a sense of security and relaxation; experiences within bad-me are accompanied by mounting anxiety; not-me experiences are enshrouded with intense anxiety. The self-system uses this rudimentary organization of experience in the infant's efforts to control anxiety, by attempting to limit awareness to experiential content within good me. The self-system, by controlling access to awareness, steers a course through the child's experience; under normal circumstances, this course is always in the direction of experiences and behaviors associated with parental approval and non-anxiety, and away from areas of experience and behavior associated with parental anxiety. As the child matures, the functioning of the self-system becomes more complex. It no longer draws simply on the control of awareness for the minimization of anxiety, but employs a whole set of processes, which Sullivan terms "security operations." The latter function by distracting attention from the "point of anxiety" onto other mental content which feels safer and more secure, often imparting an illusory sense of power, stature, and specialness. Most security operations include "an extravagant, superior formulation of the self" to aid in overcoming anxiety (1940, p. 121). Through these devices, the self-system tends to perpetuate the shape which the self took during early childhood, and thus to perpetuate its "isolation" within the personality. New kinds of experiences and needs, drawn from bad-me and not-me, arouse anxiety and hence are avoided. The person tends to stay within those areas of the personality which are relatively free from anxiety.

One of the most prevalent of the self-system's security operations entails the evocation of fictitious others. Relations of most people tend to be dominated by "illusory 2-group patterns." As the self-system anticipates anxiety and threats to self-esteem in relations with others, fictitious patterns are superimposed on experience; these consist of an image of the self and a corresponding image of the other. (Such patterns might include: the self as helpless yet deserving / the other as magical and merciful; the self as victimized / the other as powerful and tyrannical; the self as special / the other as admiring.) In some sense we are all continually anticipating, which entails the projection of these old illusory patterns onto all new experiences. "We attempt to foresee action; we foresee it as the activity of embodied others" (1953, p. 359). However, to the extent to which anxiety and security operations dominate life, the illusory 2-groups, borrowed from past integrations, either distort or completely obscure actual relatedness in the present.

Sullivan termed such relations "parataxic integrations," "when, besides the interpersonal situation as defined within awareness of the speaker, there is a concomitant interpersonal situation quite different as to its principal integrating tendencies, of which the speaker is more or less completely unaware" (1936, p. 23). These characteristic, compulsive, and illusory integrations are not simply fanciful, purely autistic creations (as, for example, self-object configurations in Klein's theory often are), nor are they standard patterns concerned with universal needs (as, for example, self-object configurations in Kohut's theory). The "me-you patterns," which become the basis for habitual distortions in experience, are always derived from actual, if improperly understood, experience with real others, in which the self has experienced some shreds of security or control, and which henceforth become misapplied in the face of anxiety. "From its origin in concrete experience and a real interpersonal situation, each personification has itself had a developmental history which is in turn completely understandable in terms of the functional adequacy of the person in the series of interpersonal situations through which he has had to live" (1938a, p. 79).

Thus, within Sullivan's system, *anxiety about anxiety* is at the core of all psychopathology and constitutes the basic organizational principle of the self. Original experience with anxiety, because it entails such intense helplessness and passivity, leaves behind a residue of terror and generates a phobic attitude toward experiences of even mild degrees of anxiety. The self operates solely on the need for security, based on the principle that anxiety is to be avoided at all costs and that power, status, and prestige in one's own eyes and in the eyes of others is the broadest and surest route to safety. Thus, the self, in Sullivan's use of the term, serves a negative and preservative function: it protects the rest of the personality from the threat of anxiety and preserves a sense of security in which satisfactions and pleasures may be enjoyed.

Life is lived, in Sullivan's vision, in the broad dialectic between needs for satisfaction and the need for security. Experiences entailing needs for satisfaction are essentially "selfless," requiring no particular self-reflexiveness, self-aggrandizement, or self-organization. Life based on the satisfaction of needs simply flows. Anxiety constantly interrupts this flow, and, because of our phobic terror of anxiety, a legacy from early childhood, anxiety arouses the need for security. The pursuit of security is carried out and pervaded by the operations of the self. The self steers attention away from anxiety emerging in the flow of life by creating an illusory sense of power and control over life. All security operations start out with the sense of "I," and the "power of I" imparts a sense of false domination.

Sullivan describes the workings of the self in various ways in different places throughout his work ("our proud self-consciousness"; "the noisy self"). They all reflect the narcissistic, fantastic quality which makes it possible for the self to reduce anxiety. "Each of us comes to be possessed of a self which he esteems and cherishes, shelters from questioning and criticism, and expands by commendation, all without much regard to his objectively observable performances, which include contradictions and gross inconsistencies" (1938a, p. 35). The central aim in the pursuit of security is to bolster and protect this "cherished self." Thus, there is continual tension between the pursuit of satisfactions and the pursuit of security. The former leads toward simple, constructive integrations with others and a joyful exercise of functions; the latter leads toward disintegration, nonconstructive integrations with others, and self-absorbed fantasy and illusion. "Any interpersonal situation is thus prone to stir conflict between the drive to reaffirm the importance of the self, and some other drive for satisfaction by way of cooperation" (1972, p. 72). The pursuit of security, if unchecked and unattended, crowds out the joyful pursuit of satisfactions: "the content of consciousness pertaining to the pursuit of satisfaction and the enjoyment of life is at best marginal. It is one's prestige, one's status, the importance which people feel one is entitled to . . . that dominate awareness" (1950a, p. 219).

Thus, Sullivan felt, the pursuit of security in its various forms and through its various operations, becomes the supervalent motivational principle in most people. Security operations usurp and warp interpersonal situations, making the satisfaction of needs peripheral at best. Mental health can be measured in terms of the balance between the pursuit of satisfactions and the pursuit of security: "this business of whether one is getting more or less anxious is in a large sense the basic influence which determines interpersonal relations — that is, it is not the motor, it does not call interpersonal relations into being, but it more or less directs the course of their development" (1953, p. 160).

The Models Compared

Every major feature of Sullivan's theory reflects his shift from Freud's drive/structure principles to relational/structure premises. The basic unit in classical theory is the individual psyche, and Freud's rich and incisive theorizing is framed by that focus. What are the events taking place *within* the mind? What is the ebb and flow of internal dynamic processes? Relations with others are not ignored, but interpreted in terms of, in some sense reduced to, *internal* mental events vis-à-vis internally arising, drive-related processes. Past relations with others are contained in psychic structures; they have become absorbed into and function as forces within the individual psyche. Current relations with others, including the analytic relationship, are understood as transferential reflections of internal processes, an occasion for the projection of internal events and struggles.

The basic units in Sullivan's interpersonal theory are the interpersonal field and the relational configurations that derive from it. The individual psyche, in this view, is a part and reflection of a larger whole, and is inconceivable outside of a social matrix. To grasp the nature of experience one must consider it *within* that environing medium. One may study a plant by separating it from the soil, sunlight, water, carbon dioxide, and other features of the environment in which it lives and is in perpetual exchange. Useful data may emerge from such a study, but they are incomprehensible unless viewed in the context of the plant's necessary environment. The very tissues constituting the plant have been drawn from the environment and cannot be understood apart from it. Likewise, the very stuff of experience, the ingredients of individual functioning is composed of relations with others, past and present, real and imagined. The separation of a "personality" from its network of interpersonal configurations is merely a verbal trick, an art of "perverted ingenuity" (1930, p. 258). The human organism, Sullivan stresses over and over, can only be grasped within the "organism-environment complex" and is therefore incapable of "definitive description in isolation" (1950a, p. 220). Personality, or the patterning of interpersonal situations, develops from and is composed of relations with others, and is made manifest only in the context of an interpersonal relationship: "everything that can be found in the human mind has been put there by interpersonal relations, excepting only the capabilities to receive *and elaborate* the relevant experiences. This statement is also intended to be the antithesis of any doctrine of human instincts" (1950b, p. 302).

The distinction between the drive/structure underpinnings of Freudian theory and the relational/structure underpinnings of Sullivanian theory concerns the basic constituents of experience, the difference between a theory of mind composed of drive-derivatives and a theory of mind composed of relational configurations. Sullivan's theory has also been compared to classical theory on the basis of the distinction between an "interpersonal" versus an "intrapsychic" approach. This distinction, important in its own right, does not parallel, but is secondarily related to the more basic distinction between the drive/structure and relational/structure models. Whereas the latter distinction concerns constituents, the distinction between intrapsychic and interpersonal theories concerns the origin of those constituents of experience and the predominant sphere of inquiry into their functioning.

Drive/structure model theories are necessarily intrapsychic—the drives by definition originate within the individual mind; the obvious focus of inquiry into drive-derived processes is within the fantasies, wishes, and impulses of the individual. Relational/structure model theories can be either intrapsychic or interpersonal in focus. Some theories within this model view relational configurations as built-in to the human mind prior to experience. Klein, like Freud, sees life as unfolding from the inside outward, but in her theory it is primitive, universal, internally arising object relations (instead of drives) that emerge, clash with social reality, and are then blocked, channeled, and contained. Her focus of inquiry, as we shall see, is likewise intrapsychic, on fantasies, wishes, fleeting and shifting impulses. Other theories within the relational/structure model view relational configurations as derivative of actual experiences with others and are hence interpersonal as well as relational. In Sullivan's view, we are born, develop, and live in the context of relations with others, and our experience is composed of and concerned with the patterning of those relations. His focus of inquiry emphasized the interpersonal, what people *do* with each other. Fairbairn, as we shall see, developed a third version of the relational/structure model in which an interpersonal theory of the origin of relational patterns is combined with an intrapsychic focus on internal fantasies and structures.

Sullivan's relational/structure premises concerning the constituents of experience result in an approach to the issues of motivation, anxiety, and the organization of the self that differs markedly from Freud's. For the latter, drives arise through bodily tensions; originally narcissistic, they are directed toward others only secondarily through vicissitudes of experience. Some "needs for satisfaction," according to Sullivan, concern the regulation of bodily processes; however, they are conceptualized throughout in terms of organism/environment regulation and exchange, not in terms of an internally focused reduction of tension. Many of the needs for satisfaction originate entirely and autonomously within the emotional realm, using the body as a vehicle for expression. Whereas Freud's "drives" are generally depicted as inherently abrasive to the social order, constituting a "seething cauldron" of chaotic and dangerous energies, Sullivan's "needs for satisfaction" are, by definition, relational. At every point in development, needs for satisfaction draw the individual into relations with others. Sullivan does not posit, as does Klein, a precognition of an "object" within the infant's experience. The infant does not "know" of the mother and her functions prior to his experience of her. Yet, the "object" is implicit in Sullivan's concept of "integrating tendencies." The infant's experience of need calls out a reciprocal experience of need in the mother. The infant's needs for satisfaction thus presuppose, are contingent upon, and, in some sense, evoke an other.

Freud sees the body's "erogenous zones" as the "source" of drive components; Sullivan sees the body's "zones of interaction" not as the source of motivation, nor as its centerpiece, but as a vehicle of other needs, more interactional in nature. The child desires relations with others; the zones provide the pathways to these relations. Developmental epochs, for Sullivan, are not organized around or dominated by a sequence of shifting predominant zones. The crucial developmental shifts concern the emergence of needs for different forms of relatedness, reflecting greater complexity and intimacy, independent of the body zones through which they might be expressed and channeled. The "need for security" in Sullivan's system is likewise inherently relational. The need for security constitutes the need to be free from anxiety. For Freud, anxiety is associated with the press of drive; security represents the control and regulation of drive tensions. For Sullivan, anxiety is purely relational in origin; the original danger situations are constituted not by a flooding of sensations and drive pressures (a dread of instincts) but by anxiety picked up from significant others through the empathic linkage. Similarly, later anxiety is not provoked by the threat of conflictual drive derivatives but with the threat of the emergence of aspects of the self or experiences with others associated with anxiety in the interpersonal field.

Within the drive/structure model, psychic structure is a product of patterns of drive discharge and regulation. The coloring and texture of the individual personality are contingent upon these predominant patterns of drive gratification and defense. In Sullivan's system, the self is organized around relational configurations: the child shapes, patterns, and distorts his own experiences, behavior, and self-perception to maintain the best possible relatedness with significant others; painful, anxiety-provoking aspects of early relations with significant others are unavoidably structured into the self, which is composed of a collection of prominent "me-you" patterns loosely held together by a set of rationalizations and illusions. Early experience is organized into relational patterns; these are subsequently employed by the self-system in the pursuit of security. The self-system maintains its strategies of safety and control, anticipating that new experience with others will always repeat the relational patterns of the past (foresight).

In classical drive theory, intrapsychic conflict is predetermined and universal, reflecting the inevitable clash between psychosexual and aggresive drives and social reality. For Sullivan, both the qualitative and quantitative factors in personality organization derive exclusively from the particulars of the interpersonal matrix within which early development takes place. What becomes associated with anxiety depends on the character of the parents and other family members. Sex may be anxiety-provoking in one family, tenderness may be anxiety-provoking in another. The distribution of content into the three rudimentary organizations (good-me, bad-me, and not-me) is not in any sense universal but is contingent solely on the particulars of the interpersonal matrix. The quantitative balance, the "economic factor" (to borrow Freud's phrase), is for Sullivan, once again, contingent solely upon interpersonal rather than constitutional factors. A person growing up in a family where anxiety is relatively minimal and circumscribed will have a broadly ranging good-me and hence a fairly resilient self, and only a narrow, circumscribed area of dissociated experience. A person growing up in a family where anxiety is pervasive and evoked in many areas of life will develop a narrow range of anxiety-free activity, and a heavily weighted set of dissociated areas. The content and the extent of conflictual areas of the personality are determined, not by universal or particular constitutional factors, but by the character of the parental figures and their relationships with the child.

Although Sullivan views personality organization and psychopathology as products of the residues of relations with others, he objects to terms such as "introjection" or "incorporation" which describe these residues in concrete, structural language (1953, p. 166). This difference in language sets him apart from the versions of the relational model developed within the British school. This objection to and concern over the dangers of reification in psychodynamic language was a product of Sullivan's philosophical pragmatism and operational methodology as well as his early horror at the ease with which Kraepelinian psychiatrists used concepts referring to invisible processes to obscure meaningful events and situations.

Although it highlighted certain misuses of language and theory by pointing to the dangers of reification, operationalism was not in itself a viable, feasible methodology. (See Suppe, 1977, pp. 18–20, for a critique of Bridgeman's concept of operationalism in its application within the natural sciences.) All psychoanalytic theory rests on a priori philosophical assumptions which it brings *to* the data. All psychoanalytic theory presumes invisible, hypothetical processes and events which are not susceptible to observation or experience. All psychoanalytic theories must "furnish" the unconscious, although Sullivan's decor is perhaps more rustic and sparse than most. Despite his concerns, Sullivan could not completely avoid giving names and descriptions to hypothetical intervening variables linking past interpersonal situations with current experiences and functioning. He often uses the concept of anxiety in precisely such a fashion, and at several points he hints at, and then backs away from, formulating internal "structures."

> The self grows by learning techniques for . . . removing threats of anxiety from the significant people . . . To do that, you have to have memory. . . . recollection appears in the form of a feeling of unpleasant anticipation, which, in turn, comes to be called by the name of guilt, or shame . . . So if you wish, you can talk about the significant person having been introjected and becoming the superego, but I think you are apt to have mental indigestion. (1956, p. 232)

Sullivan stresses repeatedly that the self-system functions on the basis of memory and foresight; foresight entails the anticipation that future interactions will conform to past experience. Thus, implicit in his theory is the view that past relations with others are retained within the mind, and that these residues shape the anticipation and often the actual perception of present and future relations.

> Sometimes in the fantasies of patients one comes across diagrammatic fragments . . . of a significant person from many years before — the significant person is still there, and still acts in the fashion that was originally relevant. This sort of thing is a caricature, in a way, of the manner in which the surviving imprints of a past situation may act very suavely in interfering with an impulse. (1953, p. 233)

The words he selects to designate residues of past relations and memories — personifications, diagrammatic fragments — serve the same function in his system as the term "internal object" serves for most of the authors within the British school. Sullivan, ever wary of metaphors being mistaken for actuality, chooses words that suggest process and function rather than language suggesting substance and structure.

Erich Fromm: Humanistic Psychoanalysis

Erich Fromm fashioned a version of the relational model which, although compatible with Sullivan's on most fundamentals, is quite different in sensibility and emphasis. The salient differences are largely a consequence of Fromm's broad goal throughout his work: the integration of Freud's psychodynamic theory of the unconscious with Karl Marx's theory of history and social criticism (Fromm, 1962, has a fascinating autobiographical account of his roots in the two traditions). Fromm's synthesis rests on the premise that the inner life of each individual draws its content from the cultural and historical context in which he lives. Social values and processes are instituted and perpetuated by each of us in our struggle to fashion a solution to the problems posed by the human condition. An essential connection between psychodynamic understanding and social criticism is thus the basis for Fromm's version of the relational model.

Fromm addressed many contemporary psychoanalytic issues decades before they were popularized by other theorists. He pointed to the importance of "narcissism," which currently dominates the literature, more than forty years ago (1941). He introduced the concept of "symbiosis" (1941) years before Mahler. He considered the role of agency and responsibility (1941) recently brought into the analytic mainstream by Schafer and Shapiro. He described the use of sexuality and perversions in the service of maintaining a fragile sense of self, an interpretive approach currently being developed by adherents of Kohut's "self psychology" (Kohut, 1977). Yet Fromm's contributions to the development of psychoanalytic thought have gone unrecognized in many quarters, precisely because of his insistence on the interpenetrability of psychodynamic understanding and a broader sociopolitical view of history. This emphasis makes it easy for critics to dismiss him as a social philosopher rather than a psychoanalytic theorist. The problem has been further compounded by Fromm's own proclivities and style as an author: the greater portion of his written legacy is couched in terms of social philosophy. Nevertheless, he was an astute psychoanalytic clinician, and close reading of his work reveals a clear intent to illuminate the psychodynamic struggles of the individual and the major dimensions of the psychoanalytic situation. Unfortunately, the volume on psychoanalytic technique that Fromm promised his students year after year never materalized, so, full appreciation of his contribution to the relational model necessitates consideration of his larger vision of culture and history in order to draw out its psychodynamic implications.

Fromm, like Sullivan and Horney, felt that the major weakness of Freud's psychoanalytic theory was failure to place his observations within a larger view of history and cultural evolution. He argues (1970) that Freud's central insights concern the importance of *hypocrisy*. Freud's patients thought of themselves as—and to a large extent acted like—the proper Victorian ladies and gentlemen their society asked them to be. Underneath this "false consciousness" Freud discovered all sorts of sexual and aggresive fantasies and motives dominating their internal life. For Fromm, Freud's salient discovery was of man's capacity for distorting the reality of his own experience to conform to socially established norms.

The most striking feature of Freud's discoveries, Fromm argues, was not *what* his patients repressed in order to integrate themselves into society (the specific sexual and aggressive impulses) but the fact that so much of themselves, major dimensions of their experience, was renounced. Freud had unearthed the extraordinary extent to which people distort their naturally evolving experiences to accommodate themselves to their human environment, the family and culture into which they are born. Vast areas of experience are disowned by all people through the process of socialization, and the loss of this experience is subsequently rationalized and covered over through complex processes of repression, self-deception, "bad faith," or, in Schafer's (1976) recent language, "disclaimed action." *Why* is so much given up? Freud had understood the necessity for repression as residing in the fundamentally antisocial nature of human passions. People are bestial, driven by dark and inhumane motives; integration into any ongoing society necessitates the control, renunciation, and transformation of these motives.

Fromm argues that Freud's great error was obscuring the centrality of his discoveries concerning self-deception in the service of social conformity by taking the content of the particular hypocrisies within Victorian culture, which happened to involve sex and aggression, and extrapolating a universal and unidimensional motivational theory out of them. "Classical" Freudian thought, according to Fromm, has been dominated by this misplaced emphasis on content as opposed to the structure of self-deception. As a result, the focus of analysis shifted away from the relation between the individual and the world of other people, toward a focus on what were presumed to be forces arising out of the individual himself—the drives and their derivatives. The theoretical premises of the drive model have overshadowed Freud's original clinical observations concerning interpersonal and social relations.

Marx's view of history and cultural transformation offered Fromm an alternative explanation for Freud's discoveries. According to Marx, man, unlike nonhuman animals, lacks an inherent tie to nature; he is not genetically equipped to react to his environment in preprogrammed ways. The nature of man as a species is *not* uniform and predetermined; it develops slowly over the course of history. Through a lawful sequence of necessary and evolving socioeconomic structures, history makes possible the development of man's productive forces, constituting his essence as a species and determining his position vis-à-vis nature. Only at the end of history does man become complete; the split between man and nature is healed and a social order allowing the full flowering of human potentials becomes possible.

In Fromm's view, the lifeline of the individual follows a similar progression. It is only before birth that the human organism is at one with nature, literally embedded within the maternal environment. Through birth, each individual is expelled from this paradisical harmony into a world in which he has no apparent place. Thus, the central feature of the human condition is that, once born, each individual is fundamentally alone. The slowly dawning realization of this separateness is the salient dimension of the development of human consciousness. This realization is difficult and frightening. With no inborn program for living, life offers a dizzying freedom and anxiety-filled sense of isolation. Each individual attempts to overcome this state by trying to reestablish the attachments and involvements with others which were once his by virtue of his embeddedness within his mother's body and nurturing care.

Over the course of development, new forms of attachment must be found. Fromm believes that in developing these new pathways to others a fundamental choice must be made between two basic alternatives. One possibility, the "productive orientation," entails a progressive, rational, and individuated response to circumstances. The fact of separateness is acknowledged and accepted, and relations with others proceed on the basis of intimate yet differentiated involvements. The other possibility entails denial of the reality of one's separateness and of individual responsibility for fashioning one's life. A wide variety of regressive, neurotic orientations may be relied upon, and Fromm argues that the differences among them are less salient than the similarity of their essential function: they all provide illusions and fantasies that enable the patient to avoid the actuality of his separateness and support the pretense that he continues to reside in the earliest state of blissful security.

Within Fromm's relational model the inner life of the individual is dominated by powerful passions and illusions. The passions derive not from body-based drives but from the desperate and profound struggle to overcome aloneness. These passions are irrational to the extent to which they draw on "regressive" solutions to the human condition: the denial of separateness and vulnerability. Denial in turn operates through various illusions—the belief in magical substances, powerful saviors, strategies for self-protection. The illusions draw on infantile fantasies and operate as a magical bastion against the reality of life; their purpose is not pleasure, but an imagined safety. The various symptoms and behaviors that constitute the fabric of neurosis and character disorder are consequences of the basic underlying stance toward the world and other people.

Fromm has argued for a parallel between the flow of human history and the individual life span. Mankind moves from the harmony with nature of our animal ancestors, to the incompleteness and alienation created by human consciousness, to the sequential and progressive development of historical societies, ending in a *truly* human society. The life course of the healthy individual moves from prenatal harmony, to the expulsion of birth, to the acceptance of aloneness and finitude, ending in a truly productive flowering of his or her potential. The parallel between these sequences is, Fromm suggests, much more than an intellectual curiosity; the issues involved in human cultural history as a whole become central to the inner life and psychodynamic struggles of each individual.

Because we have not reached the end of history that Marx envisioned, no existing human society is designed to facilitate the full development of human lives; each is designed to do the work of history, to develop capacities and technologies for material production. For societies to play their roles in this historical progression, certain types of citizens are required. Feudalism required serfs and lords; nineteenth-century capitalism, capitalists and workers. Twentieth-century capitalism, Fromm suggests, requires consumers. Socially necessary character types are not imposed by external forces upon individuals. Rather, societies become structured so that individuals are drawn into a view of the world and their place in it which enables them to want to do the work which their particular society at its particular point in history requires. In Fromm's words, "the subjective function of character for the normal person is to *lead him to act according to what is necessary for him from a practical standpoint*" (1941, p. 310; italics in original). The result is a citizenry of individuals "*wanting to act as they have to act*" (1955, p. 77; italics in original).

Why are these socially fashioned character types so compelling that most individuals truncate the richness of their experience in an effort to adapt themselves to them? Fromm's answer hinges on his depiction of the existential condition of each individual and his Marxist view of history. On the one hand, man's essential aloneness and helplessness predispose him to accept the roles offered by the society in which he lives. On the other hand, because a truly human society has not yet evolved, the roles that societies have to offer embody largely regressive solutions to the existential dilemma. Because they offer clear-cut solutions, prescribed behaviors, and codes, the "escape from freedom" made available is very compelling. Socially fashioned, regressive solutions are introduced to the child through parents who, Fromm argues, operate by virtue of their *own* character structures as the agents of social necessity. The winning of parental love and respect entails the adoption of social patterns of behavior at the expense of developing one's own emergent individuality. The power of repression derives not from a fear of punishment or dread of instincts but from the fear of social ostracism.

To the extent to which an individual has been able to face his own situation clearly, rationally, and productively he is healthy.* To the extent to which he has fashioned his own, idiosyncratic, regressive solutions from the interpersonal context of his own nuclear family, he is neurotic. To the extent to which he has appropriated the regressive solutions that his particular society offers, involving illusory union, security, and certainty, he suffers from what Fromm calls a "socially patterned defect," or the "pathology of normalcy." Fromm terms those aspects of experience which are disclaimed as the price of participating in society the "social unconscious." Thus, at the heart of the patient's struggle for an authentic existence are society's lures and the dread of aloneness.

As Maccoby puts it, Fromm views character as "a solution forged over time" (1972). Fromm draws explicitly and extensively on Freud's *descriptions* of character, but reinterprets the underlying psychodynamic issues in relational terms. The oral personality becomes the receptive personality; the analsadistic becomes the exploitative personality; and the anal-retentive becomes the hoarding personality. The key issue is not an underlying component drive, but the predominant mode of relatedness to others and the illusory effort to create a refuge from life. For the oral personality, for example, the central dynamic is understood to be the establishment of a receptive orientation toward the world and others, in which magical properties are attributed to something outside the self—food, love, sex, ideas; life becomes organized around the longing to receive and ingest the magical substance. From Fromm's point of view the patient is oral because he is receptive; oral pleasures are a vehicle for the maintenance of a receptive stance toward life. The motivational core is the perpetuation of a position vis-à-vis others in which magic is always on the outside, temporarily granted and ingested but never owned and consolidated. Orality is a metaphor for receptivity. What Freud attributed to a biologically determined drive organization, Fromm ascribes to relational configurations, "an attitude toward the world in the language of the body" (1941, p. 320).

Healthy development is predicated upon coming to terms with the

---

*An interesting controversy on this point developed between Fromm and Herbert Marcuse, who also attempted to integrate the Marxist and Freudian traditions. Marcuse is critical of Fromm's contention that one *can* disengage from one's society and live authentically, arguing that the only possible freedom from historically conditioned social constrictions is through social and political revolution. This debate represents a reemergence of a long-standing dialogue during the nineteenth century between the anarchists (Fromm's claim for the possibility of authentic existence at *any* point in history) and the doctrinal socialists (claiming that authentic existence is possible only at the "end of history," through social transformation).

loss of the "primary ties" of infancy, because only then is it possible for one to establish an intimacy with others based on differentiation and mutuality. For the neurotic, differentiation means aloneness, and recognition of the loss of the primary ties is avoided at all costs. Because the dread of isolation underlies all psychopathology, the central feature of neurosis is the perpetuation of the illusion of embeddedness or merger with others. In its clinical application, Fromm's distinction between progressive and regressive modes of relatedness resembles: Sullivan's distinction between relationships based on the need for satisfaction and relationships based on the need for security; Fairbairn's distinction between good object relations and ties to bad objects; Winnicott's distinction between the true self and the false self on a compliant basis; and Kohut's distinction between a true object relation and a relationship to a self-object. In these different versions of the relational model, varying in tone and emphasis, the other is experienced as a functional part of the self in an effort to escape a dreaded sense of isolation and emptiness.

According to the oral tradition emanating from Fromm's students and analysands, his clinical work was characterized by an empathic inquiry into the self-distortions and self-deceptions engendered by the patient in his efforts to maintain what seemed to be the best possible connections with significant others. In families where the child is not loved and valued in his or her own right, a compliant identification with parental values and an appropriation of their own illusions of magical safety seem to offer the only viable forms of human connection. Fromm saw the patient as capable of much more, and this sense of the richness and range of human potentials hidden beneath the veneer of social adaptation is apparent in all his writings. A deep sense of optimism and urgency and a belief in the ever-present potential of the patient to respond to the truth about himself and to live a richer, more authentic existence were among his greatest contributions to the practice of clinical psychoanalysis.

Sullivan and Fromm: A Comparison

Although the theories developed by Sullivan and Fromm both operate within the relational/structure model, they are markedly different in emphasis and in their approach to certain key issues. Many of these divergences result from the contrasting views of Sullivan and Fromm concerning the nature and historical place of society with respect to individual human development and difficulties in living. Fromm's critique of social mores and institutions derives from the Marxist tradition and his experience as an emigré from Nazi Germany. He sees society as dangerously luring the individual from fully authentic existence. Sullivan's attitude toward modern society is characterized by a marked ambivalence. Deep loneliness as a child and his early years of working with the ravages of social isolation in his schizophrenic patients led him to a critique of social institutions and many features of contemporary life. However, Sullivan was convinced that adaptation to and integration into contemporary society, despite its failings, is *essential* to mental health. No matter how irrational the culture, the process of becoming human necessitates living within it. Mental health, he insists, in a manner which sets him off markedly from Fromm, includes a "comfortable adaptation to . . . the social order of which one is a part" (1940, p. 57). In fact, for Sullivan, the greatest damage caused by the irrationality and heterogeneity of modern cultural mores is precisely the difficulties they place in the way of cultural adaptation. "The terrible isolation of the many is the peculiar characteristic of our people, the nucleus of their mental disorders" (1972, p. 329). Whereas Fromm sees adaptation to one's society as the broadest, most universal form of neurosis, Sullivan sees acculturation as the sine qua non of a fully human life.

The contrast between Sullivan's belief in the impossibility of escaping the social milieu and Fromm's belief in the necessity for so doing underlies much of the divergent emphases in their versions of the relational model. Sullivan stresses the need to establish and maintain relations with others despite their unavoidable cost to self-integrity. The child is born into a family and must bend himself out of shape (although not necessarily irreversibly) to reduce anxiety in his relations with others. This is not a choice, but a developmental necessity. The shape which the self-system takes on during childhood is preserved, through various security operations, throughout life. Sullivan's approach is intrinsically developmental—the neurotic operations of adult life represent childhood patterns and solutions achieved at specific developmental epochs. Fromm, by contrast, sees the establishment and maintenance of infantile relations with others not as a developmental necessity but as a regressive defense. Neurotic relatedness, like social conformism, is tempting but resistible, alluring in its fictitious promises but in the long run productive only of despair. For him, neurosis is fundamentally a *choice*. In this sense his approach is intrinsically nondevelopmental: the neurotic operations of adult life are regressive evasions of the anxieties inherent in fully individuated living.

Sullivan looks at life from a longitudinal perspective: the self-system operates through patterns laid down in childhood and adolescence and is understandable only within the broad overview of the individual's history of relations with others. Fromm looks at life cross-sectionally: the individual applies illusory solutions to the existential condition in which he finds himself. These solutions, developed within the context of his early relations with others, function as a short-sighted distraction from life, a compulsive salve to unaddressed pain within the human condition.

Sullivan is a determinist: the person is a product of past interpersonal integrations, which are preserved in memory and continually restructured through foresight. Foresight, in his theory, is an automatic scanning activity, projecting past situations onto the present and future and thereby influencing motivation. (Sullivan does not consider whether one can choose whether or not to exercise foresight.) One foresees only what one has experienced; one can never wrench oneself out of the history of one's relational experience. Fromm, on the other hand, is an existentialist: the person is continually choosing, forward or backward, living authentically or languishing in illusions.

Although Sullivan never commented on Fromm's work, Fromm, particularly in his later writings, became increasingly critical of Sullivan's theory (1955, p. 130; 1970, p. 31); this critical line was extended by Wolstein (1971) and Klenbort (1978). Sullivan is seen as presenting a view of man as empty, desperately seeking security, simply filled in by surrounding interpersonal and cultural values. Sullivan's protest against the "illusion of unique individuality" is felt to betray the conformistic nature of his theory, making Sullivanian thought, along with Hartmann's ego psychology, a psychology of bourgeoisie adjustment. The authentic uniqueness of each individual, so basic to Fromm's vision, is thus denied. This criticism, we believe, is based on a misreading of Sullivan's statements regarding "individuality" and a failure to differentiate between his concept of the self, which is explicitly narcissistic and conformistic, and his characterization of the rest of the personality, which contains many constructive, unique, and authentic features. Sullivan uses the phrase "illusion of unique individuality" in reference to the claim to "specialness" with which the self adorns itself in its struggle against anxiety. Each of us, he suggests, considers himself as uniquely special, self-contained, different from others by virtue of a particular wisdom, talent, deficit, or victimization. "This amounts to a delusion of unique individuality, related to beliefs in one's omnipotence and omniscience, and is only a very complex and personally misleading expression of the real unique individuality of each psychobiological organism—an individuality that must always escape the methods of science" (1936, p. 16).

This conviction of illusory uniqueness and specialness, drawing heavily on the competitiveness and ambition left over from the juvenile era which Sullivan feels dominates our particular society, operates as "the very mother of illusions, the ever-pregnant source of preconceptions that invalidate almost all of our efforts to understand other people" (1938, p. 33). The self, thus defined, is not to be confused with the person as a whole. In Sullivan's theory of personality there is a continual and central dialectic between the self-system, essentially negative in function, and the other positive forces within the personality, reflecting the basic thrust of the human organism toward health and growth (1940, p. 97). At the beginning of each developmental epoch the diffuse forces toward growth and health within the personality can break through the static, regressive self and create new possibilities (1953, pp. 147, 192). Those who criticize Sullivan's theory as conformistic mistake his formulations regarding the self-system, which is conformistic by definition, for his theory of man.

The Frommian critique, although inaccurate in its characterization of Sullivan's views, points to a major area of omission and weakness in his theory: the failure to provide a framework for viewing organizational processes in nonpathological functioning, the failure to provide a theory of health. Sullivan suggests that in the absence of the tyranny of anxiety, the self would expand to include the entire personality. The self-system, as he has characterized it, no longer necessary, would presumably cease to exist. However, Sullivan is very vague and inconsistent about what this ideal state of health would be like. In the one passage in his lectures in which he does speculate on the nature of the self in an ideal society (both rational and consistent), he vacillates. First he suggests that such a wholly rational situation would generate no self-system at all; then he suggests that because specialization of function is necessary in any advanced society, both anxiety and a self-system would be unavoidable; finally he decides that in such an ideal culture the self-system would certainly be different: "for all I know, there would not be evolved . . . anything like the sort of self-system that we always encounter" (1953, p.168).

Sullivan's definition of the self-system solely in terms of its antianxiety function has left a gap in his theory regarding the organization of the self in nonpathological functioning. Is there any patterning or organization of the personality in health? Is it meaningful to speak of a "self" apart from security operations and the avoidance of anxiety? Is nonpathological functioning best characterized as a formless, self-less flow? Sullivan's failure to address these questions limits his contributions to a theory of psychopathology rather than a more general psychology.

The differing versions of the relational/structure model generated by Sullivan and Fromm provide a rich complementarity; in certain ways each corrects some of the deficiencies in the other. Sullivan constructed a developmental history of the ways in which relations with others are patterned into the personality. His greatest contributions lie in his intricate analysis of the workings of anxiety and security operations, the often subtle shifts in attention, presuppositions, and feelings which protect the self in relations with others and underlie most difficulties in living. The most problematic area in his work, in addition to the inconsistent and often cumbersome quality of the language he employs in his effort to avoid structural metaphors, concerns his deterministic approach to the issue of the will and his failure to provide a framework for viewing nonpathological, authentic functioning. Fromm's version of the relational/structure model provides a larger cultural and historical framework for viewing both psychopathology and healthy, authentic strivings. His use of language is much clearer, although he employs broader strokes, often without the necessary clinical and psychodynamic elaboration. Fromm never fully developed the implications of his approach to the particulars of clinical psychoanalysis, and his work lacks the detailing of relational processes which Sullivan provides. Like most writers influenced by the existential tradition, he fails to provide a compelling developmental framework and has trouble with the childhood precursors to the capacity for choice. (Compare the efforts of Schafer, 1978, p. 194, and Shapiro, 1981, to grapple with this knotty conceptual problem.) Thus, there is a need, despite the obvious differences in their approaches, for a critical synthesis between relational model theories like Sullivan's, which stress developmental origins, and relational model theories like Fromm's, which stress the struggle for authentic selfhood.

Part Two

Alternatives

But Love has pitched his mansion in
The place of excrement;
For nothing can be sole or whole
That has not been rent.

      —W. B. YEATS,
        "Crazy Jane Talks with the Bishop"

5   Melanie Klein

Before 1919, when Melanie Klein's first psychoanalytic publication appeared, there was a curious gap in psychoanalytic research and practice. Freud's initial inquiry into the meaning behind the neurotic symptoms of adults had led to an elaborate system of unforeseen and rather staggering hypotheses concerning the emotional life of children. Yet at the time Klein began her direct investigations with children, Freud's theories remained largely extrapolations back into childhood from adult memories and fantasies. Freud had conducted a secondhand analysis of "Little Hans" through instructions to Hans's father; Hug-Hellmuth had conducted some preliminary, largely educational work with latency-age children. But no psychoanalyst had attempted to apply the techniques of psychoanalysis to children, either to ameliorate difficulties in living or to test out Freud's developmental theories firsthand.

Klein had been living in Budapest between 1910 and 1919, where her fascination with Freud's writings led her to seek psychoanalytic treatment with Ferenczi. Upon his suggestion she began to apply psychoanalytic principles and techniques to the treatment of children. This project was long overdue, and the early reports of Klein's work aroused considerable interest within the psychoanalytic community. Karl Abraham invited her to work at the Berlin Psychoanalytic Institute; her brief analysis and tutelage with Abraham ended with his illness and death in 1925. That same year Klein was invited by Ernest Jones to present her work in England; she moved there shortly afterward and worked and wrote in England until her death in 1960.

Klein's intellectual and political lineage within the psychoanalytic community could not have been more pure. In Ferenczi, Abraham, and Jones, she was sponsored by the three most prominent and influential of Freud's collaborators. (Ferenczi, only years later, long after his association with Klein, was to lose favor with Freud.) Nevertheless, beginning shortly after she settled in England, Klein's work split the British Psychoanalytic Society and eventually the international psychoanalytic community. Although she herself presented her work as a simple extension of Freud's theories, involving no fundamental innovations, she was denounced by many psychoanalytic authors for distorting and betraying basic principles of sound psychoanalytic theory and practice. The divergence, which began in the mid-1920s with a disagreement between Klein and Anna Freud concerning technique in child analysis, expanded during the 1930s and 1940s into a major ideological schism. The British Psychoanalytic Society is still split among "A Group" (loyal to A. Freud), "B Group" (followers of Klein), and the "middle group" (those who, like Winnicott, did not choose either side). The often acrimonious and mutually devaluing dialogue between these two lines of psychoanalytic theorizing has persisted down to the present.

Many of Klein's defenders regard her contributions as largely consistent with Freud's original investigations and minimize differences, which they regard simply as extensions and perfections of Freud's concepts. Critics regard Klein's formulations as tangential to the major currents within Freudian thinking and as highly speculative and fantastic. The debate is compounded by stylistic characteristics of Klein's writing. Her prose is dense with descriptions of primitive fantasy material. At the same time, she writes with great forcefulness and certainty, often resulting in overgeneralizations and hyperbole. In addition, there are major unacknowledged shifts in basic principles and emphases during her career as a theorist. This mixture of phenomenological detail, overstatement, and unannounced change in viewpoint has resulted in a body of work which is extremely rich, complex, and loosely organized. The style of her writing seems at times to reflect a texture reminiscent of the primary process thinking that constitutes so much of the content of her work.

The failure of many critics to provide a close and balanced reading of Klein's ideas and the misleading quality of some of her own rhetoric have resulted in widespread misconceptions concerning Klein's work. Foremost among these are: that she focuses exclusively on aggression at the expense of other motives, and that she neglects the importance of real people altogether at the expense of fantastic and phantasmogoric creations of the child's own mind. Amid the swirl of controversies and antipathies surrounding Klein's contributions, there is understandably little consensus either as to the precise nature of her views or to her place within the history of psychoanalytic ideas.

We will demonstrate that Klein *both* remained true to, and departed from, Freud's vision and has served as a key transitional figure between the drive/structure model and the relational/structure model. Her major contributions center on her often subtle yet fundamental reformulations concerning the nature of the drives themselves, and the origin and nature of "objects."

Phases of Klein's Theory

The psychoanalytic treatment of children poses considerable technical difficulties. To analyze anyone, one must gain access in some fashion to their experience and fantasies. Free association provides such access in the psychoanalysis of adults, but because children are often less verbal than adults and generally more mobile, direct application of the technique of free association is not possible. Klein attempted to engage her first patients by talking with them, but it soon became clear that the verbal medium was limited — a more probing approach to the child's fantasies and internal life was required. The observation and interpretation of play provided that access. Play serves a central function in the child's psychic economy, Klein felt, representing an enactment of the child's deepest unconscious wishes and fears. Although sometimes the child plays by himself, often the therapist is enlisted and assigned parts — now the naughty child punished by the patient, now the loving parent rewarding the patient, and so on. By observing and interpreting the articulation and assignment of these roles, Klein was able to help the child work through various conflicts, relationships with others, and disparate identifications.* Armed with the instrument of play interpretation, she was eager in her early papers to investigate Freud's hypotheses concerning infantile experience.

The most striking feature of the early papers is their exclusive focus on libidinal issues, even more so than in Freud's own work, where, with his proclivity for balanced, dualistic formulations, psychosexuality is always juxtaposed with other motivational themes. Klein saw genital, oedipal sexuality in every nook and cranny of the child's world. Letters and

---

*A view of the analytic process as consisting of the continual and shifting assignment of self-other configurations became the basis for Kleinian contributions to the theory of analytic technique with adults as well, leading to particular emphasis on transference and countertransference.

numbers have sexual meanings (strokes and circles in the construction of the figures representing penis and vagina). Arithmetic (division as violent coitus, for example), history (fantasies of early sexual activities and battles), and geography (interior of mother's body) draw upon sexual interests. Music represents the sounds of parental intercourse. Speech itself symbolizes sexual activity (the penis as tongue moving within the mouth as vagina). The world of the child in all its aspects represents genital sexuality writ large: "ego-activities and interests . . . have fundamentally a genital symbolic, that is to say, a coitus significance" (1923, pp. 82–83).

Libidinal development for Klein is closely related to the child's drive to know.* The child develops elaborate fantasies concerning the inside of the mother's body and the mysteries it contains—including food, feces, babies—and, as Klein believed by 1928, fantasies of the father's penis. The outer world stands for the mother's body, and Klein portrays the young child as an intense and eager explorer. Because the drive to know is so central and powerful, and because it emerges before the child develops even minimal facility with language, it is invariably frustrated, resulting in intense longings and rage. *All* inhibitions for Klein, at this point in the development of her ideas, derive from castration fears, anticipations of punishments for the pursuit of sexual satisfaction and knowledge, and *all* psychopathology is caused by a consequent repression of aspects of childhood sexuality.

Although Klein felt that she had uncovered compelling evidence for Freud's developmental theories, discrepancies did arise in terms of dating. Whereas Freud viewed the Oedipus complex as the culmination of infantile sexuality, arising only after the sequential unfolding of earlier, pregenital organizations, Klein's data suggested a much earlier onset of oedipal interests and fantasies. She placed the inception of oedipal feelings at successively earlier points, eventually locating their origins in the first year of life, around the time of weaning. She argued that the disruption in the connection of the baby with the mother brought about by weaning and toilet-training precipitates a turn to the father in the form of genital fantasies and, in the boy, a subsequent return to the mother on a genital rather than oral level. Whereas Freud saw the superego as arising in the resolution of the oedipal phase at the

*Within "ego psychology," following Hartmann, intellectual curiosity is not just a function of drive but has roots within the primary autonomous sphere of the ego, motivationally separable from the drives. Klein derives *all* curiosity from a knowledge-seeking component of the libido. This difference is central to many of the divergences between these two branches of psychoanalytic thought, particularly with regard to analytic technique. A third approach was developed by Bion, who elevates the pursuit of knowledge to an independent and predominant motivational status.

end of the childhood era, Klein's investigations revealed earlier superego figures, in the form of harsh, critical self-accusations accompanying the earlier oedipal fantasies.*

A second phase in Klein's views began with a marked shift in emphasis from libidinal to aggressive issues, in which she took her lead from Freud. Prior to 1920 Freud had considered aggression variably to be an aspect of libido or of the self-preservative instincts. In *Beyond the Pleasure Principle* (1920a) he established aggression as an independent energy source in its own right and speculated about its origins in a pervasive biological self-destructive tendency he termed the death instinct. Klein gradually absorbed and greatly expanded Freud's new focus on aggression. By the early 1930s the importance of aggression in her writings overshadows all other motives. In every aspect of emotional life, libidinal interests are now seen as less central, less conflictual, and, in many ways, as reactive to aggressive motives. Earlier, Klein had considered the child's interest in the contents of the mother's body to be motivated by pleasure and knowledge; now she views the motive as possession, control, and destruction: "the dominant aim is to possess himself of the contents of the mother's body and to destroy her by means of every weapon which sadism can command" (1930, p. 236). Sadism has no shortage of weapons.

Klein's view of the very nature of the Oedipus complex changed from a struggle over illicit pleasures and the fear of punishment, to a struggle for power and destruction and the fear of retaliation. Libidinal impulses do not become problematic in themselves, she now argued, until the later stages of the Oedipus complex—long after the early development of the child's relations to the parents. "It is only in the later stages of the Oedipus conflict that the defence against the libidinal impulses makes its appearance; in the earlier stages it is against the accompanying *destructive* impulses that the defence is directed" (1930, p. 249; italics in original). The child feels anxiety and guilt not because of lust but because of the aggressive fantasies that accompany his libidinal impulses. The child's emotional life centers around paranoid anxiety—the

*Klein's views on infancy are, for the most part, *not* based directly on work with "preoedipal" children. Her youngest patient was 2¾ years of age, and most of the children she uses as examples are considerably older, comfortably within the oedipal range as Freud had defined it. The presumption of oedipal impulses within the first two years, despite what Klein acknowledges is little overt indication of such impulses, derives mostly from the content of such fantasies in older children, particularly the predominance of oral themes. The early dating is based on the premise that orality is the central libidinal component within the first year of life (1932, p. 212). Klein was extrapolating back from the data of older children to their earlier years, much in the way Freud had used data from adults to determine infantile experiences in general.

fear of a massive and deadly retaliation by the mother's and the father's penis (inside the mother), revenging the destruction that the child has effected, in his fantasy, on the parents, particularly on their sexual union. Primitive, inherent destructiveness has replaced the pursuit of pleasure and knowledge as the driving force in life and as the hub of psychic conflict.

The vision of the mind proposed by Klein in 1932 contains many significant and innovative extensions of Freudian theory. Most salient among these are her approach to phantasy and her development of the concept of internal objects. Freud had described fantasy as a specific mental process which emerges as a consequence of frustration. In his system, fantasy and direct gratification are alternative channels. Klein slowly but pervasively extended the role of phantasy in psychic life, introducing several features which were either absent or minimal in Freud: elaborate *unconscious* phantasy, apart from specific, conscious compensations for frustrated desire; a reservoir of unconscious images and knowledge for phantasy to draw on, possessed by the child by virtue of a phylogenetic inheritance; phantasy which serves not as a substitute for, but as an accompaniment to, actual gratification. (It has become customary to use the spelling "phantasy" to designate the broader meanings of the term within Kleinian theory, and we have employed this usage where possible.) This new set of meanings for the term "phantasy" was developed gradually and without fanfare, and it was not until Isaacs' paper "On the Nature and Function of Phantasy" was presented in 1943 that the extent of this expansion was articulated. Isaacs posits the view, later endorsed by Klein, that phantasy constitutes the basic substance of all mental processes. This extension of the concept from a discrete, substitutive process to the very stuff of mental life was to become a key element in Klein's reformulation of the concept of drive.

A second Freudian concept greatly expanded by Klein was the notion of "internal objects." Freud's depiction of internal parental "voices," images, and values had remained essentially limited to the superego, internalized during the resolution of the oedipal crisis. Klein's expansion of the concept was bound up with her broadened usage of phantasy. In her depiction of the Oedipus complex, the child's mental life is filled with elaborate, mostly sadistic phantasies concerning his parents. In successive papers Klein had described more and more complex phantasies specifically concerning the mother's "insides." The child desires to possess all the riches he imagines contained in the mother's womb, including food, valued feces, babies, and the father's penis. He imagines and destroys, in phantasy, the parents' perpetual intercourse with each other, which he conceives of as an exchange of precious nurturative substances not accessible to him. He imagines a similar interior to his own body, where good and bad substances and objects reside, and he is preoccupied with an "ever-renewed attempt (a) to get hold of 'good' substances and objects (ultimately, 'good' milk, 'good' faeces, a 'good' penis and 'good' children) and with their help to paralyze the action of the 'bad' objects and substances inside its body; and (b) to amass sufficient reserves inside itself to be able to resist attacks made upon it by its external objects" (1931, p. 265). A complex set of internalized object relations are established, and phantasies and anxieties concerning the state of one's internal object world are the underlying basis, Klein was later to claim, for one's behavior, moods, and sense of self.

The third phase in Klein's work extends from the mid-1930s to 1945, during which time her focus shifted back again to libidinal themes. However, whereas her early work on libidinal issues emphasized the classical drive/structure focus on sensual, body-based pleasure and sexuality, her treatment of these issues at this later point concerns the more complex emotions of love and the desire for reparation. (Segal suggests that the accidental death of Klein's son in 1932 precipitated this renewed interest in love, loss and reparation [1979, p. 74]). Although there had been brief mention of the concept of reparation in 1929 (1929, p. 235) and some discussion of these issues in the *Psychoanalysis of Children* (1932), they do not move into the center of Klein's concern, attaining equal footing with aggression, until the formulation of the concept of depressive anxiety in 1935. In earlier work she had depicted the central fears of the infant as paranoid in nature; the child attempts to ward off the dangers of bad objects, both internal and external, largely by keeping images of them separate and isolated from the self and the good objects. Thus, the key feature of this early organization of experience, which Klein in 1935 termed the "paranoid position," involves the separation of good objects and good feelings from bad objects and bad feelings.

Klein (1935) suggests that in the second quarter of the first year of life the infant develops the capacity for internalizing whole objects (as opposed to part and split objects), and this precipitates a marked shift in the focus of the child's psychic life. The child is able at this point to integrate the previous split perceptions of the mother, to perceive that there is only one mother, with good and bad features. If there is only one mother, it is she who is the target of the child's rages, not a separate "bad mother." It is his beloved mother, both as an external, real figure and mirrored as an internal object, whom the child destroys in an orgy of malevolent phantasies during periods of frustration and anxiety, which Klein links particularly to frustrations in weaning. She terms the horror and dread concerning the fate of the whole object whom the child fears he had destroyed "depressive" anxiety. Whereas paranoid anxiety involves a fear of the destruction of the self from the outside, depressive anxiety involves fears concerning the fate of others, both inside and outside, in the face of the phantasied destruction created by the child's own aggression. As a result of his rages in the face of oral frustration, the child imagines his world as cruelly depopulated, his insides as depleted. He is a sole survivor and an empty shell. The child attempts to resolve his depressive anxiety and the intense guilt that accompanies it through "reparation," the repair of the mother through restorative phantasies and behaviors. He attempts to recreate the other he has destroyed, to employ his phantasied omnipotence in the service of love and repair. Klein makes it very clear that the child's concern for others does not consist simply of a reaction formation against his destructiveness, nor is it simply anxiety deriving from dependence on the object. The concern for the fate of the object is an expression of genuine love and regret, which develops, as Klein later suggested, along with a deep gratitude for the goodness the child has received from the mother. (By 1948 Klein argues that depressive anxiety and guilt actually begin in the earliest relationship to the breast, but do not achieve central focus until the introjection of a whole object in the second quarter of the first year [1948, p. 34].)

The centerpiece of Klein's motivational system has shifted. In the first phase the pursuit of sexual pleasure and knowledge is the central focus; in the second, the attempt to master persecutory anxiety situations, to gain reassurance against the dangers of destruction and retaliation takes on preeminent importance. In this third phase, crucial in Klein's transition from the drive/structure model to the relational/structure model, anxiety about the fate of the object and attempts to restore it, to make it whole again through love, become the driving force within the personality. "The attempts to save the love object, to repair and restore it, attempts which in the state of depression are coupled with despair, since the ego doubts its capacity to achieve this restoration, are determining factors for all sublimations and the whole of the ego-development" (1935, p. 290). The object is no longer simply the vehicle for drive gratification but has become an "other" with whom the infant maintains intensely personal relations.

Klein extended the primacy of the depressive position to subsume the Oedipus complex itself, which is redefined and now portrayed largely as a vehicle for depressive anxiety and attempts at reparation (1935). Depressive anxiety is never fully overcome, she suggests: the fate of one's objects in the face of one's own conflictual feelings remains a central concern throughout life. All loss is experienced as a result of one's own destructiveness and as a retaliation for past hatefulness and injuries. Through loss, the world and one's own insides are experienced as depleted and desolate. One's love and capacity to create and protect good relations with others are felt to be impotent and paltry. Good experiences with others, by contrast, augment the belief in the power of one's love and reparative capacities. Hatefulness and malice can be accepted and forgiven; others can be approached with a sense of hope and possibility. Real other people are extremely important in Klein's later formulations. The child regrets the damage he feels he has inflicted upon his parents. He attempts to repair that damage, to make good, over and over again. The quality of his relations with his parents and the quality of his subsequent relations with others determine the sense he has of himself, in the extremes, either as a secret and undiscovered murderer or as a repentant and absolved sinner.

Critics who depict Klein's theory as focused exclusively on hate and destructiveness often misread her formulations concerning the depressive position as suggesting that the depressive position is a relatively rare developmental achievement, possible only with the overcoming of the pervasive splitting operations during the earlier paranoid phase. In this reading, depressive concern for others is a later and markedly secondary phenomenon. Yet, Klein points out over and over that the "infantile depressive position is the central position in the child's development" (1935, p. 310). Each individual, including schizophrenic and paranoid persons, has introjected *whole* objects and thus struggles with depressive anxiety. A person living within a paranoid organization has retreated in the face of depressive anxiety over the damage he feels he wreaks on those he loves. Such a person is not incapable of loving; underneath the splitting, malevolence, and so on, is a "profound love" (1935, p. 295). In the deepest levels of schizophrenia, Klein argued in a late paper, is despair over "being dominated by destructive impulses and about having destroyed oneself and one's good object" (1960, p. 266). It is this centrality which Klein grants to love and reparation that led Riviere, one of her earliest collaborators, to suggest that the contributions on reparation are "perhaps the most essential aspect of Melanie Klein's work" (1936a, p. 60).

The major project in the fourth and final phase of Klein's work, extending from the 1946 paper "Notes on Some Schizoid Mechanisms" to her death in 1960, is an attempt to balance and synthesize her later work on depression and reparation with a deepened consideration of her earlier focus on paranoid processes. Although she had written of splitting processes earlier (see discussions of "distributing" superego imagoes,

1932, p. 215), splitting takes on a new prominence in the latest phase of her work. Whereas Klein's earlier discussions of splitting had concerned splits and dispersals of objects (good and bad, internal and external), she speaks in 1946 of splitting as a feature of the ego as well. Splits in objects precipitate and correspond to splits within the ego. The influence of Fairbairn's work on ego-splitting in the early 1940s is explicitly acknowledged—in fact, Klein adds his term "schizoid" (referring to splits in the ego) to her earlier depiction of paranoid processes, resulting in a new term, "paranoid-schizoid position," to describe the organization of experience pervaded by persecutory anxiety. The concept of "projective identification" was developed to describe extensions of splitting in which parts of the ego are separated from the rest of the self and projected into objects. In projection proper, as Freud had originated and Klein uses the term, *discrete impulses* are attributed to objects; in projective identification the attribution concerns actual *segments of the ego*. Consequently, projective identification is a more interactional concept than the Freudian concepts of both projection and identification. There is a much closer relation to the object, which now "stands for" the projected aspect of the self. (See Meissner, 1980, for an incisive critique of the usage by Klein and her followers of the term "projective identification.")

A final major concept undergoing significant development in the last phase of Klein's career is "envy." Although references to envy are found as early as *The Psychoanalysis of Children*, it was not until the publication of *Envy and Gratitude* in 1957 that it was granted a position of central importance, both in understanding psychopathology and in relation to the treatment process. Klein's formulation of the origins of envy are rooted in her presupposition of constitutional aggression. She suggests that early, primitive envy represents a particularly malignant and disastrous form of innate aggression. All other forms of hatred in the child are directed toward the *bad* objects. These are experienced as persecutory and evil (largely because they contain, via projection and projective identification, the child's own sadism), and the child in turn hates them and phantasizes their torture and demise. Envy, by contrast, is hatred directed toward *good* objects. The child experiences the goodness and nurturance which the mother provides but feels it to be insufficient and resents the mother's control over it. The breast releases the milk in limited amounts and then goes away. In the child's phantasy, Klein suggests, the breast is felt to be hoarding the milk for its own purposes.

Klein distinguishes envy from greed. In the latter, the infant in his voraciousness wants to have *all* the contents of the good breast for himself, regardless of the consequences for the breast, which he imagines leaving "scooped out" and sucked dry. For the greedy infant, as for the farmer in the fable of "The Goose that Laid the Golden Eggs," destruction is a consequence of greed, not a motive for it. In envy, the infant wants to destroy the breast, to spoil it, not because it is bad, but because it is good. It is precisely the existence of those riches, their goodness, outside the control of the infant, which he cannot tolerate and therefore desires to spoil. The enormous damage that such envy causes, Klein suggests, results from its undermining of early splitting. In nonenvious hatred, destruction is wreaked upon the bad objects; the good objects are protected by splitting, and consequently the infant can feel, at least at times, protected and safe. As a consequence of envy the infant destroys the good objects, splitting is undone, and there is a subsequent increase in persecutory anxiety and terror. Envy destroys the possibility for hope.

Although Klein derives early envy from constitutional aggression, it can be more economically derived from other factors: the frustration of the child's intense and greedy needfulness (which as Klein herself repeatedly points out, greatly exceeds any possibility for complete fulfillment); the frequent presence of intense anxiety or inconsistency in the mothering figures (as described by Sullivan); and the primitive nature of the child's cognitive capabilities, particularly in conceptualizing time and space (as demonstrated by Piaget). The condition of intense needfulness and dependency upon an anxious and inconsistent caretaker, when living a moment-by-moment sensory-motor existence seems to make early aggression unavoidable, apart from any presupposition of innate aggression.

Klein's description of envy has considerable explanatory power in relation to the most difficult patients in psychoanalysis, those who seem unable to gain anything positive from the analytic experience, manifesting what Freud termed the "negative therapeutic reaction." Freud had pointed to the operation of unconscious guilt. Klein's formulation appears closer to the phenomenology of certain patients, who express (often only after considerable analytic work) not a sense of being undeserving, but a hatred of "good" itself. They experience in their envy a sense of malice toward the analyst, connected precisely with their sense of his potential goodness, effectiveness, or love, only incompletely accessible to them and doled out at the analyst's pace or whim. Resistance in analysis can serve as a vehicle for the spoiling of the analyst's powers, his capacity to help. Each interpretation is turned into something useless or hurtful; through envy the patient systematically destroys all hope, precisely because the sense of possibility is painful and intolerable. Only through the interpretation of the workings of the envy itself, Klein suggests, can the patient free himself from this malicious and spiteful sabotage of the analysis as well as of his life with people in general.

In this final phase, as Klein works toward a synthesis of her earlier contributions, she envisions life as a struggle between the integration created by love and reparation, on the one hand, and the splitting, disintegration, and spoiling created by hatred and intense envy, on the other. Holding the object together, in its good and bad aspects, is painfully difficult: depressive anxiety and guilt must be faced, and the limits of one's love and the reality of ambivalence must be acknowledged. An abundance of hate makes the wholeness of the other difficult to sustain and necessitates swings into paranoid-schizoid mechanisms, in which good and bad are split, resulting in disintegration and depletion. Klein's final vision of the human condition is of man struggling toward the integration of himself and his experience of others despite the suffering it necessarily entails, against the pull toward fragmentation created by his own destructiveness and envy.

The Origin and Nature of the Object

Klein depicts the mental life of the child and the adult as consisting of a complex tapestry of phantasied relations between the self and others, both in the external world and within the imaginary world of internal objects. Where does the content of the patient's perceptions and phantasies of objects, both external and internal, come from? Klein devotes considerable effort to this question, and there has been much controversy concerning her formulations. Her critics (for example, Guntrip, 1971) accuse Klein of depicting the objects of human passions as phantasmagoric, solipsistic creations, with no necessary connection to real people. Her adherents dismiss these criticisms, pointing to Klein's frequent mention of the importance of real others.

This unresolved controversy derives from Klein's having developed several quite different formulations concerning the origins of objects, all extremely innovative. One or another of these explanations dominates her writing at any particular time. At times she attempts to integrate some of them, but only incompletely and suggestively. Klein's failure to acknowledge this diversity of formulations and to provide a compelling synthesis to account for the origin of objects causes much of the confusion regarding her work. Further, much additional and unnecessary confusion has resulted from efforts by her disciples and her detractors to present her views as if they were comprehensive and internally consistent.

In the most prevalent and widely known Kleinian view concerning the origin of objects and the approach characteristic of the early writings, she suggests that objects are inherent in and thereby created out of the drives themselves, independent of real others in the external world: "the child's earliest reality is wholly phantastic" (1930, p. 238). In this formulation Klein argues that perceptions of real others are merely a scaffolding for projections of the child's innate object images. How is this possible? How can the child know of others and the outside world before he encounters them in experience? At various places in her writing Klein proposes different explanations concerning the generation of object images. One explanation involves a novel understanding of the nature of desire itself. This approach, implicit throughout Klein's writings, was finally argued explicitly by Susan Isaacs in 1943. Isaacs suggests that desire implies an object of that desire; desire is always desire for something. Implicit in the experience of wanting is some image, some fantasy of the conditions leading to the gratification of the wanting. (This understanding bears some relation to the principle within philosophical phenomenology that all thought is "intentional"; see Brentano, 1924). In Freudian metapsychology the drives are uninformed about the nature of objects and reality; they contain no information about potential vehicles for their gratification. This objectlessness persists until objects are thrust upon the infant and become associatively linked with drive gratification. For Klein the drives possess, by virtue of their very nature as desire, inherent, a priori images of the outside world, which are sought for gratification, either in love or destruction.

Klein bases her presupposition of knowledge of objects separate from and prior to experience on certain more speculative passages in Freud's own work, where he posits a phylogenetic inheritance containing specific memory traces and images. This line of thought, betraying Jung's influence, is developed most fully in *Totem and Taboo* at the peak of Jung's impact on Freudian theory, and is a minor theme appearing now and again in Freud's later writing. Klein's use of the concept is much broader and more systematic. She argues the existence not just of specific phylogenetic memory traces and images but of an inherent, broad set of images and phantasied activities such as breasts, penises, the womb, babies, perfection, poison, explosions, and conflagrations. The earliest object relations of the child are relations with images of body parts which operate, Klein suggests, as "universal mechanisms" (1932, p. 195), without the child's necessarily having experienced the actual organs in reality. Only later do the child's images of objects take on aspects of the real objects they represent in the outside world. It is toward these a priori images that the child's drives are directed, both lovingly and hatefully, and they serve as a substratum and scaffolding onto which later experiences accrue. In her later writing Klein extended the principle of a priori knowledge and images of objects to whole objects as well: "the infant has an innate unconscious awareness of the existence of the mother . . . this instinctual knowledge is the basis for the infant's primal relation to his mother" (1959, p. 248).

The second explanation accounting for inherent, phantastic early objects involves the earliest channeling of the death instinct, which, Klein argues, *must* take place if the infant is to survive. We have seen that Klein, following Freud, felt that the infant is threatened by destruction from within immediately following birth. Freud had suggested that Eros, or the life instinct, intervenes and rechannels the death instinct. He proposed two mechanisms for this rescue operation: most of the destructiveness is turned outward into sadism toward others; some remains as primary erotogenic masochism. Klein proposes a third mechanism: an additional part of the death instinct is deflected or projected (she varies her language in different accounts) onto the external world. Thus, Eros actually phantasizes an external object, projects part of the death instinct onto it, and redirects the remainder of the destructiveness outward toward this newly created object. To preclude the experience of a world populated solely by bad objects, a portion of the life instincts likewise is projected, creating a good object toward which love is then directed. The nature of the good object, like the bad objects, is determined by the child's own motivations, as he generates a belief in the existence of kindly and helpful figures—a belief that derives from the nature of his own libido. Thus, in this view, the first objects of the drives are extensions of the drives themselves—their content is derived from the content of the child's own impulses, which are now experienced as directed toward him by an external object. "By projection, by turning outward libido and aggression and imbuing the object with them, the infant's first object-relation comes about. This is the process which . . . underlies the cathexis of objects" (1952a, p. 58).

This view of the child's earliest objects as creations whose purpose is the containment of his own drives was developed by Klein in her earliest papers to account for the harsh, primitive, superego figures which she discovered accompanying early oedipal phantasies in the first years of life. This explanation seemed to account for the fact that the child imagines punishments whose content matches his own aggressive phantasies. The child lives in dread of his objects' destroying, burning, mutilating, and poisoning him, because these activities dominate his own phantasies toward them and therefore constitute the substance of his projections onto them. Thus, in the child's psychic economy, as on the Lord High Executioner's list, the punishment always fits the crime. The world of the child, both internal and external, is populated by creatures whose nature reflects the child's own motivations. Thus, the child's fear of his early objects is proportional to the degree of his own aggressive impulses. "External reality is mainly a mirror of the child's own instinctual life . . . peopled in the child's imagination with objects who are expected to treat the child in precisely the same sadistic way as the child is impelled to treat the objects" (1936, p. 251).

In a third explanation for the existence of inherent, phantastic early objects, Klein suggests that the first experience of objects, internal and external, grows out of perceptual misinterpretation. She proposes that the child's experience of the workings of the death instinct within is *perceived* as an attack by something foreign, apart from any specific mechanism of projection per se or any specific knowledge or image of dreaded objects. The death instinct is "felt as fear of annihilation (death) and takes the form of fear of persecution . . .[it] attach[es] itself at once to an object — or rather *it is experienced as* the fear of an uncontrollable overpowering object" (1946, p. 4; italics ours). The nature of the child's experience leads him to construe the existence of objects. Klein did not limit this formulation to the death instinct but suggests that any frustration of bodily needs — the physical sensations, the tension, and the discomfort — are experienced by the child as foreign bodies or as attacks produced by foreign bodies. In a later paper she suggests that pleasurable sensations such as comfort and security are "felt to come from good forces" (1952a, p. 49). Thus, all sensations are personified and attributed to good and bad objects: "in the very earliest stage every unpleasant stimulus is related to the 'bad,' denying, persecuting breasts, every pleasant stimulus to the 'good,' gratifying breasts" (1935, pp. 305–306n). Riviere extended this approach to feelings of rage, suggesting that the tensions constituting rage are experienced as bad internal objects. She also suggests that the child naturally personalizes all frustrations into a presumption of a depriving other: "internal privation and need are always *felt* as external frustration" (1936a, p. 46).

Klein's claim that the content of objects is inherent in the organism and created independently of the outside world rests on three different formulations: objects are inherent in desire in the form of constitutional, universal knowledge and images; objects are created immediately to "deflect" the death instinct from self-destruction; objects are conjured up to explain the phenomenology of the child's earliest sensations.

Despite Klein's premise concerning the a priori nature of the earliest objects of the drives, she stresses, even in her early work, the role of experiences with real others in the external world in modifying and transforming these inherent images. She approaches the process of the blending of object images in several different ways. At some points she suggests a temporal layering sequence in which early harsh and primitive objects, generated out of the child's own numerous and largely sadistic phantasies, are overlaid by later images of the parents as kind and helpful. Gradually, over time, the early figures are transformed, softened by the images of the real parents (1932, p. 217). At other points Klein suggests that early objects derive partially from real, external figures, but that the realistic perceptions are distorted through the child's projections of his own impulses onto them. These early images are "constructed on the basis of the real oedipal objects and the stamp of the pregenital instinctual impulses." Thus, around a kernel of real perception is elaborated a mirror image of the child's own motives. These object images contain features of the real mother and father, but grossly distorted, resulting in figures of "the most incredible or phantastic character" (1933, p. 268).

A third approach to the problem of blending posits a more fluid mechanism of perpetual cycles of projection and introjection. Early internal objects of a harsh and phantastic nature are constantly being projected onto the external world. Perceptions of real objects in the external world blend with the projected images. In subsequent reinternalization the resulting internal objects are partially transformed by the perceptions of real objects. Klein suggests that the early establishment of harsh superego figures actually stimulates object relations in the real world, as the child seeks out allies and sources of reassurance which in turn transform his internal objects. This process is also the basis for the repetition compulsion, which involves a constant attempt to establish external danger situations to represent internal anxieties (1932, p. 170). To the extent to which one can perceive discrepancies between internally derived anticipations and reality, to allow something new to happen, the internal world is transformed accordingly, and the cycle of projection and introjection has a positive, progressive direction. To the extent to which one finds confirmation in reality for internally derived anticipations, or is able to induce others to play the anticipated roles, the bad internal objects are reinforced, and the cycle has a negative, regressive direction. In these depictions of the structuring of relations with others on the basis of characteristic anxiety situations, and in her brief mention of the role of anticipation and the induction of others to play desired roles, Klein is venturing into the kind of approach Sullivan employs (see, for example, Klein, 1964, p. 115).

In her work on the depressive position Klein's formulation concerning the origin of objects differs considerably from her earlier stress on in-herent, a priori object images; in this view, internal and external objects derive from the child's experience with real others in the outside world. Klein suggests that real others in the infant's external world are con-stantly internalized, established as internal objects, and reprojected onto external figures once again. She does not seem to consider such in-ternalization a defense mechanism per se, but rather a mode of relating to the outside world: "the ego is constantly absorbing into itself the whole external world" (1935, p. 286). Internal objects are established corresponding to real external others, as "doubles." Not just people, but all experiences and situations are internalized. The child's internal world "consists of innumerable objects taken into the ego, corresponding partly to the multitude of varying aspects, good and bad, in which the parents . . . appeared to the child's unconscious mind . . . they also represent all the real people who are continually becoming internalized" (1940, pp. 330–331).

This view of objects, particularly internal objects, as constituted from the beginning by perceptions of real others was elaborated by several of Klein's collaborators. Riviere notes that the term "introjection" is best not restricted to a defense mechanism, that it "operates continuously from the first dawning perception of 'something' external to 'me'" (1936a, p. 51). Heimann further extends the range of this process of in-ternalization, seemingly making it synonomous with perception in general: "When the ego receives stimuli from outside, it absorbs them and makes them part of itself, it introjects them" (1952a, p. 125).

Klein's formulations of objects as phantastic and internally derived were developed during the period in which aggression was her major focus, while the view that objects are synthesized out of absorptions of experience with real others was developed during the period in which depressive anxiety and reparation were her major focus. This is not hap-penstance. When Klein's focus was on aggression, it was bad or hateful objects that she was most concerned with. Her papers on depressive anx-iety, on the other hand, focus more on the good objects and their feared destruction. She has a tendency to see bad objects as internally derived, that is, as arising from the child's own drives, and good objects as ab-sorbed from the outside, from the ameliorative effect of the parents' ministrations. Unfortunately, at each point in her writing her formula-tion concerning the origin of objects is postulated as a universal mechanism for the origin of all objects, resulting in considerable confu-sion and incongruent concepts. Klein's tendency to derive good objects from the outside and bad objects internally stems from her view of psychopathology as arising from internal, constitutional sources and her parallel minimization of the importance of parental anxiety, ambivalence, and character pathology.

Major Metapsychological Shift: The Nature of the Drives

Klein's use of the concept of drive poses a paradox. On the one hand, her entire motivational system rests on drives and her writing is replete with references to them. She saw her emphasis on drives as providing the central link to Freud's work, and this emphasis has earned her the reputation, particularly among her critics, as an "id" psychologist par excellence. On the other hand, Klein's work has served as a key transition to later theorists such as Fairbairn and Guntrip, who have abandoned the drive model altogether. How is it possible that Klein's work seemingly extends and elaborates classical drive theory, yet also serves as a bridge to its abandonment, a transition from the classical drive/structure model to subsequent relational/structure model views? The answer lies in the manner in which her formulations alter, in subtle yet far-reaching fashion, the very nature of the drives as psychic phenomena.

Although other persons are clearly central to many of Freud's clinical concepts, the "object" is the least intrinsic, most "accidental" feature within his metapsychological formulations concerning the nature of the drives. The source, the aim, and the impetus are all inherent aspects of the drive; the particular object is serendipitously tacked on through experience. All of the most important psychic processes are produced by excesses or deficiencies of gratification; the object is merely the vehicle through which gratification is either obtained or denied. In the earliest developmental epochs in Freud's system (the states of autoerotism and primary narcissism), the infant is essentially autistic and the libido lacks any attachment to objects apart from the ego itself. The object in Freud's theory remains temporally secondary and always functionally subordinate to the aims of drive gratification.

For Klein the object is more basic and essential; drives are inherently and inseparably directed toward objects. This shift is directly reflected in her critique of Freud's concept of narcissism as a primary and recurrent objectless state. Klein conceives of the drives as more tightly bound to objects. The infant, she argued, has a much deeper and more immediate relation to reality than previous psychoanalytic theory has credited him with. Her objection to the concept of primary narcissism has considerably more importance than what at first glance appears to be a minor theoretical refinement. Narcissism had been applied, within classical psychoanalysis, as an explanatory concept with regard to many clinical phenomena, ranging from tics (Ferenczi, 1921) to schizophrenia (Freud, 1914a), and as a tool for understanding rigid resistances within the psychoanalytic situation itself (Abraham, 1919). Klein and her collaborators took issue with these explanations. They argued that seemingly narcissistic manifestations such as tics (Klein, 1925), schizophrenia (Klein, 1960), and extreme resistance in analysis (Riviere, 1936b) are *not* objectless states but reflect intense relations to objects, generally *internal* objects. For Klein, the content and nature of relations with objects, both real other people and phantasied images of others imagined as internal presences, are *the* crucial determinant of most important psychical processes, both normal and pathological. She argued that Freud's "narcissistic libido" reflects not a cathexis of the ego itself but of internal objects and thus replaced Freud's distinction between narcissistic libido and object libido with the distinction between relations with internal versus external objects.

Klein's premise of primary object-relatedness has considerable importance beyond the general clinical utility of the concept of internal objects; it represents a fundamental shift in vision concerning human motivation and mental processes in general. Freud's view of drives as originally and most deeply objectless necessitates a dichotomous and layered vision of the psychic apparatus. At the base is the "seething cauldron" of the drives, directionless and isolated from the outside world, operating through loose and fluid primary process thinking. The ego, operating through more organized, reality-oriented, secondary process thinking, is *required* to impart direction, structure, and continuity. The functions of the ego are thus superimposed upon the primary motivational energy of the drives, organizing mental events and orienting them toward reality.

For Klein the drives themselves possess, through their inherent object-relatedness, many of the features which in Freud's theory were the province of the ego and the secondary process. The drives are oriented toward others, toward reality, and contain information concerning the objects from whom they seek gratification. It is, she writes, "my contention that the infant has from the beginning of post-natal life a relation to the mother . . . which is imbued with the fundamental elements of an object-relation, i.e. love, hatred, phantasies, anxieties and defences" (1952b, p. 49). This primary relationship to others contrasts with Freud's view that the child turns to reality, and so to his mother, only as a consequence of the frustration of his original drive demands, and only with the development of secondary process thinking. The very building-blocks of mental life in Klein's theory are different from those in Freud's. For Klein the basic units of mental processes are not packets of objectless energy, but relational units *ab initio*. Implicit in her reformulation of the properties of drives is the notion that all psychic energy is inherently directional and structured: "there is no instinctual urge, no anxiety situation, no mental process which does not involve objects, external or internal; in other words, object relations are at the *centre* of emotional life" (1952b, p. 53; italics in original).

It is not only with respect to their orientation toward objects that Klein's "drives" differ from Freud's. Their very nature is different. For Freud the drives originate as physical forces, although they have psychological manifestations and consequences. For Klein the drives are essentially psychological forces, which utilize the body as a vehicle of expression. This implicit alteration in the nature of drives is subtle, yet it has had enormous importance for the subsequent history of psychoanalytic ideas. It is masked by Klein's efforts to remain loyal to Freud and to employ his language. It is therefore necessary to get underneath the language, to look at the differences between Klein and Freud in their fundamental grasp of the texture of human experience.

In Freud's system the drives begin as tensions within physical, bodily tissues. The body is their source, their point of origination. This physical tension affects the psychic apparatus — the mind — whose basic function is to give the body what it needs, to eliminate drive tensions and preserve a state of homeostatis. Drive tensions manifest themselves through wishful impulses, the gratification of which reduces the tension within the bodily source of the drive. It is through wishful impulses, therefore, that the drives make a demand on the mind for work. Inherent in each component instinct is an "aim," an activity which will reduce the tension at its "source." If direct gratification of the original "aim" of the drive is possible, this is the most economical route to tension-reduction. If direct gratification is not possible, aim-inhibited gratification or sublimation is the next most economical route. Within Freud's system all our most complex and personal emotions such as love and tenderness, as well as hatred, are derived from the basic building-blocks, packets of bodily tension. They are ultimately vehicles for tension reduction.

Klein does not underemphasize the importance of the body in the experience of the child and the adult. Body parts and functions play a central and pervasive role in her formulations. Yet the body has a different function vis-à-vis the drives. For Klein the body is not the source of the drives, but the vehicle for their expression. The drives themselves are fundamentally directional psychological phenomena, constituting complex emotions. Aggression does not refer to a directionless, objectless destructive energy which becomes attached to objects secondarily for the purpose of gratification. Aggression in Klein's system is an informed, personal, purposive hatred, bound up with specific relations with specific others. The child envies the mother her self-contained goodness which remains out of his control; he wants to ruin it, to spoil it. He is jealous of her unborn babies and her possession of father's penis and plots their demise. He rages against his parents' imagined mutual gratifications in the face of his own frustration and exclusion and imagines a spiteful and ironic revenge and triumph.

Libido, in Klein's usage, is likewise directed, organized, personal, and complex. The child's love of his parents and siblings, she goes to considerable lengths to explain, is not limited to desire, but entails deep caring. This caring is an inherent feature of the earliest relationship to objects: "feelings of love and gratitude arise directly and spontaneously in the baby in response to the love and care of his mother." Caring is not motivated merely by the child's dependence on his objects for drive gratification but involves a "profound urge to make sacrifices" (1964, p. 65), to make others happy, out of genuine sympathy for them.

In Klein's formulations, feelings of love are in no way aim-inhibited derivatives of frustrated impulses but fundamental features of psychic life in themselves. In fact, she suggests that it is out of love for his objects that the child is concerned with inhibiting the more destructive of his impulses, and he seeks his parents' aid in developing such control (1964, pp. 74–75n). The approach Klein takes to the Oedipus complex in her late work provides a measure of the extent of her movement from Freud with regard to the basic motivational properties of the drives. She suggests that he has "not given enough weight to the crucial role of these feelings of love, both in the development of the Oedipus conflict and in its passing . . . the Oedipus situation loses in power not only because the boy is afraid . . . but also because he is driven by feelings of love and guilt to preserve his father as an internal and external figure" (1945, p. 389). Thus, in Klein's formulations, the dialectic between the boy's love for his father and his desire to preserve a good relationship with him, on the one hand, and his hate, jealousy, and envy, on the other, constitutes the central conflict within the Oedipus complex, replacing the central position Freud had allotted to the conflict between the pursuit of drive gratification and castration anxiety (the fear of the loss of the organ which provides drive gratification). Libido and aggression for Klein are not groups of component instincts but personal, directional emotions.

Where, then, does the body come in? The body, in Klein's theory, if not the originator of the drives, is the most effective means of their expression. Picture the young infant as seen by Klein. He experiences profound love, overwhelming hate, and desolate dread and horror in relation to those around him; yet, he has no verbal or motoric means for expressing these passions. He cannot speak them; he cannot act them out, except in very crude and inchoate fashion. His understanding of the workings of the world is limited essentially to his own body. Therefore, the parts and functions of his body become signifiers in a primitive grammar of physical expression. He uses this bodily lexicon to put into effect his driving passions of love and hate. Hate (or the death instinct) uses the body's resources as weapons. Each body part and each bodily function is experienced, when the child is hating, as a powerful means for the destruction of those around him and inside him. Riviere catalogs the child's physical armamentarium:

> Loose motions, flatus and urine are all felt to be burning, corroding and poisoning agents. Not only the excretory but all other physical functions are pressed into the service of the need for aggressive (sadistic) discharge and projection in phantasy. Limbs shall trample, kick and hit; lips, fingers and hands shall suck, twist, pinch; teeth shall bite, gnaw, mangle and cut; mouth shall devour, swallow and kill (annihilate); eyes kill by a look, pierce and penetrate; breath and mouth hurt by noise, as the child's own sensitive ears have experienced. (1936a, p. 50)

Love (or the life instinct) uses the body's resources as gifts. Each body part and each bodily function is expressed, when the child is loving, as a powerful means for pleasing and restoring those around him and inside him. Love, in its drive to make up for past sins and damage, "draws on libidinal phantasies and desires" (1952c, p. 74) as a reassurance that the object is still alive, and that a loving exchange is still possible.

In the Kleinian system the same body parts and functions are employed both by hate and by love. Feeding can be used to represent either a depletion of, or a loving union with, the mother; urination can express hateful destruction through conflagration or a grateful and reciprocal offering to the mother of nutritive fluids; defecation can represent explosive (early anal) or poisonous (late anal) malice or a reparative offer of valuable objects to replace the mother's stolen babies. In Freud's theory this would not be possible. The original motive for him proceeds from the tension in the body part itself, which seeks its release in a specific "aim." Psychological derivatives of that drive are bound to and colored by that aim. The "intention" of the drive is provided by the body part itself, which generates the meaning. In Klein's usage the motive is supplied by the feeling, the passion, which selects available body parts and functions for its expression. Bodily impulses serve, in Isaacs' words, as the "vehicle of instinct." For Klein bodily processes do not instigate drive tensions; the drives, psychological in nature, give meaning to bodily events to express their aims. Meaning is generated not in body parts and mechanisms but in emotional experiences she terms "drives." The "intention," or meaning of the activity, is not determined *by* the bodily source, but is imparted *to* the bodily activity by the drives.

Because Klein was concerned throughout her writing with establishing continuity with Freud, this basic shift in understanding of the nature of drives is not addressed explicitly. The closest she comes to contrasting herself with Freud directly on this fundamental issue is in a discussion of the nature of objects. She suggests that, for Freud, the object is always "the object of an instinctual aim," whereas in her own usage it signifies "in addition to this, an object-relation involving the infant's emotions, phantasies, anxieties and defences" (1952b, p. 51). In many other places, particularly in the later papers, Klein makes it clear that her concept of drive concerns not merely the reduction of bodily tensions, but rather a fuller, passionate relatedness to another person: "Gratification is as much related to the object which gives the food as to the food itself" (1952d, p. 96). Playing at the breast is as important as the feeding itself, and provides a "loving conversation between mother and baby" (1952d, p. 96). The nature of the child's desire for the mother transcends physical gratification and entails a fuller, more personal recognition. The child "not only expects food from her but also desires love and understanding" (1959, p. 248). The breast itself is not experienced by the child merely as a physical object or a means to bodily gratification, but as the "prototype of maternal goodness, inexhaustible patience and generosity" (1957, p. 180).

Despite these clear differences in conceptualizing the nature of drives, Klein argued that her usage derives from and is consistent with Freud's concepts of life and death instincts, although Freud himself and most of his followers did not fully adhere to these formulations and integrate them into existing theory. Critics of Klein argue that this aspect of Freud's musings on life and death instincts were intended as a philosophical speculation on larger, biological forces in life in general, not as theoretical concepts meant to be applied directly to clinical phenomena. Paula Heimann (1952b) countered this argument. Although acknowledging Freud's ambivalence about this aspect of his own theorizing, she points to places in his late work where he *does* apply the concepts of life and death instincts to clinical phenomena.

It strikes us that this debate, because of the preoccupation with legitimacy, is beside the point. Freud may have used concepts of life and death instincts to illuminate clinical facts, but he never suggested that these forces have a *phenomenological* basis in experience. For him the life and death instincts were conceived of as properties of biological tissue tending toward the creation and the breaking apart, respectively, of complex biological structures. As such, they give birth to, or are manifested in, libido and destructiveness, which carry out the tasks of connecting things or disconnecting things respectively. For Freud, libido and aggression, not the life and death instincts, are the originators of experience, in the bodily tensions through which they arise. For Klein, on the other hand, the life and death instincts are contained within, and in fact originate, personal experience. Libidinal and aggressive phantasies are from the outset "the mental expression of the activity of both the life and death instincts" (1952a, p. 58). Love and hate, their respective representatives, are the basic motivational forces within the Kleinian system. This *shift from a philosophical to an experiental level* constitutes Klein's essential departure from Freud's formulations.

Klein's approach to classical Freudian principles concerning the structural, genetic, and economic points of view highlights some of the implications of the shift in her use of the concept of drives. In Freud's structural model the ego is neutral in relation to the drives. Its task is to negotiate a balance among the id, the superego, and the outside world. Although Klein retains Freud's structural language, the ego in her approach is a major protagonist within internal dynamic struggles, closely identified with love and the life instinct. The existence of the ego in the first place is credited to the life instinct and its need for an ally in thwarting the death instinct: "the ego is called into action at birth by the life instinct" (1958, p. 238). The very nature of the ego betrays its origins—"the ego's urge toward integration and organization clearly reveals its derivation from the life instinct" (1952a, p. 57). As the ego becomes more and more identified with love and reparation, the id becomes the embodiment of hate. *"The ego is identified with the sufferings of the good objects"* (1935, p. 293; italics in original), and by virtue of this identification, becomes antagonistic toward the id, fearing the destruction of itself along with all good objects.

These structural revisions derive from Klein's reformulations concerning the nature of the drives. For Freud, libido and aggression are structureless, directionless energies; they *require* a motivationally neutral but reality-oriented ego to negotiate between them and the outside world. The central human struggle, for Freud, is between drive gratification (sexual and aggressive) and the demands of social reality. For Klein, libido and aggression are inherently oriented toward the outside world, as personal, structured passions. Therefore, Freud's distinction between the id and the ego, between free-floating energy and a neutral mediator, does not apply in her system. The central conflict in human experience, for Klein, is between love and hate, between the caring preservation and the malicious destruction of others. Love and hate are already object-related and therefore have an unmediated connection to social reality. Thus, Klein implicitly redefines the structural terms as well, using the now unnecessary distinction between id and ego to represent, in a largely redundant fashion, the more basic struggle between hate and love, in which the id stands for hate, and the ego for love. Klein's altered usage of Freud's structural concepts betrays her view of the drives not as asocial energic charges lacking structure and direction but as antithetical, object-related passions.

Klein's approach to developmental sequences similarly reflects her altered understanding of drives. For Freud the components of the drives unfold in a sequence of aims based on tensions in body parts. The psychosexual stages reflect a maturational sequence in which different portions of the libido, each with its own bodily source, emerge and establish a temporary dominance, leading ultimately to the hegemony of genitality. Klein suggests that the psychosexual "phases" are not distinctly sequential, that the various stages overlap and merge into each other (1928, p. 214; 1945, p. 387). She replaces the term "stages" with "positions," suggesting patterns and groupings of anxieties and defenses. Different positions reflect different patterns of organizing experience, a differing positioning of loving and hateful relations with others. In the paranoid-schizoid position, loving relations and hateful relations are kept separate from each other; in the depressive position, loving and hateful relations are unified. The move from a concept of stages to the concept of positions again reflects a redefinition of drives from packets of energy unfolding in a sequence of predominant bodily zones to drives as relational patterns, whose intensity and antipathy necessitate different organizational patterns.

Klein's treatment of energic concepts also reflects the innovative shift in her usage of the concept of drive. The drives for Freud are finite amounts of energy; they are treated as physical substances, having specific quantities. Therefore, the more libido or aggression directed outward, the less inward; the more expended in direct gratification, the less available for sublimation or aim-inhibited activities; the more directed toward one person, the less available for others. For Freud, if real gratification is available, no fantasy takes place; if energy is expended in fantasy, less drive energy is available for real gratification. Not so with Klein. Without explicitly announcing that she is doing so, she changes all of Freud's basic economic principles. In Klein's system, the energy of the drives is not finite and preset. Phantasy is not merely a compensation or substitute for real gratification; it is also an accompaniment of actual satisfaction. Libidinal and aggressive gratification is directed inwardly (toward internal objects) and outwardly (toward real others) at the same time; they are directly rather than inversely related to each other. Love for one object does not limit, but increases love for others. In adult love, for example, the beloved is loved not instead of the original oedipal objects but in addition to them. The love is accompanied by unconscious phantasied oedipal gratification.

Klein views human experience as fluid, kaleidoscopic, and multitextured. From her earliest papers she suggests that for the child, the world represents the mother's body, with its phantasied riches and horrors. All activities and relations within the world have simultaneous, multilayered, infantile libidinal and aggressive meanings and draw on sublimations of libidinal and aggressive motives. Isaacs extends this approach to the very process of thinking: *"Reality-thinking cannot operate without concurrent and supporting unconscious phantasies"* (1943, p. 109; italics in original). Thus, the principles of energy regulation established by Freud are weakened to the point of nonexistence within the Kleinian system. Once again, her approach to energic issues reflects a concept of drives not as finite, body-derived parcels of energy but as complex, multitextured, passions involving others.

Contributions and Limitations of Klein's System

Paula Heimann (1952b) suggests that the death instinct is a stepchild within psychoanalytic theory, second in acceptability and status to the life instincts, which, because of Freud's earlier development of the libido theory, constitute his firstborn. In many respects Melanie Klein herself is a stepchild of Freudian psychoanalysis. An adversarial relationship was established between her and Anna Freud concerning the most truly "psychoanalytic" approach to the treatment of children.* Freud, in his almost complete refusal to acknowledge Klein's contributions, clearly bestowed the mantel of legitimacy upon his biological daughter. Perhaps partly as a result, continuity with and loyalty to Freud was a central preoccupation within Klein's work. (The fact that her elder sister was the favorite of her admired and beloved father must have had some bearing on this.) Her disciples and detractors have also focused on the

---

*A. Freud (1927) took the position that psychoanalysis is not possible with young children; because they are still unformed and tied to the parents, a true transference and deep oedipal analysis cannot develop. She urged a supportive and educational stance on the part of the analyst and considered Klein's more purely analytic approach inappropriate and dangerous. Klein took the position that transference and oedipal material develop spontaneously in work with children and urged a neutral, purely interpretive stance. She argued that A. Freud's educational approach splits the transference, driving the negative transference underground. The absence of a fully analytic situation is a *result* of A. Freud's methods, Klein argued, not a reasonable justification for them.

issue of legitimacy and selected supporting passages from Freud's mammoth and constantly changing opus. This preoccupation has served as a distraction from an appreciation of Klein's important contributions to the history of psychoanalytic ideas as well as from the truly problematic aspects of her theoretical system.

Klein was responsible for many important theoretical and clinical innovations. She was a key figure in the shift in emphasis within the psychoanalytic literature to the study of the earliest relationship between the infant and the mother before the full development of the oedipal constellation in later childhood. Her discovery of early introjects and identifications, her expanded appreciation of phantasy, and her development of the concepts of internal objects and the internal object world provided powerful clinical tools for the psychoanalytic investigation of these earliest object relations. Her formulations concerning primitive persecutory anxieties, early defenses dominated by splitting and its elaborations, and depressive anxiety and reparation have contributed greatly to the study of dynamic processes within psychotic, neurotic, and normal mental functioning. Her development of play technique and her incisive descriptions of the insidious workings of greed and envy and their centrality in establishing the most intransigent resistances in the psychoanalytic situation have greatly added to the range and efficacy of psychoanalytic technique. Klein's key place in the history of psychoanalytic ideas derives not only from these specific contributions but also from her role in shifting broad, metapsychological perspective. She places object relations at the center of her theoretical and clinical formulations. The organization and content of object relations, particularly relations with the fluid and complex world of internal objects, are the central determinants of experience and behavior.

Klein takes from the drive/structure model the premise that the major constituents of mental life originate in the individual organism and unfold in a maturational sequence, at which time they come to be modified and transformed through interactions between the individual and the world of others. Libido and aggression, for her as for Freud, are motivational energies within the individual, whose properties are constitutional givens, determined a priori: man is understood to be driven by these forces, propelled by internal pressures. In this sense only, Klein is very much an "id psychologist." However, she redefines the *nature* of these interior forces. She redefines the essential properties of the drives themselves and, by so doing, sows the seeds from which developed the relational/structure model theories of the "British School." Drives are no longer directionless, tension-producing stimuli which become secondarily attached to objects serving as the vehicle for their gratification.

Drives for Klein contain objects as a constitutive part of their nature; libido and aggression are inherently directional longings aimed at specific eidetic images. It is in this sense that the frequent characterization of Klein as an "id" psychologist, in contrast to the ego psychology of the American Freudian school deriving from Hartmann and A. Freud, is fundamentally misleading. The ego in her system is underdeveloped, because the drives, in Klein, contain many of the properties carried by the concept of the "ego" in ego psychology. Drives for her are not discrete quantities of energy arising from specific body tensions but passionate feelings of love and hate directed toward others and utilizing the body as a vehicle of expression. *Drives, for Klein, are relationships.*

Klein's depiction of the relationships that dominate emotional life—the paranoid-schizoid position, the workings of envy, the depressive position—are powerful and incisive; they constitute her greatest contribution to clinical psychoanalysis. However, she presents them as constitutional and universal, a direct and predetermined result of the nature of the drives, particularly of constitutional aggression. It is as if each of us begins life by being born into the same play, in which the cast of characters is standard and the script well-established and unchanging. The parents as real people are of central importance, but in tightly circumscribed and unidimensional ways. They are important as representatives of universal human attributes—a mother with breasts, a father with penis. The actuality of their anatomy both corroborates and transforms the child's inherent a priori imagoes and phantasies. The parents are also important in their physical reality largely because they survive. Their perpetual reappearance, despite the child's murderous phantasies, strengthens the child's belief in his own restorative capacities and aids in the development of reality testing.

Klein tends to see the effect of the parents on the child as uniformly positive, as a source of loving and nurturative images that serve as a counterpart to the child's own inherent aggression. Although in case illustrations she occasionally mentions some more personal or characterological feature (a mother's depression, lack of warmth, dislike for the child), such features never appear in formulations concerning internal object relations, where the cast of characters is always composed of *universal* images, benevolent or malevolent body parts, babies, victims, survivors, and executioners. The richness and detail of the parents' personalities is missing, and the impact of the parents as real others is measured on a continuum of greater or lesser amelioration of the child's own aggression. Bad objects are internally derived. Good experiences with the parents transform these bad objects into more benign, whole objects. The origins of psychopathology lie in the child's own aggression, which may or may not be able to be rectified by parental care. What is missing here is the possibility that problematic features of the parents' own personalities, the parents' own difficulties in living, may contribute in a more direct and immediate way to the original establishment of bad objects and thus to the beginnings of psychopathology in the child.

Klein does not allow for the impact of the parents' character defects or particular strengths. This omission seems particularly striking given her account of the continual presence of infantile conflicts in adults, and in the complex and intense feelings underlying parenting (1964). For example, in her discussion of the depressive position, Klein links the child's concern about parental damage to the child's own aggressive fantasies toward the parent. The child destroys the parent in fantasy, then becomes concerned about and regrets the damage inflicted. What Klein does not consider, in her characteristic fashion of deriving all salient emotional factors from inside the individual's own mind, is the extent to which depressive anxiety and guilt often derive from actual parental suffering and difficulties. Children are often extremely sensitive to parental anxiety and depression. The developing personality of the child invariably becomes enormously entangled in the sufferings of the parents. Similarly, reparative fantasies often tend to revolve around hopes for restoring and transforming actual parental pain and deficiencies ("If I succeed, I redeem my father, making up for his deep sense of personal failure" or "If I remain a saintly person, my mother's depression will finally lift and she will be able to live"). It was left to Fairbairn and Winnicott, less encumbered by loyalty to the drive/structure model, to extend Klein's compelling delineation of the child's struggle with love and hate past his own internally generated fantasies to include the child's perceptions of and involvement with the parents as actual persons in their struggles with life.

All the problematic areas within Klein's system derive in one way or another from her transitional position within the history of psychoanalytic ideas. Klein has two concerns: on the one hand, she provides powerful and incisive descriptions of the fundamental organizations of object relations and emotional life; on the other hand, she wants to preserve the notion that all significant constituents of mental life are internally given. This dual focus makes it necessary for her to account for the presence of complex relational constellations within very early developmental phases. Her adherence to the concept of the death instinct, her presupposition of extensive constitutional knowledge and imagery, and her attribution to the infant of elaborate cognitive capacities at or shortly before birth are the three areas within her theory most persistently challenged by critics. These three principles combine to serve Klein's dual purpose. Early cognitive resources and a priori knowledge are employed by the ego to ward off the threat to survival posed by the death instinct, generating both good and bad object images and early defensive organizations. The world of object relations is thus invented under the threat of internal pressures. In our opinion, Klein's depiction of the basic organizations of early object relations does not stand or fall with the premise of constitutionality and the controversial areas within her work which support that premise. Her depiction of early object relations provide powerful tools for understanding the psychodynamics of older children and adults, whether or not they accurately portray the early months of the newborn's experience.

The assumption of constitutionality in the patterning of early object relationships is a remnant of Klein's allegiance to the drive/structure model; it was abandoned, to varying degrees, by many subsequent theorists influenced by her. Some authors, like Fairbairn, Guntrip, and Bowlby, abandon the language of drive theory explicitly and derive object relations completely from the child's experience with the actual parents. Likewise, most of the major authors who have maintained Klein's frame of reference more fully derive patterns of early object relations more from the child's actual experience with the parents as *particular* people (Bion, 1957; Meltzer, 1974; Rosenfeld, 1965; Segal, 1981). Racker, for example, has explicitly modified Klein's developmental model, deriving paranoid and depressive anxieties not from vicissitudes of drive but from the child's experience of wanting and needing the mother's love with such extreme intensity (1968).

A final weakness in Klein's system also derives from her position midway between the drive/structure tradition and her growing use of relational/structure assumptions and formulations. There is in her work considerable fuzziness concerning the relationship between phantasy and the establishment of character or psychic structure (see Fairbairn, 1952, p. 154; Modell, 1968, p. 120; Kernberg, 1980, p. 42). Klein's depiction of mental life is characterized by an enormous fluidity. Images of objects, both internal and external, constantly emerge from the drives themselves. Perceptions of reality are continually absorbed and brought to bear on internal phantasies and experiences. How does a patterned existence emerge from this rich, kaleidoscopic fluidity? How does the personality become organized into patterns or structures which have durability and constancy? If phantasy life is so rich and chaotic, what mechanisms are responsible for the selection of those phantasies which take on central dynamic significance or pathogenic properties? Klein leaves an unfilled gap between her vivid and fluid account of the phenomenology of experience and the organization of personality and behavior. Segal suggests that the most enduring features of the internal object world are the ones that have been phantasied with the greatest frequency. The simple accretion of phantasy seems, at best, an incomplete explanation for the development of character.

The lack of clarity in Klein's system concerning the relationship between phantasy and structure is reflected in a fuzziness concerning the precise nature as well as the ultimate fate of internalizations. On the one hand, Klein described internalizations as phantasies; the child or the adult imagines someone or part of someone inside him. Such a phantasy is usually motivated by the desire to derive gratification from the object or to control it. On the other hand, Klein suggests that the child internalizes *all* his significant others, in fact all of his experiences. In this formulation, developed further by Heimann, the distinctions between phantasied objects, perception, and memory become blurred. Are durable phantasies of internal objects kept separate from day-to-day perceptions of others? (Klein at points suggests such a layering, for example, in her concept of an "inner super-ego" in which original internal objects are established and kept separate from more realistic perceptions of others.) Or, is there a continual transformation of all phantasied internal objects through a constant intermingling with current perceptions? (Klein at points suggests such a perceptual blending in the development of internal replicas or duplicates of real others.) Klein does not sufficiently distinguish or articulate the relationship among: current perceptions of real others; relatively durable representations of others (object relations); phantasies of internal objects; and identifications with internal objects which serve as a focus for the organization of various functions within the personality (as in Freud's description of the superego).

The ambiguity in Klein's formulations concerning structure is further illustrated when we consider the fate of internalizations. On the one hand, Klein has, from her earliest papers, linked internal objects with superego formation: "The incorporated object at once assumes the functions of a super-ego" (1932, p. 184n). The superego is thus constituted by an "assembly of internalized objects" (1940, p. 330). On the other hand, beginning in 1946, Klein places great emphasis on the role of internal objects in the development of the ego itself: "The first internal good object acts as a focal point in the ego. It counteracts the processes of splitting and dispersal, makes for cohesiveness and integration, and is instrumental in building up the ego" (1946, p. 6).

Are internal objects constitutive of the ego, the superego, or both? In one of her last papers Klein offers two suggestions, themselves incompatible, aimed at clarifying this problem. First she proposes that the superego is formed later in development from a splitting of the ego. This approach seems to contradict much of her data concerning early, harsh, and critical parental imagoes. Second, she suggests that the ego and superego share different aspects of the same good object. A quality of contrivance in both these proposals highlights the dilemma Klein faced in her efforts to squeeze the richness of her account of the varied phantasies and identifications of the child into Freud's original dichotomy between ego and superego. (See Segal, 1979, p. 103, for a further consideration of inconsistencies in Klein's use of the term "superego.")

Freud's structural model developed out of drive/structure premises. It illuminates psychic conflict between drive impulses and social reality and is inextricably bound to Freud's original formulations concerning the nature of the drives. Character structure for Freud is constituted by patterns of drive and defense. For him, the distinction between the ego and the superego is a distinction between the regulatory functions of the psychic apparatus and the parental imagoes that have been internalized to aid in the regulation. In Klein's system drive regulation has been replaced by a complex web of relations with others, real and imagined. Character for Klein is constituted by phantasies concerning internal objects, derived from the inherent object-relatedness of love and hate. Internal object relations constitute the basic substructure of experience and the stuff of the entire personality. The dichotomy between ego and superego, based on their different positions vis-à-vis the drives and their function with respect to drive regulation, simply does not fit in Klein's system. Klein generally tries to use the distinction to differentiate between internal objects which have been digested into the self (the ego) and internal objects which have retained a relatively distinct and foreign quality within the self-experience (the superego). But the simple dichotomy does not work. Klein's ill-fated attempt to force the complexity of her account of internal object relations into the drive/structure framework of classical structural theory is largely responsible for her failure to bridge the gap between her depiction of phantasy and a compelling account of patterned, structured character-formation.

Of late I have been increasingly able to catch, if I listen attentively, the sound of the sobs . . . which broke out only when I found myself alone with Mamma. Actually, their echo has never ceased: it is only because life is now growing more and more quiet round about me that I hear them afresh, like those convent bells which are so effectively drowned during the day by the noises of the streets that one would suppose them to have been stopped for ever, until they sound out again through the silent evening air.

—PROUST, *Remembrance of Things Past*

6 W. R. D. Fairbairn

In a series of dense and fertile papers written during the early 1940s, W. R. D. Fairbairn developed a theoretical perspective which, along with Sullivan's "interpersonal psychiatry," provides the purest and clearest expression of the shift from the drive/structure model to the relational/structure model. Fairbairn's physical and collegial semi-isolation in the psychoanalytic provinces of Edinburgh and a background of study in philosophy and divinity facilitated his bold and far-reaching reconsideration of the conceptual edifice within which psychoanalytic theory operates. His strategy contrasts sharply with Sullivan's, who sidestepped Freudian psychoanalysis and developed his own language and conceptual framework. Fairbairn's approach also contrasts sharply with the strategies of other British theorists such as Klein and Winnicott, as well as those within the tradition of American ego psychology, all of whom, in one way or another, attempted to preserve as much as possible of classical theory.

Fairbairn begins in the very heart of Freudian metapsychology, with the libido theory and the theory of psychosexual development, and challenges its basic assumptions and principles. His immediate focus was not on the clinical practice of psychoanalysis. In fact, he felt that most analysts would be rightfully indignant at the suggestion that they minimized concerns about relations with other people in their work with patients. Rather, his concern was with their failure to apply their clinical experience with patients to the most basic of their theoretical principles.

Fairbairn argues that the fundamental assumptions and conceptual underpinnings of the libido theory and the theory of psychosexual development represent misplaced emphases and basic misunderstandings concerning human motivation and experience.

The relative unfamiliarity with Fairbairn's work among practicing analysts and the paucity of direct references to his ideas in the psychoanalytic literature is not commensurate with the significance of his contribution within the history of psychoanalytic ideas. There appear to be several reasons for this oversight, in addition to his physical isolation and the political considerations stemming from his disavowal of orthodox libido theory. First, Fairbairn came to intellectual maturity in a climate dominated by Klein's extensions of Freud's theory. His early papers were written from a Kleinian point of view, and even his later papers employ much of her language, particularly the lexicon of terms referring to internal object relations. However, critics who tend to lump his work together with hers under the general category of "object relations theory" or the "British School" have overlooked the fact that Fairbairn changed the meanings of all the major terms and concepts he borrowed from Klein; his broad vision of human experience differs in fundamental respects from hers.

A second factor contributing to the minimal recognition accorded Fairbairn's contributions is that the only comprehensive presentation of his views is that of Guntrip (1961, 1971). The latter had a great interest both in proselytizing for the point of view he and Fairbairn held in common and in emphasizing his own particular emendations and extensions of Fairbairn's ideas. Consequently, he had a tendency to gloss over problematic areas and inconsistencies in Fairbairn's writings. Also, a central principle in Fairbairn's understanding of psychopathology is that all portions of the ego are always joined with objects. In fact, psychopathology is understood fundamentally as the ego's attempt to perpetuate old ties and hopes represented by internal objects. Guntrip, on the other hand, stresses, in all forms of psychopathology, the ego's withdrawal from objects (both external and internal) altogether. This provides a very different understanding of the nature of psychopathology. Yet, Guntrip presents his views as merely an elaboration and inevitable extension of Fairbairn's theory, obscuring their fundamental differences. For readers who know Fairbairn's work only through Guntrip's presentation, it is difficult to tease out the distinctive contribution of Fairbairn's ideas.

A third set of reasons for Fairbairn's relative obscurity has to do with his writing. Although he did pull together his major contributions into a single volume, he did not rework them into a coherent and comprehensive theory but left them in their original chronological order and form.

Consequently, the reader is faced not with a single theory but with a series of different formulations, with varying yet related focuses, circling again and again over the same territory, yet not wholly consistent with each other. Fairbairn points out several times that he is offering "not the systematic elaboration of an already established point of view, but the progressive development of a line of thought" (1951, p. 133). This mode of presentation has advantages and disadvantages. Among the former are the excitement and interest with which the student of Fairbairn's work can recreate and reconsider the sequence of issues with which he struggled. On the other hand, the finished body of work has a patchwork quality; the relationships among his various concepts are often fuzzy and poorly delineated.

Another problem with Fairbairn's writing is his tendency to be abstract and overly systematized. He deals with broad theoretical issues, often without filling in the clinical referents and implications. He seems fascinated with the intricacies of theory construction itself, often on aesthetic grounds or for the number of logical permutations and combinations which the theory provides (1944, p. 128). Amid the welter of detail, technical terms, and intricate, highly schematic distinctions, the power of his work, in both its clinical and its theoretical implications, can be missed.

Theory of Motivation

At the center of Fairbairn's broad and varied contributions lies his critique and reformulation of the classical theory of motivation—the drive theory. The basic motivational unit within drive theory is the impulse. Impulses are derivatives of drive tensions; they provide the energy which fuels all activities of the psychic apparatus. Fairbairn pointed out that although Freud's later work stressed the functioning of the ego and the superego, the more social dimensions of the personality, and that although Klein's work had elaborated a complex theory of internal objects, the source of motivational energy for both classical and Kleinian theory remained the instinctual impulse. The psychology of the ego and its objects had been superimposed upon the earlier psychology of impulses. Fairbairn argued that the basic assumptions upon which the drive theory rests are erroneous and misleading; in the broadest sense he saw his work as entailing a "reinterpretation of Freud's views on the basis of a differing set of underlying scientific principles" (1946, p. 149). The first step in this reinterpretation was the "recasting and reorientation of the libido theory" (1941, p. 28).

Within Freud's system the most salient and constant characteristic of the functioning of the psychic apparatus is its propulsion toward tension-regulation, otherwise known as the pleasure principle. The ultimate goal of all impulses is a reduction in bodily tension, experienced as pleasure.* The original impulse has no direction — it is a quantum of tension waiting to be reduced. The most pliable and interchangeable aspect of the impulse is the object. Impulses become directed toward external objects only when these objects present themselves and prove useful in reducing tension.

Fairbairn focused his disagreement with drive theory on two basic principles: libido is not pleasure-seeking but object-seeking; and impulse is inseparable from structure. The first of these can be understood as an extension of Klein's emendations of drive theory. Klein argued that objects were not added onto impulses secondarily through experience but were built into the impulses from the start. For her, despite the subtle and covert changes in the nature of the concept of drive, the fundamental aim of the impulse is still ostensibly pleasure — the object is merely a means toward that end. Fairbairn reverses this means/end relationship. He argues that the object is not only built into the impulse from the start, but that the main characteristic of libidinal energy is its object-seeking quality. Pleasure is not the end goal of the impulse, but a means to its real end — relations with another.

The second and closely related principle upon which Fairbairn rests his revision of libido theory is the notion that energy and structure are inseparable. For Freud the impulses are packets of energy distinct and separate from the ego, the agency which, along with the superego, uses the energy for various physical and psychical activities. The assumption that energy is separable from structure underlies Freud's distinction between different psychic agencies in his structural model — a structureless id, with directionless energy, and an ego with processes and mechanisms for using energy, but with no energy of its own. Fairbairn argues that this separation of energy from structure derives from a nineteenth-century physics world view in which the universe is conceived of as a "conglomeration of inert, immutable and indivisible particles to which motion was imparted by a fixed quantity of energy separate from the particles themselves" (1944, p. 127). This separation of structure from function, of mass from energy, is not at all consistent with twentieth-century physics, in which mass and energy have been demonstrated to

---

*Freud had revised this conception in his later work to regard pleasure not as the consequence of a simple reduction of tension but as the consequence of a particular rhythm of increases and decreases in tension, although he never revised his basic metapsychology accordingly (1924a). Descriptions of drive theory in this chapter refer to drive theory at the time Fairbairn was writing, and do not reflect subsequent changes in Freudian thinking.

be one and the same. In this sense, Freud's motivational theory is seen as anachronistic in its basic assumptions of the properties of matter and energy.

From Fairbairn's point of view, Freud's distinction between id and ego and his view of the impulse as directionless energy secondarily attachable to objects entails a misuse of language. Human beings operate through certain characteristic processes. We can make a linguistic distinction between these processes and the energy we assume fuels them. However, such a distinction between two aspects of a set of seamless experiences and activities does not necessarily imply that the energy and the activities are in fact separable in reality, belonging to different agencies in the mind, each with its own rules and principles of functioning. From Fairbairn's point of view, what classical metapsychology does is to take the human person who *is* energy operating in directional ways (toward objects) and to superimpose upon that human process an artificial distinction between the activities and the energy presumed to be fueling them. (See Schafer, 1968, for a critique of the language of drive theory along somewhat similar lines.) As a consequence of this linguistic operation, one is left with a set of energyless structures (the ego) and a pool of structureless energy (the id). Adherents of this view argue that one *must* have an energy/id principle—what else would drive the machinery of the psychic apparatus? For Fairbairn, however, the view of the ego as an apparatus, as structures without energy, is a linguistic distortion of the original energized and structured human activity. Hence there is no separation of ego from id. There is no pool of directionless energy which becomes secondarily oriented toward objects. Ego structures have energy—*are* energy—and that energy is structured and directed toward objects from the start. Impulses cannot be separated from these structures and the object relations which they enable the ego to establish. The only meaningful use of the term "impulses," Fairbairn argues, is to describe the activities, the dynamic aspects, of such structures (1944, p. 88).

What difference does it make if libido is understood to be object-seeking rather than pleasure-seeking, if impulses are understood to be constitutive of ego structures rather than separate from them? The abstractness of the language can mislead the reader into thinking of these as Talmudic and arcane theoretical distinctions. What Fairbairn is suggesting, however, is really a fundamentally different view of human motivation, meaning, and values. According to the classical drive/structure model, the human infant is born fundamentally unrelated to others, seeking tension-reduction; he becomes related to others only secondarily, because of their utility in reducing his tensions, providing him pleasure. Fairbairn suggests that the infant is oriented toward others from the beginning, and that his relation-seeking has adaptive roots in his biological survival.

Newborn animals of other species demonstrate various prepro-grammed, instinctive behaviors bonding them to their mothers. The human infant lacks most of these stereotyped, preprogrammed patterns. Fairbairn argues that the human infant is just as oriented toward reality, the mother, as are lower animals, but that without the preprogrammed instinctive behaviors, his path to the mother is more "roughly charted" (1946, p. 140). The apparent chaos and random behavior of the early months does not reflect a primary "narcissistic" or autoerotic stage in which the infant is not directed toward objects for fulfilling his needs. The apparent randomness simply reflects inexperience. Without built-in patterns, Fairbairn reasoned, it takes the human infant time to learn *how* to make contact and organize his relations with his mother.

The theoretical shift Fairbairn is proposing has implications not just for the earliest months of life but for a view of the essential forces in adult motivation as well. Fairbairn is suggesting that behavior and ex-periences of human beings are not derived from a set of directionless tensions seeking release, not constructed out of a thirst for various bodily pleasures which become secondarily altered and transformed into socially acceptable and desirable behaviors. He is suggesting that human experience and behavior derive fundamentally from the search for and maintenance of contacts with others. "The clinical material on which this proposition is based may be summarized in the protesting cry of a patient to this effect — 'You're always talking about my wanting this and that desire satisfied; but what I really want is a father'" (1946, p. 137). Psychopathology is understood not as deriving from conflicts over pleasure-seeking impulses, but as reflective of disturbances and in-terferences in relations with others. The analytic process is understood not as consisting of a resolution of unconscious conflict over pleasure-seeking impulses, but as a process through which the capacity for mak-ing direct and full contact with real other human beings is restored. Thus, the change in theoretical principles of motivation that Fairbairn is proposing is not trivial; it provides a different conceptual framework for viewing the entirety of human experience.

What happens to pleasure in Fairbairn's system? Surely bodily zones which provide intense sensual experiences play an important role in human affairs. Fairbairn does not negate the importance of pleasure, but he places it in a different context, in which it is seen as a means to an end, a "signpost to the object" (1941, p. 33), rather than as an end in itself. The body provides the opportunity for various types of sensual pleasures and activities, mainly through the erogenous zones, which are used by the object-seeking ego as occasions for contact, modes of relatedness with others. The zones are not seen as producing packets of tension demanding release but as providing pathways to the object. The first object for the infant is the mother's breast, and he seeks contact with it to ensure his own survival and development, both biologically and emotionally. He "looks for" the breast, and his built-in oral reflexes enable him to relate to and use it. The mouth becomes the salient "zone" in the early months of life, because it is the part of the infant's body most suited, through adaptation for survival, to make contact with the breast as well as to exchange pleasure with it. He uses his mouth in the service of his "breast-seeking."

Likewise, the crucial aspect of healthy maturity is a capacity for a rich and intimate mutuality with another. The genitalia offer themselves as perhaps the most intense and felicitous medium for such exchange. However, whereas in the Freud/Abraham developmental scheme, "genital primacy" was seen as the crucial development, with the maturity of relatedness a secondary derivative of this psychosexual achievement, Fairbairn argues that it is the capacity for intimacy that is crucial and primary, with the possibility of truly genital functioning a consequence of this ability to relate intimately and with mutuality. (Similar revisions of the concept of genital primacy were made several decades later within the ego psychological school; see Ross 1970, Lichtenstein, 1977, and Kernberg, 1976.) In the classical model the zones and their tensions dictate the quality of relatedness. For Fairbairn, relations with significant objects are primary; the zones are simply channels and instruments of those relations. "It is not the libidinal attitude which determines the object-relationship, but the object-relationship which determines the libidinal attitude" (1941, p. 34). The zones provide various means through which the libido relates to objects, and Fairbairn suggests that the libido chooses the best of what's available, the zones of "least resistance."

How does Fairbairn account for purely hedonistic behavior, seemingly motivated by pleasure-seeking with no regard for relations with particular objects? He sees this not as reflecting a baseline in human motivation but as a secondary consequence of a breakdown in the more basic search for pleasurable relations *with an other*. The infant is reality-oriented (object-oriented) from the start; pure pleasure-seeking is reflective of a deterioration of natural (object-related) libidinal functioning. The use of pleasure by tension-release serves as a safety-valve; it functions not as a means of achieving true libidinal aims but as a "means of mitigating the failure of these aims" (1946, pp. 139–140). (Kohut was later to term such purely pleasure-seeking impulses "disintegration products.")

From the vantage point of Fairbairn's motivational theory, the classical libido theory has limited explanatory power. For him, libido theory takes various processes which are channels and techniques for regulating the object-relations of the ego and confers upon them the status of ultimate casual, motivational powers. *Classical theory mistakes the means for the ends.* In a paper on hysteria, Fairbairn characterizes the process of hysterical conversion as the substitution of bodily tensions for emotional states (1954). Emotional deprivation and longings are transformed into physical tensions and needs. The classical theory of erotogenic zones is a product of an hysterical conversion process. The theory accepts the ruse used by the ego in focusing on impersonal bodily tensions, relegating the more basic strivings and struggles for relatedness with objects to a secondary status.

The question might be raised as to why Fairbairn retains the term "libido" at all, since he uses it to signify a general characteristic of human experience — its orientation toward and need for relations with others — rather than a specific form of energy or sensuality. His retention of the term perpetuates the sense of libido as an entity, separate from the person himself, making demands upon him. In a reply to such a criticism by Balint, Fairbairn took a further step toward abandoning the classical term altogether: "I would now prefer to say that it is the individual in his libidinal capacity (and not libido) that is object-seeking. This reformulation is designed to avoid any appearance of hypostatization of instincts" (reprinted in Guntrip, 1961, p. 305).

What is the nature of the "objects" toward which the libido is striving? Within classical drive theory the object facilitates the attainment of the ultimate aim of the impulse — the reduction of tension. Just about anything can become the object of an instinctual impulse — another person, a body part of another person, a part of the subject's own body, a piece of the inanimate world, and so on — contingent solely on having been associatively linked with the reduction of the tension of the impulse. "Natural objects," or "primary objects," for Fairbairn, that is, objects which the libido seeks prior to any deprivation or interference, are simply other people. Like Sullivan, he felt that there is a naturally unfolding, maturational sequence of needs for various kinds of relatedness with others, from infantile dependence to the mature intimacy of adult love. If relations with others were nonproblematic, if satisfying contacts could be established and maintained, psychology would consist simply of the study of the individual's relations with other people. However, Fairbairn felt that this is not the case with modern man. Relations with others, particularly the earliest needs of infantile dependence on maternal figures, become unsatisfying, "bad." Fairbairn suggests that the one large factor in this general deprivation has been civilization's interference with the mother-infant bond. The young of other animals are in direct physical contact with mothers for as long as their physical helplessness and dependency require. With humans, because of the numerous other domestic, economic, and social claims on the mother, this intense and unbroken contact is seldom possible.

The consequence of what Fairbairn regards as an unnatural separation is that early relations with objects become "bad," or depriving. It becomes too painful to long for and depend on an object which is physically or emotionally absent a good deal of the time. Therefore, the child establishes internal objects inside himself, which act as substitutes and solutions for unsatisfying relationships with real external objects. These objects are wholly compensatory, unnatural, and not dictated by the biological object-seeking nature of libido (1941, p. 40). The greater the degree of interference and deprivation in relations with its "natural" objects, real people, the greater the need for the ego to establish relations with internal objects. Thus, for Fairbairn, while psychology is the "study of the relationships of the individual to his objects," psychopathology is the "study of the relationships of the ego to its internalized objects" (1943a, p. 60). The internal objects within his theory are by definition psychopathological structures. Fairbairn does not address himself to the question of the mechanisms through which positive, healthy experiences with real, external people are registered within the psyche and facilitate ego growth. In this sense his theory of object relations, like Sullivan's formulations of the self-system, explicates the nature of psychopathology, but leaves vague and ambiguous the foundation and mechanisms of healthy growth.

What is the role of aggression in Fairbairn's theory of motivation? Fairbairn put great stress on the clinical importance of aggression. For him, as in post-1920 Freudian theory, aggression is not just a component or transformation of libido but draws on its own distinct energy. This energy, although qualitatively different from libido, exists only as a potential, not a "drive" demanding expression. Aggression uses specific bodily equipment (most notably the teeth and biting) to elaborate its aims. However, in contrast to Klein and to adherents of the classical dual-instinct theory, Fairbairn felt that aggression is not a primary *motivational* factor. Rather than arising spontaneously, it is a reaction to the frustration of the primary motivational aim—the striving for contact with objects. Thus, aggression is not "natural," but a secondary derivative of the failure of satisfying object relations. Although aggression has no primary motivational force in Fairbairn's system, it does assume an enormous clinical significance. Because of the widespread and disruptive impact of civilization on the natural development of the mother-infant dyad, intense aggression is a crucial factor with which the ego must deal in its struggle to maintain good object relations.

Theory of Development

In Fairbairn's view the central feature of emotional development is a natural, maturational sequence of relations to others. Psychopathology is characterized by disturbances in this natural sequence of relations, a proliferation of relations with compensatory internal objects, and a consequent internal fragmentation. Some of the details of this sequence, particularly with respect to the circumstances leading to the establishment of the first internalization, vary in Fairbairn's presentation from one paper to the next (see Mitchell, 1981).

For Fairbairn, human emotional development traverses several stages. As with Klein's concept of "positions," and in contrast to the classical theory of psychosexual stages, Fairbairn's stages are not based on a maturation of bodily zones of sequential prominence, but on the maturation of differing modes of relations with others. What changes is not the body part, serving as the focus of instinctual tension, but the quality and complexity of relatedness to others. Fairbairn sees this sequence as composed of three broad phases: the earliest period of infantile dependence; a transitional phase; and a state of maturity which he terms "mature dependence." Because the middle phase serves wholly as a bridge, Fairbairn's view of normal development consists essentially of a gradual process through which an infantile, dependent manner of relations to others is replaced by a capacity for adult mutuality (1941, p. 34). The key element in this transition is the process of separation.

Fairbairn's depiction of the psychological state in the earliest months of the child's life centers around the experience of merger with the mother. (His focus here strikingly anticipates major features of the approach which Margaret Mahler was to develop two decades later.) He suggested that the earliest months of life are characterized by the perpetuation of the mental state existing before birth, in which the child is in such total merger with the mother as to "preclude his entertaining any thought of differentiation from the maternal body, which constitutes his whole environment and the whole world of his experience" (1943b, p. 275). Fairbairn terms the mode of relatedness through which the infant experiences contact with others during this time "primary identification," which he defines as "the cathexis of an object which has not yet been differentiated from the cathecting subject" (1941, p. 34n). The inclination to merge with the mother derives from the infant's total and unconditional helplessness and dependency. His survival is contingent upon the mother's presence and ministrations, and he experiences himself either at one with her, or striving to be at one with her, through the major relational modalities available to him—sucking, taking, incorporation. The earliest months of life, characterized by classical theorists as consisting of a "primary narcissism," in which all of the child's love is self-directed, are for Fairbairn characterized by a total merger with the mother, a "state of identification with the object" (1941, p. 48). The infant is intensely involved with others; the crucial feature of these infantile relations with objects is lack of differentiation from them.

Fairbairn designates the full development of emotional health as the stage of "mature dependence." Healthy adults are emotionally interdependent upon each other, in contrast to the largely skewed dependence of infancy. In maturity the dependency is conditional, with other objects always potentially available, as opposed to the unconditional dependence of the infant on his sole objects—the parents. In mature dependence the emphasis shifts from taking to giving and exchange, "by a capacity on the part of a differentiated individual for cooperative relationships with differentiated objects" (1946, p. 145). As already noted, Fairbairn does not view genitality as the basis for adult intimacy but as one channel for its expression. The ideal healthy adult would have no need for compensatory attachments to internal objects, with libidinal energy fully available for contact and exchange with real other human beings. Fairbairn stresses that such a total state of health, however, is only a theoretical possibility.

The transitional phase bridges relations with objects based on infantile dependence and relations with objects based on mature dependence. It entails a renunciation of compulsive attachments to objects based on primary identification and merger in favor of relationships based on differentiation and exchange. This is an enormously difficult developmental step, and one which is never fully complete. The great fear here is of separation and loss of objects altogether. From Fairbairn's point of view the ego, with its object-seeking libidinal qualities, requires objects to survive. To achieve maturity, the child must renounce his dependent relations with his actual, external parents and experience himself as fully differentiated and separate from them, and he must renounce as well his intense attachments to his compensatory internal objects, which have provided him with whatever sense of security and continuity was missing in his real relationships with his parents. In order for this crucial process to take place, the child must feel loved as a person in his own right and believe that his own love is welcomed and valued. Optimism regarding the likelihood of this mutual love between differentiated people makes it possible for him to release his viselike grasp on the objects of his infantile dependence and become his own people, capable of mutual relatedness in the world of real people.

With the renunciation of infantile internal objects, the splitting of the ego is overcome and the original integrity and richness of the ego restored. If the sense of hopeful possibility is lacking, if the child feels that the renunciation of his infantile attachments to his parents and internal objects may not result in new, richer relations but in an isolation and lack of contact, the attachments remain, and the transitional phase is never completed. The anxiety over separation is simply too great. The central conflict of the entire transitional phase, and, therefore, the central, core conflict underlying all psychopathology, is between the developmental urge toward mature dependence and richer relations, and the regressive reluctance to abandon infantile dependence and ties to undifferentiated objects (both external and internal), for fear of losing contact of any sort.*

Anal and phallic dynamics are redefined in Fairbairn's developmental scheme; they are no longer considered to be "organizations" in their own right, but vehicles for the child's struggles within the transitional phase between the desire to abandon infantile attachments and internal objects and the urge to cling to infantile attachments and internal objects. Fairbairn suggests that anal and phallic fantasies provide suitable techniques through which the ego can express these conflictual relations to internal objects, experienced as contents. Feces and the penis take on oral meanings. Longings to hold onto infantile internal attachments are conveyed through anal retentive fantasies; the urge to be free of such internal ties are conveyed through anal explosive fantasies. Phallic fantasies are also employed in the service of oral dynamics; sexual intercourse is experienced as an essentially oral transaction. The genitals of the object

---

*The details of the processes characterizing the transitional phase constitute one of the weakest and least developed aspects of Fairbairn's theory. He worked out a tentative approach in the first of the papers marking his break with libido theory (1941), focusing on the struggle of the ego to control and separate from the early internal objects of infantile dependence. He introduced the concept of the "dichotomy of the object"—a separation between good or satisfying aspects of the parents which have become internalized, and the bad or ungratifying aspects of the parents which have become internalized—and attempted to link various combinations of "techniques" through which the ego experiences these internal objects with corresponding styles of neurotic psychopathology. In addition to being highly schematic and oversimplified, this early theory suffered from major ambiguities which Fairbairn never resolved. He dropped it in his later work, although he retained some broad features of the transitional stage concerned with the regulation of objects of infantile dependence, particularly internalized objects.

are identified with the breast, and the genitals of the subject with the mouth.

Psychic Structuralization

In 1944 Fairbairn began to work out the implications for psychoanalytic structural theory of his innovations in motivational and developmental theory. He envisions a unitary, integral ego with its own libidinal energy, seeking relations with real external objects. If these relations are satisfactory, the ego remains integral and whole. Unsatisfactory relations with natural, external objects necessitate the establishment by the ego of compensatory internal objects. The splitting of the ego is a consequence of this proliferation of internal objects, since different portions of the ego remain related to different internal objects. This attachment and devotion by the ego to its internal objects causes a fragmentation of the original, integral ego.

Fairbairn writes as if he has simply modified Freud's concept of the ego. The most notable of these modifications is the attribution to the ego of its own energy, rather than energy siphoned off from the id. However, the very nature of Fairbairn's "ego" is different in every fundamental respect from the use of the term in Freudian structural theory. In the latter, "ego" refers to a set of functions, including the regulation of drive energies coming from the id and the negotiation of the demands and interests of the id with those of the superego and the outside world. As Guntrip has pointed out, Fairbairn's ego is not "the superficial, adaptive ego of Freud . . . formed on the surface of a hypothetical impersonal id as its adjustment to outer reality. Fairbairn's 'ego' is the primary psychic self in its original wholeness, a whole which differentiates into organized structural patterns under the impact of experience of object relationships after birth" (1961, p. 279). Fairbairn's use of "ego," when compared to contemporary writers within the Freudian tradition, is much closer to their use of the term "self" in a functional sense (Jacobson, 1964, Kohut, 1977; Gedo, 1979).

Because he retains an old term with a strikingly different meaning, Fairbairn does not directly address some of the more controversial and difficult aspects of his structural theory. What does it mean, for example, to say that the ego is originally a unitary, integral whole? This view contrasts with most other psychoanalytic developmental theories, in which the ego, or self, is viewed as a developmental achievement, out of a state of "undifferentiation" or "unintegration." In Guntrip's explication of Fairbairn, he at points describes this original unity as referring to a state of "ego potential" (1971, p. 93), apparently meaning that which is possible but does *not yet* exist, and at other points as referring to what he calls the "dynamic center" or "heart" of the personality. These definitions are puzzling, both within Fairbairn's original formulations and in Guntrip's explications. If the "wholeness" of the original ego refers to potential, it would appear inaccurate to suggest that it does exist at birth. If ego refers to the center or "heart" of the personality, what does it mean to have such a center "split" through distortions in object relationships? Does one then have two or three centers or hearts? As with his retention of the term "libido," Fairbairn's preservation of the term "ego," while radically changing its meaning, has led to some unclarity.

In Fairbairn's view the relationship to the mother has two fundamental features: a gratifying component and an ungratifying component. The ungratifying aspect is further separable since it consists of not just rejection, but rejection following some sense of hope or promise. Thus, the child has three different experiences of mother: gratifying mother; enticing mother; and depriving mother. As the original relationship to the real, external mother becomes unsatisfactory, it is internalized. The result, however, is not a single internal relationship, but three, corresponding to the three features of the external relationship with the mother. The three internal objects which are separated out Fairbairn terms: the ideal object (the gratifying aspects of the mother); the exciting object (the promising and enticing aspects of the mother); and the rejecting object (the depriving, withholding aspects of the mother). As each of these features of the mother is internalized and established as an internal object, a piece of the outer-directed, integral ego is split off from its original unity and bound up in an internal object relationship with it. The piece of the ego that remains bound to and identified with the exciting object, which is, therefore, perpetually seeking and longing for the enticing promise of relatedness, Fairbairn terms the "libidinal ego." The piece of the ego that remains bound to and identified with the "rejecting object" and is therefore hostile and derisive toward any possible contact or gratification, Fairbairn terms the "anti-libidinal ego" (an earlier term for this structure was the "internal saboteur"). The remainder of the original ego, which Fairbairn terms the "central ego," is bound to and identified with the "ideal object," the comforting and gratifying aspects of the relationship with the mother. The central ego is also that part of the ego which is still available for relations with real people in the external world.

An essential principle in Fairbairn's structural system is that ego and object are inseparable. To be of importance, an object must have a piece of the ego attached to it. An object with no corresponding portion of the ego is emotionally irrelevant. The ego is unthinkable except as bound up with objects. It grows through relations with objects, both real and internal, like a plant through contact with soil, water, and sunlight. Objects are necessary for the ego to survive and flourish. An objectless ego is a contradiction in terms, much in the way Sullivan argued the impossibility of a "personality" outside an interpersonal field. As aspects of the original, unsatisfying relations with the mother are split off and internalized, pieces of the original, integral ego are diverted from their original direction toward real, external people and follow them inside. These split-off portions of the ego (the libidinal ego and the anti-libidinal ego), which Fairbairn calls "subsidiary egos," are unavailable for real object relations and remain bound up with the compensatory internal objects. The exciting object and the rejecting object are "bad" objects, in Fairbairn's sense of the term, in that they are ungratifying. The ego maintains relations with these bad internal objects in an effort to control them and to preserve its relations with the real mother uncontaminated by frustration, rage, and ungratified longings.

As noted earlier, the child also internalizes a good object, the "ideal object," which is composed of those features of the mother that remain after the overexciting and overrejecting portions are separated out. The internalization of this object is the result of a secondary development which Fairbairn terms the "moral defense." The central ego strives to live up to the ideals of the ideal object. The assumption of the central ego is that, if these ideals are met, relatedness and contact will be forthcoming; this striving for moral perfection serves as a distraction and defense against the cathexis of the "bad" internal objects by the subsidiary egos. The residue of the central ego, following the splitting off of the subsidiary egos and the central ego's defensive cathexis of its own internal object (the ideal object), is employed in the service of relations with real people in the external world. Psychopathology results from this fragmentation of the ego and the devotion of the resulting portions of the ego to their internal objects at the expense of relations with real people.

Fairbairn's account of the relations among the internal objects and their corresponding subsidiary egos becomes quite intricate and detailed, and it is possible to consider only the highlights. Freud's dual motivational principles of libido and aggression have been replaced by a single motivational principle—libido—and a powerful reaction to libidinal frustration—an "anti-libidinal" factor. The "libidinal ego" is that part of the child's original ego which has not given up the unsatisfied longings and demands of infantile dependence. It is the repository of hope and, in its attachment to the exciting object, remains bound to images of unfulfilled promises, enticements, and potentials for contact with the mother that were never brought to fruition. The libidinal ego longs for union with the exciting object, as an internal object relation, because the longing for real gratification from the real mother has become too painful. The libidinal ego, therefore, remains in a perpetual, deprived relationship with the exciting object. The promise is kept alive, but fulfillment is impossible.

The anti-libidinal ego is the part of the ego that becomes the repository for all the hatred and destructiveness which accumulate as a consequence of the frustration of libidinal longing. The anti-libidinal ego is attached to and identified with the rejecting object, the aspect of the mother experienced as depriving and withholding. The anti-libidinal ego represents the part of the ego which, because it was not gratified by the enticements of the mother, identifies with her depriving and withholding features. Much of the rage contained in the anti-libidinal ego is directed toward the exciting object — the promises and enticements of the mother. Another target of this rage is the libidinal ego, because of its identification with the exciting object. The anti-libidinal ego hates the libidinal ego for its hope, for continuing to perpetuate the belief that the promises of the mother may yet be fulfilled. The anti-libidinal ego continually attacks the exciting object for its false promises, and the libidinal ego for its naive hope and devotion. These internal attacks by the anti-libidinal ego are responsible for self-destructive, self-punitive aspects of psychopathology. The anti-libidinal ego is the enemy of hope, particularly of hope for anything meaningful with other people. It hates and punishes the libidinal ego for any attempts to get something from others, and it hates the other person who offers the possibility of relatedness. Thus, in the psychoanalytic situation, a period of increased contact between a severely disturbed patient and the analyst is often followed by venomous hatred by the patient, of himself and of the analyst. In Fairbairn's terms, this is the anti-libidinal ego punishing the libidinal ego and the exciting object — both the subject and object of possible relatedness.

Fairbairn's structural theory, a relational/structure theory, differs in several distinct and innovative ways from classical Freudian structural theory, a drive/structure theory. The latter locates conflict as taking place among the functions represented by the id, ego, and superego. The superego is fueled by instinctual impulses organized around internalized images of parental figures, while the id is understood to be the source of impulses derived from drive tensions. The ego negotiates among the demands for impulse gratification from the id, the guiding and prohibiting impact of the internalized aspects of the parents in the superego, and the requirements of the outside world. Thus, within the classical model the basic format for understanding human conflicts is a struggle between impersonal impulses or bodily tensions, on the one hand, and internal objects also fueled by instinctual tensions, on the other. The ego serves as an arbitrator with no clearly defined interests of its own, apart from achieving relative internal harmony and good standing with the outside world. In Fairbairn's model all the major protagonists in internal struggles are essentially relational units, composed of a portion of the ego and a portion of the child's relations to the parents, experienced as an internal object. Conflict takes place among these three ego-object components (libidinal ego/exciting object; anti-libidinal ego/rejecting object; central ego/ideal object).

Eliminating the anthropomorphization and reification inherent in both models sharpens the differences between them. The essential struggle in the classical Freudian model involves conflicts stemming from the person's instinctual impulses, some of these being mediated through internal representation of his early relations with his parents. The essential struggle in Fairbairn's model involves the person's irreconcilable loyalties in his longings for and identifications with various features of his significant others, in the outside world and as they have been internalized in an effort to control them. The problem for Freud is the inherent opposition among instinctual aims and between instinctual aims and social reality; the problem for Fairbairn is that the person cannot maintain the integrity and wholeness of his experience of himself within his necessary relations with others and is forced to fragment himself to maintain contact and devotion to the irreconcilable features of those relations.

As a consequence of this difference in fundamental assumptions concerning human experience, any attempt to correlate the three major structures in Fairbairn's structural model with the three agencies in the classical model is misleading. Although the libidinal ego and the id both manifest themselves in the form of longings and wishes, the former is inherently object-related, and bound to specific and personal features of the early relationship with the parents (what they seemed to offer and promise but did not supply), while the id is by definition structureless and directionless.

Freud's ego, with no energy of its own, is developed on the surface of the structureless id. All of Fairbairn's "egos," including the central ego, have energy of their own and are directed toward and bound up with objects. Freud's superego and Fairbairn's anti-libidinal ego both refer to internal objects that manifest themselves through self-punitive aspects of mental functioning. However, the superego's attacks are essentially moral, the pressure of social constraints against antisocial drive derivatives, while the attacks of the anti-libidinal ego are premoral and derive from the child's identification with the rejecting aspects of his early relations with his parents. He identifies with these aspects of the parents through the anti-libidinal ego because he cannot have them, and he becomes the self-punitive enemy of any hope for gratification (embodied in the libidinal ego). The functions to which Freud's term "superego" refers, including punishing and ideal features, are carried, within Fairbairn's model, by the activities of the anti-libidinal ego and the rejecting object, combined with the ideal object.

Further important differences between Fairbairn's approach to psychic structure and Freud's concern the understanding of oedipal dynamics and the point in development when the basic components of internal experience are established. In Freud's theory the major features of psychic structuralization are completed only with the dissolution of the oedipal conflict, with the internalization of the superego. By contrast, Fairbairn argues that the "universal endopsychic situation" is established in all essential respects in the earliest relations with the mother. The tripartite splitting of the ego with its corresponding objects results from the child's earliest struggles to maintain good relations with the mother and persists throughout life.

For Fairbairn the relationship with the father simply recapitulates the earlier relationship with the mother. The child seeks object-relatedness with the father, also based upon infantile dependency. As in his relationship with his mother, he experiences the father as both gratifying and ungratifying. Therefore, as the relationship with the father likewise proves itself to be less than wholly satisfactory, various features of the father are internalized. As with the mother, the child constructs an exciting object, a rejecting object, and an ideal object—all out of features in his experience of his father. There are thus two sets of each of these objects: one derived from the relationship with the mother, the other from the relationship with the father. The child's ego combines these two sets of objects through processes of layering and fusion to form a single exciting object, a single rejecting object, and a single ideal object; these are now complex, composite structures, derived from relations with both parents. The child then projects the images of the exciting and the rejecting objects onto the parents. Most often the parent of the opposite sex becomes the exciting object, seen as seductive and enticing; the other parent is the rejecting object, seen as interfering, malevolent, and rivalrous. Fairbairn suggests that the choice of which parent represents the exciting object and which the rejecting object is determined partly by the biological sex of the child and partly by his emotional relationships with his respective parents.

The splitting of the exciting and rejecting features between the two parents simplifies the child's world, giving him a clearer sense of what he seems to need and what seems to interfere with his needs. What he really needs of course is a fuller emotional contact with both parents, and what really interferes with this is the parents' relative unavailability and his own consequent hostility toward his own needs. A further process sometimes takes place involving the sexualization of these needs, resulting in the experiences and feelings which Freud had termed "oedipal." Fairbairn suggests that sometimes the emotional longings concerning infantile dependency are experienced as sexual in nature. This is essentially a defense, often provoked by seductiveness in the parent, in which the infantile dependent longings are disguised as a precocious genitality. At bottom, however, what is desired is not sexual gratification as such, but contact and nurturance. For Fairbairn the oedipal situation is nothing new, simply a set of further elaborations of the earliest search for basic relatedness and contact. The structuralization of the ego into its three major components, each attached to an object, is established in the oral-dependent relationship with the mother, persists throughout life, and underlies all psychopathology; "the role of the ultimate cause, which Freud allotted to the Oedipus situation, should properly be allotted to the phenomenon of infantile dependence" (1944, p. 120).

Theory of Psychopathology

Fairbairn's writings contain two different approaches to psychopathology that were never reconciled. In earlier papers (1940 and 1941) he views psychopathology as dichotomous—derived from two basic fixation points, early oral and late oral. The crucial determinant of later pathology is the phase of infancy during which the child fails in his effort to establish good object relations. This failure entails the child's experience that he is unloved by the mother, or that his love for the mother is not felt and valued by her. If the failure is experienced in the early oral phase, he feels that his *love* is at fault—the parent must have been driven away by the child's own intense dependency and neediness. Such a fixation at the early oral period results in essentially schizoid dynamics: the child withdraws from relatedness because he feels his love, his oral greed, is bad.

What is distinctive about the late oral phase is the development of biting and the potential for aggression. If the failure of early object relations is experienced at this later point, the child feels that his *hate*, his natural reaction to the frustration of his object-seeking, is to blame. He feels he has driven the parent away through his own destructiveness. Fairbairn suggests that such a fixation at the late oral period results in depressive dynamics, as described by Klein. Thus, in his first theory of psychopathology, Fairbairn suggests that all forms of psychopathology are defenses against oral conflicts and anxieties, either of a schizoid or a depressive nature, centering on a fear of one's own love or on a fear of one's own rage respectively. This theory allowed him to maintain some continuity with Kleinian theory, while at the same time breaking away from it in certain important respects. He retains Klein's view that there are two distinct phases during infancy, with two separate dynamic struggles resulting in two fundamentally distinct forms of psychopathology. Fairbairn also retains, almost whole cloth, Klein's characterization of the second phase—the depressive position. It is in his description of the early oral phase that Fairbairn introduces his own innovations. He sees the central issue here to be not aggression and hate, but intense dependency and frustrated love. The problem of aggression enters later and, even then, not as an autonomous instinctual pressure but as a reaction to frustration. This stress on the earliest libidinal strivings for contact with the mother was expanded, in Fairbairn's later work, to become the underlying issue in all psychopathology.

In 1943 Fairbairn began his consideration of psychopathology from a different starting point. He suggests that the initial internalization of objects derives from the intensity of the child's need for relatedness and the consequent dilemma posed by parents who are emotionally absent, intrusive, or chaotic. The child cannot do without parents, yet living in a world in which parents, the constituents of one's entire interpersonal world, are unavailable or arbitrary is unbearably painful. Therefore, according to Fairbairn, the first in a series of internalizations, repressions, and splits takes place, based on the necessity for preserving the illusion of the goodness of the parents as real figures in the outside world. The child separates and internalizes the bad aspects of the parents—it is not they who are bad, it is he. The badness is inside him; if he were different, their love would be forthcoming. Every child needs to feel that his parents understand the world, are just and dependable. If he does not experience them in these ways, he transfers the problem into himself. He takes upon himself the "burden of the badness." The "badness," the undesirable qualities of the parents—that is, the depression, the disorganization, the sadism—are now in him. These "bad" features become bad objects, with which the ego identifies (through primary identification). The child has purchased outer security at the price of sacrificing internal security plus illusory hope. When the child experienced the "badness" as outside, in the real parents, he felt painfully unable to make any impact at all. If the "badness" is inside him, he preserves the hope of omnipotent control over it.

These internal object relations are the core of the repressed. Memories are repressed as well, because they are associatively linked to the "overexciting" or "overrejecting" aspects of the parents. The memories are dangerous because they bring close to consciousness the powerful internal relationship with the "exciting object" and the "rejecting object," the patient's continual longings for and identifications with these objects. Impulses and fantasies are repressed also, not because of some danger inherent in them as such, but because they are directed toward exciting and rejecting aspects of the parents and threaten to bring into awareness the entire constellations of the internal object relations. Hence, at the core of the repressed, and at the center of all psychopathology, lies the repression of bad objects.

In 1943 Fairbairn distinguished qualitative and quantitative differences among the types of pathology based upon: the extent of bad objects and degree of badness of the objects; the extent of the ego's identification with the bad objects; and the nature and strength of the defenses protecting the ego from the objects. By 1944 he had added to his theory of the repression of bad objects the view that portions of the ego follow these objects into repression resulting in a splitting of the ego. Subsequently, the severity of psychopathology was understood to be contingent upon the extent of this splitting, that is, the relative portions of the central ego split off into the libidinal ego and the antilibidinal ego. The degree of pathology depends on how much of the ego is still available for real and potentially fulfilling relations with others, and how much is bound up with ungratifying, unreachable aspects of the parents which have become enshrined internally. Guilt is seen as arising secondarily, through the "moral defense." The child experiences himself as morally bad in order to open up the possibility of becoming morally good, to regain good relations with the object. This marks the distance Fairbairn has come from his first theory of psychopathology, where, with its Kleinian influence, guilt in connection with aggression is seen as a basic and primary phenomenon of the late oral stage.

Although Fairbairn never explicitly abandoned his early dichotomous approach to psychopathology, a close reading of his work leads to the conclusion that he did so implicitly. In his 1941 theory, early and late oral fixations lead to schizoid and depressive characters respectively. Schizoid dynamics center on a splitting of the ego itself, while depressive dynamics center on ambivalence and guilt. As we have seen, in his later work Fairbairn argues that the ego is universally split, resulting in the "basic endopsychic situation." This splitting of the ego into libidinal ego, anti-libidinal ego, and central ego underlies *all* psychopathology. The early separation between schizoid and depressive fixations has been replaced by a more unified theory of psychopathology based on ego-splitting and schizoid dynamics. The second theory of psychopathology is more purely relational and experiential than the first, where the distinction between early oral and late oral is based on defenses against specific impulses. Thus, while the first theory of psychopathology preserves ties to the drive/structure model, the second theory of psychopathology operates wholly within the relational/structure model. Although in his later work Fairbairn does not directly disavow the earlier theory (nor does Guntrip in his presentations of Fairbairn's work), he does raise questions about the emphasis Klein places on depression, which he finds "difficult to reconcile with my own experience," and suggests that many patients diagnosed depressive are really misdiagnosed schizoids (1944, p. 91). In addition, in the context of his later views, depression is clearly a secondary and derivative form of psychopathology; depressive guilt follows from the internalization of the ideal object through the moral defense subsequent to the original schizoid splitting caused by the internalization of bad objects.

Fairbairn's second theory of psychopathology, in which attachments to bad objects are seen as constituting the core of the repressed and underlying all pathology, has broad applications in many areas of clinical practice and analytic technique. One major feature of this approach is its illumination of the clinical phenomenon which Freud termed the "repetition compulsion." This brings us full circle to the advantages which Fairbairn felt his own motivational theory held over classical drive theory.

Perhaps the most broadly characteristic feature of all psychopathology is its self-defeating quality. Pain, suffering, and defeat are structured into the patient's life and experienced again and again. This feature characterizes psychopathology across the entire continuum: from the neurotic character who chooses unresponsive or sadistic love objects again and again, or behaves toward them to ensure their lack of response or sadism, to the depressive who seems to suffer the deprivations of early mothering over and over again, to the schizophrenic whose primitive childhood terrors haunt his adult life. Why?

Freud had difficulty accounting for this aspect of life within the framework of classical drive theory. According to the latter, man is hedonistic—he seeks pleasure and the avoidance of pain. If this is so, how can one account for the systematic structuring of pain and the methodical disavowal of pleasure which is constitutive of all forms of psychopathology. If humans operate on the basis of the pleasure principle, why are not unpleasant experiences and early childhood miseries simply dropped rather than repeated throughout adult life? Neurotics, as Fairbairn puts it, "cling to painful experiences so assiduously" (1944, p. 84). Freud termed this phenomenon the "repetition compulsion" and initially attempted to account for it in several different ways within the framework of the pleasure principle: the suffering in psychopathology represented punishment for forbidden wishes; suffering itself was inherently sensually pleasurable (masochism); the libido picks up "clichés" of loving which remain attached to it throughout later life; and so on. However, Freud himself considered these attempts to account for the repetition compulsion within the framework of the pleasure principle to be insufficiently persuasive, and in 1920 he argued that the repetition of painful early experiences operates "beyond the pleasure principle" and is an instinctual characteristic of mental functioning, derivative of the death instinct.

Fairbairn felt that his own view of libido as object-seeking provided a much more economical explanation for this characteristic feature of psychopathology. The essential striving of the child is not for pleasure but for contact. He *needs* the other. If the other is available for gratifying, pleasurable exchange, the child will enter into pleasurable activities. If the parent offers only painful, unfulfilling contacts, the child does not abandon the parent to search for more pleasurable opportunities. The child needs the parent, so he integrates his relations with him on a suffering, masochistic basis. Fairbairn felt the child attempts to protect what is gratifying and control what is not gratifying in the relationship with the parent by establishing compensatory internal object relations. It is in the "obstinate attachment" (1944, p. 117) of the libidinal ego to the exciting object that the child preserves his hopes for fuller, more satisfying contact with the parent. The emptier the real exchange, the greater his devotion to the promising yet depriving features of his parents which he has internalized and seeks within. In addition, he preserves his childhood terror that if he disengages himself from these internal objects, he will find himself totally alone.

It is the experience of these internal object relations and the projection of them onto the outside world that produces pathological suffering within human experience. Love objects are selected for or made into withholders or deprivers so as to personify the exciting object, promising, but never fulfilling. Defeat is orchestrated again and again to perpetuate the longing and need of the libidinal ego for the fulfillment of the promise of the exciting object. Success is equated with a betrayal of that promise, as if the libidinal ego had no need of it anymore, and hence threatens to rupture those internal ties. Depression, terror, and futility represent the ego's identifications with "bad" aspects of the parents which could not be reached through real exchange with the parents in the external world and thus were taken inside. Psychopathology persists, old pain returns, destructive patterns of integrating relations with others and experiencing life are perpetuated—because beneath the pain and the self-defeating relations and organizations of experience lie ancient internal attachments and allegiances to early significant others. The re-creation of the sorrow, suffering, and defeat are forms of renewal of and devotion to these ties. Reluctance to betray these attachments through new relations and allegiances impedes constructive change in living and results in a central and often the most intransigent resistance in psychoanalysis.

Fairbairn and Klein

Much of Fairbairn's writing is overtly addressed to Freud; the differences between his concepts and classical Freudian theory are openly acknowledged and argued. Klein is a more shadowy, but equally present figure. Fairbairn made extensive use of her language and many of her concepts; he was actively, although often covertly, struggling to disengage himself from her views. Melanie Klein had altered Freudian theory in fundamental ways that pointed in the direction of a relational/structure theory of motivation, development, and psychopathology, without herself taking the final step and abandoning the classical drive/structure model. Klein continually weaves object-relations concepts and issues into traditional drive and impulse language and the classical lexicon of body parts. Fairbairn takes the final step, freeing his account of the interrelations between people from classical impulse psychology altogether.

Many of the central features of Fairbairn's theory stand in sharp contrast to Klein's theoretical system. One fundamental difference concerns the nature of fantasy. Phantasy for Klein is the earliest and most basic activity of the mind: it constitutes the direct, unmediated manifestation of the instincts themselves. Thought concerning external reality and real people is secondary and derivative of earlier phantasy processes, and therefore all of the child's and the adult's experiences, both positive and negative, are accompanied by phantasy. For Fairbairn, fantasy is not primary, but substitutive. The child from the start is oriented toward reality and actual relations with others. Fantasy represents a secondary compensation for a failure of these actual relations. Thus, for Klein, with one theoretical foot in the drive/structure model, phantasy is a primary component of the drives themselves. From Fairbairn's more purely relational/structure point of view, fantasy constitutes a retreat from the more basic motivational push toward establishing and maintaining relations with real other people.

A second and closely related difference concerns the nature of the internal object world. For Klein, the internal object world is a natural, inevitable, and continual accompaniment of all experience. Internal objects are established at the beginning of psychological life and become the major content of phantasy. The internal object world for Klein is the source both of life's greatest horrors and of its deepest comforts. For Fairbairn, internal objects are neither primary nor inevitable (theoretically). They are compensatory substitutes for unsatisfactory relations with real, external objects, the "natural," primary objects of libido. For him, relations with internal objects are inherently masochistic. Bad internal objects are persistent temptors and persecutors; good internal objects do not offer real gratification, merely a refuge from relations with bad internal objects.

As a consequence of these differences concerning the nature and origins of internal objects, Fairbairn and Klein differ about the content of internal objects as well. In most of Klein's formulations the internal objects are constructed around imagoes that are part of the instincts a priori. Here, once again, her retention of aspects of the drive/structure model influences her treatment of the nature of object relations. The "good breast," the "bad breast," and so on are universal imagoes which are part of the constitutional biological human equipment. External contributions and experiences modify these imagoes in circumscribed and specific ways. For Fairbairn, who breaks totally from the drive/structure model, the content of internal objects derives completely from real, external objects, fragmented and recombined, to be sure, but always deriving from the child's experiences of his actual parents. Whereas in Klein's view phantasied relations with internal objects constitute the bedrock of all experience, for Fairbairn such relations represent a secondary retreat from disturbances in relations with real people, toward whom man is more fundamentally directed.

A third major area in which Fairbairn and Klein differ is their view of the ultimate source of pathology or suffering in human experience. For Klein, again operating partially within the drive/structure model, the root of evil lies in human instincts, particularly the death instinct and its derivative, aggression. The great dilemma for the child in both the paranoid-schizoid position and the depressive position is the safe discharge of his aggression. The earliest anxiety for the child is persecutory; he experiences the threat of his own demise as the victim of his own projected aggression. For Fairbairn, on the other hand, operating purely within a relational context, the root of psychopathology and human suffering is maternal deprivation. Ideally, perfect mothering results in a whole, nonfragmented ego, with its full libidinal potential available for relations with actual, external objects. Inadequate parenting poses grave threats to the integrity of the ego. The central anxiety for Fairbairn involves the protection of the tie to the object in the face of deprivation, and all psychopathology is understood as deriving from the ego's self-fragmentation in the service of protecting that tie and controlling its ungratifying aspects. The differences in their views of the ultimate source of evil is reflected in the different meanings of the term "bad object" in the theories of Klein and Fairbairn. For Klein the "badness" of an object, whether internal or external, refers to malevolence, deriving ultimately from the child's own inherent destructiveness, projected onto others. By contrast, "badness" for Fairbairn means depriving. The "bad" object is the one which frustrates the object-seeking of the libido by its absence and unresponsiveness. For Klein "bad objects" are reflections, creations derived from the child's own inherent and spontaneous destructiveness. For Fairbairn "bad objects" are aspects of the child's parents which make them unavailable to him and frustrate his inherent longing for contact and relatedness.

Klein's influence on Fairbairn's work was considerable. Her study of the internal object world opened up avenues of inquiry and conceptualization which made possible the development of Fairbairn's own contributions. Nevertheless, although Fairbairn retained much of her language, the meanings of the terms shifted, and the major assumptions of his theory stand in stark contrast to her approach. Her emphases on phantasy, on inevitable and perpetual internal objects, and on the horrors of instinctual destructiveness are countered by Fairbairn's emphases on reality, the primary world of real others, the compensatory nature of internal objects, and the destructiveness of parental deprivation. Fairbairn's greatest contributions are in areas that distinguish him most strikingly from Klein—as the architect of a purely relational/structure model. His account of the conflicts accompanying the child's earliest relations with significant others, the internalization of disturbing aspects of those relations, and the centrality of the resulting internal object relations in all forms of psychopathology—these contributions impart to Fairbairn's work a lasting place and a seminal role in the history of psychoanalytic ideas.

Fairbairn and Sullivan

Sullivan and Fairbairn differ in many ways—in intellectual ancestry, use of language, philosophy of science, and sensibility. Sullivan's work is distinctively American: pragmatic, operationally oriented, focused on what people *do*. He eschewed speculations about processes *inside* the mind, hidden from public view. Fairbairn's intellectual roots go back to Greek and European philosophy, with their fascination with the abstract. His immediate psychoanalytic forebear was Melanie Klein, whose theory is rich and loose in speculations about internal psychic processes. Fairbairn focused on events and structures inside the mind, and he developed a complex internal psychic morphology. Nevertheless, Sullivan and Fairbairn developed a grasp of the nature and the constituents of human experience which is strikingly similar in fundamentals in areas crucial for psychoanalytic models.

Both Sullivan and Fairbairn object to the focus on *the* person, *the* psyche within classical psychoanalytic theorizing, arguing that this establishes an artificial and misleading basis for viewing human experience, rending it from its relational setting. Sullivan suggests that one cannot understand *a* personality in isolation. The only meaningful context for grasping the fundamentals of human experience is what he termed the "interpersonal field." Fairbairn likewise argues that it is conceptually meaningless to speak of a person outside the context of the history of the person's relations with others, that it is "impossible to gain any adequate conception of the nature of an individual organism if it is considered apart from its relationships to its natural objects; for it is only in its relationships to these objects that its true nature is displayed" (1946, p. 139). For both theorists the concept of "drives" is an artifact, a consequence of the isolation of the person from his relational context, from which his experience and behavior take their meaning.

From this common starting point, Sullivan and Fairbairn take similar approaches to each of the major issues basic for psychoanalytic models. The fundamental motivational force is understood to be the search for and establishment of relations with others. For Sullivan the human being is constructed in such a way that the expression and gratification of his own needs for "satisfaction" intrinsically draw him into relations with others. Fairbairn also clearly establishes the need for relations with others as the fundamental motivational principle in his concept of libido (redefined as the energy of the ego) as "object-seeking." Throughout his writing Fairbairn stresses the inseparability of ego from its objects; an objectless ego is, for him, a contradiction in terms.

Sullivan and Fairbairn approach development similarly, viewing the salient process not as the sequential emergence of component drives but of needs for new forms of contact and relatedness with others. For Sullivan, each new developmental epoch is initiated with the introduction of a need for a new mode of relation—from playmates like oneself, to more specific intimacy with one other person, to heterosexual love. Fairbairn's developmental theory also consists of a sequence of different forms of relations with others, moving from "infantile dependence" to "mature dependence."

In the areas of psychic structure and psychopathology there are important differences between Sullivan and Fairbairn in terms of language and emphasis. Nevertheless, their basic principles overlap—the child shapes, structures, and distorts his own experience, behavior, and self-perception to maintain the best possible relatedness with the parent; psychopathology is a consequence of disruptions in these early relations. The personality of the child shapes itself in complementarity with the personalities of the parents. Areas in the child which are complemented by nonanxious, emotionally available areas in the parents' personalities become developed and expand. Areas in the parents' personalities which have a disruptive impact on the relations with the child become encased within the child's personality and are not available for his use in subsequent relations with others. Fairbairn, with his preference for structural concepts, stresses the internal residues of these early interactions—the internal object relations. The strength of his version of the relational model lies in his delineation of the experience and the fantasies patients have of their own internal worlds. Sullivan, with his preference for operational concepts, stresses the tendency of the person to avoid anxiety, based on anticipations from past experience. The strength of Sullivan's version of the relational model lies in his delineation of the intricacies of what patients *do*, in their perpetuation of their characteristic patterns of behavior.

Although different in language, tone, and clinical application, the interpersonal theory of Sullivan and the object relations theory of Fairbairn overlap in basic premises; taken together, they constitute the purest expression of the relational model. For both Fairbairn and Sullivan the personality itself is understood to derive from the residues of exchanges with others. Objects are no longer merely targets or inhibitors of drive; they no longer function merely vis-à-vis discharge processes. Relations with objects, internal and external, constitute the primary dynamic processes within mental life and are built into the very texture of psychic structure. The striving toward the establishment and maintenance of relations with others becomes a motivational force (the activity of the individual is not to be understood as instigated by the need to discharge drive, but as a movement toward a specific mode of relatedness with another person) as well as the major constituent of the "stuff" of psychic structure. In the relational model, drives as Freud defined them drop out entirely. Their role in motivation, development, psychic structure, and psychopathology is assumed by relations with others, real and imaginary.

Limitations of Fairbairn's System

The several areas of unclarity and salient omission in Fairbairn's theory that we have noted result from two characteristic features of his approach: singleness of focus and a tendency to overreact in rejecting drive theory. Central to almost all his formulations is an emphasis on the child's total dependence on significant others. Early disturbances around dependency constitute the psychological bedrock for all subsequent emotional events, and all relationships are evaluated within the context of their function as gratifiers of dependency needs. Thus, objects are either "good" (emotionally available to dependency needs) or "bad" (unavailable to dependency needs). Relationships are characterized either by the continual search for infantile gratification (infantile dependence) or have transcended infantile forms of gratification (mature dependence). Two important areas of omission result from this narrowness of focus. First, all "objects" short of "mature" objects are substitutes for the mother of early infancy. Fairbairn does not allow for the possibility that parents fulfill important developmental functions other than gratification for infantile dependency, such as encouraging separation, setting boundaries and controls, reflecting infantile grandiosity, or introducing the child to the world. In this sense his theory loses much of the richness of the classical psychosexual scheme, in which different stages reflect different needs and require different parental roles. Also, Fairbairn underplays the potentially different developmental role of the father, with its own features distinct from the relationship with the mother. The father is at best a poor substitute for the mother, a "parent without breasts" (1944, p. 122).

Another consequence of Fairbairn's unifocality is that his treatment of the role of internal as well as external objects is limited to their function with respect to the vicissitudes of infantile dependence. Internal objects are established to compensate for the lack of full gratification of infantile dependence. Because of this function, the earliest and dynamically most fundamental internal objects are "bad" (emotionally ungratifying). And the only function of "good" internal objects is as a moral refuge from "bad" internal objects (through a process termed "moral defense"). Although Fairbairn argues that good relationships are longed for and required for healthy development, he does not account for the residues of good experiences and gratifying relationships, the establishment of healthy identifications, authentic values, and so on. There is no place for good internal objects which function apart from defenses against bad internal object relations. As L. Friedman puts it, Fairbairn "leaves us with no meat to hang on the bones of attachment" (1978a, p. 542).

How are good experiences recorded and structured, making possible greater relatedness and emotional complexity? Clearly the mechanism for the storage of good experiences may be very different from the account Fairbairn provides of the establishment of internal objects as the result of bad early relationships. Yet, he neither accounts for the former process nor addresses this distinction. Thus, one is left with the choice of assuming either that Fairbairn believes that good relationships leave no structural residues, which would be difficult to fathom, or that his theory of object relations is limited to psychopathology and falls short of working as a general psychology.

A second characteristic of Fairbairn's approach underlying some of the problems we have noted in his theorizing is his tendency to develop formulations in sharp, dialectical opposition to problematic areas in Freudian and Kleinian theory. Fairbairn's major philosophical objection to Freudian theory is what he argues is its mechanistic, atomistic, and depersonalized language and metapsychology; one of his major objections to Kleinian theory is the great stress it places on constitutional aggression and instinctual excess. Many of Fairbairn's formulations stand in direct opposition to these features of Freud and Klein, and most of them are well-articulated and compelling. However, certain of Fairbairn's emphases seem unpersuasive and might be understood as a romantic overreaction to the mechanistic and pessimistic aspects of Freudian and Kleinian thought. We have noted, for example, that Fairbairn's concept of an originally integral and whole ego is poorly articulated, difficult to grasp, and puzzling from a developmental point of view. Further, his implication throughout is that internal disharmony (splitting) is bad, and that a whole, integral ego is the most desirable of mental states. This seems to overlook the possibilities of productive conflicts, creative confusion, and mutually enriching partial identifications.

A closely related issue is Fairbairn's clear implication that parental deprivation is at the root of all difficulties in living. If the parents respond fully to the child's infantile dependence, ego-splitting and the establishment of internal objects are avoided and the ego presumably retains its pristine wholeness. Although Fairbairn does indicate at some points that such total parental availability is an impossibility, he does not regard this as suggesting that infantile dependence is, by its very nature, ungratifiable. Rather, he suggests that the parents' failure to provide complete gratification is a product of their own psychopathology, perhaps as a result of the stresses and multiple demands of modern life, leading to an infinite regression ending presumably only with Eve (whose difficulties in living could only be the result of some divine imperfection). This view, although internally consistent, seems unpersuasive and overly simplistic.

In Freud's early theory of neurosis, adult seductions of innocent children were seen as the sole causative agents of psychopathology. Subsequent to his discovery of a lack of verisimilitude in the "memories" of his patients, he tended to underemphasize the role of adult psychopathology in generating neurosis in children, focusing instead on what he argued were biologically based drive impulses and fantasies generated from within the child's own psyche. Klein's theory is the ultimate extension of this conceptual line, where the objects of the child's world derive almost entirely from internal sources; relations with actual, real others play only a modifying, refining role. Fairbairn's work constitutes a return of the dialectical pendulum on this issue. In stressing the pristine integrity of the original ego and placing the blame for all difficulties in living on parental psychopathology, he overlooks such important issues as: the insatiable and sometimes incompatible features of infantile needs; temperamental differences among infants and between infants and their particular caretakers; and distortions and misunderstandings of experience resulting from primitive perceptual and cognitive capacities. (Fairbairn, like Klein, tends to presuppose rather accurate, complex, and discerning mental processes in the young infant.) In Guntrip's exposition and extension of Fairbairn's theory these romantic features become more and more prominent, crowding out, in the process, other important aspects of Fairbairn's innovative formulations.

Afterword: The Relational/Structure Models of Balint and Bowlby

Fairbairn's contributions operate fully within the relational/structure model. His "object relations theory of the personality," however, is only one of many possible relational/structure theories. Several other theorists within the British school have generated conceptual models which are similar and, in many respects, complementary. Among the more interesting and influential are the approaches of Michael Balint and John Bowlby.

Balint was an analysand and disciple of Ferenczi. (As the analyst of Klein, Balint, and Clara Thompson, Ferenczi was an important figure, directly or indirectly, in the psychoanalytic lineage of all the major relational model innovators, within both the American interpersonal school and the British school of object relations.) According to his own account, Balint considered the schism between Freud and Ferenczi in the years prior to the latter's death in 1931 as a "tragic" event of monumental proportions (1948, p. 243). The larger project within Balint's contributions seems to have been fueled by an effort to heal that split, first by developing further Ferenczi's own work on early maternal deprivation, and second by reconciling that work with mainline psychoanalytic theorizing. Ferenczi had been more and more involved in his final years with a consideration of the deleterious impact of parental deficiencies on young children, and with the highly controversial attempt to remedy these deprivations within the psychoanalytic situation. Balint reports that certain of his patients, like Ferenczi's, attempt to remedy their own early deprivations by involving or coercing the analyst into granting them unconditional love which they had been deprived of in childhood. This recurrent phenomenon led Balint to the conviction that the search for "primary object love" underlies virtually all other psychological phenomena.

Object relations, Balint argues, are present from the beginning of life. Rejecting the concept of primary narcissism, he suggests that "relationship with the environment exists in a primitive form right from the start" (1968, p. 63). Following Ferenczi, he characterizes this earliest object relation as "passive object love," the wish to be loved totally and unconditionally. (In later writings Balint suggests that prior to a focus on specific objects, the infant, and even the fetus, is oriented toward the environment as an "*harmonious, interpenetrating mix-up*" of "primary substances" [1968, p. 66; italics in original].) The pursuit of primary love represents not only the first and most basic form of object relations, but in some sense underlies all others. Particularly in civilized cultures where, Balint suggests, the mother-infant tie is severed too early, the remainder of life becomes a search for restitution, and passive object love becomes the "final aim of all erotic striving" (1935, p. 50).

All of the major psychodynamic and motivational features which are primary and central to the drive/structure model are seen by Balint as secondary, compensatory derivatives of the failure to obtain sufficient primary love. Narcissism is a "roundabout" way of attempting to provide for oneself what was not provided by others (1952, p. 248). Aggression is a reaction to the lack of primary love, not a primary drive in its own right (1951, p. 128). Sensual, body-based gratifications are substitutive replacements for what is missing in terms of primary love, derived from whatever partial contacts the parents are able to offer: "If it [the child] gets something, it becomes, as it were, moulded by the gratification received . . . anal-sadistic, phallic, and finally genital object relations—have not a biological, but a cultural basis" (1935, p. 50). Even the most mature form of object relations—genitality (which Balint calls "active object love," replacing drive/structure terminology with a relational structure term)—represents a roundabout attempt to secure primary, passive love. One loves the other in a disguised effort to be loved, totally and unconditionally, in return. The hope for finally attaining primary love remains "forever the final goal of all erotic striving" (1937, p. 82). Thus, Balint grants relational needs primary theoretical status: "This form of object relation [primary object-love] is not linked to any of the erotogenic zones; it is not oral, oral-sucking, anal, genital, etc., love, but is something on its own" (1937, pp. 84–85). Balint's extension of Ferenczi's contributions carries him to a position whose broad outlines are quite similar to Fairbairn's and seems to call for a sharp break with drive/structure tradition.

However, unlike Fairbairn, Balint does *not* discard drive/structure theory. Although he has argued that sensual strivings are derivative of relational needs, Balint alternately reinstitutes sensual pleasure-seeking as having primary motivational status in its own right. He chastises Fairbairn for abandoning libido theory, arguing that libido has two fundamental tendencies—that it is *both* pleasure-seeking and object-seeking (1956). Thus, despite his own reformulation of the nature and function of drive impulses, Balint continues to employ the term "id" and the language of drive theory as if they had the same referents they have in Freud's work. Balint's critique of Fairbairn seems baffling in light of his own redefinition of the pleasure-seeking aims of libido as derivatives of disturbances in object-relating. A return to Balint's project of reconciling Ferenczi and Freud will shed light on this dilemma.

The major point of controversy between Freud and Ferenczi concerned the latter's modifications of psychoanalytic technique to encourage and gratify regression, which Freud regarded as dangerous and ill-fated. Balint's position with regard to the dual nature of libido seems largely aimed at resolving this dispute. He distinguishes between "benign" and "malignant" regression, the former aimed at "recognition," the fulfillment of primary relational needs, and the latter aimed at "gratification" of instinctual craving. As a further extension of this dichotomy, he distinguishes psychopathology deriving from early disturbances in object relations ("the basic fault") from psychopathology deriving from conflict (over instinctual wishes). These distinctions are puzzling in the context of Balint's argument that instinctual cravings themselves derive from disturbances in early object relations; according to the logic of his theory, *all* regression and psychopathology must concern disturbances in object relations, some forms of which entail a further breakdown of object-seeking into sensual cravings and rage and revenge as disintegrative substitutes.

Balint's distinction does serve his larger political purpose, however. It allows him to preserve Freud's drive/structure theory and his wariness toward gratification (Freud was dealing with malignant regression, the pursuit of infantile instinctual gratification), while justifying Ferenczi's focus on early object relations and his provision of gratification (Ferenczi was dealing with "benign" regression, in which relationship, not pleasure, is the goal (1968, p. 144). Although Balint clearly developed a theoretical system *alternative* to and conceptually incompatible with Freud's drive/structure theory, he nevertheless continues to juxtapose it, to mix it together, with classical theory, largely through what appears to be politically motivated diagnostic distinctions. This strategic use of diagnosis allows Balint to maintain what we have termed a "mixed models" theory, in which relational/structure premises are introduced and maintained alongside earlier drive/structure premises. This mixing strategy has reappeared most prominently in recent years in the work of Heinz Kohut.

Over the past twenty-five years John Bowlby has developed a version of the relational/structure model closely related to Fairbairn's work. Although supervised by Klein and analyzed by Joan Riviere, Bowlby, like Fairbairn, abandoned Klein's efforts to preserve classical drive theory and sought to redefine radically the basic principles within which classical theory operates. Like Fairbairn, Bowlby sees classical theory as ensconced in an anachronistic framework borrowed from nineteenth-century physics and biology. Unlike Fairbairn, he explicitly looks outside the range of psychoanalysis to areas within contemporary biology, for his basic premises, drawing on ethology and the Darwinian theory of natural selection and presenting what he characterizes as a "new type of instinct theory" (1969, p. 17).

Bowlby suggests that "instinctive" behavioral systems underlie much of the emotional life of man and have developed because they were conducive to survival. The system with which he has been almost exclusively concerned is the array of behaviors and experiences constituting the child's "attachment" to the mother. Bowlby suggests that "attachment" is mediated through five component instinctive responses: sucking, smiling, clinging, crying, and following, organized into a complex system of internal controls and feedback, resulting in proximity-maintaining behavior (1969, p. 180). This system was "selected" during the early evolution of the human species because it made survival more likely; children in the proximity of the mother are less vulnerable to predators. Thus, the child's attachment to the mother is part of an "archaic heritage" whose function is species survival. Bowlby took issue with the predominant trend within classical psychoanalytic theorizing to view the child's tie to the mother as a derivative, secondary development, contingent upon the mother's function as the gratifier of the child's physiological and sensual needs. The mother does not become important because she gratifies, he argues; she is important from the start.

Much of the early controversy concerning Bowlby's work centered around the question of whether young children experience true grief in the face of prolonged separation from or loss of the mother. A. Freud took the position that the earliest relationship with the mother is constituted wholly by her function as need-gratifier and is thus "governed by the more primitive and direct dictates of the pleasure-pain principle" (1960, p. 58). Thus, the child's relationship to the mother, prior to the acceptance of the reality principle, partial control of id tendencies by the ego, object-constancy, and so forth, lacks the affectual ties and specificity which constitute true object love. Early reactions to loss, A. Freud argues, are not true mourning, but transient reactions to the anticipation of deprivation persisting only until a new need-gratifying object presents itself. Bowlby argues that the attachment to the mother is primary, and not derivative of the mother's function as need gratifier. He suggests that young children react to the loss of the mother with true mourning, betraying the power of their primary attachment. He argues that more classical observers of children do not place full significance on what he claims are the clear and unmistakable signs of mourning in young children because classical drive theory has trouble accounting for the intensity and specificity of early attachments. He further suggests that A. Freud has attempted to "squeeze the new observations within the framework of existing theories, especially those of primary narcissism and of the primacy of bodily needs" (1960, p. 30).

Bowlby extends the concept of attachment to serve as the basis for a reconsideration of all basic areas within classical theory: all anxiety, phobic and otherwise, is related to separation from the mothering figure; dependency is understood in terms of anxious attachment; anger is a response to separation (1973); the core of all defenses is a deactivation of the need for attachment (1980). Emotional struggles and difficulties of all sorts derive from disturbances in the early attachment to the mother and subsequent objects of attachment: "Whether a child or adult is in a state of security, anxiety, or distress is determined in large part by the accessibility and responsiveness of his principal attachment figure" (1973, p. 23). Confidence in the availability of attachment figures, Bowlby suggests, underlies emotional stability; anticipations of such availability are built up slowly throughout childhood and adolescence and are generally stable throughout later life; expectations of availability of attachment figures are accurate reflections of actual experiences with parents.

Bowlby's theorizing operates entirely within the relational/structure model and is closely related to the theories of Sullivan and Fairbairn.* Among his most important contributions is his exploration of the interface between psychoanalytic theory and data and related disciplines (most recently, information-processing theory). Because of these efforts to place psychoanalytic data within an extrapsychoanalytic framework, however, Bowlby's theory cannot stand as a distinctly and purely psychoanalytic model per se. He understands much of human experience and behavior in terms of its function in species survival. This leaves his account of the *meaning*, to the individual, of the experiences and behaviors involved in attachment, separation, and loss underdeveloped. He writes at times as if *experiences* and fantasies of relationship and loss are epiphenomena, as if the instinctive, behavioral systems which are our archaic heritage simply operate *through* us, blindly, automatically, concretely: "Complex sequences of behavior are regarded as due to the sequential activation and termination of behavioral units, their sequential appearance being controlled by a superordinate behavioral structure organized as a chain, as a causal hierarchy, as a plan hierarchy, or as some integrate of them all" (1969, p. 1972). In Bowlby's account, the meaning of the object to the person is often subsumed under a description of the distribution of instinctive behavioral systems, a kind of behavioral economics.

A closely related feature of Bowlby's system is that his theory of object relations tends toward the concrete, the actual physical absence or presence of the mother. "The child's tie to his mother is a product of the activity of a number of behavioural systems that have proximity to mother as a predictable outcome" (1969, p. 179). Although in his later

---

*Bowlby acknowledges these correspondences (1973, pp. 273–275), but repeatedly criticizes Fairbairn for linking attachment to feeding and orality. This criticism seems to miss Fairbairn's emphasis that orality is not the cause but the channel for early object-relatedness, and that later relationships employ other channels.

work, Bowlby increasingly acknowledges the importance of *emotional* absence, inaccessibility, and nonresponsiveness, he does not integrate these more subtle aspects of relationship into his broader theory. Nor does he account for the emotional need for and meaning of attachment and relationship in the development of a distinctly human self, as do Fairbairn, Winnicott, and Sullivan. Bowlby's observational data and ethological framework need to be filled in with concepts drawn from more purely psychoanalytic and experiential relational/structure theories.

7   D. W. Winnicott and Harry Guntrip

Klein and Fairbairn were system-builders. Each constructed a broad and novel vision of human experience and difficulties: Klein, in her slowly evolving, piece-by-piece redefinition and refocusing of Freudian theory; Fairbairn, in his dramatic refutation of Freud's work. Winnicott and Guntrip, by contrast, were concerned with single issues. Both declared allegiance to prior traditions: for Winnicott, his own personal blend of Freudian and Kleinian thought; for Guntrip, Fairbairn's recently fashioned object relations theory. Yet each felt that the tradition he emulated had omitted one crucial area of concern and attempted to correct that oversight.

Winnicott and Guntrip present their own contributions as circumscribed and limited, mere emendations of earlier theoretical traditions. Winnicott's formulations concerning the emergence of the self, however, provide a foundation for developmental theory radically different from that of his Freudian and Kleinian predecessors. Guntrip's formulations concerning ego regression move Fairbairn's object relations theory in a direction which diverges from some of its most basic premises.

D. W. Winnicott

Winnicott, an extremely innovative and influential contributor to the development of psychoanalytic theory and practice, has provided an intricate, subtle, and often powerfully poetic account of the development of the self out of its relational matrix. The form and manner of his work parallels some of his central thematic concerns in two striking ways. First, Winnicott's prose has an elusive quality. Almost all of his papers were originally presented as talks, and their style reflects an informality more suitable to the spoken than the written word. Each is short, with often scintillating clinical observations loosely strung together with pithy, almost epigrammatic theoretical formulations. The central themes are generally presented in the form of evocative paradoxes that entice the reader playfully. The arguments are more discursive than tightly reasoned; Winnicott follows his presentations where they take him. Because of this elusiveness, Masud Khan, his editor and foremost disciple, has aptly characterized his style as "cryptic."

A second striking feature of Winnicott's presentation is his curious manner of locating himself with regard to psychoanalytic tradition. Winnicott claims great allegiance to his theoretical forebears, particularly Freud and, to a lesser extent, Klein. He presents his own contributions as a continuation of their work, which he describes in reverential terms. In fact, the central thrust of a rather scathing review by Winnicott and Khan (1953) of Fairbairn's work is a criticism of the latter's rejection of Freud's metapsychological formulations. However, Winnicott preserves tradition in a curious fashion, largely by distorting it. His interpretation of Freudian and Kleinian concepts is so idiosyncratic and so unrepresentative of their original formulation and intent as to make them at times unrecognizable. He recounts the history of psychoanalytic ideas not so much as it developed, but as he would like it to have been, rewriting Freud to make him a clearer and smoother predecessor of Winnicott's own vision. This tendency to absorb and rework the concepts of others is reflected in Khan's description of Winnicott's impatience with reading: "'It is no use, Masud, asking me to read anything! If it bores me I shall fall asleep in the middle of the first page, and if it interests me I will start re-writing it by the end of that page'" (1975, p. xvi). Harold Bloom (1973) has suggested that each major poet within the Western tradition distorts the vision of his most prominent predecessors to make room for his own personal vision. Winnicott's manner of positioning his own innovative and important contributions vis-à-vis the psychoanalytic tradition suggests such a process more than any of the other theorists considered in this volume. He could have been describing his own approach to psychoanalytic tradition when he says: "Mature adults bring vitality to that which is ancient, old and orthodox by re-creating it after destroying it" (1965b, p. 94).

These formal characteristics of Winnicott's writing—his elusive mode of presentation and his absorption yet transformation of theoretical predecessors—parallel his central thematic interest: the delicate and in-

tricate dialectic between contact and differentiation. Almost all his contributions center around what he depicts as the continually hazardous
struggle of the self for an individuated existence which at the same time
allows for intimate contact with others. Winnicott's depiction of the
healthy self rests upon one of his many paradoxes—through separation,
nothing is lost, but rather something is gained and preserved: *"This is
the place that I have set out to examine,* the separation that is not a
separation but a form of union" (1971, p. 115; italics in original). The
achievement of such a state is by no means easy; the development of the
self is fraught with dangers. How does the child discover himself within
his mother's care without losing himself to her? How can the child differentiate himself yet retain maternal resources? How can one communicate without being depleted, be seen without being appropriated,
be touched without being exploited? How can one preserve a personal
core without becoming isolated? The formal and stylistic characteristics
of Winnicott's presentation reflect these issues. He entices, baffles, and
provokes his readers, valuing them highly but never confronting them
directly. He reveres his theoretical forebears, prizing continuity with
them; yet, he refashions and reshapes their work radically according to
his own imagery and vision. Lack of contact with others as well as total
accessibility to others pose, for Winnicott, grave dangers to the survival
of the self.

Winnicott was a prominent pediatrician prior to and throughout his
career as a psychoanalyst, and his deep familiarity with babies and
mothers pervades and informs his approach to psychoanalytic issues. He
began his ten-year analysis with Strachey in 1923, three years before
Melanie Klein's move to England; like Fairbairn, he was deeply influenced by her work. His second analyst, Joan Riviere, was among Klein's
closest collaborators, and he was in supervision with Klein herself between 1936 and 1940. Winnicott felt that Klein's work overlapped some
of his own early observations and helped him resolve issues with which
he was struggling. He had worked with children who seemed never to
have reached a stable and differentiated oedipal stage; in his early work
on feeding disorders he had been struck by the predominance of greed
in infants and the centrality of fantasies in young children concerning
their own "insides" and the "insides" of the mother (1936, p. 34).
Klein's depiction of early phantasies, anxieties, and primitive object
relations spoke directly to Winnicott's earliest concerns.

In 1945, following an incubation period involving considerable
clinical work both with children and with psychotics, Winnicott began a
series of papers which marked his departure from Freudian and Kleinian
theory. Freud had illuminated neurosis; Klein had explored depression.
His own work, Winnicott suggests, is an emendation, an application of

prior psychoanalytic concepts to the relatively uncharted area of manifest psychosis. This diagnostic distinction was to lose meaning as the approach Winnicott developed broadened into a general theory of development and psychopathology markedly at variance with the formulations of Freud and Klein. The processes leading to the development or the inhibition of the self are depicted and understood solely in the context of the interaction between the child and the environmental provisions supplied by significant others. Thus, despite his protestations of continuity and allegiance, Winnicott's work constitutes an approach to human experience which rests solidly within the relational/structure model.

The Emergence of the Person

Winnicott's most important contributions to psychoanalysis begin with his observation that classical theory and the psychoanalytic treatment of neurosis take something very basic for granted: that the patient is a person. By this he means it is assumed that the patient has a unified and stable personality available for interactions with others. Freud, Winnicott suggests, presupposed the "separateness of the self and a structuring of the ego" (1960a, p. 41). Because of this presumption, two major problems have been overlooked: patients who are not "persons," either because of manifest psychosis or because they only *appear* to interact with others; and those features of the analytic situation which bear most directly on early developmental processes facilitating the emergence of personhood. These were precisely the areas Winnicott set out to explore. Almost all of his major contributions concerned the conditions making possible the child's awareness of himself as a being separate from other people, and he approaches this problem from different angles, through different formulations, and in different contexts.

The mother provides experiences which enable the incipient self of the infant to emerge. The latter begins life in a state of "unintegration," with scattered and diffuse bits and pieces of experience. The infant's organization of his own experience is preceded by and draws upon the mother's organized perceptions of him. The mother provides a "holding environment" within which the infant is contained and experienced: "an infant who has had no one person to gather his bits together starts with a handicap in his own self-integrating task" (1945, p. 150). Winnicott termed the state of devotion that characterizes the mother, enabling her willingly to offer herself as an attentive medium for her baby's growth, the state of "primary maternal preoccupation." He regards the mother's absorption in fantasies of and experiences with her baby as a natural, biologically rooted, and adaptive feature of the last trimester of pregnancy and the first several months of the baby's life.

In addition to "holding," the mother "brings the world to the child" and, in Winnicott's view, this function plays a crucial and intricate role in development. The infant when excited conjures up, or, more precisely, is on the verge of conjuring up, an object suitable to his needs. Ideally it is precisely at that moment that the devoted mother presents him with just such a suitable object — the breast, for example. This is the "moment of illusion." The infant believes he has created the object. Over and over the infant hallucinates, the mother presents, and the content of the conjuring approximates more and more closely to the real world.

> the infant comes to the breast when excited, and ready to hallucinate something fit to be attacked. At that moment the actual nipple appears and he is able to feel it was that nipple that he hallucinated. So his ideas are enriched by actual details of sight, feel, smell, and next time this material is used in the hallucination. In this way he starts to build up a capacity to conjure up what is actually available. The mother has to go on giving the infant this type of experience. (1945, pp. 152–153)

In the "moment of illusion" the infant's hallucination and the object presented by the mother are taken to be identical. The infant experiences himself as omnipotent, the source of all creation; this omnipotence, Winnicott suggests, becomes the basis for the healthy development and solidity of the self. (Kohut was later also to argue that the basis for a healthy self lies in the opportunity for a prolonged experience of infantile omnipotence.) The necessity for maternal devotion in this process is apparent. The mother's empathic anticipations of the baby's needs and her precise timing are crucial. To make illusion possible, "a human being has to be taking the trouble all the time to bring the world to the baby in understandable form" (p. 154). The simultaneity of infantile hallucination and maternal presentation provide the repetitive experiential basis for the child's sense of contact with and power over external reality.

Healthy development requires a perfect environment, but only briefly. By perfect, Winnicott means a mother whose maternal preoccupation makes possible a very close and accurate sensitivity to her infant's needs and gestures. As Winnicott describes it in his later writing, the mother functions as a mirror, providing the infant with a precise reflection of his own experience and gestures, despite their fragmented and formless qualities. "When I look I am seen, so I exist" (1971, p. 134). Imperfections in the reflected rendition mar and inhibit the child's capacity for self-experience and integration and interfere with the process of "personalization." When the mother is able to resonate with the baby's wants and needs, the latter becomes attuned to his own bodily functions and impulses, which become the basis for his slowly evolving sense of self. The failure of the mother to actualize the child's gestures and needs undercuts the child's sense of hallucinatory omnipotence, constricting his belief in his own creativity and powers and driving a wedge between the evolution of the psyche and its somatic underpinings. "The mind has a root, perhaps its most important root, in the need of the individual, at the core of the self, for a perfect environment" (1949a, p. 246).

Another approach Winnicott takes to the same issues is his consideration of the conditions necessary for the development of the capacity to be alone. He suggests that it is extremely important for the mother not only to shape the world to the infant's demands but also to provide a nondemanding presence when the infant is not making demands or experiencing needs. This makes it possible for the infant to experience needlessness and complete unintegration, a state of "going-on-being" out of which needs and spontaneous gestures emerge. The mother's nondemanding presence makes this experience of formlessness and comfortable solitude possible, and this capacity becomes a central feature in the development of a stable and personal self. "It is only when alone (that is to say, in the presence of someone) that the infant can discover his own personal life" (1958b, p. 34).

Fortunately for everyone involved, the mother's exquisite responsiveness is not necessary for very long. Once hallucinatory omnipotence is firmly established, it is necessary for the child to learn the reality of the world outside his control and to experience the limits of his powers. What makes this learning possible is the mother's failure, little by little, to shape the world according to the infant's demands. As the mother recovers from her maternal preoccupation and becomes interested once again in other areas of her life, the child is forced to come to terms with what he cannot do, cannot create, cannot make happen. These harsh realities are assuaged by a push within the child toward separateness. Thus, the mother's ego coverage and responsiveness decrease in fine syncrony with an increase in the exercise of active ego functions on the part of the infant. As the infant matures, the mother does not actualize his wishes so much as receive and respond to his gestures. An increasingly greater differentiation and interaction characterizes their relationship. The early mother who materializes the infant's passive hallucinatory wish gradually gives way to the mother who responds to needs which are now actually expressed through gestures and signals. The mother's "graduated failure of adaptation" (1949a, p. 246) is essential to the development of separation, differentiation, and realization.

Winnicott suggests that deficiencies in maternal care, more specifically the failure to provide a perfect environment and its graduated withdrawal, have a debilitating impact on the emotional development of the child. Maternal failures are of two kinds: inability to actualize the hallucinatory creations and needs of the infant when he is in excited states; and interference with the infant's formlessness and unintegration when he is in quiescent states. Both kinds of maternal deficiencies are experienced by the child as a terrifying interference with the continuity of his own personal existence, and both result in the experience of the "annihilation of the infant's self" (1956a, p. 304). The infant's personal existence is rooted both in his formless states and in his omnipotent creative gestures. Ideally, the mother is the medium for formlessness and the instrument of omnipotence. Any interference with these functions is experienced by the infant as an "impingement." Something from the outside is making claims on him, demanding a response. He is wrenched from his quiescent state and forced to respond, or he is compelled to abandon his own wishes, to accept prematurely the feeble and unrealistic nature of his own demands, and to mold himself to what is provided for him.

The major consequence of prolonged impingement is fragmentation of the infant's experience. Out of necessity he becomes prematurely and compulsively attuned to the claims and requests of others. He cannot allow himself the experience of formless quiescence, since he must be prepared to respond to what is asked of and provided for him. He loses touch with his own spontaneous needs and gestures, as these bear no relation to the way his mother experiences him and what she offers him. Winnicott characterizes the resulting fragmentation as a split between a "true self," which becomes detached and atrophied, and a "false self on a compliant basis." The "true self," the source of spontaneous needs, images, and gestures, goes into hiding, avoiding at all costs the possibility of expression without being seen or responded to, the equivalence of complete psychic annihilation. The "false self" provides an illusion of personal existence whose content is fashioned out of maternal expectations and claims. The child becomes the mother's image of him. The "false self" comes to take over in some sense the caretaking functions which the environment has failed to provide. The "false self" covertly protects the integrity of the "true self"; it functions "to hide the true Self, which it does by compliance with environmental demands" (1960b, p. 147). The false self draws on cognitive functions in its anticipations of and reactions to environmental impingements, resulting in an overactivity of mind and a separation of cognitive processes from any affective or somatic grounding (1949b, pp. 191–192).

Winnicott regards the formation of "transitional objects" as another aspect of this larger process entailing the development of the person. The most important dimension of transitional phenomena is not the objects themselves, but the nature of the relationship to the objects, representing a developmental way station between hallucinatory omnipotence and the recognition of objective reality. The emergence of the person entails a movement from a state of illusory omnipotence, in which the infant, through the mother's facilitation, feels he creates and controls all features of the world he lives in, to a state of objective perception, in which the infant accepts the limits of his powers and becomes aware of the independent existence of others. The move between these states is not a one-way, linear progression; both children and adults continually vacillate between them. Winnicott contrasts these two different states starkly with each other: solipsistic subjectivity with objective perception; the inner world with the world of outer reality; the world of "subjective objects" over which one has total control with the world of separate and independent others. Relations with transitional objects constitute a third, intermediary, and transitional realm between these two worlds.

How is it possible for an object to be neither under illusory, omnipotent control nor part of objective reality? Herein lies the paradox which is the essence of transitional experiencing. Winnicott suggests that what is necessary for the establishment of a transitional object (such as a blanket or teddy bear) is a tacit agreement between the adults and the baby not to question the origin and nature of that object. The parent proceeds as if the baby had created the object and maintains control over it, yet also acknowledges its objective existence in the world of other people. Thus, the parent who understands this paradox allocates the object to neither of the two realms, and the agreement not to challenge the baby's special rights and privileges over his object creates the transitional realm. The transitional object is neither under magical control (like hallucinations and fantasies) nor outside control (like the real mother). Transitional experience lies somewhere between "primary creativity and objective perception based on reality-testing" (1951, p. 239). Because of this ambiguous and paradoxical status, transitional objects help the baby negotiate the gradual shift from the experience of himself as the center of a totally subjective world to the sense of himself as a person among other persons. Transitional experiencing is not merely a developmental interlude, but remains a cherished and highly valuable realm within healthy adult experience. It is here we can let our thoughts wander, concerned neither with their logic and validity in the real world nor with the threat that our musings will lead us into a totally subjective, solipsistic realm, causing us to lose the real world altogether. Transitional experience is rooted in the capacity of the child to play; in adult form it is expressed as a capacity to play with one's fantasies, ideas, and the world's possibilities in a way that continually allows for the surprising, the original, and the new. In transitional experience, we maintain access to the most private wellspring of our thoughts and imagery, without being held accountable for them in the clear and harsh light of objective reality.

In later writings Winnicott depicts yet another feature of the emergence of the person, based on the distinction between "object-relating" and "object usage." These formulations highlight his understanding of the function of aggression and destruction in the process of separation. "Object-relating" is defined as subjective, projective experiencing in which the other is under the infant's illusory control. "Object-usage" is the perception of and interaction with the other as independent and real, outside the infant's omnipotent control. Once again, Winnicott tries to focus our attention on the precise mechanisms which make this transition possible, and once again they revolve around a paradox. The child "destroys" the object because he has begun to experience it as separate and outside his subjective control; the child "places" the object outside his omnipotent control because he is aware of having destroyed it. Thus, the child "uses" and "destroys" the object because it has become real, and the object becomes real because it has been "used" and "destroyed." The survival of the object is crucial. The mother's nonretaliatory durability allows the infant the experience of unconcerned "usage," which in turn aids him in establishing a belief in resilient others outside his omnipotent control.

For Winnicott the emergence of a healthy, creative self is contingent upon the specific environmental provisions he has grouped under the term "good-enough-mothering." These provisions make it possible for the infant to start "by existing and not by reacting" (1960b, p. 148). They make possible the affective shift from infantile dependence to independence and the cognitive shift from omnipotent conception to realistic perception. They determine the structure, coherence, and vitality of the person's sense of self: "individuals live creatively and feel that life is worth living or else . . . they cannot live creatively and are doubtful about the value of living. This variable in human beings is directly related to the quality and quantity of environmental provision at the beginning or in the early phases of each baby's living experience" (1971, p. 83).

Ideally, the true self, nurtured in a nonimpinging environment, represents "the inherited potential which is experiencing a continuity of being, and acquiring in its own way and at its own speed a personal psychic reality and a personal body-scheme" (1965b, p. 46). Ideally, human experience entails the generation of spontaneous impulses and expressions, while the true self "does no more than collect together the details of the experience of aliveness" (1960b, p. 148). Yet, even under the best of circumstances, Winnicott suggests, personhood is a fragile and tenuous phenomenon, and there is always tension between subjective experience and objective reality. We all begin life completely dependent on our caretaker's recognition and facilitation of our wishes and gestures to provide even the chance for us to know and become ourselves. This total dependence necessitates a total vulnerability to nonresponsiveness and intrusions, which are experienced as annihilations of personal continuity. The inevitable residue of this vulnerability is a private citadel of subjective reality held forever inaccessible to public, objective light. "At the centre of each person is an incommunicado element, and this is sacred and most worthy of preservation" (1963, p. 187). No matter how firmly anchored in objective reality the person is, no matter how fluidly and resiliently one negotiates the gap between subjective creativity and objective externality, the fear of the exploitation of the true self persists as the deepest dread and therefore there remains a "noncommunicating self, or the personal core of the self that is truly isolate." "The question is: how to be isolated without having to be insulted" (1963, pp. 182, 187). Winnicott's answer to this question is reflected in the substance as well as the stylistic qualities of his contributions to psychoanalytic ideas, in the tension in his own work between openness and elusiveness, directness and cryptic ambiguity, loyalty to tradition and the destruction and rearrangement of that tradition.

Winnicott and the Models

Winnicott's innovative contributions to psychoanalytic thought operate within the relational/structure model. There is no such thing as a baby, he insists, only a nursing couple. The concept of the mother-infant unit, brought along from his experience in pediatrics, led him to establish his frame of reference not in processes taking place solely within the child, but in the relational field between the child and the caretakers: "The centre of gravity of the being does not start off in the individual. It is in the total set-up" (1952, p. 99). With an emphasis greatly reminiscent of Sullivan, Winnicott declares the uselessness "in describing babies in the earliest stages except in relation to the mother's functioning" (1962a,

p. 57) and the impossibility of understanding psychopathology by viewing the individual as an "isolate" (1971, pp. 83–84). Although physical holding and ministrations are of tremendous importance in the holding environment, in Winnicott's view the relationship between mother and infant consists of complex and mutual emotional needs and is not essentially physical. In fact, he explicitly rejects Mahler's term "symbiosis" as "too well rooted in biology to be acceptable" (1971, p. 152), stressing instead the interactional, emotional nature of the exchange between mother and child. In his system various aspects of the early relationship between the infant and the mother serve as the foundation for the differentiation and structuralization of the self.

Winnicott's strategy for positioning himself vis-à-vis the drive/structure tradition, given his relational/structure framework, might be characterized as one of benign neglect. He did not, like Fairbairn, abandon the use of the drive theory altogether. Nor did he, like Jacobson, Kernberg, and other figures within American ego psychology, attempt to blend relational concepts with the older drive/structure framework. Rather, he establishes object relations on a footing that is autonomous and separate from instinctual processes. In classical drive theory, object relations are derivatives of the vehicles for drive gratification and defense. In Winnicott's theory, the earliest object relations consist of interactions between developmental needs within the child and maternal provisions offered by the mother, entirely separate from drive gratification. He does not challenge the drive concept directly, but he crowds it out, relegating it to a peripheral and secondary status.

According to Winnicott, the child *needs* relatedness with the mother. This need for contact consists of a built-in orientation and anticipation rather than a set of specific a priori images of the kind Klein had suggested; there is a readiness and expectancy rather than an object itself. Play "enables the baby to find the mother" (1948a, p. 165), and, despite his reluctance to align himself with Fairbairn's work, Winnicott speaks of a "drive that could be called object-seeking" (1956b, p. 314). The infant needs the maternal provisions which define good-enough mothering including: an initial perfectly responsive facilitation of his needs and gestures; a nonintrusive "holding" and mirroring environment throughout quiescent states; the collusive agreement to respect transitional objects; survival, despite the intensity of the infant's needs; and the failure to retaliate against the destructive features of object-usage. Winnicott differentiates the need for these maternal provisions from instinctual wishes: "a need is either met or not met, and the effect is not the same as that of satisfaction and frustration of an id impulse" (1956a, p. 301).

These relational needs are a developmental imperative; if they are not met, no further meaningful growth can take place.

Winnicott emphasizes the separation between key relational processes and the drives. "There is a relationship between the baby and the mother . . . it is not a derivation of instinctual experience, nor of object relationship arising out of instinctual experience. It antedates instinctual experience, as well as running concurrently with it, and getting mixed up with it" (1952a, p. 98). In classical drive theory the capacity to enjoy life is rooted in the possibility for drive gratification and sublimation. Winnicott emphasizes the priority of relational processes leading to the emergence of the self.

> We now see that it is not instinctual satisfaction that makes a baby begin to be, to feel that life is real, to find life worth living. In fact, instinctual gratifications start off as part-functions and they become *seductions* unless based on a well-established capacity in the individual person for total experience, and for experience in the area of transitional phenomena. It is the self that must precede the self's use of instinct; the rider must ride the horse, not be run away with. (1971, p. 116)

How can drive gratification provide a seductive distraction from more basic developmental needs? Here the distance Winnicott has come from the drive/structure model is apparent. In the latter, drive gratification constitutes the underlying foundation for, and the latent, essential nature of, object relations. Even within Klein's work, gratification is essential to the development of object relations. The mother *becomes* "good" through a good feed; the infant loves the mother by swallowing and internalizing her. The mother *becomes* "bad" by frustrating the infant. Winnicott has separated these two realms. The self emerges and becomes structuralized through relational experiences with specific maternal provisions. What is crucial in these provisions is the *position* of the object, the mother's function in "holding" the infant, actualizing his gestures, surviving his attacks, and so on. According to Winnicott, gratification by itself does little to affect the position of the object; maternal provisions are independent of the mother's function in satisfying instinctual needs. "A baby can be *fed* without love, but lovelessness or impersonal *management* cannot succeed in producing a new autonomous human child" (1971, p. 127). The satisfaction of instinctual needs can, in fact, be offered as a substitutive distraction. The infant can be "'fobbed off' by a satisfactory feed" (1963, p. 181).

> It must be understood that when reference is made to the mother's adaptive capacity this has only a little to do with her ability to satisfy the in-

fant's oral drives, as by giving a satisfactory feed. What is being discussed here runs parallel with such a consideration as this. It is indeed possible to gratify an oral drive and by so doing to *violate* the infant's ego-function, or that which will later on be jealously guarded as the self, the core of the personality. A feeding satisfaction can be a seduction and can be traumatic if it comes to a baby without coverage by ego-functioning. (1962a, p. 57)

Thus, although Winnicott preserves the concept of instincts, they are relegated to a secondary and peripheral status in development. His greatest concern vis-à-vis physically based instinctual wishes is that they can become a means for interference with more basic developmental needs (1952b, p. 225).

Winnicott's approach to psychopathology and treatment reflects relational/structure premises. Mental health in his view is constituted by the relative integrity and spontaneity of the self. Psychopathology (apart from a politically aimed diagnostic slight of hand to be considered shortly) entails corruption and constriction in the movement and expression of the self. The necessary and sufficient factor responsible for mental health is appropriate parental provisions—good-enough mothering. Winnicott defines psychosis specifically as an "environmental deficiency disease"; yet all psychopathology within his system involves impairment in the functioning of the self and is thus, by definition, a product of parental deficiency. The parents' personalities, Winnicott demonstrates over and over throughout his clinical illustrations, have an enormous impact on the development of the child, and parental pathology, when it interferes with the provision of nurturance and proper infant care, reverberates clearly in the psychopathology of the child: "the child lives within the circle of the parent's personality and . . . this circle has pathological features" (1948b, p. 93).

Winnicott's relational/structure understanding of the nature of psychopathology is reflected in his treatment of the phenomenon of regression. Regression, he suggests, is not a return to points of libidinal fixation or specific erotogenic zones. Regression represents a return to the point at which the environment has failed the child. Appropriate parental provisions are the sine qua non of emotional growth; where they are missing, development stops, and the absent developmental "needs" dominate subsequent living. Developmental needs are very different from "wishes" derived from drives. Needs are a developmental necessity; nothing else can happen until they are filled. Within the drive/structure model, regression is pathological and dangerous in that it provides a surfeit of infantile gratification. In Winnicott's version of the relational/structure model, regression is a search for missing relational experiences. "The tendency to regression in a patient is now seen as part of the capacity of the individual to bring about self-cure" (1959, p. 128).

Winnicott sees the curative factor in psychoanalysis, not in its interpretive function, but in the manner in which the analytic setting provides missing parental provisions and fills early developmental needs. The function of psychoanalysis is to compensate for parental failures in adaptation, and "to provide a certain type of environment" (1948a, p. 168). The person of the analyst and the analytic setting "hold" the patient; in the reliability, attentiveness, responsiveness, memory, and durability of the analyst, the aborted self of the patient becomes unstuck and continues to grow. Winnicott also sees the psychoanalytic process in terms of mutual play between patient and analyst; when the patient is constricted in this capacity, the analyst functions to rekindle it (1971, p. 38). Whereas Freud's major emphasis in discussing the liberating value of psychoanalysis is on the freedom *from* illusion, Winnicott emphasizes the increasing freedom to *create* illusion, and this is intimately tied up with the capacity to play (R. Bank, personal communication).

Winnicott defended himself against orthodox critics who charged that his approach to treatment is too regressive and too gratifying of infantile wishes, by arguing that gratification in regression is the result not of libidinal satisfaction, but of the fact that the "self is reached" (1954, p. 290). This view of treatment is an outgrowth of, and consistent with, his relational/structure assumptions concerning maturation, development, and psychopathology. Specific relations with a maternal caretaker are essential to the development of the person. When provided, they set the child free to grow and function freely as a person in the world; when they are missing, the incipient self is ensnared and imprisoned, wrapped in a protective cocoon, hidden from the world of others experienced as unsafe for authentic and spontaneous living. Only if the appropriate facilitating environment is provided can the true self be reached and allowed to continue its growth.

Winnicott and the Tradition

Winnicott is very careful throughout his writings to place himself within the earlier tradition of psychoanalytic ideas. The two figures he was most concerned with, both explicitly and implicitly, were Klein and Freud. Winnicott took considerable pains to present his contributions as a continuation of, not a departure from, their systems, and criticized Fairbairn for directly challenging Freud's drive theory. Yet his own formulations operate wholly within the relational/structure model—and this posed serious political problems. Despite the relational nature of his concepts,

Winnicott aligns himself with Klein and Freud through a combination of assimilation, distortion, and strategic avoidance.

Winnicott's use of Klein's theory reflects a marked ambivalence. On the one hand, several of her concepts and emphases provided key intellectual tools in the development of his own thought. The notions of an inner world, internal objects, primitive greed, the importance of phantasy—all these concepts occupy a central place within Winnicott's system. He openly acknowledged this debt and as late as 1948 defended Kleinian theory against its critics, most notably Glover. On the other hand, Winnicott began directly challenging Kleinian theory as early as 1941. That year he took objection to the notion of a priori knowledge and imagery of the father's penis (1941, p. 63). In 1949 he argued that birth is not experienced in terms of the projection of aggression—"the stage has not yet been reached at which this means anything" (1949b, p. 185). In 1959 he suggests that the concept of the death instinct is "unnecessary" (1959 p. 127). And in a retrospective review of Klein's contributions he suggests that her attempt to date complex cognitive processes earlier and earlier in infancy "spoilt" her later work (1962b, p. 177).

Winnicott's broadest critique of Klein's system concerned her emphasis on internal processes at the expense of relations with real others; his major theoretical departure from her vision lies in his stress on the interpersonal environment. In Winnicott's theory of mind, object relations are rooted in and constituted by both the mother's performance of caretaking functions and her character. His major criticisms of Kleinian concepts address her attempt to derive object relations from inherent, constitutional sources such as a priori object images and innate aggression. What Klein derives from constitution, Winnicott derives from environmental provisions and failures.

"Melanie Klein represents the most vigorous attempt to study the earliest processes of the developing human infant *apart from the study of child-care*. She has always admitted that child-care is important but has not made special study of it" (1959, p. 126; italics in original). As a pediatrician and director of a child psychiatric clinic, Winnicott was much more aware of battering and neglecting mothers than was Klein, who had a fashionable West End practice. This difference undoubtedly bears on the difference in the weight they give to the reality of parental behavior and character (James Grotstein, personal communication).

In his challenge of the central pillars of Klein's theory, Winnicott became disaffiliated with the Kleinian group; in later years, he seems to have regarded this with a touch of bitterness and regret. "I never had analysis by her, or by any of her analysands, so that I did not qualify to be one of her group of chosen Kleinians" (1962b, p. 173)—a puzzling statement, given his analysis with Joan Riviere. Winnicott used his position as a member of "c-group" within the British Psychoanalytic Society (devotees of neither Klein nor Anna Freud), to attempt to heal the split within the society and reconcile Kleinian formulations with main-line Freudian theory.

Despite Winnicott's open departure on many issues, the treatment of Klein in his writing reflects a considerable effort to demonstrate his continuity with her views. The major device employed to preserve continuity is his tendency to reinterpret Klein's formulations into a more fully relational/structure framework. At times Winnicott's alterations are openly acknowledged. For example, he maintains Klein's emphasis on unconscious phantasy as the pervasive underpinning of mental life, but he explicitly separates phantasy from presuppositions concerning a priori knowledge. For Klein, with closer ties to the drive/structure model, phantasy is primarily an internal phenomenon, generated by the drives and related to the world of real others only secondarily. In Winnicott's system the primacy of phantasy is preserved but the content is altered. "Fantasy is more primary than reality, and the enrichment of fantasy with the world's riches depends on the experience of illusion" (1945, p. 153). For him phantasy is oriented toward personalized reality from the start, manifesting itself in a readiness to develop illusions of control over what the real world actually provides. Through phantasy the infant is poised, at the "moment of illusion," for relational interchange with the outside world.

At other points Winnicott's alteration of Klein's formulations is much more covert. For example, he considered Klein's development of the concept of the depressive position to be her greatest contribution to the history of the psychoanalytic ideas; it "ranks with Freud's concept of the Oedipus complex" (1962b, p. 176). By introducing personal, as opposed to social, sources of the sense of guilt, Winnicott felt that Klein had opened up a whole new realm of psychoanalytic investigation concerned with the "idea of an individual's value," in addition to questions of "health" (1958a, p. 25). Nevertheless, in presenting Klein's formulations, he changes them. The development of the capacity for concern (Winnicott prefers the term "concern" to Klein's "guilt") is presented as a feature of the transition from infantile omnipotence to objective perception and relationship. In this transition the synthesis is effected between the two different "mothers" within the infant's experience: the caretaker, environment mother, who provides the holding function in quiescent states, and the "object" mother, who is the victim of the infant's "ruthless" fantasies and attacks in excited states.

In his greedy excitement, Winnicott suggests, the infant uses the mother with no regard for her feelings or even survival. He is aware only of his own wishes. The depressive crisis is precipitated by the realization that the mother who is the object of these excited states is also the mother who provides the holding environment between excitements, the mother the infant depends on and loves. This synthesis and realization arouses a deep concern for the mother. Two aspects of maternal functioning are crucial, according to Winnicott, for the infant to sustain and integrate the capacity for concern. First, the mother must survive the excited states and "hold" the situation in time, so that the child can come to trust her durability and perceive the less-than-omnipotent destructiveness of his own needs and phantasies. The mother's survival demonstrates the resistance and resiliency of the real world in the face of the infant's wants and demands. Second, the mother must provide the baby with the "opportunity to contribute," to make up to the mother, to console her. Only if reparation is possible can the guilt the child feels over his destructive impact be tolerated and the capacity for concern emerge.

In Winnicott's reworking of Klein's formulations concerning the depressive position, several basic changes are apparent. He views depressive anxiety and guilt as much more directly concerned with the person of the real mother than did Klein. The child cannot simply "repair" the mother in fantasy and play, but needs to be given the "opportunity to contribute," to console the mother in actuality. This poses difficult problems for children of inconsolable, depressed mothers. "Their task is first to deal with the mother's mood . . . creating an atmosphere in which they can start on their own lives" (1948b, p. 93). The depressive position, therefore, is more fully grounded in the child's actual interpersonal world. Further, the very issue at the heart of the depressive position is different in Winnicott's formulations. Klein had depicted depressive anxiety as arising from the integration of the good breast (the repository of the child's projected love plus gratifying experiences with the mother) with the bad breast (the repository of the child's projected hate plus frustrating experiences with the mother). Without acknowledging that he is changing anything, Winnicott depicts depressive anxiety as arising from the integration of the environment mother (who "holds" the infant in quiescent states) with the object mother (who is the victim of the infant's greedy appropriations in excited states). These are not simply parallel constructions.

Klein's formulation reflects the residues of the drive model notion that the central task of early psychic development is the regulation and integration of internally arising drive energies; Winnicott's formulation reflects the more fully relational model notion that the central task of early psychic development is the integration of various caretaking functions provided by the mother. To employ Klein's concepts without openly modifying them, it is necessary for Winnicott to misread them. This becomes most clear in his discussion of the function of aggression. "I have used the expression primitive love impulse, but in Klein's writings the reference is to the aggression that is associated with the frustrations that inevitably disturb instinctual satisfactions as the child begins to be affected by the demands of reality" (1958a, p. 22). To modify Klein's work by deriving aggression from actual experiences of frustration is not only possible, but is a compelling alteration. To present such modifications as Klein's own view obscures the fundamental differences between Klein and Winnicott with respect to their basic, underlying presuppositions.

Guntrip reports that Winnicott urged him to "have your own relation to Freud and not Fairbairn's" (1975, p. 151). In another context Guntrip implies that Winnicott himself actually had two relationships to Freud, one public and one private. Privately, he suggests, Winnicott acknowledged his departure from Freud's drive-based approach to psychopathology in the direction of a more relational view. "We disagree with Freud," Guntrip reports Winnicott as saying. "He was for 'curing symptoms.' We are concerned with whole living and loving persons" (Mendez and Fine, p. 361). Why was this open divergence not reflected in Winnicott's writings? Winnicott, Guntrip suggests, was "clinically revolutionary and not really interested enough in pure theory to bother to think it out." This assertion is puzzling if one examines references to Freud in the work of Winnicott, who takes great pains, at times involving elaborate and intricate argumentation, to proclaim himself at one with Freud in all respects. His relationship to Freud cannot be, as Guntrip asserts, the product of laziness or disinterest; rather, it appears to be the result of a systematic strategy by Winnicott to present his contributions as a direct continuation of, rather than a marked departure from, Freud's work. The major devices used in these efforts were a systematic misreading of Freud's formulations, and a use of diagnostic distinctions which give the appearance of preserving Freud's theory of neurosis intact.

Let us consider several of the more striking of Winnicott's misreadings of Freud. Freud's concept of primary narcissism is a stumbling block for any relational/structure model, since it explicitly presupposes that the infant is at first *not* oriented toward others, thereby making object relations secondary and derivative phenomena. Both Klein and Fairbairn directly challenged the concept of primary narcissism, the former by arguing the presence of internal object relations inherent in narcissism, the latter by arguing that libido is directed toward reality and others from the start. Winnicott takes a different tack: he recognizes the difficulties Freud's concept poses, then says he prefers to think that Freud did not really mean what he said. Winnicott quotes Freud's reference to the infant as a "completely narcissistic creature . . . totally unaware of her [the mother's] existence as an object." He goes on to remark, "I like to think that Freud was feeling round this subject without coming to a final conclusion because of the fact that he lacked certain data which were essential to the understanding of the subject" (1949b, p. 175). Despite the total absence of any such tentativeness in Freud's writing, Winnicott proceeds to use the concept of "primary narcissism" *as if* it did not imply an early objectless state, but was in fact equivalent to his own antithetical view of the early dependence of the infant on the mother.

The presupposition of an innate aggressive drive is one of the twin pillars of Freud's "dual-instinct theory." Klein preserved and extended this concept; Fairbairn explicitly rejected it. In Winnicott's work there is no aggressive drive of the sort Freud had formulated, yet he continues to use the term extensively. Winnicott achieves the appearance of continuity with respect to the concept of innate aggression by simply adopting the term and redefining it. He emphasizes the importance of aggression throughout his work, employing Freud's term as if it carried the same meaning. Yet, at several points he notes that aggression and destruction do not entail anger or hate. "Aggression" for him refers not to a specific instinctual drive, but to a general vitality and motility. He equates it with a life force and argues that "at origin, aggressiveness is almost synonymous with activity" (1950, p. 204). He suggests that it consists of a need for something to bump up against, something outside the self to be encouraged and struggled with: "it is the aggressive component that . . . drives the individual to a need for a *Not-Me* or an object that is felt to be *external*" (1950, p. 215). The "destruction" in Winnicott's late work on object-usage is thus an innocent, nonbelligerent desire for engagement: "this destructive activity is the patient's attempt to place the analyst outside the area of omnipotent control, that is, out in the world." The aggressive drive "creates the quality of externality" (1971, pp. 107, 110).

Winnicott's treatment of Freud's theory of oedipal guilt provides another example of forced continuity. In Freud's theory the Oedipus complex is constituted by the clash between instinctual forces driving the child toward incestuous and murderous impulses, on the one hand, and the fear of retaliation by the real parent and later by the superego, on the other. It is a product of the tension between the press of drive and the fear of retribution from social reality. Winnicott describes Freud's Oedipus complex quite differently:

> In the simplest possible terms of the Oedipus complex, a boy in *health* achieved a relationship with his mother in which instinct was involved and in which the dream contained an in-love relationship with her. This led to the dream of the death of the father, which in turn led to the fear of the father and the fear that the father would destroy the child's instinctual potential. This is referred to as the castration-complex. At the same time there was the boy's love of the father and his respect for him. The boy's conflict between that side of his nature which made him hate and want to harm his father, and the other side by which he loved him, involved the boy in a sense of guilt. (1953a, p. 17)

This description is an account of the Oedipus complex as modified by Klein's formulations concerning the depressive position. Freud's conflict between drive (both libidinal and aggressive) and social reality has been replaced by Klein's conflict between love and hate. (Freud sometimes also speaks of ambivalence in connection with oedipal conflicts, but an ambivalence derived from constitutional bisexuality, body-based and drive-derivative, rather than the more fully emotional ambivalence Klein and Winnicott depict.) Klein explicitly addressed the differences between her account of the oedipal crisis and Freud's. Winnicott does not; he rewrites Freudian theory through a Kleinian perspective, preserving an illusion of consensus and unbroken tradition.

A final example of his systematic misreading of Freud is provided by Winnicott's argument that the most novel and innovative of his contributions were actually implicit in Freud's work all along:

> It would appear to me that the idea of a False Self . . . can be discerned in the early formulations of Freud. In particular I link what I divide into a True and False Self with Freud's division of the self into a part that is central and powered by the instincts (or by what Freud called sexuality, pregenital and genital), and a part that is turned outwards and is related to the world. (1960b, p. 140)

This is an extremely misleading parallel. Winnicott's distinction between the true and false self contrasts authentic and spontaneous living with compliant, overly adaptational living. Freud's distinction between the id and ego contrasts primitive, asocial, undirected impulses with a necessary knowledge of and facility with the outside world. Freud's distinction does not address itself to the issue of inauthenticity, which is at the center of Winnicott's concern. A comparison between the two concepts is interesting and revealing. Freud's concern, consistent with the drive/structure model, is with the division between drives and regulatory functions, between energy and its organization and use. Winnicott's concern, consistent with the relational/structure model, is with different forms of relation between self and others. Placing Winnicott's formulations beside Freud's, one can see the distance he has moved from the drive/structure model. Winnicott is concerned with minimizing that distance.

The second device used by Winnicott to position himself in continuity with Freud's work is found in his approach to diagnosis. In one of the earliest papers in which he put forth his original views (1945) Winnicott makes a tripartite distinction among categories of mental disorder: pre-self disorders (psychotics, schizoids, borderline cases, and false selves)—a dysfunction within the earliest, most primitive object relations; depressive disorders—difficulties with inner-world issues involving conflicts between love and hate as characterized by Melanie Klein; whole person disorders (neurosis)—oedipal conflicts as characterized by Freud. This classificatory system reflects Winnicott's relation to tradition: Freud was right with respect to neurosis; Klein was right with respect to depressives; Winnicott takes as his own province the relatively unexplored area of psychotic and borderline-psychotic phenomena.

By 1954 he has placed the "majority of so-called normal people" in the middle group, as Kleinian depressives (1954b, pp. 276–277). The third group, Freudian neurotics, now consists only of "quite healthy people" who have managed to establish a stable and vital enough self to be confronted with the oedipal problems Freud had described. By 1956 the middle classification of Kleinian depressives has dropped out, and the majority of sufferers from mental dysfunction are understood to be grouped in the first category, those who, as a result of deficiencies in parental provisions, lack an integrated, vital self. Winnicott has come to use the false self concept as a single diagnostic principle, representing a continuum of psychopathology from psychotic states, in which the false self has collapsed, to nearly healthy states, in which the false self mediates selectively and sparingly between the true self and the outside world (1960b, p. 150). The other category of human beings, that realm within which Freudian theory still applies, is no longer regarded as a form of psychopathology at all. In neurosis, adequate parenting has produced a healthy self. "True neurosis is not necessarily an illness . . . we should think of it as a tribute to the fact that life is difficult" (1956c, pp. 318–319).

What is Winnicott accomplishing with these shifting diagnostic distinctions? Initially he portrays his work as an application of Freud's concepts to a realm of pathology not considered by Freud. As his work developed, however, it became apparent that Winnicott was proposing not an extension, but an *alternative* to Freud's approach. He is offering a framework for understanding psychopathology which, firmly rooted in the relational model, is at odds with classical formulations based on drive and defense. Thus, the diagnostic group Winnicott takes as his own gradually swells; that left to Freud gradually shrinks. It is necessary for Winnicott's political positioning of himself in continuity with Freud, however, for him to designate neurosis as a phenomenon adequately understood only within the framework of classical drive theory. However, because Winnicott's own system is so comprehensive and so much at odds with drive/structure principles, it is not easy for him to allow Freud's theory a meaningful place. In fact, the manner in which he depicts Freud's view of neurosis is itself badly distorted. He defines neurosis as "the illness that belongs to intolerable *conflict* which is inherent in life and in living as whole persons" (1959, p. 136). Neurosis, he suggests, is the fate of individuals who have had adequate parenting and hence possess a stable and vital self. Their struggles concern universal instinctual conflicts, and their own constitutional excesses and deficiencies, balances and imbalances. Neurosis is the province of the "individual," the "personal factor," in contrast to false-self disorders, which are the product of environmental deficiencies.

Freud, despite his emphasis on constitutional factors, *never* separated neurosis from environmental factors. In fact, the interaction between constitutional and environmental factors formed one of Freud's "complemental series" and is at the heart of his understanding of the development of psychopathology. Further, Freud did not view neurotics as existential heroes, as Winnicott suggests, but distinguished very clearly between neurotic suffering and the "common unhappiness" of everyday life. In separating out "neurosis" as a preserve in which Freud's theory remains unchallenged and merely amended, Winnicott perpetuates not Freud's original vision, but a distorted icon.

Harry Guntrip

Guntrip has been the foremost historian, synthesizer, and popularizer of the study of object relations within the writings of Klein, Fairbairn, and Winnicott. His particular vantage point as an analysand of both Fairbairn and Winnicott, the larger historical context he provides, and the fluidity and lucidity of his prose (in comparison with that of the other major British theorists) all contribute to the effectiveness of his overview and synthesis. Guntrip's enthusiastic expositions of Fairbairn's work, in particular, were largely responsible for drawing attention to the latter's contributions.

Guntrip not only surveyed and synthesized the work of his predecessors, however; he also moved the theory in a very specific direction, according to his own unique vision of human experience and suffering. In 1960 he introduced what he characterized as a modification and extension of Fairbairn's theory of ego-splitting and object relations. This "extension" radically alters the thrust of Fairbairn's approach and generates clinical hypotheses antithetical to those derived from his system.

The Emergent Synthesis and the "Regressed Ego"

Guntrip's history of psychoanalytic ideas is first and foremost a moral history. From the ministry and pastoral counseling he turned to psychoanalysis in search of a deeper, psychologically more sophisticated approach to human experience. But the scientism and the antipathy toward religion he discovered in Freud's work was disturbing to him. Guntrip came to understand Freud as torn by an internal tension between his clinical observations, which were concerned with persons and relationships, and the depersonalized, biologistic theoretical edifice he had constructed in accordance with the mechanistic, Helmholtzian intellectual milieu surrounding him. Guntrip sees the drive theory, the formulations concerning the "psychic apparatus," and the functional analysis of the ego as products of the dehumanizing currents within Freud's intellectual environment, and therefore as unacceptable and dangerous.

> While Freud hovered between a psychology of the organism and a psychology of the person, a theory of instincts and a theory of object relations, his theory *in toto* remained fundamentally oriented to biology. Thus, he makes character dependent on the organic maturing of the sexual instincts rather than dealing with sexual functioning as controlled by the extent to which character has matured in human relationships. Moreover, his radical subordination of objects to the role of mere means to the gratification of instincts is unsatisfactory from a sociological and from a human point of view, since it treats of personal relationships on a subpersonal level. (1961, p. 29)

Guntrip's moral critique of Freud is deep and far-reaching and extends to modern science and technology as a whole. "Science has to discover whether and how it can deal with the 'person,' the 'unique individual,' we will dare to say the 'spiritual self' with all the motives, values, hopes, fears and purposes that constitute the real life of man, and make a purely 'organic' approach to man inadequate." The stakes are high; what hangs in the balance is the "final fate of mankind. If nuclear physics threatens us with the possibility of universal destruction, genuine psychodynamic understanding, if only it be given time to work quietly, gives at least a realistic hope of new life" (1961, pp. 15–16).

Guntrip's own innovation in theory and practice centers on his development of the concept of the "regressed ego." Fairbairn had described fragmentation of the ego as resulting from the compensatory establishment of internal objects as substitutes for relations with real others. According to him, pieces of the ego remain attached to these internal objects, siphoning off libido from the increasingly emptied central ego, which remains directed toward real others in the external world. He understands the schizoid sense of emptiness and weakness as reflecting the withdrawal of energy from the real world into the world of internal object relations.

Around the time that Fairbairn's terminal illness forced the premature ending of Guntrip's analysis with him, Guntrip began to develop the view that "ego-weakness" is reflective not just of the withdrawal of libido from external objects, but of the withdrawal of libido from objects altogether, whether external or internal. He argues that Fairbairn's "libidinal ego," which acts as the repository of all disappointed longings and hopes for contact and nurturance, undergoes a "final split." Part of it remains attached to the "exciting object," as Fairbairn had described, perpetually seeking relatedness. Another part becomes split off from the exciting object and becomes even more withdrawn, renouncing object-seeking altogether. This "regressed ego" is constituted by a profound sense of helplessness and hopelessness. The depriving experiences with real others have produced a fear of and antipathy toward life so intense and pervasive that this central portion of the ego has renounced all others, external and internal, real and imaginary; it has withdrawn into an isolated, objectless state. In this flight from life, Guntrip suggests, the regressed ego seeks to return to the prenatal security of the womb, to await a rebirth into a more hospitable human environment. Thus, regression entails a flight and a longing for renewal. When the flight aspect is more prominent, the regression is experienced as a longing for death—relief from conflictual relations with external and internal objects. When the hope aspect is more prominent, the regression is experienced in connection with a return to the protection of the womb.

After some initial unclarity about the relationship of his own formulations to Winnicott's work (1969, p. 74), Guntrip concluded that his concept of the "regressed ego" includes *both* the split-off portion of the libidinal ego in flight from all objects as well as all "unevoked potentials" (Winnicott's "true self"), which because of maternal deprivation have never been fully experienced or expressed in relation to others in the first place. Guntrip further pieces together aspects of Fairbairn's and Winnicott's concepts with his own formulation as follows: when maternal deprivation is experienced as "tantalizing refusal" (Fairbairn's "exciting object"), the result is an active oral libidinal ego bound to internal objects; when maternal deprivation is experienced as simple neglect or impingement (Winnicott), there is a more pronounced retreat into a passive, withdrawn state where the ego is in hiding and potentials never develop (1969, p. 70).

In Guntrip's view the regressed ego exerts a powerful pull out of life, both from the world of real others and from the world of internal object relations. He attributes to this regressive pull an increasingly more central role in the dynamics of all psychopathology. The lure of the regressed ego threatens to deplete the total personality, plunging the patient into isolation and dysfunction. Guntrip suggests that the early traumas generated by inadequate mothering are essentially frozen in time: the helpless and terrified infantile ego, overwhelmed by unrequited longings and dread of abandonment, remains alive within the regressed ego, in the heart of the personality. "Ego-weakness" is both the experiential product of regressive longings which perpetually tug at whatever ego is left attached to objects as well as an actual structural impairment, reflecting the helpless terror of the infant, encased in the heart of the personality, generating a perpetual sense of inner dread and vulnerability. In the face of the constant threat of total depersonalization and disorganization, reasoned Guntrip, the ego continually struggles to remain attached to life. All mental life and involvements with others, real and imaginary, operate most basically as a defense against regressive longing. Thus, the concept of the "regressed ego" becomes a conceptual black hole, swallowing up everything else. Conflictual relations with others and masochistic attachments to bad internal objects serve as the ego's protection against regression. Oral, anal, genital fantasies reflect "a struggle . . . to 'stay born' and function in the world of differentiated object-relations as a separate ego," as defenses against the central part of the personality that has "gone back inside." The dangers threatened by the regressed ego constitute the "tap-root" of all psychopathology; all forms of pathology are defenses against the "schizoid problem." Psychoanalytic treatment is a controlled "exhaustion illness" (1969, pp. 79, 53, 215, 78). All defensive attachments to objects, real and imagined, are relinquished; the weak and helpless infantile ego emerges; and the largely maternal relationship with the analyst, through "replacement therapy," allows the ego to reintegrate and enter the world on a positive basis.

Guntrip's Divergence from Fairbairn
In championing Fairbairn as an alternative to Freud, Guntrip blurs fundamental differences between his own approach and Fairbairn's, and this obscures important conceptual issues and clinical choices. One broad difference is their overall approach to the history of psychoanalytic ideas. Fairbairn and Guntrip both begin with a critical evaluation of classical drive theory, but their critical basis is quite different. Fairbairn's objections rest on conceptual and pragmatic grounds: the presuppositions of pure pleasure-seeking and the separation of energy from structure are anachronistic and misleading; his own theory of endopsychic structure is closer to the clinical data, more economical, and provides more interpretive possibilities. Guntrip's objections to the classical tradition are less conceptual than moral and aesthetic. Freud's "theories of instinctive sex and instinctive aggression have done as much harm to our general cultural orientation in this century, especially in the atmospheres engendered by two world wars, as his opening up of the field of psychotherapy in depth has done good" (1971, p. 137).

Guntrip objects to Freud's motivational theory (man as governed by impersonal drives), to machine metaphors, and to the presupposition of innate aggression. His fundamental concern is with the ethical implications of Freud's language and system.

> Where does the difficulty about Freud's position lie? It is not that his description of the actual sexual situation of civilized man in our time is inaccurate . . . His picture of the state of sexual frustration inside marriage, and its wider repercussions . . . is both true and challenging. Large numbers of human beings experience a strong and persistent pressure of sexual need either conscious or repressed, and the upsurge of sexual impulses, in a way that finds no gratification within the limits of monogamous marriage and civilized sexual morality . . . The question concerns the *interpretation* to be put upon these strong sexual impulses. If they are indeed solely manifestations of an innate, constitutionally powerful instinct, then we have little option but to tolerate rebels or to endure the spread of neurosis. (1969, p. 71)

Guntrip believes the conclusions Freud's theory produces regarding human possibilities too grim. He considers drive theory degrading to mankind and, on that basis, unacceptable. He sees the shift toward the study of the ego and the emphasis on its resources in Freud's later writings as moving psychoanalytic theory in a more acceptable direction. "Here, truly, is a reprieve for and a reinstatement of the ego of ordinary consciousness to a position of dignity from which Freud's earlier, biologically oriented, instinct-theory threatened to dethrone it" (1969, p. 100). This teleological approach to theory is a bit like criticizing the "big bang" theory of the origin of the universe because of its implications for the eventual fate of the cosmos. Schafer points out that in Guntrip's writings, "It sounds as if kindly theory is better theory, or a kindly theoretician a better theoretician" (1976, p. 118). This seems an apt characterization, and constitutes a distinct and significant departure from Fairbairn's concerns.

Guntrip's most important departure from Fairbairn's system centers on his claim that the regressed ego constitutes the "core" of all psychopathology. Although he suggests that this concept is simply an extension of Fairbairn's formulations, a closer look reveals it to be a radical shift in a direction leading to antithetical clinical hypotheses and interpretations. Guntrip's premise is that the dominant dynamic pull within human experience is a total retreat from others, real and imagined, in a deep longing for a "return to the womb." This is a puzzling formulation, even on its own terms. What are the ingredients of such a longing? Since Guntrip does not explicitly suggest the existence of prenatal memories (as Winnicott does), fantasies of a withdrawal to a completely nurturative, supportive environment can only derive from elaborations of pieces of actual experience with caretaking figures. Unless it is a memory, a longing for a return to the womb can only be a metaphor for or fantasy of perfect mothering. Guntrip states emphatically that the regressive flight seeks objectlessness, and he distinguishes regressive fantasies concerning a return to the womb from fantasies concerning the breast precisely on that point. However, it is not clear why the womb, any more than the breast, represents an objectless state rather than a particular form and representation of "exciting object." It is not clear why the regressed ego is seen as withdrawn from all objects rather than seeking a particular fantasied object of an infinitely perfect and totally supportive nature. Another reading of Guntrip's theory of regression would be to regard the "womb" as a biological metaphor standing for a psychological and developmental state of undifferentiation, not so much objectless as pre-object. This reading brings it very close to formulations concerning an early undifferentiated matrix in the work of Jacobson, Loewald, and others within the ego psychological tradition. Again, such an approach is a marked departure from Fairbairn, who emphasizes the child's object-relatedness and reality-orientation from the start.

Guntrip emphasizes regression and withdrawal exclusively — which seems both unconvincing and at odds with the basic thrust of Fairbairn's work. He points out that flight is a ubiquitous reaction to conflict and deprivation and amasses various clinical examples revolving around a wish to retreat and escape. He then argues that this regressive pull toward flight is not simply reactive and transitory, but so pervasive and powerful that it becomes the dominant motivational thrust within the personality. All other motivations, all relations with external and internal objects, become defensive bastions against this regressive pull. This conclusion is novel and startling. It is one thing to say that flight is a reaction to difficulty; clearly withdrawal from others in the face of deprivation, anxiety, and conflict is a common response, and Guntrip's depiction of schizoid withdrawal is a clinically useful account of the phenomenology of such reactions. However, it is something else altogether to argue that flight is the predominant motivation in human experience. Surely this does not coincide with Fairbairn's view. Fairbairn had argued that attachments to objects are so necessary and adhesive that bad objects are relinquished only when good object relations are experienced as a real possibility. Compulsive attachments to bad objects are maintained, since objectlessness is impossible, both conceptually and experientially. For Guntrip, objectlessness is not only possible; the threat of depersonalization and devitalization created by the lure of regression to an objectless state is the deepest and most pervasive anxiety within the psyche.

Guntrip has stood Fairbairn on his head by subtly reversing priorities. In Fairbairn's system, object-seeking, the need for contact and relation, is primary; for Guntrip, withdrawal is primary, and object-seeking is a secondary defensive reaction against the terror of regressive longing. For Guntrip, the regressed ego abandons objects. For Fairbairn, the ego can never rid itself of objects; it is by its very nature entangled with them. Fairbairn sees even the most regressed and seemingly withdrawn behavior as deriving from powerful ties to internal objects. (For example, he [1954] suggests that in "auto-eroticism" the genitals symbolize objects; libido is always object-related.) He considers the greatest resistance in psychoanalysis to be the libidinal attachment to bad objects. Guntrip considers the greatest resistance in psychoanalysis to be the terror of regressive ego weakness and depersonalization. In line with this reversal, he uses the designation "ego psychology" in his later writings to characterize his point of view. "Object relations theory" has become a more superficial layer of analysis: "'*depression* has to be understood . . . from the point of view of object-relations,' i.e., the need and struggle to retain object-relations (guilt being an object-relation), but . . . *the deeper problem of regression* which it masks, has to be understood 'in terms of ego psychology'" (1969, p. 144). Guntrip retains the complexities of prior theory, but he reinterprets the fundamental function of all dynamic processes in terms of defending against regression.

To highlight the clinical implications of the difference between Fairbairn and Guntrip in understanding psychopathology and resistance, let us consider a piece of autobiographical material provided by Guntrip himself. In a posthumously published article (1975) he presents a moving and candid retrospective consideration of the significance in his life of his personal analyses with Fairbairn and Winnicott, which centers around his own internal struggle with regressive longings. Guntrip differed with Fairbairn's interpretations of this material, and his dissatisfaction with the latter's approach led him to formulate his own innovative concept of the "regressed ego." (Kernberg, 1980, argues that Guntrip's unresolved transference toward Fairbairn was responsible for his tendency to distort the latter's ideas.)

Guntrip portrays his mother as a woman who, deprived of maternal care and compelled to take care of younger siblings, approached the experience of motherhood with a sense of duty and deep resentment. She nursed Harry, her firstborn, in the hope that nursing would forestall a second pregnancy. She refused to nurse her second son, who subsequently died, at which time she renounced all sexual relations and devoted herself to a business career. Guntrip, according to his mother's account, walked into her room at the age of three and a half to discover his dead brother on her lap. He subsequently developed a severe, mysterious illness. He was sent away from the mother to an aunt, where he recovered, but he remained for several years sickly and demanding. Guntrip suffered a complete amnesia for the experiences surrounding his brother's death. Yet one major indication of their importance in his later life was a recurrent "illness" involving total exhaustion that would develop following the departures of close fraternal figures. Between "illnesses" he was compulsively active and preoccupied with work.

Themes and images about death, tombs, buried men, and so on recurred in dreams throughout his life. Although Guntrip had sought analysis to aid in the recovery of these early memories and the cure of the psychogenic illnesses which he felt derived from them, the memories had remained inaccessible during his two analyses. They finally emerged in a series of dreams in his later life, when both Fairbairn and Winnicott were dead. The dreams were precipitated by a retirement forced upon him for reasons of health, which he experienced as a surrender to his mother's wishes to destroy him or to let him die. They consist of a series of images of the mother as immobile, unreachable, frozen, and, finally, a figure with no face, arms, or breasts, holding on her lap the dead baby brother. Guntrip understood these images as the reemergence from repression of the memories of his mother as paralyzing, aloof, and totally schizoid. The dreams were followed by a mood state consisting of a dull, mechanical, lifeless apathy—a final, diminishing echo of the earlier illnesses of collapse.

What is the nature of the images of Guntrip's mother as frozen and mutilated? What is the dynamic significance of his exhaustion illness? From Guntrip's point of view, the images and illness represent the final retreat of the schizoid "heart of the self" from life, because of gross and terrifying maternal deficiencies. This interpretation derives from his revision of Fairbairn's theory, proposing a final schizoid split in which the center of the self detaches itself completely from objects and renounces life. The exhaustion illness represents a desperate escape from the horrifying visage of the mother and the dead brother. Throughout his analysis he felt that Fairbairn shed little light on these problems. He reports that Fairbairn founded his interpretations on "oedipal" dynamics, on what he felt were Guntrip's attempts to get his mother to mother him. Guntrip does not explain or elaborate Fairbairn's thinking on this point; nevertheless, it is possible to construct a Fairbairnian approach from the latter's basic theoretical principles. In Fairbairn's system, Guntrip's images and feeling states would be viewed not as an escape from his mother, but as a return to her, a longing for the reestablishment of his early connection to her, in her depression and aloofness, her morbidity and desolation—an unconscious yet tenacious holding on to her. This holding on is reflected in a dream Guntrip recounts, illustrating in the most concrete and literal terms Fairbairn's notion of object tie: "I was working downstairs at my desk and suddenly an invisible band of ectoplasm tying me to a dying invalid upstairs, was pulling me steadily out of the room. I knew I would be absorbed into her. I fought and suddenly the band snapped and I knew I was free" (1975, p. 150). In Fairbairn's system the "invisible band" is the object tie which Guntrip actively, although unconsciously, perpetuates, despite his counterdepressive defenses and disclaimers.

The implications of these alternative interpretations are quite different. From Guntrip's point of view, his mother was unable to support life, and his perception of this was horrifying and traumatic. Although he tried to win her love later in childhood through provocation, his deepest fears were based on his massive flight from his mother and all other objects, a flight which manifests itself in episodic collapses. Within Fairbairn's system, the central issue is not flight from, but devotion and allegiance to, the depressed and desolate mother of Guntrip's early years. The collapses, so dreadful to him, represent a longing for a reunion with the dead and lifeless core of the mother, with whom the dead brother remains in envied union. As he expresses it in the dream, "I knew I would be absorbed into her." The faceless mother is the "exciting object" which Guntrip seeks continually in his descents into exhaustion and lifelessness. Within Fairbairn's system, Guntrip has turned his profound longing for his schizoid mother (manifested in his exhaustion illnesses) into an illusion of escape from her.

Guntrip's reworking of Fairbairn poses several serious problems in its clinical application. The patient for him is an innocent and passive victim of parental deficiency. At the core of all forms of psychopathology is a helpless, frightened child who has gone into hiding. Guntrip takes considerable pains to absolve the patient of accountability for perpetuating his condition — the problem is "pre-moral" (1969, p. 10), deriving solely from primitive terror, never from conflicts or ambivalence. In this respect Guntrip's vision closely resembles Freud's earliest theory of neurosis based on infantile seduction and Rank's theory of the birth trauma. Guntrip objects to Rank's emphasis on the *physical* aspects of the birth experience rather than on the personal, emotional atmosphere provided by the mother, as well as to his call for a quick cure, a direct and immediate assault on the affective residues of the birth trauma rather than a gradual analytic working through of defenses. However, he echoes Rank's view that underlying all neurosis is an encapsulated traumatic (hysterical) neurosis which provoked and preserves a flight from life.

Guntrip's account of psychopathology and the analytic process resembles the child's fable "Sleeping Beauty." A terrible trauma has occurred in early childhood, inflicted on the passive and innocent child from the outside (a disgruntled fairy). The terror and helplessness of this traumatic event remain imbedded in the heart of the personality, awaiting a call back to life by a more hospitable environment. The self of the patient is ultimately passive; lack of good mothering produces a retreat to a lifeless withdrawal, until the analyst (the prince) awakens it from its slumber. We have noted Fairbairn's tendency to portray the patient as an innocent victim. This tendency is somewhat balanced in his system by his view of neurosis as an active perpetuation of bad object ties. Guntrip removes this balance; object ties are merely a defense against more basic fearful flight. In his system terror has replaced active allegiance as the bottom line of neurosis and the source of the greatest resistance within the psychoanalytic process.

Corollary to Guntrip's presentation of the patient as victim is his utopian premise that complete happiness, free from anxiety and conflict, is possible within human experience.

> If we imagine a perfectly mature person, he would have no endopsychic structure in the sense of permanently opposed drives and controls. He would be a whole unified person whose internal psychic differentiation and organization would simply represent his diversified interests and abilities, within an overall good ego-development, in good object-relationship. (1969, p. 425)

Proper parenting results in a perpetual internal harmony and equilibrium.

> Then the grown-up child is free without anxiety or guilt to enter an erotic relationship with an extra-familial partner, and to form other important personal relationships in which there is a genuine meeting of kindred spirits without the erotic element, and further to exercise an active and spontaneous personality free from inhibiting fears. This kind of parental love, which the Greeks called *agape* as distinct from *eros*, is the kind of love the psychotherapist must give his patient because he did not get it from his parents in an adequate way. (1969, p. 357)

Guntrip attributes the universal failure of mankind (to live up to this myth of mental health) to inadequate mothering—depriving, insensitive, or malevolent. His absolution of the patient is paralleled by a tendency to villify the actual parents, in contrast to the ideal parenting and love he calls upon the therapist to provide *"in loco parentis"* (1969, p. 350). This polarity between the good parenting of the therapist and the good life to which it presumably leads and the bad parenting of the actual caretakers perpetuates both a splitting of object relations and the transference, and a disclaiming of accountability for the active perpetuation of the neurosis. What is at stake in therapy, in Guntrip's vision, is the "saving of the ego" (1969, p. 213). Just as humane psychodynamic theory constitutes the hope for mankind, the therapist, in his view, becomes an heroic nurturative figure, rescuing the helpless patient from the terror and paralysis generated by disastrous mothering.

The Relational Model in Perspective

It would be convenient, perhaps, if the history of psychoanalytic ideas consisted of an unbroken line of progressive advances, with each new theorist standing squarely on the shoulders of his predecessor, using prior theory as a solid foundation for further, incremental exploration. Instead, the major figures within the history of psychoanalytic ideas have a complex and discontinuous relationship. Psychoanalytic theory is not simply additive; it consists of a collection of uniquely fashioned crystallizations of ideas and data, often overlapping, but with different centers and organizational principles. The authors we have considered in "The British School" do not constitute a "school" by virtue of subscribing to a set of shared beliefs, but, like a school of painters, by virtue of a shared set of problems and sensibilities.

The most fundamental common problem addressed by these theorists, as well as by theorists within the American interpersonal school, is the transformation of psychoanalytic metapsychology from a theoretical framework based on drives to a framework which makes relations with others, real and imagined, the conceptual and interpretive hub. The various versions of the relational/structure model share a common set of assumptions which set them apart from earlier drive/structure theory: the unit of study of psychoanalysis is not the individual, but the relational matrix constituted by the individual in interaction with significant others. The stuff of personality and the patterns that characterize psychopathological functioning are formed from that relational field. While physiological needs, bodily events, temperament, and other biological factors significantly affect human experience and behavior, they operate within the context of an interactive matrix and are subsumed by the preeminant motivational thrust toward the establishment and maintenance of relations with others. Each major theorist of the British school made important contributions to the movement of psychoanalytic theory from the drive/structure model to the relational/structure model. The nature and the style of presentation of these contributions, however, vary considerably; they begin with a common starting point and arrive at a common destination, but each covered the intermediate conceptual expanse differently.

Klein began her researches into the mental life of children with a total dedication to classical drive theory. However, the data yielded by her efforts were rife with powerful, primitive phantasies involving loving and hateful relations with others—both with real, external figures as well as with characters in an internal drama of passionate and tragic intensity. Her interpretive focus shifted from an early emphasis on psychosexuality, to an almost exclusive emphasis on aggression, to a more balanced view of mental life centered around a profound struggle between love and hate, restoration and destruction. Although she retained the language of drive theory throughout and presented her work as an extension of classical theory, Klein's formulations alter, in a subtle yet pervasive way, the nature and function of the drives. Drives, in her system, are bound inextricably to objects, built-in with considerable specificity to the very experience of desire itself. Mental life in health and in pathology is a complex fabric woven out of relational strands—each component is an informed and personal engagement between the self and an other, real or imagined, external or internal. Gone are the basic components of the drive/structure model—directionless impulses seeking tension reduction. Gone is the classical closed energy system in which psychic energy is finite and distributed through alternate channels. Underneath Klein's drive theory language, a new vision of the mind had begun to emerge. The pursuit of pleasure and the avoidance of pain recede into the background in this motivational framework; the struggle between hateful destruction and fragmentation, between loving restoration and integration, occupies center stage.

Klein's work made possible the contributions of Fairbairn, Winnicott, and Guntrip. Fairbairn applied her depiction of internal object relations to a thorough reconsideration of classical motivational and structural theory. He also retains some of Freud's language, though, unlike Klein, he explicitly redefines the terms. Libido for Fairbairn is not pleasure-seeking but object-seeking; psychic energy is not directionless and structureless but organized and oriented toward the reality of other people. Development, in his view, consists of a maturational unfolding of different modes of connection to other people, and all psychopathology is constituted by a failure in that development and a subsequent attachment and allegiance to infantile object ties, established as internal residues.

Fairbairn's system, although often highly sparse and schematic, represents, along with the interpersonal theory of Sullivan, the purest and most consistent formulation of the relational/structure model. Fairbairn and Sullivan view the development of personality and psychopathology from a similar perspective: the child is enmeshed in relations with others and discovers himself in interaction. This embeddedness of the child with others is the overriding feature of early development, and the need for attachment, connection, integration with others is the preeminent motivational thrust of the human organism throughout life. While Sullivan delineates this common relational vision largely by studying patterns of behavior and interaction, Fairbairn's emphasis is on intrapsychic residues of relational experience—the internal fragmentation and patterning of the personality.

Guntrip's emendation of Fairbairn's theory with the introduction of the concept of the "regressed ego" raises the *retreat* from object relations to a superordinate motivational principle, displacing Fairbairn's emphasis on attachment to objects. Guntrip's point of view, however, with its analysis of human experience and difficulties as derivative of vicissitudes of relations with others, remains as an alternative theory within the relational/structure model.

Winnicott negotiated the expanse between the drive/structure model and the relational/structure model by sidestepping rather than directly challenging classical theory. He addresses himself to the development of an integrated and experientially real self, which he suggests is a problem not explored by Freud and Klein, and antedates or underlies the kinds of issues they concerned themselves with. Winnicott delineates a set of unfolding relational needs for specific maternal provisions which have a peremptory nature; the structure of the self and the organization of psychopathology derive from the fate of these early relational needs. Vicissitudes of and conflicts concerning the drives become important, he suggests, only in the context of these more basic processes. By this device, he introduces a theory of motivation, development, structure, and psychopathology that is based on relations between the self and others and operates squarely within the relational/structure model.

In the work of Klein, Fairbairn, Winnicott, and Guntrip, object relations occupy the central focus and are understood to constitute the basic stuff of human experience. However, *the nature of the object*, its origins and qualities, is quite different in the formulations of these different theorists. Each sees particular aspects of objects as most crucial for development and psychic structure. For Klein, objects tend to have *universal* features. In many of her theoretical statements she stresses the a priori origins of object images as: part of a phylogenetic inheritance, built onto the experience of desire itself, construed from early sensations, or derived from the drives through projections. Although different in terms of frequency and severity, the content of these objects is the same for everyone—good and bad breasts, good and bad penises, babies, united parental couples. Klein stresses the importance of real people in the child's life; however, here, too, the universal features of these real objects are most important—their anatomical characteristics as representatives of the human species, their durability in the face of phantisied attacks against them, their inevitable mixture of gratifying and depriving features. The dramatis personae within the external and internal object worlds is standard.

For Fairbairn, on the other hand, objects are highly specific and personalized. Internal objects are fashioned exclusively out of the particular features of the child's actual experience with the parents. The exciting object entices in precisely the manner in which the parent seemed to offer contact; the rejecting object attacks and withholds in precisely the manner in which the parents failed to provide contact; the ideal object provides contact precisely through the parents' actual pleasures and values. Fairbairn's structural theory parallels Sullivan's account of the formation of the self-system in this crucial respect. The personality of the child is patterned and organized in direct complementarity to the character of the parents, their actual behavior, appearances, subtle differences in responsiveness to the child, and so on. Even in light of this specificity, however, Fairbairn's categories are uniform and narrow. He sees the superordinate need of the child as the longing for emotional nurturance. "Good" objects are those features of the parents that provide for infantile dependence; "bad" objects are the features of the parents that fail to provide fully for infantile dependence. Other areas of the parents' personalities, unrelated to the issue of dependency, fade into the background. Sullivan, in contrast, considers many different features of parent-child interactions in addition to needs for early nurturance, and he extends his relational analysis beyond early infancy to later childhood and adolescence. Guntrip further narrows Fairbairn's singleness of focus in this regard; maternal nurturance for the very young infant assumes an exclusive focus and all subsequent development and psychopathology serve as reactions against failures in the earliest maternal contact.

For Winnicott the nature of the object is also constituted by early maternal provisions, but these are somewhat more varied. The child has built-in needs for: a holding environment; mirroring; the actualization of his omnipotence; the opportunity for object-usage; the toleration of the ambiguities of his transitional experience; the opportunity to console. The child's early objects are prepatterned according to the templates provided by the child's own developmental needs. However, Winnicott, like Fairbairn, also brings the particularities of the actual parents into prominence. The specific characterological features of the parents which stand in the way of their fulfilling their caretaking functions become crucial for the child; the consolation of the actual parent in terms of his or her own difficulties in living becomes a concern and a prerequisite to the child's further development.

Partially because of the difference in conceptualizing the origins and nature of objects, there is a marked difference in sensibility regarding private, personal fantasy between Klein and Winnicott, on the one hand, and Fairbairn and Guntrip, on the other. Klein and Winnicott regard the inner world of idiosyncratic fantasy as the most basic level of experiential reality and the external world of real others as a secondary, although important, realm. For Klein, phantasy, generated out of the drives themselves, constitutes the bedrock of experience; primitive phantasies dominate early development and phantasies concerning one's internal object world underlie the sense of self and the nature of reality. The internal world, in her system, provides life's greatest resources and deepest torments. Winnicott likewise stresses the depth, beauty and primacy of the most private experiences. Subjective reality is the basis for all creativity prior to the transition to the objective external world; one's deepest being is removed from contact with others, remaining forever isolate.

Fairbairn and Guntrip, by contrast, regard the inner world of internal object relations as secondary and compensatory. In their view, the child is oriented from the beginning toward contact with the parents as real people. The turn inward, the establishment of internal object relations (Fairbairn), and the regression of the ego (Guntrip) are substitutive replacements for what is missing in actual relations with the parents. Thus, although internal object relations are crucial to the understanding of psychopathology in the systems developed by Fairbairn and Guntrip, internal object relations are considered to be essentially masochistic and defensive rather than the underlying foundation and resource Klein and Winnicott take them to be.

In devising a relational model theory, the central concern of each author has been to provide a compelling and clinically useful account of the origins and development of relations with others. However, abandoning the drive/structure model as a theoretical base creates other problems which each relational theorist must address. The classical drive theory provides a way of conceptualizing the source of psychic energy, the principles upon which the mind becomes patterned or structuralized, and the phylogenetic endowment which the child brings to his experience of the world. In abandoning drive theory, relational model theorists must provide alternative solutions to these issues, and the manner in which they have approached them varies considerably.

In the drive/structure model the energy which fuels mental phenomena is drawn from transformations of drive tensions. To eliminate the drive concept is to eliminate the energy source, and a new source, or a new way of conceptualizing the problem, is necessary. Klein deals with this question by retaining the language of drives as energic forces, while changing their meanings into relational configurations. Libido and aggression become constellations of loving and hateful affects, images, and relationships respectively. Drives still fuel mental phenomena, but drives are impulses toward different relational patterns. Winnicott, although he does not address himself at length to this issue, tends to adapt a similar strategy—for example, by redefining aggression as motility or a kind of élan vital. Thus, aggressive energy becomes a relational thrust which is either facilitated by the mother or squelched, turning it into destructiveness. Both Sullivan and Fairbairn present more radical challenges to the classical theory of psychic energy. For them, the separation between mind as a set of structures and energy as the fuel which drives them is fundamentally misconceived. Mind *is* energy. For Sullivan the self is not a quasi-entity, but a dynamism, a pattern of energy transformation; for Fairbairn ego structures are energic, manifesting themselves in relational impulses.

In the drive model, the mind is forged out of the necessity for drive gratification and regulation. To eliminate the drive concept is to eliminate the basis for the patterning of mental phenomena, and a new basis for that patterning is provided by each relational theorist. For Klein psychic structure is derivative of phantasy. The world of internal objects develops out of early relational needs, and its organization, set by the predominant, recurring phantasies, underlies the individual's experience of himself and his interpersonal world. Fairbairn, Sullivan, and Winnicott all see the personality as patterned around the necessity for maintaining the best possible connection with the parents. For Fairbairn disturbances in object relations necessitate the establishment of compensatory internal objects, and these become the kernels of different components of the personality. For Sullivan the self becomes organized first for the purpose of avoiding anxious interactions with caretakers, and subsequently for maintaining levels of anxiety at a minimum. Winnicott portrays the structuralization of the self into true and false dimensions as a consequence of the child's dual need to engage the parents through the caretaking which is provided, yet to protect the self from being overwhelmed or exploited. Hence, each relational theorist derives psychic structure not from the need to regulate drive tensions but from central relational needs.

In the drive/structure model the infant is portrayed as equipped with a complex phylogenetic inheritance, both drives and innate ego capacities. These inborn, physiologically based characteristics set a prior cast to the individual's life, contributing both to character formation and to the direction in which psychopathology develops. The world of reality and actual others becomes relevant and meaningful to the extent to which they approximate (either through fulfillment or frustration) the various needs derived from the drives. In abandoning the drive concept, each relational theorist also necessarily disassociates himself from this particular manner of assigning to the body and to the physiological endowment of the infant a central role in the development of personality and psychopathology. In fact, adherents of classical drive theory often criticize relational model theories on the grounds that they constitute an extreme and naive environmentalism, viewing mental life as a simple registering of external events. In this view, relational model theories, by abandoning the drive concept, omit the central role of the body in human development and the importance of innate factors in general.

Physical sensations are the basis for all experience. The infant's life is dominated by physiological needs; bodily images and preoccupations pervade much of later psychopathology. The difference between the approach to the body in relational model and drive model theories is not in terms of *whether* the body is important, but *in what way*. Bodily needs are not viewed, as they are by drive structure theorists, as the originator of important *psychological* intentions and meanings. Bodily events and processes are regarded instead as providing a language for experience, a vehicle for the expression of intentions and meanings, relational in nature. Thus, in Klein's theory bodily tensions do not create motives which demand actions to relieve tensions; the child loves or hates, and uses bodily processes to express these motives. Fairbairn characterizes erogenous zones as "channels" to the object; Sullivan stresses the manner in which "zones of interaction" color the different experiences of the infant with the caretaker. Sullivan grants bodily tensions (as the major source of the infant's "needs for satisfaction") a prominent place in his theory. They are the major force drawing the infant into interpersonal configurations with caretakers. However, what is important psychologically is not whether such needs are gratified or frustrated but the quality of the interaction, the anxious or nonanxious nature of the relationship. Similarly, Winnicott emphasizes the importance of physical handling in early experience, not in providing specific forms of gratification but in expressing and mediating caring and responsiveness. Relational model theorists tend to regard the body not as generating independent psychological motives which shape experience and behavior but as the major medium of exchange between the infant and his or her caretakers. This is not to deny that the body manifests independent physical needs for food, oxygen, and so on, interference with which has grave consequences. For relational/structure theorists, these independent physical needs do not in themselves play a significant etiological role in shaping personality and psychopathology, whose major determinants are the vicissitudes of more purely relational considerations. "Average expectable" physical care is presumed. The human infant is viewed as an organism whose experience is fully mediated through the body and whose means of expression are limited to bodily events and processes, yet whose psychological nature is dominated by a search for connection, attachment, engagement with other human beings. It is this search that subsumes and imparts meaning to all other dimensions of human life.

Does the abandonment of the drive concept and the view of the body as the vehicle for, rather than the cause of, psychological motives suggest that in the relational/structure model all innate factors have been eliminated? Do the purer and more explicit relational theories like Sullivan's and Fairbairn's regard personality and psychopathology as a direct, unmediated product of input from others, registered on an organism that brings nothing significant to experience, a psychological blank slate?

Within learning theory, the earlier account (Skinner, for example) of all experience as a product of learning, with no contributions from innate factors, has been superseded by the concept of "prepared" or "directed" learning, in which experience is understood to register on an organism oriented with a priori sets of expectations, "wired" in a particular fashion (see Konner, 1982, pp. 26–29). Similarly, each relational theory posits, either explicitly or implicitly, a motivational thrust toward interpersonal engagement, a "drive" toward object-relatedness. Experience with significant others becomes important not simply because environmental influences are powerful and the baby is responsive but because the baby is "looking" for certain kinds of experiences, primed for specifically human engagement.

In Sullivan's principle that "needs for satisfaction" operate as integrating tendencies, in Fairbairn's assertion that "libido is object-seeking," in Bowlby's claim that the infant is preprogrammed for attachment is the common premise that the infant brings to his experience an elaborate phylogenetic endowment. However, that inheritance is understood to consist not of an array of loosely organized body-based tensions but of a complex, coherent set of interests, sensitivities, and expectations which draw the infant into human relationship. Spitz's studies (1965) demonstrated that the infant prefers the human face to all other visual stimuli. A long line of subsequent research findings have catalogued the exquisite synchrony between the infant's inborn visual, auditory, tactile preferences and rhythms and physical attributes of human caretakers as well as their intuitive responsiveness to the baby. This discovery of innate factors in the baby's experience does not pose a problem for relational model theories; rather it supports its central premise.

The child is primed for certain kinds of experience. What happens after that experience is encountered? Do relational model theorists suggest that experience, interchanges with others, are recorded in a direct, unmediated fashion? Do they presume that the account which the adult maintains of parental figures, for example, is wholly veridical, an undistorted replica of the actuality of those parents? Here too, the answer is "no." Both Sullivan and Fairbairn assume that the infant brings to his or her experience not only expectations but particular a priori principles for organizing that experience. Sullivan delineates a developmental sequence of "prototaxic," "parataxic," and "syntaxic" modes (bearing some resemblance to Piaget's stages of cognitive development) in which all experience is registered. In his theory, psychopathology is not a simple reflection of actual events; it is a complex transformation of events processed and refashioned through different perceptual and cognitive organizational patterns. Similarly, Fairbairn's account of the formation of endopsychic structures does not presume a direct transfer from actual experience to internal residues. Experience with caretakers undergoes a complex sequence of splitting and recombining operations. The content of internal objects is derived from actual experience, but experience that has been transformed according to an innately given set of organizational processes.

We have considered innate expectations and organizational principles which are fairly standard from one baby to the next. What of those innate features which vary from baby to baby? A growing body of research on temperamental differences in young infants suggests that constitutional differences are stable over time and important influences on personality development (Thomas and Chess, 1980). The drive/structure model accounts for these considerations in terms of different distributions of drive energies (and in later ego psychology, through different constitutional strengths of autonomous ego functions). Is there room in the relational/structure model for innate temperamental differences? Observations of such differences are not inconsistent with relational model premises (although they are often neglected by relational model theorists). The relational model highlights the caretakers' success or failure in meeting the infant's relational needs, in providing nurturance, bonding, a "facilitating environment." What causes failure in these efforts? Early infant researchers tend to characterize such discordances in terms of a lack of "fit" between the particular mother and the particular infant (Stern, 1977). Each baby brings to encounters with caretakers his own particular rhythm of engagement, level of activity, distinct affective and behavioral displays. Each caretaker brings to his encounter with the baby his own style and intensity of responsiveness, attention span, level of interest, anxieties, and so on. The fullest delineation of infant/caretaker interactions, the most complete relational model account, would take into consideration all these factors, viewing the relational residues of the child as a complex blend of temperamental and experiential influences continually interpenetrating each other. Discordances in these interactions would be understood to represent a lack of fit between the coparticipants.

Thus, a consideration of innate constitutional factors is not outside the interpretive realm of the relational/structure model, not inconsistent with its basic premises. However, these factors *are* the least developed area of relational structure theories. Other than Bowlby's important efforts to ground his theory of attachment in biological principles, the inherent characteristics, expectations, and rhythms of relational needs tend to be only vaguely and globally described by relational model theorists. The inherent organizational principles through which experience is coded and retained have been delineated only incompletely. The greatest area of relative omission has been in the consideration of temperamental differences among babies. Sullivan and Fairbairn both write as if the only crucial variable is the caretaker, anxious or not, emotionally available or not. They do not emphasize the extent to which the caretaker's responsiveness or lack of responsiveness is keyed to the *particular* baby's style and rhythm. For example, Sullivan traces the caretaker's anxious responses to the baby's various behaviors back to the caretaker's own difficulties in living. He does not consider that different babies might display more or less of particular behaviors which are likely to set off the caretaker's anxiety. Although they are not compelled to by the premises of their model, relational/structure theorists *do* tend to deemphasize constitutional factors and treat the character and emotional presence of the caretaker as the major determinant of personality development.

What are the reasons for this imbalance? First, the two purest relational model theories, those of Sullivan and Fairbairn, are explicitly theories of psychopathology, not general theories of personality development. Sullivan provides no account of the organization of the self apart from the need to avoid anxiety; Fairbairn provides no account of the structuralization of the self apart from the establishment of compensatory internal objects. Both blame psychopathology on parental failure. This does not imply that innate features of the child are unimportant for a general theory of human development, only that they are not a crucial determinant in creating psychopathology per se. Second, the history of psychoanalytic ideas, like that of most intellectual disciplines, tends toward broad dialectical swings. Freud's early seduction theory placed full responsibility for neurosis on molesting caretakers. His realization of the apocryphal nature of his patients' seduction "memories" led to the development of the drive/structure model, in which psychopathology unfolds from the innate recesses of the child's mind. Klein's formulations of a priori object images and relationships represent the furthest swing of the pendulum in this direction. The contributions of the relational model theorists, both of the interpersonal and British traditions, constitute a reaction to this feature of Freudian and Kleinian thought. Although the principles of the relational/structure model itself do not demand it, they tend to portray the infant as fairly uniform and innocent, with the blame for psychopathology set back once again on the parents. We expect that this slant will disappear as the influence of early infant research on relational model theory increases, with its stress on the interactive nature of temperamental and experiential variables.

Part Three

Accommodation

Thus, from the war of nature, from famine and death, the most exalted object which we are capable of conceiving, namely, the production of the higher animals, directly follows. There is grandeur in this view of life with its several powers, having been originally breathed by the Creator into a few forms or into one; and that, while this planet has gone circling on according to the fixed law of gravity, from so simple a beginning endless forms most beautiful and most wonderful have been, and are being evolved.

—CHARLES DARWIN, *On the Origin of Species*

8 Heinz Hartmann

A theory of object relations, if it is not to be phantasmagoric and mythological, must include constructs which provide for a relationship between the individual and external reality. Reality is the field within which people and things exist, and for the individual to know his objects he must have access to it. Accounting for this knowledge is a requirement for any theory that would attribute significance to relations with other people. To the extent that this influence is understood as operating from the earliest developmental eras, ties to reality must be understood as existing from the beginning of life.

Reality is thus a necessary constituent of a psychoanalytic theory of object relations. It is not, however, a sufficient one. A focus on external reality exclusively can lead to a theory that is reductionistically behavioral rather than psychoanalytic. Psychoanalysis is distinguished from other psychologies by its requirement for additional explanatory concepts to account for an inner world of process and experience through which relationships with other people are mediated and exert their influence. Freud's concept of instinctual drive was designed to serve just this theoretical function.

The relationship between a theory which takes account of reality and one which grants primary importance to object relations is further complicated by the fact that to speak of reality is not necessarily to grant particular importance to the people who exist within it. The world can be approached with broad strokes, as embodying the conditions required for human growth and survival. People in this view are relevant only insofar as they are the carriers of some of the necessary conditions; many aspects of object relations thus remain at the theoretical periphery. This is the case with the drive/structure model as Freud left it. Because motivation was understood as originating in internal processes (drives and their vicissitudes), the objects themselves entered the system only in relation to these, as facilitators, inhibitors, or targets. Despite his recognition that the prolonged period of helplessness of the human infant results in a heightened attachment to caretaking figures, Freud saw this attachment as evolving secondarily from the child's need for the conditions which caretakers can provide (Bowlby, 1958). Involvement with objects remains secondary throughout life, because the quality of the relationship itself continues to derive primarily from the demands of the operative drive.

Even in this limited sense, psychoanalysis was a long time in granting reality any substantial role in its theory of personality or of psychopathology. Once Freud discovered that his patient's account of childhood seductions were untrue, he renounced his interest in real events in favor or explanatory concepts predicated on fantasy and on endogenously determined instinctual processes. Mental life was understood as originating with drive demands; the psychic apparatus functioned, under the sway of the pleasure principle, only insofar as drive pressed toward discharge. Freud's definition of drive as a "demand made upon the mind for work" (1905a, 1915a) indicates that all behavior (ranging from diffuse motor discharge to rational action, from highly evolved technical thinking to dreams and neurotic symptoms) is motivated by the press of drive. The drives and their topographic realm, the system Ucs., occupied the interest of psychoanalytic theorists for many years. Consciousness, as one among several organs of perception, had a limited explanatory role in the system. Reality was of little interest, since the system Ucs. (and, in the structural model, the id) was understood as that part of the psychic apparatus most sheltered from the external world (see Arlow and Brenner, 1964).

With the advent and elaboration of the structural model, new problems arose concerning the individual's relationship with reality. Freud's clinical insights into the significance of unconscious defenses and the unconscious sense of guilt led to a formulation in which the ego played a greater role than it had previously in the overall psychic economy. Since the ego is that part of the mental apparatus that is in contact with the outside, Freud began to place increasing emphasis on its strength and, correspondingly, on the role of reality. In 1926 internal danger situations were understood as deriving from external ones, and a specific aspect of ego maturation (parallel to the maturational determinants of the libidinal drives) was understood to shape the experience of anxiety. In 1937 constitutional ego elements (parallel to the maturational determinants of the drives and independent of them) were given a role in the determinations of patterns of defense. The ego was gaining strength vis-à-vis the superior powers of the id.

During the last years of Freud's life, other theorists operating within the framework of classical psychoanalysis contributed to the movement toward recognition of the ego's strengthened role. Nunberg's concept of the ego's synthetic function (1930) depicted the ego as assimilating and binding together, rather than merely as driven by, the various internal and external forces acting upon it. Waelder's principle of multiple function granted the ego a powerful executive role, an "active trend toward the instinctual life, a disposition to dominate or . . . to incorporate it into its organization" (1930, p. 48). Anna Freud's (1936) volume pictured the ego as having a powerful armamentarium of defenses at its disposal in its inherent battle against the drives.

The increased interest in the ego and appreciation of its strength against other sectors of the personality were a measure of the new psychoanalytic interest in reality, in some ways a return to the interest which Freud had shown prior to the full development of the drive/structure model. At the same time, the focus on reality was furthered by the proliferation of direct psychoanalytic observations of children and of both normal and pathological child development. Freud himself had noted that the study of early childhood leads to an appreciation of the actual relationship between the child and his mother (1933, p. 120). The systematic study of children demonstrated that the outside world, particularly the world of adults in the child's environment, significantly influenced development more directly than had previously been imagined. Moreover, this influence was apparent at earlier developmental stages than had previously been assumed, that is, earlier than the time of the Oedipus complex. Anna Freud's (1936) concepts of "identification with the aggressor" and "defense against reality situations" are examples of the ideas that challenged a monistic conception of motivation as dependent exclusively on internal drives and their vicissitudes. She derives the specific behaviors constituting these defenses from specific constellations of external conditions: the aggressor who is identified with is, at least to some extent, a figure in reality; defenses against reality (for example, against the child's small size and slight power) originate with a realistic situation.

Heinz Hartmann's work originated within this context of the expanding appreciation of the role of the ego and of reality. His contributions to psychoanalysis have been discussed and appraised by many authors (Rangell, 1965; Benjamin, 1966; A. Freud, 1966; Loewenstein, 1966; Guntrip, 1971; Blanck and Blanck, 1974; Schafer, 1976). Our purpose is to consider his work from one point of view only: his contribution to modifying the drive/structure model to accommodate new information about the role of object relations. Seen from this angle, Hartmann appears as a transitional figure. Throughout his writings his concern is to provide a more significant and more immediate theoretical place for reality, and many of his modifications of and additions to existing theory are best understood in this light. The body of his work has the effect of modifying each of the classical metapsychological points of view to enhance the role of reality and of its spokesman, the ego, in the determination of human motivation. Nevertheless, Hartmann's commitment to the drive model is unwavering. As a result, his observations of the dynamic significance of object relationships are often accompanied by warnings not to overemphasize their impact as compared with that of other aspects of growth and development. His approach to reality represents a balance between the need for theoretical preservation and the need to encompass newly emerging data. Reality, painted in broad strokes, consists of a set of conditions, an ecological system with which the organism must interact.

Hartmann approaches psychological development as a problem of evolution and adaptation. His interest is in developing those aspects of Freud's theory which delineated the mechanisms that enable man to survive in his environment. Therefore, the specific contributions of significant other people in the individual's life are approached only tentatively, and then only in his later writings. But in his delineation of reality and in his depiction of man's capacity for dealing with it, Hartmann stretches the canvas on which subsequent theorists will paint the picture of the motivational role of object relationships. Without his contributions there could have been none of the later, more highly articulated integration of data concerning object relations which characterizes the subsequent history of the drive/structure model.

Throughout his career Hartmann was well aware of the radical alternatives to drive theory which were being proposed during the 1930s and 1940s by Sullivan, Fromm, Thompson, Horney, and others, and he was unwilling to follow them in abandoning a fundamental commitment to maintaining the theory of drive at the conceptual center of psychoanalysis. He argued strongly against the perspective of the culturalist school, accusing Fromm and Thompson of simplifying and abbreviating the complex structure of Freud's thinking (Hartmann, Kris, and Loewenstein, 1951, pp. 86–92). Hartmann's goal went beyond mere criticism, however; he attempted as well to incorporate their insights into the framework of the drive model. This required him to develop an umbrella concept or set of concepts to account for reality relations and for certain aspects of motivation, while leaving the essence of the classical model unaltered. Hartmann's style throughout his writings, therefore, is to add to the theory where others modified it. In adopting this approach, he set a model of theoretical accommodation which has been followed by subsequent drive theorists, notably Mahler and Jacobson.

Hartmann's personal and family background suited him well for the role of conservator and compromiser in the debate over psychoanalytic models. In the description of his biographers, the Eisslers, he was an intellectual aristocrat, with a family tradition of scientific and academic achievement dating back many centuries (Eissler and Eissler, 1964). On his father's side this tradition is traceable to the astronomer and historiographer Adolf Gans (1541–1613), who was personally acquainted with both Kepler and Tycho Brahe. Hartmann's paternal grandfather was a well-known professor of literature and a politician who served as a deputy in the German parliament after the Revolution of 1848. His father, Ludo Hartmann, was a famed historian who held a full professorship in history at the University of Vienna and after the First World War became Austrian ambassador to Germany. Hartmann's maternal grandfather, Rudolf Chrobak, was the professor of obstetrics and gynecology described by Freud in his *History of the Psychoanalytic Movement* as "perhaps the most eminent of all our Viennese physicians" (1914b, p. 13).

Hartmann's training, in addition to the then current medical curriculum, included much work in philosophy and the social sciences, highlighted by intensive study with the sociologist Max Weber. With this background, and with a personal history that included frequent contact with the outstanding scientists and scholars of the day, he developed a profound respect for and commitment to prevailing intellectual tradition. His approach to the body of Freud's theories, in which originality (certainly by no means lacking in his work) must always be tempered by a conservative or, perhaps more aptly, preservative attitude toward the past, reflects his family history and the milieu in which he grew up. Particularly evident are the influence of his father and grandfather, both intensely involved in the work of government. Much of Hartmann's writing reads like the work of a constitutional scholar. Such scholars cannot challenge the body of what has been written; the Constitution itself is a given. By interpretation of meaning and application of the "givens" to previously unforeseen or unexplored situations they can, however, significantly alter the impact of the document on which they are commenting. This Hartmann has done with Freud's psychoanalysis. A large number of his papers are entitled "Comments on" or "Notes on" one or another aspect of psychoanalytic theory, as if his contribution was aimed at explication alone. Although these commentaries do let stand the essence of the theory, their net effect is to open it to possibilities never before considered.

Psychoanalysis: A General Psychology

In its broadest terms, Hartmann's expansion of theory is served by his emphasis on developing psychoanalysis into a "general psychology" rather than a theory more narrowly limited by its focus on psychopathology. This early goal of Freud's (see *Project for a Scientific Psychology*, 1895a; see also Hartmann, 1958), had been deemphasized in light of his subsequent interest in psychopathological, and especially psychoneurotic, phenomena. The study of the oedipal neuroses, Hartmann suggests, leads to an appreciation of intrapsychic conflict as a primary etiological factor, and it highlights the significance of drive, which is a concept well suited to account for conflict (Hartmann, Kris, and Loewenstein, 1951). Thus, for many years psychoanalysis attended almost exclusively to drive, conflict, and their ultimate manifestation as neurotic symptoms. There is little concern in Freud's writings with non-pathological development and behavior; the theory lacks, especially in its earlier form, a psychodynamic of normality. Although some "normal" phenomena are considered—notably dreams, jokes, and parapraxes—they are those which can be explained by the model of neurosis. Even the personality of neurotics, insofar as it is not implicated in their symptoms, receives scant theoretical treatment.

For Hartmann, psychoanalysis has both broad and narrow objectives (1939a, 1950b). The focus on psychopathology, and consequently the almost exclusive concern with conflict, represents the narrow approach. There is an equal need, he feels, to embrace broader goals, to return to Freud's original intention of creating a general psychoanalytic psychology. Seen from the broader point of view, psychoanalysis must become a theory of the total personality; it must account for normal as well as pathological phenomena. This involves the theory in what had traditionally been the subjects of investigation of nonanalytic (that is, descriptive) psychologies, issues such as adaptation to the environment, achievements, ego interests, and the more general area of rational as well as irrational action. Hartmann sees the normal as intimately related to the pathological, arguing that "we do not feel that we can handle a patient's neurosis without dealing with its interaction with normal functioning. We feel that in order fully to grasp neurosis and its etiology, we have to understand the etiology of health, too" (1951, p. 145). It is toward this end that the study of the ego and of the individual's existence in a real world occupy the center of Hartmann's theorizing.

Hartmann employs his distinction between the two levels of psychoanalytic theory by broadening the classical approach to phenomena such as action, intellectualization, fantasy, and values. Action is not a basic concept within the traditional psychoanalytic approach because "in the study of intra-psychic conflict, action can be temporarily bracketed" (1939a, p. 86). Moreover, "structurally and genetically, action is derived from more fundamental human properties" (1950a, p. 91). Action, defined as behavior in the world of reality, is of interest from the narrow psychoanalytic perspective only insofar as it is a reliable indicator of underlying psychodynamic states of affairs. The attempt to broaden the application of the theory, requiring that more attention be paid to connections between the individual and the real world, forces action closer to what Hartmann calls the "center stage" of theorymaking. Thus, a concept of psychoanalysis as a general psychology points the way to a theory that accounts for how people get along in the world; it must become in part a theory of action. Sullivan and others influenced by the philosophical tenet of operationalism view action, because it is subject to direct observation, as the major focus of theorizing. Intrapsychic conflict, constituting a nonoperationally definable extrapolation from what can be publicly observed, is by definition excluded. Hartmann rejects this restriction, but his attribution of a central theoretical role to action does enlarge the emphasis given to the interaction between man and his outer world.

Similar considerations underlie Hartmann's distinction between the broad and narrow approaches to intellectualization (as a special instance of defense). The function of intellectualization as a means of conflict resolution (the narrow perspective) had been much studied by psychoanalysts before the appearance of his work. From this point of view, intellectualization is one of the ego's mechanisms of defense, a method of dealing with unacceptable drive demand. Interest in intellectualization would, consequently, focus on its role as cause or result of pathological processes. To this approach (the relevance of which he does not deny), Hartmann adds that intellectualization has action implications, that is has an impact on the individual's relation to reality. In addition to its function in opposition to the drives, intellectualization must be analyzed as a potentially constructive, reality-oriented approach to problems. Seen from the broad perspective of psychoanalysis, the behaviors constituting many of the mechanisms of defense may be understood as serving an adaptive function in addition to their role in conflict resolution (1939a).

Hartmann's treatment of fantasy parallels and complements his approach to intellectualization. From the narrow perspective, fantasy is construed as a regressive, pathological phenomenon (especially in adults), since it involves withdrawal from reality and abandonment of secondary process thinking. It can also be understood, however, as furthering, via detour processes, the individual's relation to reality. The use of imagery in fantasy may enable one to approach problems from a fresh perspective; it may suggest solutions that would not have resulted from more logical thought. By permitting temporary withdrawal from a reality situation which, as a result of specific pressures, inhibits problem-solving, fantasy can create an environmental "breathing space" from which one can return with new and creative adaptive possibilities. These aspects of the analysis of fantasy processes can be considered only when the broader objectives of psychoanalysis are taken into account, and they do not eliminate the need to analyze psychopathological aspects of fantasy. As with intellectualization, aspects of the process operating on one side or another of a conflict situation must be understood. Hartmann's approach does not alter this central theoretical tenet of Freud's model. Instead, it adds a complementary point of view.

The scope of psychoanalytic inquiry is broadened in Hartmann's discussion of values. These are no longer understood simply as a way of coping (via reaction formation and other defensive structures) with drive demands. They also may be understood, from the new perspective, as facilitating social cooperation and thereby serving individual or species survival. In this respect, "there are moral motivations which have the full dynamic significance of independent forces in the mental economy" (1960, p. 40). Man's needs dictate that his environment support social cooperation, and certain of the values prized by society serve that need. These values are thus the result of social (adaptive) rather than intrapsychic pressures, a view which once more opens the model to a consideration of external influence.

Psychoanalysis Redefined

The broadened approach to the scope of psychoanalytic theory required that Hartmann reconsider the definition of psychoanalysis as a science. Freud's latest definition of the field addressed its subject matter:

psychoanalysis is the study of unconscious processes (1926c). This clearly excludes some of the considerations that Hartmann attempts to introduce. Since the broad approach to psychoanalysis extends the field beyond unconscious processes, he must posit a definition that goes beyond the idea of the unconscious as a central defining characteristic. Hartmann's strategy is to produce one with no notion of subject matter whatsoever. Rather, he argues, psychoanalysis is defined by its specific scientific methodology and by three characteristics: its biological orientation; the explanatory nature of its concepts; and the metapsychological points of view. Each critically affects Hartmann's approach to theoretical change, particularly with respect to the broadened role of reality and of object relations.

The study of man can be approached from many points of view. Man is simultaneously a biological organism, a social organism, an economic organism, and so on. We have argued that Freud's drive/structure model can be, but need not be, read from a biological/mechanistic point of view. From among the possible alternatives, Hartmann makes a deliberate choice to approach man as a biological organism and to interpret Freud in this light (see the commentary of Schafer, 1976). Hartmann's endorsement of Freud's biological perspective places him in direct opposition to analysts of the interpersonal school, who were developing their critique of Freud at the same time he was working out his own theoretical vision.

As early as 1927, Hartmann formulated the view that in psychoanalytic thinking the "concept of the person is constructed much like the biological concept of the organism" (1927 [1964], p. 29). The human individual is born adapted to certain conditions, to an "average expectable environment." Other people in the child's world provide or fail to provide those conditions and are theoretically significant mainly with respect to this function. Like Freud, Hartmann derives object relations from the survival needs of the infant, from the child's need to maintain his biological equilibrium. He states: "We may not yet fully appreciate how fruitful it is that the foundation on which Freud built his theory of neurosis is not 'specifically human' but 'generally biological,' so that for us the differences between animal and man . . . are relative" (1939a, p. 28).

For Freud the central meeting point of purely psychological and purely biological concepts is the theory of instinctual drive. He frequently defined drive as a concept on the border of the psychic and the somatic (1905a, 1915a) and traced the source of drive to the body. The advent of ego psychology, however, led many psychoanalysts toward social and even sociological thinking, since the ego is derived in part from social sources and is the mediating structure for social behavior. For these theorists (the adherents of various interpersonal approaches, for example), reality is social reality, and the ego, as its spokesman, must be talked about in the language of the social sciences. Hartmann takes a strikingly different stance, criticizing the culturalists for failing to realize that "The 'biological' is neither limited to the innate nor identical with invariant traits in man" (Hartmann, Kris, and Loewenstein, 1951, p. 90). For him the ego as much as the drives is a product of biology. He argues that the study of the ego extends the biological relevance of psychoanalysis by providing a potential meeting ground for analytic concepts and those of brain physiology (1950c). Approached from this angle, the ego is viewed as the organ of adaptation, of synthesis, of integration, and of organization. It is responsible for the maintenance of homeostasis (1959) and provides the human organism with central functional control (1952). The function of control is no less biological than that which is controlled (the drives), and it is the functional and adaptational aspects of the operation of the ego that are stressed when it is approached from the biological point of view. The ego has biological roots as well, and Hartmann embraces and expands Freud's late suggestion (1937) of the constitutional nature of many ego characteristics.

The implication of Hartmann's approach for his understanding of object relations is clear in his way of conceptualizing the relationship between a mother and her infant. As he puts it, "we can characterize the relationship between mother and child as a biological relationship, or we can characterize it as a social one" (Hartmann, Kris, and Loewenstein, 1951, p. 93). One can analyze the transactions between mother and child as deriving primarily from a social bond between the two or from the child's need for physical survival (Hartmann, 1944). For Hartmann, as he brings the influence of the external world more to bear on psychoanalytic theorizing, the emphasis is always on the infant's need to adapt in order to survive. In this sense, the role of human relationships per se must always be secondary; they must be subordinated to the survival conditions which they represent. The personal characteristics of other people in the child's world remain peripheral to the central concerns of the theory.

The second aspect of Hartmann's definition of psychoanalysis is that its concepts are explanatory rather than merely descriptive. The concepts of nonpsychoanalytic psychologies can describe behavior with great precision and even elegance without providing the underlying constructs to explain the occurrence of the behavior. Psychoanalysis, by contrast, is occupied not with the description of psychic content but with what is causal, with the formulation of laws (1927; 1927 [1964]). Consequently, it approaches behavior from a different point of view than do other psychologies; its focus is not on what is descriptively similar but on that which dynamically and genetically stems from common roots (Hartmann, 1958; Hartmann and Kris, 1945). Anality, for example, is a genetic and explanatory concept which serves to establish a meaningful relationship among descriptively disparate behaviors: orderliness, stinginess, obstinacy, and reaction formations against them (Hartmann, 1934–35; Hartmann, Kris, and Loewenstein, 1951). The central psychoanalytic construct of instinctual drive is one which has explanatory power without necessarily being descriptive (Hartmann, 1948). The concept explains the occurrence of various behavioral phenomena, yet lacks specific descriptive or experiential referents.

Since by definition psychoanalysis is a science of explanation, concepts which are not explanatory must be of secondary interest. This includes what Hartmann calls the "phenomenological details" of human experience (1939a). The meaning of the relationships an individual has with other people is, as it was for Freud, determined by the biological needs and capabilities of the individual as organism. Because of this central premise the "specifically human" aspects of object relations for Hartmann must be subordinated to the theoretically primary concepts of the "generally biological." The new explanatory power given to the ego and its functions, with the concomitant emphasis on adaptation as a motivational supplement to the force of instinctual drive, remains within the framework of biological primacy, in contrast to other theorists who emphasize the specifically human aspects of ego development (Guntrip's "person ego"). Moreover, Hartmann's emphasis on the explanatory priority of biological concepts leads him to a relative underestimation of the role of the superego within the psychic economy.

Hartmann's third criterion in his definition of psychoanalysis is its reliance on the metapsychological points of view. Freud (1917b) defined metapsychology as the study of the assumptions on which psychoanalytic theory is based, and he explicitly formulated three sets of assumptions. The dynamic point of view assumes that there are forces active in the mind, at times convergent and at times opposed, and that behavior is the result of the interplay among them. The economic point of view states that the quantities of energy attached to a particular psychic tendency determine what will become of it. The topographic assumptions state that the impact of psychic events on behavior is determined by the relation of these events to consciousness.

Hartmann (1952) preserves metapsychology as the defining framework for psychoanalysis, but he argues that the advent of interest in the psychology of the ego had a major impact on each of the points of view. Dynamically, the ego is seen as stronger in its opposition to the drives. The ego for Hartmann has its own set of motives, independent of those of the id or superego, derived exclusively from the need to live in the real world. Adaptive tendencies, ego interests, and moral imperatives are motivational forces in their own right. Economically, Hartmann argues that the theory must consider not only the magnitude of energy but also its quality. The ego can "choose" among libidinal, aggressive, and more or less deinstinctualized energies to fuel its functioning, thereby increasing its range and powers. In his latest writing, Hartmann alludes to a primary ego energy, present from birth and in no way derived from instinctual drive (1955). The topographic point of view has been, to a large extent, replaced by a set of structural assumptions geared around the tripartite model. The ego is no longer viewed as a unitary structure formed as a differentiated part of the id. Within the structure ego there are a large number of hierarchically arranged functional units, interacting with each other as well as with the other psychic organizations. To the extent that a topographic point of view is retained, Hartmann attributes more explanatory weight to the operation of preconscious and conscious activity.

The impact of each of these changes is to enhance the power of the ego relative to the other psychic structures and to emphasize its independence from domination by the id. Hartmann also adds genetic considerations to his structural formulations. (These are often thought to constitute an independent metapsychological perspective which, along with an adaptive point of view, were introduced by Hartmann; see Rapaport and Gill, 1959.) The ego no less than the id has constitutional roots. Many of its functions are "primarily autonomous," in that they are not derived from the conflict between drive and reality. Others, which may originate in conflict, become "secondarily autonomous" by virtue of a change of function. The functioning of the ego is not only genetically determined by, but itself influences, the development of the id.

Motivation and Reality

Each of Hartmann's elaborations of the metapsychological points of view suggests an enhancement of the motivational role of reality conditions. Those aspects of motivation not derived from instinctual drive are to be explained largely on the basis of the individual's relationship to the external world. Hartmann and Kris state that "Psychoanalysis does not claim to explain human behavior only as a result of drives and fantasies; human behavior is directed toward a world of men and things" (1945,

p. 23; see also Hartmann, 1959). In formulating the principle of multiple function, Waelder (1930) had indicated that every action simultaneously serves both internal and external demands. However, like others of Hartmann's predecessors within the drive model, Waelder stopped short of extending this principle into a systematic theory of motivation. He concludes his presentation with the statement that "the drive for instinctual gratification [is], as a rule, the motor for what occurs" (1930, p. 52). While acceptable in the context of the narrower goals of psychoanalysis as a psychology of conflict, Hartmann's psychoanalysis in the broader sense must account as well for actions which are rational and geared toward adaptive needs, and for the rational and adapted components of all action. Here reality contributes its own contingencies; it imposes its own requirements on the individual's choice among various potential behaviors. These requirements are mediated by the system ego, which acts to translate external conditions into internal forces. (A similar statement could be made with regard to the superego, but this structure remains more closely related to the original drives than does the ego.) Different behaviors differentially reflect the influence of inner and outer forces. As Hartmann puts it, "Action may predominantly serve the ego; or it may predominantly serve the gratification of instinctual needs; it may also be mainly in the service of the superego" (1947, p.42).

In light of these considerations, Hartmann extended the principle of multiple function so that, in the case of a given behavior, primary motivational influence may be attributed to any of the psychic structures. His concept of "ego interests," including the desire for wealth, for social status, for professional success, and so on, illustrates this approach. The ego interests are not at the center of investigation for psychoanalysis in the narrow sense because "they play no essential part in the etiology of neurosis" (1950c, p. 135). They "follow not the laws of the id but of the ego. They are working with neutralized energy and may . . . put this energy against the satisfaction of instinctual drives" (p. 137). Like the demands of the id, they may be opposed by the superego (1960). Thus, not only can considerations of reality become motivating forces in their own right, but, as mediated by the ego, they can actually oppose the demands of drive.

Hartmann's presentation of the ego interests is reminiscent of but significantly transcends Freud's early discussion of narcissism and narcissistic aims (1914a, 1917c, 1923b). In Chapter 4 we showed that once the ego has captured object libido it can use this energy in pursuit of its own aims, which include the retention of feces, preservation of the penis in the face of castration fears, and, in the case of narcissistic object choice, selecting a person on the basis of being loved rather than loving. Each of these aims may, like Hartmann's ego interests, oppose and even conflict with more directly expressed libidinal impulses — the clearest example is the conflict between oedipal wishes and castration anxiety. The distinction between the two concepts goes to the core of Hartmann's theoretical emendations. When Freud first postulated the concept of narcissism (during the period when he was operating within the framework of the topographic model), the ego was not viewed as an articulated structure within the mind; rather, the term referred to something like the "self" or the "whole person." Because of its theoretically shadowy status, it was not clear just where the ego "got" the aims which it could impose on captured libido, although the aims themselves are organized around the preservation of the integrity of the body and/or the "self."

Hartmann's specification of the psychology of the ego fills in the gaps in Freud's concept of narcissistic aims. The ego is a specific structure with a developmental history partially determined by its interaction with the world of reality. The ego interests evolve out of a need to live in and to succeed in the real world; they are the motivational consequence of the impact of external reality. Although they are genetically derived from the id (and therefore linked to the earlier narcissistic aims), the ego interests have undergone a change of function that brings them exclusively under the domination of the ego. The specificity which was lacking in Freud's theory of the operation of narcissistic aims has been supplied by Hartmann. It derives from the individual's relationship to reality and is mediated by a structure (the ego) dedicated to the task of adaptation.

Hartmann's reconsideration of the motivational influence of reality requires that he examine anew the channels through which man relates to the external world. Until his very last writings Freud believed that the psychological equipment of the infant at birth consists entirely of drives (1905a, 1911a). Drives are affected by reality only insofar as the experience of frustration intrudes itself upon the infant. The aim of drive is always discharge, and so long as hallucinatory evocation of an object provides an opportunity for discharge — so long as frustration does not intervene — channels to the external world need not develop. These channels appear only under the impact of frustration-induced conflict. Viewed from the standpoint of motivation, they are secondary structures that exist only in the service of conflict resolution. This position they retain throughout the life of the individual. The impact of reality is secondary as well, a point underscored by Freud's statements that the object is the most variable characteristic of drives (1905a, 1915a). Even self-preservation, a necessity that appears to require an inherent relatedness to the external world, is carried by the drives. In his original dual-instinct theory Freud (1905a) proposed a self-preservative drive that guaranteed survival. In his later theory this function is carried by aspects of both the sexual and aggressive drives (1920a). One result of Freud's modification of his drive theory is that self-preservation disappears as an independent unit in the conceptual schema (Hartmann, 1948).

Because Hartmann's central theoretical goal is to integrate considerations drawn from the study of reality into psychoanalysis without disturbing the fundamental premises of the drive/structure model, he is faced with two major tasks: he must posit channels from the individual to the external world that are more direct than those suggested by Freud; and he must protect the drive concept from theoretical modifications drawn from the study of reality, thus avoiding the change in tone and substance which characterize the relational/structure model. Accordingly, he introduces new constructs that broaden but at the same time shelter the core concepts of the drive model. The most central of these "sheltering" constructs is adaptation. Psychoanalysis, Hartmann argues, requires consideration of "conduct adapted to reality" (1939b, p. 14). The concept of adaptation, borrowed from biology, is rooted in the need for physical survival. Three characteristics define the "well-adapted" man: he must be productive; able to enjoy life; and possessed of an undisturbed mental equilibrium. Although these criteria appear to transcend physical survival needs, for Hartmann each has a specific, biologically determined survival value. A concept of primary psychological need—that adaptation may be required for the attainment of other than physical necessities—receives little attention in his theory. Considerations such as those raised by Spitz's (1945, 1946) studies of infants' needs for maternal care and tenderness beyond the satisfaction of physical requirements are not integrated into Hartmann's concept of adaptation.

In sharp contradistinction from Freud, he sees the ego's connection to reality as beginning prior to the influence of frustration. Channels to the outside are present *ab initio*. The impact of the external world is immediate, from birth or before, and primary in the sense of not having to work through the mediating influence of drive satisfaction or frustration. This impact is guaranteed by the biologically determined fitting in of the ego and its environment (1956a).

Man is born with some existing adaptive capacities and with others that will appear as the result of maturation. This is a "generally biological" consideration for Hartmann; the same could be said of animals. Animals in fact have instincts which, because they are highly developed at the time of birth, guarantee their survival. The relative lack of differentiation of the psychic apparatus of the lower species insures that pleasure remains closely associated with self-preservative activities. Although such a connection is not entirely absent in man, Hartmann argues that the tie between the two is weaker. Both the ego and the id of man are derived phylogenetically from the instincts of animals, as products of differentiation (1950c). One consequence of this is to increase "the alienation of the id from reality" (1939a, p. 48; see also Hartmann, Kris, and Loewenstein, 1946). Drive in man comes more under the sway of the pleasure principle (it demands discharge without regard for attendant consequences), while the reality principle, with its adaptive implications, is mediated by the ego (1948, 1956a). A critical distinction between the instincts of animals and the drives of man is that only the former are capable of reaching their goal without the intervention of the structure ego (Hartmann, Kris, and Loewenstein, 1949). One consequence of Hartmann's formulation is that the drives remain as sheltered from reality as they were in Freud's system. At the same time, the process of differentiation through phylogeny results in an ego which emerges in man as a "very highly differentiated organ of adaptation" (1939b, p. 13; see also 1948, 1950c, 1952; Hartmann, Kris, and Loewenstein, 1946).

Hartmann's strategy here has been to introduce a set of functions, the adaptive capacities of the ego (more accurately, of the ego elements of the undifferentiated matrix), which from birth onward carry the weight of the individual's relationship to reality. The external world, therefore, can exert a direct influence on mental functioning from the outset of life. But this formulation allows Hartmann to retain Freud's drive theory in unmodified form: the drives still seek discharge as their aim and obey the dictates of the pleasure principle as originally defined. Motivation is thus derived from two independent sources: the (unchanged) drives which relate to reality only secondarily, and those adaptive capacities of the ego which are inherently related to the environment.

The Environment

What is the nature of the environment to which man must adapt? Here the biological and social levels of conceptualization meet in Hartmann's thought. Biological considerations, as we have seen, determine the need for adaptation, and biological mechanisms guarantee its occurrence. But the external world to which the human organism must adapt is unquestionably a social world. The framework for Hartmann's presentation of this issue is spelled out in his monograph *Ego Psychology and the Problem of Adaptation*: "the task of man to adapt to man is present from the very beginning of life. Furthermore, man adapts to an environment part of which has not, but part of which has already been molded by his kind and himself . . . Thus the crucial adaptation man has to make is to the social structure, and his collaboration in building it" (1939a, p. 31). The point of intersection of the biological and social comes in the concept that adaptation to the social environment is guaranteed by innate psychic structures, at least insofar as the environment is within the "average expectable" range. Man in this view is not quite a social animal, but he is an animal innately equipped to become part of an ecological system that has strong social ingredients.

The environment in Hartmann's theory is a limiting factor. It can prevent, without being able to encourage (except in a restricted sense to be mentioned shortly), specific developmental outcomes. It is tempting to find similarities between the concept of an "average expectable environment" and Winnicott's "facilitating environment" (1965a). Some similarities do in fact exist, particularly in a negative sense. In each case the role of the environment is most striking (from the standpoint of subsequent psychopathology) when it interferes with maturational processes. It is the differences between the concepts, however, that prove more illuminating. For Winnicott the environment generally coincides (at the outset of life) with the person of the mother, typically the "good-enough mother." This specificity constitutes a critical departure from Hartmann's perspective. In Winnicott's theory it is the task of the "good-enough mother" to respond to the biological and psychological needs of the infant in a way that will allow maturational processes to proceed without interference and, ultimately, for the true self (notably a "specifically human" construct) to emerge and to flourish. The environment in this sense actively "finds" the child and responds to him in a way that promotes a fitting together that is true to the child's innate potential. Environmental response—the specific behavioral and emotional reactions of the child's earliest objects—plays the critical role in shaping human development.

For Hartmann the environment is less personified and, at least insofar as it is of the "average expectable" kind, more passive than in Winnicott's view. The emphasis is placed not on a particular quality of responsiveness from the parents, but on characteristics that are innate in man's psychological (and biological) endowment. The fit between organism and environment is patterned essentially phylogenetically, rather than being forged for each infant in the reciprocal exchange between himself and his caretakers. Human biology (which for Hartmann includes the evolution of cultural tradition), rather than specific ontogenetic experience with people and its derivatives, carries the task of adaptation.

Hartmann's approach stops short of the relational model, since the relation to reality is not fully interactive in Winnicott's sense. Lacking a theory of such interaction, there is no way for the specific characteristics of the objects to exercise specific influence on the course of development (along the lines of Winnicott's "false self"). What can be influenced is the mode of adaptation effected by the individual. There are three possible ways of fitting in with the environment: changing oneself to meet environmental demands (autoplastic); making changes in the environment itself (alloplastic); and the intermediate course of finding a more favorable environment. But even here there is not much room in the conceptual structure for the sort of reciprocity upon which one could build a theory of motivation in Winnicott's sense. The "average expectable environment" is a "generally biological" concept; Winnicott's "facilitating environment" is "specifically human."

The most important contribution of the environment in Hartmann's sense is that it provides the conditions necessary for physical survival. The lack of these conditions — physical deprivation — can adversely affect psychological development. Within a very broad range of emotional behavior on the part of the objects, however, the environment can remain within the "average expectable" range, and will not decisively alter the developmental outcome. People in the world are important, and Hartmann holds that at birth the "most essential part of the new environment is the infant's mother" (Hartmann, Kris, and Loewenstein, 1946, p. 37). But even this importance accrues on the basis of the mother's carrying or mediating requisite survival conditions. The importance of the mother to her infant is explained in the same sentence with the statement that "she controls the physical properties of the environment, providing shelter, care and food." The environment, then, is a much broader concept for Hartmann than it is for Winnicott: "Both mother and father play a dominant role in the vicissitudes of the child's relations to reality. But I think that the concepts both of reality and of the reality principle as presented by Freud are of a far more general nature. The child's concepts of reality can be followed through the vicissitudes of object relations and conflicts. But 'the reality concept of psychoanalysis' cannot be defined by these" (1950a, p. 245n).

Pleasure and Reality

Theorists who choose to remain within the drive model are faced with the task of integrating data derived from the study of early object relations into a motivational framework predicated on the drives. Specifically, if one is committed to the view that man is motivated essentially by the pursuit of pleasure which is contingent upon the discharge of drive, one must demonstrate how reality experiences can affect the pleasure sequence. Hartmann devotes a large portion of his writing to this problem, and his model of theoretical accommodation has been followed by subsequent authors within the school of American ego psychology. The issue can be broken into two components: what is the impact of reality on the pleasure sequence? what is the impact on the pleasure sequence of specific experiences with other people?

Early in his writings Hartmann asks "why certain modes of behavior have greater pleasure potentialities than others," responding that "the psychology of instinctual drives does not completely answer this question" (1939a, p. 43). His first, tentative answer follows in the same volume, where he states that "We may have before us a relationship to the external world which, *as an independent factor*, regulates certain prerequisites of the pleasure principle (p. 44; italics ours). Here, as with his concept of the ego interests, Hartmann enters an area which had been left unexplored during Freud's period of theoretical accommodation. Once he abandoned the identity of the pleasure and constancy principles, Freud was left with considerable indeterminacy as to just what gave rise to pleasurable feelings (1924a). Hartmann introduces the possibility that reality itself may have a primary influence on the experience of pleasure. This concept has more radical theoretical implications than the use so far described, in which reality is introduced into the motivational system (via the idea of adaptation) as a supplementary construct. In this sense, reality operates as an independent partner of the drives, which continue to operate solely under the influence of Freud's regulatory principles.

The broadening of the concept of the pleasurable is given sporadic and usually sketchy expression throughout Hartmann's writings. If his work is viewed as a whole, he appears to be confronting a dilemma he cannot quite resolve. He is committed to preserving the classical viewpoint, with its emphasis on pleasure deriving from the discharge of libidinal drive, yet he is faced with observations that he cannot ignore. In 1949 he admits that "It seems unavoidable to assume that the very fact of discharge of aggressive tension is pleasurable" (Hartmann, Kris, and Loewenstein, 1949, p. 77). And in 1956 he returns to the question raised in 1939 by arguing that the development of the ego not only places conditions on how pleasure is to be experienced (via institution of the reality principle and the consequent demand that discharge be delayed), but also plays a decisive role in the determination of what is to be experienced as pleasurable. The stages of ego development, he states, lead to changes of pleasure conditions similar to those brought about by the sequence of libidinal phases. And, "there is no denying that a reassessment of pleasure values does take place, a differentiation according to their various sources, which one may well describe as a modification of the pleasure principle, or perhaps as a partial domestication of the pleasure principle—different from the reality principle in the stricter sense" (1956a, p. 248).

Characteristically, Hartmann does not underscore the extent to which these views, although instigated by Freud's own late uncertainty about the nature of pleasure, constitute a radical modification of classical metapsychology. Two new considerations have been added to the libidinal aspects of the pleasure sequence: the vicissitudes of aggressive drives and considerations deriving from reality as mediated by its psychic spokesman, the ego. The "partial domestication of the pleasure principle" by the ego allows that structure, with its intimate relationship with the external world, not only to delay discharge but also to speak to the very issue of what is considered pleasurable. The fact that discharge of aggressive as well as libidinal tension may be experienced as pleasurable allows the ego, in its executive function, to pick and choose among various pleasure-yielding possibilities. In Freud's theory, even in light of the late ambiguity, the role of reality with respect to pleasure is simply to facilitate its attainment by permitting discharge or to require its postponement through the medium of the reality principle. Reality remains outside the pleasure sequence; it is in this sense that the characterization of Freud's theory as "intrapsychic" is most accurate. Object relations a fortiori remain at the periphery of the theory of motivation.

Hartmann's insights into the inherent connection between pleasure and reality open a path to the integration of object relations into the motivational structure of the drive model. His preservative attitude toward classical theory, however, leads him to minimize the implication of his observations. In fact, he adopts a theoretical strategy in which a new "generally biological" consideration is added to the existing structure in order to account for the new data. The framework for this new explanatory principle is spelled out in *Ego Psychology and the Problem of Adaptation*: "The requirements for the survival of the species can take a form, in the mental development of man, which may be independent from the pleasure principle—and from a reality principle that is secondarily derived from it—and can even regulate the possibilities of pleasure gain. A similar assumption may be made for the needs of self-preservation . . . *The reality principle in the broader sense* would historically precede and hierarchically outrank the pleasure principle" (1939a, pp. 43–44; italics ours).

The "reality principle in the broader sense" is taken up again in 1956, where its functions are more clearly described. The reality principle in the narrower sense (in its classical usage) refers to "a tendency to wrest our activities from the immediate need for discharge inherent in the pleasure principle." In the broad sense the reality principle "indicates a tendency to take into account in an adaptive way, in perception, thinking, and action, whatever we consider the 'real' features of an object or a situation" (1956a, p. 244).

The distinction between the broad and narrow constructions of the reality principle is the distinction between reality remaining external to or entering the pleasure sequence. In its narrow sense, the external world can influence only the timing of drive discharge. In the broader sense, it enters the system by affecting that which is perceived as pleasurable. But Hartmann himself does not go very far with this distinction. Significantly, the concept of the reality principle in the broader sense does not appear in his writings between 1939 and 1956, as he was nearing the end of his career. This indicates that he was fully aware of the potential disruption implicit in the concept and did not want to follow through its implications.

The introduction of reality into the pleasure sequence leads to the second question: what impact do the child's specific experiences with other people have on the pleasure sequence? This is an area in which Hartmann's contributions can be ambiguous, and one in which his views changed over the course of his career. Quite early in his writings he indicated an awareness of the possible environmental influence on subsequent development beyond its ability simply to meet the child's physical needs, stating, "the nature of the environment may be such that a pathological development of the psyche offers a more satisfying solution than would a normal one" (1939b, p. 16). The implication of this thought, not elaborated at that time, is that specific environments, insofar as they depart from the "average expectable" kind, can produce specific psychopathological outcomes. No explanation is offered of how this may come about, although Hartmann's conceptual framework would lead to the conclusion that environmental effect must be exercised either through its influence on the adaptive behavior of the child or through modification of the pleasure conditions within the psychic economy. In fact, Hartmann made no effort to answer the questions raised by his remark for the next seventeen years. In the interim his focus with respect to object relations was on pointing suggestively to some aspects of pathologically significant interaction between parent and child, always explaining these in terms of drive theory.

In 1945 Hartmann took issue with Freud's (1937–1939) suggestion that the ubiquity of castration fears among little boys in the absence of ubiquitous castration threats must be the result of aspects of racial memory. This may be accounted for by "veiled aggression of the adult against the child," which as it appears in the phallic period is in turn dependent upon "the total attitude of the environment toward the child's anaclitic desires" (Hartmann and Kris, 1945, pp. 18–19). The role of parental attitudes, especially unconscious ones, is stressed again a year later, when he argues that deprivation of the child by the adult—for example, inhibition of a desired activity—does not necessarily lead to aggression. The unconscious attitude of the depriving parent, on the other hand, may elicit aggressive responses (Hartmann, Kris, and Loewenstein, 1946). Observations such as these have led authors such as Sullivan, Mahler, and Kohut to suggest theories in which the total personalities and specific psychopathology of the parents bear decisively on the development of the child. Hartmann rejects explanation on this level. His view that the attitude of the parent rather than the fact of deprivation elicits aggression is predicated on the idea that "One distracts a child best by loving attention. Cathexis directed toward action is thus transformed into object cathexis" (Hartmann, Kris, and Loewenstein, 1946, p. 43).

At this point Hartmann started to bring data from the study of early object relations to bear on his developmental schema. He states that "the two processes, differentiation of psychic structure and relation of the self to external objects, are interdependent" (Hartmann, Kris, and Loewenstein, 1949, p. 77). Again, "while the development of object relations is codetermined by ego development, *object relations are also one of the main factors that determine the development of the ego.*" The impact of object relations on ego development derives partly from "the psychological characteristics of the relevant figures of [the child's] environment" (Hartmann, 1950b, pp. 105, 108; italics ours). But in the same paper, Hartmann criticizes the interpersonal school for suggesting a one-sided picture of development as determined exclusively by exchanges with other people in the child's world.

As his work progressed during the early 1950s Hartmann spelled out some of the developmental influences of early object relations, especially with the mother. For example, "it appears that the nature and intensity of this relationship [with the mother] determines a large number of features in the child's subsequent development. Moreover, in some instances it has been possible to state in detail how one particular type of conflict in the mother stimulated in the child the development of a certain pattern of defense mechanism" (Hartmann, Kris, and Loewenstein, 1951, p. 92). The next year he reiterates this point, noting that "the relevance of the mother's conflicts in the shaping of the child's attitudes and defenses can sometimes be traced" (Hartmann, 1952, p. 162). But the influence of object relations is never as direct or as unquivocal as it is for other theorists; it is always mediated by their effect on the system ego and counterbalanced by biological processes of maturation as they affect both ego and drive.

It is in "Notes on the Reality Principle" that Hartmann presents his fullest statement on the impact of object relations on all aspects of the child's developing personality. Object relations, he argues, are themselves derivative of the infant's helplessness. Dependence on them "becomes an essential factor in the human child's learning about reality" and affects future development because it "is responsible . . . for typical or individual distortions of the picture of reality which the child develops" (1956a, p. 255). Other aspects of reality besides the objects have an impact on these developments, but the influence of the objects is most pronounced. Again, the influence is exercised in terms of developing ego functions, and is variable among them: perception is the least likely to be affected, language the most likely.

By influencing the child's relation to reality, people in his life can enter the pleasure sequence more directly than was possible in Hartmann's earlier formulations. Thus, "pleasure premia are in store for the child who conforms to the demands of reality and of socialization; *but they are equally available if this conforming means the acceptance by the child of erroneous and biased views which the parents hold of reality*" (1956a, p. 256; italics ours). Because the parents' distortions can have a bearing on the pleasure conditions, the personality and/or psychopathology of the parents enter the core of the child's motivational system. As a result, for example, "What the mother . . . is 'neurotically' afraid of can . . . mean 'real' danger for the child" (1956a, p. 258).

These remarks recall Sullivan's (1953) observation that the child empathizes with the mother's anxiety. It must be borne in mind, however, that Hartmann is operating out of a different conceptual system than is Sullivan. For Sullivan the central focus of the self-system is anxiety avoidance; the relationship to the anxiety of the mother is thus immediate. For Hartmann, on the other hand, the attainment of pleasure is still at the center of the theory. Even though the personal characteristics of important figures in the child's life have been brought to bear directly on the pleasure sequence, drive and its vicissitudes remain motivationally central. Moreover, Hartmann's emphasis on biological aspects of development alongside those determined by object relations leads him always to consider the role of the object as one among many influences on the child's development.

Structural and Economic Considerations

For Hartmann, as for Freud and subsequent drive model theorists, revision of the structural theory comes more easily than revision of the energic principles. This follows from the fact that the fundamental premises of the drive model—the centrality of drive itself as a motivational force, the constancy principle, and so on—are economic in nature. Therefore, Hartmann's revisions are clearest in the realm of structure. Despite his view that the ego is a "definite system" and a "structural unit" defined by the similarity of its various functions (1950c), Hartmann frequently warns against a monolithic conception of the ego (1950b), arguing that "in many instances in which we speak of 'the ego,' a differential consideration of various ego functions is indicated" (1951, p. 146). These various functions are arranged hierarchically (1939a, 1939b) and can work together harmoniously or can themselves become involved in intrasystemic conflict (1950c), for example, between defensive and nondefensive ego functions. The process of free association is one example of this hierarchical arrangement, in that one ego function (logical thought) is suspended in favor of another (the associative process). This can result in cooperation or in conflict between the two functions. Other examples of intrasystemic conflict are commonplace in analytic practice.

The idea that the ego is composed of a number of functional units, each connected in its own way with external reality, serves the theoretical purpose of strengthening the impact of the system on the overall functioning of the psychic apparatus. To employ an analogy, let us assume a legislative body which has the function only of approving or disapproving bills submitted to it by an outside agency. If this legislature always operates as a unit, its function must be restricted to saying "yes" or "no." This is the ego as originally pictured in Freud's structural model, in which it relates to the id as a "man on horseback," often guiding the id in the direction which the id wants to go (1923a, p. 25). If, however, the legislature is composed of a number of factions, each with its own concerns and willing to collaborate with or oppose the others as the situation warrants, that body will be able to demand bills more specifically tailored to its interests; the forging of a majority becomes a matter of appeasing the interests of individual factions and of various coalitions. This is the system ego Hartmann paints. Many more "points of view" are contained within the structure, and its own internecine struggles and collaborations must be considered in the shaping of any behavior.

This approach to the role of the ego is already clear in *Ego Psychology and the Problem of Adaptation*, in which Hartmann introduces the concepts of equilibrium and fitting together. Equilibrium, the harmonious functioning of various aspects of the psychic system, is one of the requisites of mental health and balance. It is necessary in four areas: (1) between drives; (2) between psychic structures; (3) between the synthetic function of the ego and other ego functions; (4) between the individual and his environment. The fourth of these we have already encountered as the concept of adaptation; it is a significant addition to the classical metapsychology. It is to the first three, which refer to harmony within the psychic apparatus, that Hartmann applies the concept of "fitting together" (1939a, p. 40). The first two, as critical aspects of smooth psychic functioning, are drawn from the work of both Freud and Anna Freud. The third, the requirement that the ego function harmoniously as a system, is another of Hartmann's additions to the theory. Moreover, as his work progressed, the requirement for intrasystemic balance was extended to embrace the many functions of the ego rather than just the synthetic function vis-à-vis all others (1951). The requirement that psychic activity satisfy the internal needs of the ego rather than just its external relations with reality and the other psychic systems (Freud, 1923a; Waelder, 1930) increases the power of the ego in the determination of all behavior.

At the risk of stretching an analogy, the picture of governmental organization can be further expanded. In the image we have suggested, the bills on which the legislature acts are submitted by an outside source and, once proposed, cannot be modified. This "outside" source in the drive/structure model is of course the id, and the "bills" are impulses fueled by the energy of the instinctual drives. Here again is an area in which Hartmann offers decisive theoretical change, although his modifications are more complex than those already mentioned.

In considering the economic point of view, Hartmann goes to the core of the psychoanalytic approach to motivation. As we have noted, this is also the one area in which he explicitly broadens the application of the metapsychological assumptions: the economic point of view is no longer concerned exclusively with quantities of energy, but with the mode of available energy as well (1953). The role of aggression as an independent source of energy and of grades of neutralized (desexualized and deaggressivized) energy is given equal weight in the theory to the role of libido. Late in his career Hartmann suggests that some of the energy available to the ego may be noninstinctual in origin, and therefore unrelated to either of the basic drives (1955). Each of these propositions, as it takes its place in the body of theory, guarantees the ego a greater latitude in the disposition of psychic energy.

With the expansion of the economic point of view, many forms of energy become available to the ego. In fact, all three psychic structures have their own distinctive energy. As early as 1948 Hartmann argues that: "we assume that once the differentiation into three mental systems has taken place, each one of these systems dispenses psychic energy . . . Of the forms and conditions of the energy used, of their origin, and their interchange, suffice it to say that the momentum to activity, the dynamic and energic aspects apply to all systems of personality, but that we find differences among the id and the ego and the superego not only with respect to their organization but also with respect to this momentum" (1948, p. 80). For a long time Hartmann remained unwilling to commit himself on the source of the various forms of energy, but he was convinced that once the ego is formed it operates with modes of energy that are independent of their origins in the id (1950c).

The question of independent energy available to the ego bears directly on the basic issue of the ego's strength against the drives. The ego in Freud's model can directly affect libido by desexualizing it; it has no such power with respect to aggression. The major thrust of Hartmann's economic contributions is to bring the quality of all modes of energy under the (partial) control of the ego. The concept of grades of deinstinctualization, which makes its first appearance in Hartmann's work, brings the ego to bear on the development and ultimate dispensation of drive energy.

Considerations such as these led Hartmann to the concept of neutralization, an expansion and reworking of Freud's theory of sublimation. Neutralization differs from sublimation in three critical respects. First, it is a continuous process rather than one called upon only under conditions of heightened drive demand; its function, therefore, is more than simply defensive. Second, neutralization involves a deinstinctualization of the two primary sources of energy, libido and aggression, rather than involving only libido as is the case with sublimation. Third, neutralization involves a transformation of the quality of drive energy itself, not merely a deflection of aim toward socially acceptable goals. (Freud's use of sublimation is ambiguous and underwent modification in this respect.)

In addition to enhancing the power of the ego, the concept of neutralization bears on the theory of the nature of drive itself. Drive possesses as an inherent characteristic the capacity to be modified by experience. Neutralized energy differs from the original energy of drive in that it is less peremptory in its demand for discharge and less instinctual in the character of its aims. Drive *develops* through the individual's relations with the external world; on this basis it acquires organization and direction (Schafer, 1968). In Hartmann's approach, while drive remains the central determinant of motivation, it can be influenced by reality.

Neutralized energy makes its first appearance in Hartmann's work in 1949 in the statement that "We are inclined to consider the contribution of neutralized aggressive energy to equipment of the ego and superego to be at least as important as that of libido" (Hartmann, Kris, and Loewenstein, 1949, p. 70). It is elaborated a year later: "Aggressive as well as sexual energy may be neutralized, and in both cases this process of neutralization takes place through the mediation of the ego (and probably already through its autonomous forestages too). We assume that these neutralized energies are closer to one another than the strictly instinctual energies of the two drives" (1950c, pp. 128–129).

In the same paper a specific use of this neutralized aggressive energy is proposed: it fuels the defensive countercathexes that ward off drive demands. This is in sharp contrast to Freud's theory of the energy of countercathexis (1915b), in which it was assumed that the energy for defensive operations is derived from cathexis withdrawn from the threatening instinctual impulse. This modification is critical in terms of the ego's strength and freedom of operation: it no longer depends for its energy exclusively on the immediately active drive. The continuous process of neutralization means that the ego has at its disposal at all times a quantity of energy with which it can oppose the demands of drive. In Hartmann's words, the concept of neutralization more adequately explains "the high degree of activity and plasticity characteristic of the ego's choice of means to accomplish its ends" (1950c, p. 132). The importance of this aspect of the use of neutralized energy is underscored in his paper on the metapsychology of schizophrenia (1953), in which failure of the capacity to neutralize aggressive energy (and therefore to build adequate defensive structures) is seen as the most significant etiological factor in the development of the psychosis.

The impact of neutralization is not felt only in situations of conflict. Many of the functions of the ego, during the course of their development, become fueled with deinstinctualized energy. Thus, "Once the ego has accumulated a reservoir of neutralized energy of its own, it will—in interaction with the outer and inner world—develop aims and functions whose cathexis can be derived from this reservoir, which means that they have not always to depend on *ad hoc* neutralizations" (1955, p. 229). The language here, in conscious parallel to Freud's metaphor in which the id is the great reservoir of libido (1923a), establishes a parallel energic system to that which is immediately dependent upon the operation of instinctual drive. We have already discussed Hartmann's concept of "ego interests," which are distinct from and can oppose drive-determined motives. In a late summary statement, he notes that "the development of ego psychology . . . broadened our views on the hierarchy of motivations" (1960, pp. 59–60). It is the concept of neutralization, and of the ego's ability to accumulate stores of deinstinctualized energy, that is the theoretical road to this broadening of the motivational system. That this modification of theoretical perspective increases the role of reality follows from the ego's intimate connection with the external world, and from its consideration of the world in utilizing its own reservoir of energy (as opposed to the id's peremptory, directionless, unmodulated use of energy).

In Hartmann's final approach to the problem of psychic energy he makes an even stronger break from the classical metapsychology than that implied by the concept of neutralization. Neutralized energy, however deinstinctualized and however much at the disposal of the ego, is genetically derived from the energy of instinctual drive. As early as 1949, however, he was unsure of the accuracy of this proposition. In a footnote to his discussion of deinstinctualization he states that "Psychic energy is here considered only in relation to instinctual drives. We do not discuss the problem of other, noninstinctual, sources of psychic energy" (Hartmann, Kris, and Loewenstein, 1949, p. 63n). A year later he returns to the problem, again refusing to take a stand: "The question whether all energy at the disposal of the ego originates in the instinctual drives, I am not prepared to answer . . . It may be that some of the energy originates in what I described before as the autonomous ego. However, all these questions referring to the primordial origin of mental energy lead ultimately back to physiology — as they do in the case of instinctual energy" (1950c, p. 130).

Five years later Hartmann does offer a possible answer to the question he has posed. Not all energy, he argues, stems from the drives, even genetically; "part of the mental energy — how much or how little we can hardly estimate — is not primarily drive energy but belongs from the very first to the ego" (1955, p. 236). In a footnote to the same paper (an indication of how tentatively he approaches the topic) he adds: "Strictly speaking, energy that from the start belongs to the ego can, of course, not be termed 'deinstinctualized' or 'neutralized.' It could be called 'noninstinctual,' and probably is best called 'primary ego energy'" (p. 240n).

We are now in a position to summarize the extent to which Hartmann's revision of the economic point of view increases the relative strength of the system ego and, as a consequence, brings reality more to bear on the psychoanalytic theory of motivation. For Freud, the ego operates exclusively with energy borrowed from the drives, especially libidinal drives; its functioning, therefore, must remain close to its instinctual impetus. With the advent of the structural model and the second dual-instinct theory, concepts such as narcissism, sublimation, and fusion loosened the connection between the goals of particular behaviors and the original instinctual aim. Hartmann continued this trend, suggesting that the ego may function with aggressive and libidinal energy of various degrees of neutralization and, finally, with noninstinctual energy that has belonged to the ego all along. By loosening its ties to specific modes of energy, the new formulation increases the ego's flexibility and the latitude of its operation: it no longer depends so heavily on the demands of the id (and the superego) as it did in Freud's model. This enhances the role of the ego as the servant and spokesman of reality; as the ego gains in strength, the motivational impact of reality increases vis-à-vis the impact of the drives.

At the same time as he expanded the framework within which reality can influence the characteristics of drive, Hartmann reaffirmed the remoteness of the id from reality. The contradiction implied, however, is more apparent than real, and is best understood as an expression of his preservative approach to the drive/structure model. The concept of neutralization allows him to retain Freud's drive theory in its genetic aspects, while integrating the impact of reality into the dynamic perspective. With the exception of primary ego energy, in Hartmann's theory all motivation continues to *originate* with the innate instincts. At the same time, the theory of neutralization became the model for later, more substantial modifications of the theory of drive by authors whose intent was preservation of the classical model. Jacobson's work increased the impact of the "object world" on the drives (even genetically) by holding that reality experience is partially responsible for the bifurcation of initial undifferentiated energy into libido and aggression (1964). Kernberg further pursued this strategy, arguing that libido and aggression themselves are constructed from building blocks consisting of good and bad experiences with other people (1976). Each of these theorists preserves ties with the drive model by retaining the motivational primacy of drive, but each takes a sequential step toward accommodation by increasing the impact of reality on its origins and ultimate characteristics. Hartmann's concept of neutralization opened the door for this particular approach to accommodation.

The operation of grades of neutralized energy available to the ego underlies Hartmann's concept of the primary and secondary autonomy of many ego functions (1950c, 1955; see also the prefiguring of these constructs in 1939a). His presentation of these ideas precedes and is clearer than his revision of their underlying economic aspects, the result of his realization that revision of the energic model of psychoanalysis posed more of a challenge to the fundamental premises of the drive model than did the suggestion of functions which operate outside the influence of psychic conflict.

The apparatus of primary autonomy are those which function independently of conflict from birth onward; secondary autonomy applies to functions which originate in conflict but which can, through change of function, come to operate independently of it in the course of development (1950c). Secondarily autonomous functions operate with neutralized energy, while the apparatus of primary autonomy are fueled by "primary ego energy" (1955). All ego functions, including those which are primarily or secondarily autonomous may, under a variety of circumstances, become involved in conflict situations—a development conceptualized from the economic point of view as deneutralization.

Hartmann first approached the problem of what he later termed autonomous functioning in 1939. His formulation in *Ego Psychology and the Problem of Adaptation*, while it does not encompass the later economic considerations, offers insight into the way in which he introduces reality as a motivational factor complementary to the drives. In this monograph he postulates the "conflict-free ego sphere," along with its developmental forerunner, the undifferentiated matrix of ego and id. Autonomous ego development, he argues, "is one of the prerequisites of all reality relations" (1939a, p. 107). The elements of the conflict-free sphere present from birth include perception, memory, motility, and association. These apparatus, which "serve to master the external world" (p. 50), follow their own maturational course. They mature in a fashion parallel to the maturation of the drives and independent of the conflicts arising from the drives. Hartmann thus generalizes Freud's (1926a) schema for the specific ego function of anticipating danger (see Rapaport, 1958).

The earliest root of the conflict-free ego functions is the undifferentiated matrix of ego and id. Hartmann disputes Freud's view (somewhat modified in Freud, 1937) that the psychic equipment of the infant at birth consists entirely of drive. The functions of the ego do not evolve out of the id; rather, ego and id differentiate out of a common source that contains the elements of both systems. This modification of the structural point of view leads to the conclusion that development is not a simple matter of the organism turning to reality only when hallucinatory gratification of drive demand fails to be experienced as pleasurable (Freud, 1911a). Now, channels relating the infant to reality exist from the outset and follow their own maturational course.

A specific developmental line leads from the ego elements of the undifferentiated matrix to the apparatus of the conflict-free sphere. This latter term is proposed to cover "that ensemble of functions which at any given time exert their effects outside the region of mental conflicts" (1939a, pp. 8–9). These functions provide Hartmann with the ongoing connection between the individual and reality. Although they typically operate with neutralized or primary ego energy, they may become involved in conflict and may also become the precursors of later mechanisms of defense (1950c, 1952, 1953; Hartmann, Kris, and Loewenstein, 1946).

Nowhere is Hartmann's strategy of introducing new concepts to supplement and preserve existing drive model theory clearer than in his concept of the "preconscious automatisms." Borrowed from somatic observations, the automatisms introduce into the motivational system a level of repetitive behavior that functions at least relatively independently of both the pleasure principle and the repetition compulsion (see Hartmann, 1933). These are behaviors that operate largely outside the influence of drive. (Early in his theory, when Hartmann was dealing with these issues, he had not turned his attention to the economic point of view. These observations are among those that led him to his later revisions.)

What motivates these behaviors? From the considerations already advanced, it is clear that non-drive derived motivation must stem from the individual's relationship to reality, from the propensity to adaptation. Indeed, Hartmann characterizes the automatisms as "under the control of the external world," arguing that they are "the lasting effects of adaptation processes" (1939a, p. 92). Their place in the psychic economy is to function as a "guarantee of reality mastery." This construction postulates direct motivational impact from reality. In this sense it is reminiscent of Anna Freud's view that defenses can be motivated by external as well as by internal (drive derived) threats, but represents an even more sweeping departure from the earlier view by invoking reality in a manner that transcends conflict entirely.

The refinement of the structural model, which occupied so much of Hartmann's attention, raised serious questions about Freud's concept of narcissism. As Hartmann notes (1950c), Freud defined narcissism as the libidinal cathexis of the ego at a time when he was working with the topographic model. The ego within that model was vaguely defined; it referred generally to the "whole person," or the "self." The more specific definition of the later model, in which the ego was viewed as one discrete system among the three that compose the psychic apparatus,

changed the apparent meaning of narcissism: it no longer referred to investment of libido in the self as opposed to in objects, but to the
cathexis of a particular mental structure. This deprived the concept of its
clinical meaning.

Hartmann accordingly undertook a redefinition of narcissism: within
the structural model it is to be understood, he argued, as the libidinal
cathexis of the self rather than of the system ego. As with many of his
contributions, this reformulation simultaneously modified and preserved existing theory. It changed the theory by bringing a concept of
the self (seen in interaction with objects) into the classical framework.
This in turn opened the way for future theorists (Jacobson, 1964; Kernberg, 1976) to erect structures in which the exchange between what
Jacobson calls "the self and the object world" are of central motivational
importance. Hartmann's view is preservative, however, in that he
defines the self as a *representation*, an experiential construct parallel to
and constructed in the same way as object representations. Because the
self is experiential, it remains a descriptive concept. In light of Hartmann's definition of psychoanalysis, in which the distinction between
descriptive and explanatory concepts plays a critical role, his use of the
self keeps it on the theoretical periphery. The explanatory (and therefore
central) concepts of psychoanalysis are still the drives and the "classical"
structures.

In pointing to the conservative aspects of the new approach, Kernberg
notes that "Hartmann in effect removed the 'self' from metapsychology"
(1982, p. 898). We agree, and suggest that he did so at least partially in
response to contemporary theorists of the relational model who were
bringing the concept much more into the heart of their theoretical
models. (This alternative usage, clearest in the writings of Sullivan,
Horney, Fromm, and Winnicott, was developed more fully later by
Guntrip and Kohut.) Hartmann's strategy is preservative in another area
as well: although he changed the object of narcissistic investment from
the ego to the self, narcissism still represents the libidinal cathexis of
something, and Freud's original energic framework is retained.

In his published writings Hartmann devoted relatively little attention to
clinical practice. However, his perspective on the process of analytic interpretation and on the therapeutic action of psychoanalysis follows consistently from the general theoretical approach we have outlined. The
essential goal of psychoanalysis remains for Hartmann, as it was for
Freud, "capturing the repressed" (Hartmann and Kris, 1945). But to
this aim of making the unconscious conscious a contemporary element is
added, deriving from the increased importance attributed to the

organizing function of the ego. It involves a revision and regulation of processes of adaptation and fitting together, with all the biologically significant consequences that this implies.

For Hartmann, psychoanalysis as a therapy not only interprets drives and their derivatives (makes the unconscious conscious) but acts on the contemporary adaptive and synthetic organization of the ego. Reality plays a greater role in therapy, a development which, according to Hartmann, follows from Freud's derivation of neurotic from real anxiety and from Anna Freud's focus on the significance of conflict with reality (Hartmann, 1951). However, just as in his developmental schema the initial relation to the external world (the state of adaptedness) is not a relation to another person as such, so the contemporary impact of the analytic process (and of the analyst) is not personal. Rather, the impact is mediated by its effects on the adaptive and organizing components of the structure ego. Hartmann does describe psychoanalysis as "a theory of self-deceptions and of misjudgments of the external world" (1939a, p. 64), but he does not mean to imply that such misjudgments are to be corrected experientially within the transference. In fact, transferential reliving of the past is therapeutic only insofar as it operates in the service of subsequent insight (Hartmann and Kris, 1945). Self-deceptions and misjudgments are to be elucidated in the analytic process, and new connections (a new level of organization and synthesis) are to take their place. Analysis acts upon and modifies the judging apparatus of the ego, and thereby facilitates the adaptive process. But the analytic setting does not constitute an object relationship in the full meaning of the term, and Hartmann rejects views such as Strachey's (1934) that provide a framework for some experiential reworking of transference distortions through the new relationship which is established with the analyst. So, while the experience of analysis is seen in broader terms than it had been by earlier theorists, with consideration given to the contemporary operation of the ego and its revision, Hartmann stops far short of approaching the process in relational terms.

Between Two Models: A Commentary

Hartmann's attempt throughout his writings to integrate new insights into the conceptual framework of psychoanalysis while preserving the essence of the drive/structure model enabled him to make crucial contributions to the evolution of the theory. It also created a series of problems. We have shown that the "broader" and "narrower" conceptions of psychoanalysis allowed him to introduce new theoretical structures to account for normal development and for adaptive behavior, while retaining the centrality of conflict (and the underlying theory of drive) in the explanation of psychopathology, and especially of neurosis. This method of letting stand existing theory "as far as it goes," while introducing new concepts to explain new observations, prefigures a strategy recently adopted by Kohut. In Kohut's work the "classical" oedipal neuroses are explained adequately by the "classical" drives and structures, while the "new" narcissistic personality disorders require a "new" conceptual psychology of the self. Similarly, Hartmann introduced a schema for the explanation of adaptive and other "normal" phenomena which, being largely outside of the realm of conflict, is quite different from the system which accounts for neurosis.

This solution raises a serious conceptual problem. A central tenet of the psychoanalytic approach has always been that health and neurosis (although not necessarily psychosis) are points on a continuum. If psychoanalysis is to be a truly general psychology, it must have a theory that accounts in unified fashion for phenomena throughout this continuum. Hartmann's theory fails in this regard, because the drives and the conflict to which they give rise constitute explanatory concepts that are adequate to one point on the continuum (neurosis) but do not fully explain another point (normal development). Hartmann is unwilling to take the step that might resolve this difficulty—bringing the external world (relations with other people) into more intimate connection with (pathogenic) intrapsychic conflict. He makes an effort in this direction when he brings object relations into the pleasure sequence, but he stops short of a full appreciation of the implications of this step for the theory of drive itself. Following the implications of this line of inquiry could lead to fundamental change in the hypothesized nature of drive (that it is pleasure seeking and at most minimally influenced by experience). Hartmann's interest in conserving classical theory makes him unwilling to commit himself to such change.

A related difficulty arises in connection with Hartmann's decision to treat psychoanalysis as a biological science, a decision which leads to the analysis of development as determined ultimately by the organism's need for physical survival. He insists that psychoanalysis is a "generally biological" rather than "specifically human" discipline. In distinguishing between man and animal, Hartmann cites three differentiating characteristics: insightful behavior, language, and use of tools. This distinction is problematic: even to the extent that these characteristics do differentiate man from animal, they merely suggest phylogenetic advances in alloplastic capacity that is relative. They are, that is, precisely those differentiating characteristics that are "generally biological." Clearly, there are other "specifically human" attributes not shared by animals, including the ability to embrace abstract ideals and values, artistic creativity, the setting of goals that are beyond biological survival, and so on. Hartmann has difficulty integrating these characteristics into his system: the strategy of supplementing Freud's model with an adaptive perspective in some ways narrows the hermeneutic approach of his theory.

Let us take as an example his discussion of the preconscious automatisms. The automatisms are "musts" for the ego, and the healthy ego "must . . . *be able to must*" (1939a, p. 94; italics in original). It is in this context that Hartmann quotes Martin Luther: "Here I stand—I cannot do otherwise." This he offers as an example of a human characteristic, one of the "relatively stable reaction-forms which are not reconsidered at every occasion" (p. 94). A statement such as Luther's, however, can only be understood as one which is made in the context of consideration and reconsideration. Such principled stands are meaningless if viewed as anything other than the highest acts of human consciousness; to attribute them to the automatized functioning of the preconscious robs them of their value to the individual making them, as well as of their inspirational potential for others. When Luther says "I cannot do otherwise," he is not talking about un-reconsidered action; he is saying that he cannot do otherwise and remain true to himself. It is hard to encompass this issue of truth to oneself within a framework in which motivation is based so heavily on adaptive needs.

Luther's statement is not adaptive in the conventional sense of the term, nor can it be adequately derived from the press of drive demand. Hartmann was aware of this area of difficulty in his theory. It is in the concepts of equilibrium, and especially of fitting together, that he opened the way for a new and more satisfactory explanation. That he left to others the task of applying his framework to such issues is the result of his continuous attempt to keep theoretical change to a minimum. But the framework *is* suggested in Hartmann's assertion that there must be a superordinate function that coordinates the process of adaptation and fitting together:

> If we encounter—as we do in man—a function which simultaneously regulates both the environmental relationships and the interrelations of mental institutions, *we will have to place it above adaptation in the biological hierarchy*: we will place it above adaptive activity regulated by the external world, that is, above adaptation in the narrower sense, but not above adaptation in the broader sense, because the latter already implies a "survival value," *determined both by the environmental relationships and the interrelations of the mental institutions*. (1939a, pp. 40–41; italics ours)

This statement recalls Hartmann's argument earlier in the same monograph that a "higher ego function" determines the choice among the three potential modes of adaptation (alloplastic, autoplastic, and seeking a new environment). For many authors of the relational model (Winnicott, Kohut, and Guntrip, among others), considerations such as these require a concept of the self as an explanatory supplement to, or replacement of, the drive/structure model. Such a structure serves just the supraordinate regulating function to which Hartmann's remarks point.

Luther's "Here I stand" is an excellent case in point. The statement simultaneously embraces and transcends considerations of adaptation in the cause of fitting together (internal harmony and truth to oneself). The search for this inner harmony and balance, regardless of the consequences for a narrowly defined adaptation, determines Luther's stand. It is that most "specifically human" of actions—one man's solution to what Lichtenstein (1977) calls "the dilemma of human identity." Hartmann's insistence on the organismic approach limits his potential contribution to the problem he so insightfully raised. The structural ego, even enhanced by its synthetic function and its executive powers, and even granted a certain amount of independent energy, is too narrowly based a concept (particularly in terms of its close relation to the drives, on the one hand, and the problem of physical survival, on the other) to provide the breadth of integrative capacity required. More specifically, no structure so near to regulation by either the pleasure principle or the repetition compulsion can satisfactorily account for the phenomena of fitting together, especially insofar as this is valued above even survival.

In light of these considerations, Hartmann emerges as a theorist caught between two models. His desire to maintain the classical model inhibits his attempt to integrate new considerations into the framework of psychoanalysis. These issues reemerge in his consideration of art, which Hartmann sees as bearing analysis from the adaptive point of view. Thus, "evolution takes two courses: one leads to rational (and ultimately to scientific) representation, the other to artistic expression . . . Art is certainly not a mere archaic residue." The perceived value of art has two roots: it "gives pleasure and is dependent on instinctual drives," and it has a "normative, ordering element" (1939a, pp. 77, 78). Art serves the demands of both id and ego. It not only gives pleasure but provides varied possibilities for synthetic solutions (compare Kris, 1952). Hartmann's view of the function of art thus expands and transcends Freud's theory that art serves to reconcile the pleasure and reality principles (1911a). Art is now given roots not only in the conflicting demands of drive and of an antagonistic external world, but serves as well the conflict-free adaptation to the world.

Here again, however, we encounter the same kind of difficulty found in the consideration of Luther's statement. Surely Hartmann's remarks on the adaptive value of art are relevant. But it strains our everyday, intuitive understanding of the experience of art, as creators or appreciators, to reduce the experience to such constructs, even supplemented by a concept of drive satisfaction. Where does the theory account for the experience of being elevated by an encounter with a work of great beauty, of being awed by the creative potential of our fellow men? The dichotomy between art and science is, from one point of view, not so strict as Hartmann would have it. One can be awed, in the artistic sense, by an encounter with scientific creation so intricate in its architechtonic and so elegant in its construction that it becomes a thing of great internal beauty. Einstein's relativity theory, not to mention Freud's psychoanalysis, can evoke such responses. The works of modern technology could be analyzed for their impact along such lines.

To understand art as more than an "archaic residue" is certainly an advantage of Hartmann's modification of psychoanalytic theory. However, here as before he has no structure to account for what is most "specifically human" in the experience of art. It may not be extravagant to assert that a major distinction between man and the subhuman species is that man alone is capable of elevation as a consequence of the experience of something greater than himself. This elevation must transcend both drive-derived pleasures and adaptive value. It must be a consequence of the encounter with an expression of the limits of human potential (thus the similarity to scientific expression). As such, it must be the work of the "higher ego function" or the superordinate function that simultaneously regulates both adaptation and fitting together. But Hartmann's theory can only point the way to these functions. Art is a "specifically human" creation, and a "specifically human" theoretical structure must be devised to account for it adequately. Hartmann lacks a precise theory of this function; his conceptualizations can only be suggestive.

This becoming one instead of two was the very expression of his ancient need. And the reason is that human nature was originally one and we were a whole, and the desire and pursuit of the whole is called love. —ARISTOPHANES, in Plato's *Symposium*

9 Margaret Mahler

The inner experience of the human infant, although it must forever elude direct observation, is by general consensus unorganized and chaotic. The child is born into a world perhaps best characterized by William James's phrase as a "blooming, buzzing confusion." He begins life in an environment that envelops him, one that he is only minimally capable of understanding or transforming. Psychoanalysts have characterized this early stage of life in different terms, as autoerotism (Freud, 1914a); primary narcissism (Freud, 1914a; Hartmann, 1950); absolute dependence (Fairbairn, 1952); and embeddedness (Schachtel, 1959). Each of these terms derives from a complex set of theoretical premises. Each addresses the phenomenon of an unorganized, undifferentiated individual living in a turbulent and unpatterned world.

Within a relatively short time, the infant becomes a child with a unique personality. He is an individual living in a world that, within limits, he has already structured in ways that make it comprehensible to him. He experiences in his own way; he reacts in his own way; he acts in his own way. He has, in short, become a person.

The task of the psychoanalytic developmental theorist is to chart the infant's path from formlessness to form. In common with all mapmaking attempts, certain choices must be made a priori. The cartographer must choose among mapping political boundaries, topographical features, climate, transportation facilities, and so on. No one map can contain all the information that might be needed. Equally accurate maps designed to different needs may look nothing alike. Some, drawn for specific purposes, do not even look like maps to those unfamiliar with their use.

Psychoanalytic developmental maps depend no less on underlying assumptions than do the products of cartographers. Freud's early developmental approach, organized around the maturational unfolding of libidinal stages (Freud, 1905a; Abraham, 1908, 1924), was predicated on the constancy and pleasure principles. The psychic apparatus was assumed to exist for the purpose of lowering the tension of drive, and drive discharge was assumed to explain pleasurable sensations. Given these a priori conceptions, it follows that the developmental map should be organized around shifts in the prevailing mode of discharge, in the predominant mode of experiencing pleasure. The theory of psychosexual stages charts this movement and is understood to form the basis of all emotional development.

The crucial movement mapped by the theory of libidinal stages begins with pleasure experienced autoerotically and ends, if successful, in the capacity for genital pleasure with an appropriate heterosexual partner. The critical event in this progression is the Oedipus complex; its successful resolution leads to the child's movement away from his earliest ways of attaining pleasure. Pleasure is no longer possible only with the original, archaic objects, self and family. The child is free to seek satisfaction from new, realistically attainable sources. This is both a loss and a gain. It is a loss because the child must realize that the original objects are not available as he once thought, or wished, they were. It is a gain because he is free to pursue what is new and good, and to pursue it in a way that is true to his own developing personality. If we are predicating a developmental map on the organizing principle of the pleasure sequence, the resolution of the Oedipus complex represents the point of separation and individuation.

The limitations of the Freud/Abraham theory of libidinal development are not to be found in the terrain it attempts to map, nor in the essential story it is designed to tell. They are to be found in the organizing principle of the map itself. Defining mature individuality as the achievement of genital primacy is like locating Chicago in terms of its relationship to a series of air navigation facilities. Doing so is not inaccurate but, unless we are airplane pilots, it probably does not tell us as much about Chicago as we would like to know. Similarly, the account of the child's movement from formlessness to form in terms of an underlying sequential unfolding of libidinal stages seems to many recent theorists to leave out a great deal that is crucial in early development. Theorists operating purely within the relational model reject the organizing principle of the pleasure sequence entirely, stressing instead the unfolding of new modes of relatedness to others. Theorists loyal to Freud, those who accept the motivational centrality of pleasure, have felt the need to add to it in the construction of their own developmental maps. Freud himself added supplementary concepts such as the shaping of psychic structure through identification and the sequence of danger situations, each of which expanded the original approach while remaining at least partly dependent on drive and its vicissitudes. Heinz Hartmann accelerated this theoretical strategy by including in his map the "problem of adaptation," which addresses the maturation and development of the individual's capacities to relate to a broadly sketched "reality." Theorists following Hartmann within the tradition of American ego psychology have attempted to fill in the concept of "reality" in much clearer detail, yet, like Hartmann, without losing sight of the role of pleasure-seeking.

Probably the most influential follower of Hartmann's strategy of expanding the drive model to encompass new dimensions of psychological development is Margaret Mahler. Building on Hartmann's schematic framework, Mahler emphasizes the *personal* aspect of reality relations. The "problem of adaptation" in her work is specifically construed as coming to terms with the *human* environment, a focus which Hartmann considered but ultimately rejected as too narrow. For Mahler, the benchmark of successful development is not the establishment of genital primacy following the resolution of the Oedipus complex. Instead, she points to a developmental movement from embeddedness within a symbiotic matrix of child-mother to the achievement of a stable individual identity within a world of predictable and realistically perceived others. She terms this process "separation-individuation" or, in her most recent formulations, "psychological birth." Thus, the organizing principle of Mahler's developmental map is based on the relations between the self and its objects, but it is a focus which is backed up with explanatory principles derived from classical drive theory.

Mahler's contributions occupy a crucial and paradoxical position within the history of psychoanalytic ideas. Her account of the child's immersion in symbiotic fusion with his mother and of a gradual, halting emergence from that fusion into independent selfhood has provided a generation of analytic theorists and practitioners with a vision of the essential struggles of childhood which is quite different from Freud's. Her child is less a creature struggling with conflictual drive demands than one who must continually reconcile his longing for independent, autonomous existence with an equally powerful urge to surrender and reimmerse himself in the enveloping fusion from which he has come. Mahler's account has a simplicity and lyrical power which has made it perhaps the most compelling vision of early childhood since Freud's depiction of the Oedipus complex, and the concept of symbiosis has been embraced not only by psychoanalysts but also by literary critics and philosophers of love (see Bergmann, 1971).

Mahler began her career in Vienna as a pediatrician; the observational basis of her work has always been the normal and pathological behavior of children. This background, allowing the observer access to personality formation and the evolution of psychopathology *in statu nascendi*, before it has been internalized and structuralized, leads naturally to an emphasis on the transactional aspects of growth and development, since it is precisely the transactions between the child and others that are being observed. Indeed, in her earliest English language papers, written shortly after her arrival in the United States in the late 1930s, Mahler stressed the importance of conscious and unconscious parental attitudes toward the child as forces in both normal and pathological development. The neuroses of childhood (Mahler, 1941; Mahler [Schoenberger], 1942), normal ego development, and the early expression of affect (Mahler, 1946) are all described as resultants of the interaction between the needs of the child and the personalities of his parents, particularly his mother. Many of Mahler's early descriptions are similar to ideas presented in Sullivan's interpersonal psychiatry: the child empathizing with the anxiety of his mother; the child's capacity to elicit tenderness from his caretakers; the child's molding himself to the expectations and assumptions of his parents, and so on.

There is, however, a fundamental tension in these early works between observation and explanation, between what Mahler sees and how she accounts for what she sees. She observes the paramount importance of the parents in their interactions with the child; she derives that importance from the parents' role as objects of the child's libidinal and aggressive drives. The function of the parents, in Mahler's classical metapsychological account, is to "give the child the object-related opportunity for channelization, i.e., utilization and amalgamation of his love and aggressive tendencies" (1946, p. 47). Thus, while the parents' personalities are understood as having considerable impact on their child's development, their influence is mediated through and made possible by their function as "objects" in the classical sense. The tension between relational observations and drive explanations makes it necessary for Mahler to bend the classical framework to contain her new perspective.

From Autism to Individuation

Mahler's original interest in the child's earliest object relations derived from her study of the severe psychopathology of childhood. Her concepts of autistic and symbiotic psychosis refer first to a disorder in which there is an inability to form a nurturing relationship with caretaking figures, second to a condition in which the child is unable to move away from that relationship (Mahler, Ross, and DeFries, 1949; Mahler, 1952; Mahler and Gosliner, 1955). From the study of these conditions she generated her vision of the normal child's developmental experience. As is true of any theory that developed over a number of years, Mahler's characterization of the main features of development have undergone considerable changes and revisions, particularly with regard to the timing and characteristics of specific subphases. Our account is drawn from her most recent systematic formulations of the process (Mahler, Pine, and Bergman, 1975).

The normal autistic phase. During the first several weeks of life the neonate seems relatively oblivious to all stimulation, with periods of sleep far outweighing those of arousal. Mahler characterizes this phase as "autistic" and infers that the infant is functioning as a closed system, at considerable remove from external reality. Freud (1911a) had argued that the infant's earliest protection against environmental impingement, which cannot be handled by the rudimentary psychic apparatus, is provided by the fact that the sense organs (the periphery, in structural terms) is initially uncathected and, therefore, inoperative. Channels connecting the infant to the external world are unawakened, not yet functional. The infant is concerned only with the satisfaction of its needs, with tension reduction, and operates according to the principle of hallucinatory wish fulfillment rather than locating possible sources of satisfaction in the external world. The newborn lacks the capacity to be aware of, much less to relate to, external objects; his experience is limited to the maintenance or disruption of physiological homeostasis, to a sequence of frustration and gratification that can equally well be "real" or hallucinatory.

The normal symbiotic phase. At the age of three to four weeks, a physiological maturational crisis occurs in which the infant shows increased sensitivity to external stimulation. This enhanced responsiveness brings with it a dim awareness of the mother as an external object, particularly with respect to her ability to aid in tension reduction. The specific smiling response to the gestalt of the human face appears with the emergence of this phase. Cathexis is now directed toward the periphery rather than exclusively inward, but "the periphery" has acquired a new meaning: it is the periphery of a "dual unity" which, from the observer's point of view, includes both the child and the mother. From the infant's perspective, there is no differentiation between the two individuals comprising the symbiotic unit; he behaves as if he and mother are a unitary, omnipotent system.

During the normal symbiotic phase the infant begins to organize experience. This is particularly assisted by maturation of the primarily autonomous functions of the ego, especially memory. Experience is initially categorized as "good," equivalent to pleasurable, and "bad," equivalent to painful. These are related, as in the autistic period, to the maintenance of homeostasis. Islands of "good" and "bad" memory traces form within the undifferentiated matrix of ego and id.

From the perspective of object relations, the autistic phase is "objectless," the symbiotic phase "preobjectal" (Mahler, Pine, and Bergman, 1975). In terms of the distribution of drive energy, both fall within Freud's epoch of primary narcissism. The symbiotic phase is critical, however, for the evolution of one's subsequent sense of the self and others, for it is the period during which the experiential precursors of self and object are laid down. This is the first phase in which, for Mahler, it makes sense to talk of the infant in psychological terms.

The differentiation subphase. From four or five months until ten months, the first of the phases of separation-individuation begins with the process Mahler calls "hatching." During this phase, the infant appears for the first time to be more or less permanently alert when awake. His earlier tendency to mold himself to his mother's body gives way to a preference for more active, self-determined positions. The infant begins to explore mother during this period, pulling at her hair, clothes, eyeglasses.

Somewhat later during the differentiation process the infant begins to search beyond the mother-child orbit, seeking out and responding to stimuli coming from a distance. There is a pattern of scanning the world outside and checking back to the mother, thus establishing the difference between "mother and other." Eventually during the differentiation subphase the infant will initiate the first breaks from passive "lap babyhood"; he will slide from his mother's lap to the floor, but will remain near her feet.

While these behavioral developments are taking place, the evolving capacities of the ego are bringing with them significant changes in the child's relationship to the object world. The child acquires the capacity to distinguish between contact perceptual and internal sensations; this permits for the first time a clear sensory discrimination between self and object. Later in the differentiation subphase the established ability to distinguish mother from other allows consistent discrimination among external objects. The principal indicator of this newly acquired ability is the appearance, at the age of six months, of stranger anxiety.

The practicing subphase. Mahler delineates two distinct periods of this second subphase of separation-individuation: early practicing, and the practicing subphase proper. Each, like the preceding phases, is ushered in by the maturation of a new physiological capacity. The earlier practicing period, beginning at about the age of ten months and gradually overlapping the differentiation subphase, begins with the dawning of the child's capacity for quadruped locomotion: crawling, paddling, climbing, and so on. The baby is now able to move some distance away from his mother, although the mother is still treated as a kind of "home base," to be returned to for what Mahler calls "emotional refueling." The child's interests at this stage spill over from the mother to the inanimate objects of the world, one of which may become a transitional object in Winnicott's (1965a) sense. Interest in the mother, and in her continuous availability for refueling, still takes precedence over interest in the world of things.

The early practicing period is the setting for three crucial developments in the establishment of separation and individuation. There is an increase in body differentiation from the mother following the ability to distance oneself from her physically. At the same time, a specific bond is formed between baby and mother based on her capacity to provide the required emotional refueling. Finally, this is a time for dramatic growth of the autonomous functions of the ego, a growth which occurs optimally in close physical proximity to the mother.

The practicing subphase proper, the period during which Mahler specifically locates the occurrence of "psychological birth," begins with the child's achievement of upright locomotion. With this development, the child's horizons widen immeasurably, and he is exhilarated by what he sees. It is, as Mahler conceptualizes it, the height of both (secondary) narcissism and object love. These are manifested in the child's pleasure in his own body and his newly achieved functioning, as well as his easy acceptance of adults other than his mother. The practicing subphase proper is the time during which "the world is his oyster," or, in Greenacre's (1957) phrase, it is the height of his "love affair with the world."

In line with his increasing body narcissism, the child's interest at this stage is concentrated on his expanding abilities, perceived by him as omnipotence. Mahler speculates that exhilaration at this time may be the result not only of the rapidly increasing abilities but also of his escape from the symbiotic embeddedness with his mother. She suggests that the frequently observed fact that the child's first steps are almost inevitably taken in a direction away from his mother points to an innate tendency toward separation which is manifested at this stage of autonomous development (1974).

Despite the rapid spurt of separate functioning during the practicing subphase proper, the new toddler's reactions to his mother do not indicate that he appreciates her as a separate person. He still treats her as a "home base," with frequent returns for emotional refueling. The advent of this subphase, however, does require certain specific responses on the part of the mother. Parallel to the child's experience of "psychological birth," the mother must be willing to relinquish her possession of the child's body if development is to proceed satisfactorily. She must be willing to allow and even to enjoy his increasing capacity to operate at a distance from her and his entrance into an expanding and exciting world. The mother's responsiveness must be tuned to the maturational and developmental pace of her particular child; she must respond to him rather than to her own preconceived ideas of what he should be like.

The rapprochement subphase. The expansion of the child's world during the practicing subphase and the enhancement of his sense of separateness does not proceed without its price. At a certain point in the middle of the second year (usually between fifteen and eighteen months) the child who has been increasingly able to function at a distance from his mother comes to the realization that, contrary to his earlier narcissistic sense of omnipotence, he is in fact a very small person in a very big world. This realization brings with it both a loss of the previously enjoyed ideal sense of self and the reappearance of a kind of separation anxiety. What is wanted is no longer forthcoming just because the need is felt or even because it is expressed. Frustration is more frequently experienced, and the imperviousness to failure that characterized the practicing subphase fades.

The rapprochement subphase is ushered in by the toddler's dawning realization that the mother is actually a separate person, one who will not always be available to help him in dealing with his newly enlarged world. Mother must now be approached on a new, higher level of interaction, characterized especially by sharing new discoveries in the "outside" world and by language. The early months of the rapprochement subphase are typified by the "wooing" behavior of the child toward his mother, in which he tries to obtain her participation in his world within the context of some recognition of his separateness.

The loss of the ideal sense of self and the realization that the world is not his oyster leads the toddler to what Mahler terms the "rapprochement crisis," lasting from approximately eighteen to twenty or twenty-four months of age. This is a very difficult, painful time, and the manner in which the child resolves his intense struggles during the rapprochement crisis determines many features of later personality development. During the rapprochement crisis the child experiences a need for help from outside but simultaneously, in the service of his consolidating separateness and individuation, needs to deny that it actually comes from another person. This leads to a behavioral picture in which intense neediness and clinging to the mother alternates with equally intense negativity and battling with her. Demands and dramatic fighting alternate, often at rapid intervals. Mahler describes the prevalent attitude of the child during this period as "ambivalent," because of his apparently conflicting affective reactions toward his mother, alternating between periods of intense neediness and powerful desires for separateness.* The child fears loss of the mother's love following his separation from her, on the one hand, and reengulfment in the symbiotic orbit resulting from his need for her, on the other.

Successful resolution of the rapprochement crisis, which brings to a head the conflict between need for the mother and need for separation and individuation, is understood by Mahler as the central developmental requirement for the avoidance of subsequent severe psychopathology. She points out (Mahler, Pine, and Bergman, 1975; Mahler, 1971) that both the splitting of good and bad representations of the mother and the coercion of her that characterize the rapprochement crisis also typify the later transference reactions of borderline patients. To traverse this period successfully thus becomes, for the more severe psychopathologies, what resolution of the Oedipus complex was in Freud's etiological understanding of the neuroses.

The rapprochement subphase, especially the rapprochement crisis, is a time during which the child is undergoing developmental and maturational changes in addition to those involving his object relationships. It is a period of rapidly changing autonomous ego functions, most notably highlighted by rapid gains in language ability and by the appearance of reality testing (compare Freud, 1925b). The child is also becoming aware of the anatomical differences between the sexes, and notions of his own gender identity are contributing to and interacting with the individuation process. Awareness of father, a member of the family who is not mother but who stands in a special relationship to the child, is increasing. And, finally, viewed from the perspective of the

---

*This ambivalence should not be taken to imply that object constancy has been attained. In fact, the rapprochement crisis is, in Mahler's schema, the period during which splitting mechanisms are at their height.

theory of libidinal development, the child is making the transition from the oral to the anal phase.

The advent of rapprochement places a new set of demands on the toddler's mother. From her point of view the onset of this phase may appear to be a regressive development. The child who a few months before had appeared to be so independent, and so content in his independence, has become more needy, more anxious, more demanding. He insists on her help but rejects it in a way that is particularly torturing. How should she respond? What she does will depend on her conscious and unconscious attitudes toward both symbiosis and separation. Some mothers welcome the opportunity to reimmerse the child in their own caretaking and in their own body, thereby stifling the drive toward separateness. Others reject the child's new dependency in the belief that "he's a big boy now," overlooking the legitimate needs of the subphase. Mahler stresses repeatedly that the mother's reaction at all subphases, and particularly during rapprochement, decisively influences the final outcome.

The phase of libidinal object constancy. This is not a subphase in the sense of the preceding three, because it is open-ended at the older end, with the results variable throughout life. The achievement of libidinal object constancy begins during the third year of life and is normally relatively consolidated by the age of three years. There are two principal tasks of this period, organized around the coparticipants in all object relationships: a stable concept of the self and a stable concept of the other must be formed. The child must attain a sense of his own individuality, as well as a sense of the other as an internal, positively cathected presence. This permits adequate functioning in the absence of the other person, a capacity that implies the achievement of intrapsychic separateness.

Libidinal object constancy presupposes but is not identical to the capacity for "object permanence" in Piaget's (1937) sense. Piaget's work focuses on the child's relations with inanimate things, and the idea of permanence indicates that things continue to exist in the child's mind even when they are not present. This capacity has been found to appear at about eighteen to twenty months, long before the development of "constancy" in the libidinal sense. The reason for this lag is that, in speaking of the constancy of the human, libidinally cathected object, we are referring to a situation far more affectively charged than is Piaget. Libidinal object constancy presupposes the unification of good and bad representations of the object as well as the fusion of the libidinal and aggressive drives with which they are cathected. These achievements depend, in Mahler's view, both on constitutional givens and on prior developmental experiences. The innate strength of drives and their vicissitudes, as well as the developmental sequelae of the first three subphases of separation-individuation, bear decisively on the events of the fourth subphase. Its successful (or relatively successful) completion marks the firm establishment of stable self-other relationships.

Throughout her writings Mahler makes it clear that separation and individuation are complementary but distinct developmental processes. Separation refers to the emergence from symbiotic fusion with the mother, while individuation "consists of those achievements marking the child's assumption of his own individual characteristics" (Mahler, Pine, and Bergman, 1975, p. 4). The two processes may proceed at a similar pace, with each facilitating the achievement of the other, or there may be relative lags — as when the capacity to move away from the mother outstrips the capacity to function autonomously (for example, to regulate tension adequately in the mother's absence). This distinction is similar to, and may interact with, the distinction originally drawn by Hartmann, Kris, and Loewenstein (1946; see also Mahler, 1958a) between maturation and development. The maturation of autonomous ego functions and of muscular abilities may lead the child into activities for which he is otherwise developmentally unready. The two poles, separation-individuation and maturation-development, are for Mahler the critical determinants of developmental outcome.

In our description of the subphases of separation-individuation we have at several points alluded to the importance of the mother's reactions to her child's changing needs and behaviors. The responses of the "optimal" mother of the symbiotic period, it is clear, are not those of the "optimal" mother of the practicing subphase, and they must again be modified with the onset of rapprochement — and especially of the rapprochement crisis. It is crucial for an accurate understanding of Mahler's contribution to psychoanalysis to appreciate the intrinsic relation between the child's changing needs and the responsiveness of his mother to these changes. The child's development results from the interaction between his subphase-specific behaviors and the mother's responses. As the child passes through the various subphases, his needs change, including his need for different modes of relatedness with the mother. Mahler's story of early development is, therefore, dyadic: analysis must take into account the contributions of each of the two principal participants. In her latest work, she even addresses the previously omitted role of the father, suggesting that the infant's feeling about himself during the practicing subphase depends on subphase-adequate responses from both parents (Mahler and McDevitt, 1982).

The requirements placed on the mother of the separating and individuating child parallel changes within the child. An initial willingness to be available as a buffer between the child and the external world, to function as an auxiliary ego and a stimulus barrier, must give way to a willingness to relinquish this closeness in favor of a higher-level relationship with an increasingly autonomous individual. Mahler's requirements for optimal mothering thus bear striking similarities to Winnicott's "good-enough mother," who is able both to achieve and to leave behind her "primary maternal preoccupation." In Mahler's framework the mother's capacity to "move with" the child is as important a determinant of character formation and pathological development as are the drives, their vicissitudes, and ego maturation. The contribution of the mother in Mahler's theory transcends the more or less serendipitous role of the "object" as gratifier or frustrator in Freud's drive model formulation.

Mahler and Hartmann

The concept of symbiosis has, over the past twenty-five years, become so embedded in psychoanalytic thinking that it is difficult today to realize how little there is in the drive/structure model to prepare us for it. Symbiosis is characteristic of the earliest preverbal period of infancy (following the initial autistic phase), a developmental epoch into which drive model theorists have been and are reluctant to venture. Even more important, it occupies a position in the theory of libidinal object relationship that is difficult to encompass within the classical metapsychology. It *is* a type of object relationship in the sense that during the symbiotic period libidinal cathexis is directed toward a "dual-unity" that includes the object (mother) as well as the self. At the same time, it *cannot be* an object relationship, because there is no or only very little differentiation between the self and the object. The drive model, especially as it stood at the time of Mahler's postulation of the concept of symbiosis, allows no such middle ground in object relations. For Freud (1914a) the antithesis between narcissistic libido and object libido is absolute: that which cathects the object is not available to the ego, and vice versa. Thus, one cannot support anything like a symbiotic phase from the libido theory approach to object relations, and yet the postulate of a symbiotic phase of normal development is a crucial part of Mahler's contribution. How can the theory of symbiosis be tied into the preexisting model? The concepts of Hartmann provided Mahler with a crucial link.

The several innovations Hartmann introduced into the drive model serve the purpose of bringing the human organism into more immediate contact with his environment. Principal among these are the concepts of adaptation and of an average expectable environment to which adaptive processes are geared. We observed that Hartmann's biological level of conceptualization leads to a theory in which both adaptation and the environment emerge as schematic concepts, a vision of an organism fitting into an ecological system. Yet, despite Hartmann's theoretical caution, it was apparent that he was moving the drive model in a direction which implicitly granted relations with others a much more central explanatory role, and thus threatened the exclusive explanatory monopoly previously held by the concept of drive. In a scathing review of Hartmann's monograph, written more than two decades after its publication, Glover (1961) warns that "metapsychologically speaking, adaptation is the history of object relations" (p. 98n). For Glover this raises the specter of a theory based on object relations rather than on drives, and thus an abandonment of psychoanalytic depth psychology. He correctly perceived that the adaptive point of view and the concomitant concept of an average expectable environment can open psychoanalytic theory to a preoccupation with object relations. Hartmann scrupulously avoided this path throughout his career, and Mahler followed his lead. The lengths to which Mahler was willing to go in *not* explicitly equating the "environment" with parental figures is revealed in an early paper in which she describes a young child who has troubled her parents with a variety of psychosomatic and psychological symptoms. The parents' reaction is described by Mahler in the following words: "The environment, extremely overanxious, consulted one doctor after another" (1946, p. 48).

Despite this early caution, Mahler was in fact the theorist who moved Hartmann's framework in the direction feared by Glover: she offered a specification and personification of the "average expectable environment." In an early paper she notes that a function of the infant's earliest motor abilities is to relate him to the mother (Mahler, Luke, and Daltroff, 1945). A year later she returns to the same point, stating that: "When the instinctual tension grows beyond a certain limit, the infant feels intense distress resulting in his automatic outburst into crying and other affectomotor spells which, *although very ineffective in serving a discharge function, do summon help*" (1946, p. 44; italics ours).

A decade later, after postulating the normal symbiotic phase, Mahler has become somewhat more specific, noting that affectomotor reactions serve to attract the mother, who can then be used as an external ego (1958). Autistic psychosis, which is phenomenologically characterized by a failure to establish a symbiotic relationship, is understood as resulting from "an intrinsic defect of the socio-biological adaptation" (Mahler, Fuhrer, and Settlage, 1959, p. 816). In her eventual theory of the separation-individuation process as a normal developmental phase, Mahler argues that the "average expectable environment" at birth consists entirely of the infant in interaction with his mother (Mahler, 1966; 1968; Mahler and McDermitt, 1968; see also McDevitt and Settlage, 1971). Thus, while Hartmann's environment is an intentionally vaguely defined "reality," Mahler's "average expectable environment" gradually becomes, over the course of the evolution of her theory, the "ordinary devoted mother" (1968).

Thus, Mahler has redefined the environment to coincide with the specific person of the mother. Simultaneously she has specified the adaptive capacities of the child: these are understood as his abilities, via affectomotor discharge, to bring the mother to him, and to use her for the purpose of reducing tension. There is a fit between the child's need for care, the mother's ability and willingness to provide care, and the child's capacity to summon the caring mother. (With characteristic pithiness and a preference for operational concepts, Sullivan [1953] describes this as the child's capacity to elicit tenderness.) Mahler's depiction of this characteristic pattern of need and response constitutes a much more specific and relational view of adaptation to the environment than that of Hartmann's original broadly sketched version.

But where does symbiosis enter the picture? Here Mahler begins with Hartmann's (1939a) citation of Freud's (1923a) ideas that man at birth suffers from two complementary deficits when compared with other animals: he is unusually physically immature, and over the course of evolution his instincts of self-preservation have decayed substantially. Hartmann argued that it is for these reasons that the ego has evolved as a specific organ of adaptation, although he preferred to leave the mechanisms of adaptation vaguely stated. For Mahler, man's difficulty has been solved by the evolution of a "species specific social symbiosis" (1958a; Mahler, Fuhrer, and Settlage, 1959), which provides for the survival needs of the child. The neonate's rudimentary ego is helpless against the world at large, but it *is* uniquely suited to deal with its environment as redefined by Mahler: it can elicit the aid of the mother who, in the capacity of auxiliary ego, supplements the infant's abilities (1967). As she puts it: "Adaptation may be regarded as beginning with the infant's fitting into his symbiotic environment. This adaptation is synonymous with his success in . . . finding 'good enough mothering'" (1966, p. 153). That the capacity to form a symbiotic relationship is a specification of Hartmann's concept of the infant's initial adaptedness to his average expectable environment, an ability determined by the biological characteristics of the human species, is clear in Mahler's statement that "even the very young baby may have to strain his innate equipment to elicit 'good enough mothering,' in Winnicott's sense [1960] from his mother" (1965, p. 164).

Thus, Mahler has specified the "capacity for adaptedness" sketched out by Hartmann as well as spelling out the first step of the adaptive process. *The capacity to adapt is the capacity to establish a specific mode of object relationship with the mother; that object relationship, symbiosis, is the first stage of adaptation.* The establishment of a symbiotic relationship requires the participation of both partners (although, as we will demonstrate, this is not unambiguous). The infant's innate capacity to summon help is successful only in the context of an average expectable environment, an "ordinary devoted mother," who is reasonably responsive. Although symbiosis is a normal developmental phase, theoretically identical in this respect to the Oedipus complex, the collaboration of the object is necessary. The symbiotic object cannot be created by the child in the sense that the oedipal objects can. Because the theory of symbiosis indicates that survival depends on events within an interpersonal field, it is inherently dyadic. The relationship to the object and the behavior of the object in reality are essential aspects of symbiosis, as well as of subsequent steps in the processes of separation and individuation.

This perspective further implies, although it does not explicitly contain, a new definition of the object. Because of the specific capacities implied in her concept, Mahler's "symbiotic object" is necessarily a person. This requirement was deliberately excluded in the theory of Freud, whose approach was continued by Hartmann's broadly sketched formulation of reality and of the environment. In expanding Hartmann's adaptive point of view, Mahler has emphasized the infant's need for specifically human relationships. Unlike Sullivan and Fairbairn, however, this need derives from survival requirements; it does not reflect a primary urge toward social affiliation.

Mahler's "ordinary devoted mother" closely resembles Winnicott's "good-enough mother." Yet, although Mahler frequently refers favorably to Winnicott's ideas, he characterized the theory of symbiosis as "too biological." His objections to Mahler's formulations illustrate the differences in their conceptual lineage, particularly in terms of Mahler's reliance on the metapsychological adaptive point of view and Winnicott's independence from it. Mahler, following Hartmann, organizes her theory around the adaptive capacities of the infant far more than did Winnicott. Thus, she notes that: "What impressed us already in the pilot study of the separation-individuation project was the great extent to which it is the normal infant who actively takes on the task of adaptation in the mother-infant interaction! Of course, the average nursing mother readily meets the major biological needs of her infant" (1965, pp. 163–164). This statement contrasts sharply with Winnicott's idea that the good-enough mother is the one who is able to locate and respond positively to the infant's nascent self. In fact, Mahler's idea that the infant adapts to the conscious and unconscious requirements of his mother reflects precisely the line of development which for Winnicott leads to a "false self on a compliance basis."

Two years later Mahler did offer a formulation of the symbiotic relationship that appears more interactive. She states that "Mutual cuing during the symbiotic phase creates that indelibly imprinted configuration — that complex pattern — that becomes the *leitmotif for 'the infant's becoming the child of his particular mother'*" (1967, p. 750; italics in original). It is clear, however, that even this construction emerges from a biological/adaptational framework as opposed to the personal/interpersonal framework of Winnicott, and Mahler preserves as her legacy from Hartmann a stress on "adaptive" operations. For Winnicott the child is born with a self which emerges in interaction with the personal care offered by his mother. For Mahler the environment/mother offers biological sustenance but also imposes conditions to which the infant must adapt. Winnicott's "personhood" is an innate given which is encouraged by the "facilitating environment"; Mahler's "personhood" is *achieved* through, among other factors, adaptation to the environment. Although Mahler's environment is personified by the mother, her theory continues to treat the mother-child relationship as an interaction between an organism and its ecological system, much as Hartmann did.

Symbiosis and Drive: A Study in Accommodation

The map Mahler has delineated for reading the essential features of the infant's development from formlessness to form differs fundamentally from the map provided by classical drive theory. For Mahler the infant becomes a person by virtue of a submersion within and emergence from the personality of his mother. The benchmarks of that development are drawn in terms of modes of relatedness rather than tension reduction. She stresses the nature of the connection between the child and his mother, whose results become the basis for psychic structure formation. Yet she remains loyal to the drive model, not in the gratuitous fashion of Winnicott, who nods to drive theory and then ignores it, but in a sincere and often painstaking effort to weave her innovations into the existing framework. This is not an easy task.

Mahler uses the term "symbiosis" with two essentially different referents; the elasticity provided by this double usage serves as her most powerful vehicle for theoretical accommodation. From the perspective we have been following, symbiosis denotes an actual *relationship* between infant and mother, with specific actions and behaviors required from both partners. Following Hartmann's adaptive point of view, symbiosis is a mode of interaction between two people which is necessary for the survival of one of them. At other points, however, Mahler makes it clear that symbiosis also denotes an intrapsychic event, a *fantasy*. She argues that it is "an inferred state . . . a feature of primitive cognitive-affective life wherein the differentiation between self and mother has not taken place, or where regression to that self-object undifferentiated state (which characterized the symbiotic phase) has occurred. Indeed *this does not necessarily require the physical presence of the mother*, but it may be based on primitive images of oneness and/or scotomatization or disavowal of contradictory perceptions" (Mahler, Pine, and Bergman, 1975, p. 8; italics ours). Seen in this way, symbiosis loses its dyadic connotation, and may even work in opposition to adaptation. Mahler continues: "The essential feature of symbiosis is hallucinatory or delusional somatopsychic *omnipotent* fusion with the representation of the mother and, in particular, the delusion of a common boundary between two physically separate individuals. This is the mechanism to which the ego regresses in cases of the most severe disturbance of individuation and psychotic disorganization" (Mahler, Pine, and Bergman, 1975, p. 45; italics in original).

We are thus confronted with a critical ambiguity: symbiosis is at once an event occurring in an interpersonal field and a fantasy which may be occurring independent of events in that field. It is at once a description of the behavior of two people and a metapsychological explanation of the behavior of one of them. This apparent contradiction is not just the result of semantic carelessness, but reflects an ambiguity which allows Mahler to set her relational concepts into existing drive theory. Her views grew out of her observations of the behaviors of both mother and child. In order to integrate these observations into the metapsychology of the drive model, she must infer an intrapsychic state of affairs that underlies the observed behaviors. *If symbiosis is to become a developmental concept on a par with the established drive model concepts (identification, the sequence of danger situations, the Oedipus complex, and so on), it must have a libidinal as well as a behavioral referent.* This requirement, implicit in Freud's writing, was articulated carefully by Hartmann.

By using symbiosis to refer both to a relationship in reality and to a libidinally determined internal fantasy, Mahler is able to create an interface between a developmental theory of object relations and drive model metapsychology. By making this conceptual leap, the theory of symbiosis and of separation-individuation becomes an independent intrapsychic developmental line.

This strategy of accommodation, though ingenious, is not without difficulties. The concept of a relationship to an object that is not yet differentiated from the self has no place within classical libido theory, because the object is by definition separate from and outside the self. Mahler needs to find some way to make it possible to have a meaningful metapsychological (as opposed to behavioral) referent for the "symbiotic object." To this end she embarks on a redefinition of the concept of the object itself.

The idea of an "object" originated as an aspect of Freud's drive theory, the object serving as the target of a (libidinal or aggressive) drive. It was only with the advent of the structural model and its elaboration in ego psychology that cognitive aspects of the formation of the object began to receive consideration, independent of the operation of drive. Even Hartmann's (1952) discussion of libidinal object constancy approaches the formation of the object from the perspective of a modification (neutralization) of the drive that cathects it. The ego aspect is little attended.

Mahler recognized the difficulties brought on by the historically one-sided approach to object formation and therefore to object relations. Children, and psychotic adults, relate libidinally and aggressively to objects which, from a cognitive and perceptual perspective, are "fantastic." These objects may be formed from fused perceptions of the self and the other person, from fused perceptions of many others, and so on. These distinctions, though unimportant from the perspective of the nature of instinctual cathexis (the id aspect of object relations), are critical from the perspective of how the object is cognitively formed (the ego aspect).

Psychoanalysis, Mahler believed, lacked an adequate definition of the object from the perspective of the psychology of the ego. In approaching this problem, she began with Freud's well-known statement that "For the ego, perception plays the part which in the id falls to instinct" (1923a, p. 25). In light of this statement, may we not define the object in terms of its place in the perceptual field? This is precisely what Mahler did in her statement that "In the broadest sense . . . we may speak of anything as an object which, in a field of interreaction, physiologically or otherwise impinges upon the organism *in utero* or in extrauterine life, as its environment" (1960, p. 184). The theoretical implications of this redefinition cannot be overstated. The concept of "object" is no longer tied to the concept of drive. The "object" which impinges upon perception is present, necessarily, from the beginning (even, Mahler notes, during intrauterine life), and relations with it do not depend necessarily on differentiation of perceptions of the self from perceptions of the "other."

This reformulation bears directly on the problem of narcissism. Freud (1914a) originally defined narcissism entirely in energic terms: it was understood as a vicissitude of the libidinal drive. Hartmann's modification of the original use of the term suggested a new object (the self rather than the ego), but retained the earlier energic basis (Hartmann, 1950a). Difficulties in integrating ego aspects of object relations into the energic framework of the narcissism concept have led in recent years to drastically new approaches. Kernberg (1976) drops the term altogether as a reference to a stage of normal development. Jacobson (1954a) originally suggested doing so, but later revived it. In Jacobson's (1964) usage, as well as in Kohut's (and in Kernberg's designation of narcissistic psychopathology), narcissism is defined not in energic but in structural/cognitive terms. Narcissism is understood as a stage of undifferentiation between self and object, as a state of "merger." The vicissitudes of libido within this matrix of merged self and object representation are not part of the definition.

Mahler's redefinition of the object concept could lead her into a sweeping revision of the idea of narcissism, but she is unwilling to suggest so fundamental a change in drive theory; her solution, therefore, represents an intermediate position. Throughout her work, Mahler makes it clear that she is following Hartmann in retaining the energic connotation of narcissism: the concept still refers to the libidinal cathexis of *something*.

From the libidinal point of view, narcissism is most applicable to Mahler's normal autistic phase, because during this phase psychic energy is turned entirely inward and the infant is without an external object. Mahler, however, includes the symbiotic phase as well within Freud's era of primary narcissism (1967; Mahler, Pine, and Bergman, 1975). This develops one aspect of the initial concept of Freud, whose use of narcissism contains its own ambiguities. On the one hand, narcissism refers to a vicissitude of libido; on the other hand, the concept of a "narcissistic object choice" describes a particular type of object relationship. We have shown that this latter, descriptive use was, within the framework of drive model metapsychology, theoretically oxymoronic. Mahler's account of narcissism contains similar ambiguities, but, unlike Freud, she has made an attempt to resolve them. This is part of her strategy of theoretical accommodation, because it represents an attempt to integrate the observed patterns of object relations into the classical metapsychological framework. She argues that during the period of symbiosis (which, descriptively, is clearly one type of narcissistic object relationship) the distribution of libido is still narcissistic because what is cathected is a "dual-unity" which includes both the infant and the mother. The idea of a dual-unity is made possible by the fact that the self and the object are still undifferentiated from the infant's point of view.

Mahler's depiction of the symbiotic phase of primary narcissism thus draws on Freud's concept of narcissistic object choice, but goes beyond it because it refers to the state of internal representations as well as external behavior. This in turn depends on her embracing a cognitive definition of the "object," because the phase is partially defined by the state of cognitive undifferentiation of self and other. Yet because she insists on retaining its energic aspect, Mahler defines narcissism as the cathexis of a still merged image of self and object.

Mahler's formulation of narcissism relies *simultaneously* on libidinal and cognitive perspectives. The effect of this dual definition is to move drive model thinking by broadening the role of the object considerably beyond its function vis-à-vis drive. This is clear in some of her reworking of Freud's thinking about the era of primary narcissism. For Freud, the infant at the beginning of life is completely self-absorbed, operating according to hallucinatory wish-fulfillment. He turns to the outside world only under the impetus of feelings of frustration of his drive-derived needs. The outside world is always seen as separate and hostile to the infant's needs; this is the meaning of Freud's (1915a) concept of the "purified pleasure ego." For Mahler, on the other hand, the first relationship to an object, the relationship of the symbiotic phase, is one of merger; the hostility directed toward the "not-I" is in fact directed toward that which is beyond the symbiotic orbit. The object, although dimly perceived, is essentially experienced as helpful, as assisting in the easing of endogenously arising unpleasurable sensations. If Mahler's infant is not innately object seeking, as Fairbairn's infant is, it is at least an important aspect of development that the earliest relationships with others are essentially positive. Accordingly, the purified pleasure ego is one of the few Freudian concepts that Mahler explicitly rejects (Mahler and Gosliner, 1955, p. 198). Her treatment of these issues exemplifies the strategy of theoretical accommodation.

Mahler's approach to the concepts of delaying drive gratification and drive neutralization further illustrates her stretching of classical theory to encompass relational processes. For drive model theorists, the capacity to delay discharge is one of the most critical achievements of early development; it is the first step in "civilizing" the animal that will become man. Freud (1911a) suggests that delay is made possible by the appearance of thinking, which he defined as a kind of trial action using relatively small quantities of energy. In turn, thinking was made possible by the conversion of free into bound cathexes; it depended solely upon a modification of the state of drive energy. Hartmann (1939a) extended this construction with the idea that the binding of cathexes already *presupposes a capacity to bind* innate to the ego and dependent upon maturational and developmental processes. He did not spell out these processes, concentrating instead on the *function* of binding. However, since the ego is by definition that part of the psychic apparatus that is in contact with reality, Hartmann's view schematically brings the environment to bear on the evolving capacity to delay.

Mahler proposes a different and innovative approach to the development of the ego in general and the capacity for delay of gratification in particular, an approach in which relational processes and drive energies are brought into a delicate balance. In discussing the application of ego psychology to behavior disorders in children, she states that "normal satisfactory ego growth is dependent almost exclusively upon the emotional relationship between child and mother, and later between child and parents" (1946, p. 46). In the same paper, however, she stays more closely within Hartmann's framework, arguing that ego formation is the result of controlled drive. These statements are not of course contradictory, although their full integration is not without its problems. We are faced with the same sort of theoretical strategy which we found in our discussion of symbiosis and narcissism. The second of Mahler's statements is a metapsychological hypothesis: it points to the mechanism underlying ego formation. The first is a statement of the conditions necessary to bring about a series of intrapsychic events. By emphasizing conditions rather than mechanisms Mahler is able to broaden the theoretical scope of the drive model.

In an early paper Mahler noted that the neonate's experience of a rhythmic alternation between states of need tension and need satisfaction leads to two developments: an awareness of his own body as distinct from mother's, and "confident expectation" directed toward the outer world (Mahler, Ross, and DeFries, 1946). The first part of this formulation, relating the sequence of frustration-gratification to the sense of owning one's body, is a classic drive model statement about ego development; it recalls Freud's remark that the ego is "first and foremost a body-ego" (1923a, p. 27). The second part appears simply to relate the sequence of frustration-gratification to the development of a particular quality of object relatedness. That more is intended becomes clear in Mahler's subsequent writing, when she states that: "when some measure of development enables the infant to hold tension in abeyance, that is to say, *when he is able to wait for and confidently expect satisfaction — only then is it possible to speak of the beginning of an ego"* (1968, p. 12; italics ours). For Hartmann (1950a; see also Rapaport, 1958) the ego is the structure that allows the delay of drive discharge, the holding of tension in abeyance. By equating this with a particular quality of interpersonal relatedness, the experience of confident expectation, Mahler stresses the interpersonal conditions that promote ego development, rather than the mechanisms involved. In this way, she brings object relations much closer to the core of the theory of ego development than had her theoretical predecessors.

In Mahler's (1967; 1968) construction the capacity to delay is built upon a specific interpersonal experience: the sense of satisfaction from the symbiotic partner. This represents at the least a specification of the environmental conditions required if the ego is to develop. But in the 1968 statement just quoted, even more is implied: there is an equation of the ability to hold tension in abeyance and confident expectation. Mahler appears to be saying that the interpersonal experience *is* the mechanism, that is, that drive is regulated via the evocation of a particular affectively charged self-other configuration (the needy infant confidently expecting satisfaction from the nurturant mother). This coincides in many respects with the formulations of relational model theorists.

Similar considerations emerge in the discussion of Mahler's approach to a related issue: the neutralization of drives. For Hartmann, who first proposed the concept, neutralization is a function of the ego; it is a mechanism by which the ego is able to affect the very nature of drive energy itself. Neutralization is an elaboration of Freud's concept of sublimation, with application to aggressive as well as to libidinal drives. Energy which has been acted upon, neutralized, by the ego is available for the ego to use in pursuing its own aims. The importance of the neutralization concept within the drive model is that it moves the theory beyond a monotonic emphasis on purely instinctual energy as a source of motivation. In Hartmann's view the relationship between neutralization and object relations is complex and broadly sketched; his most clearly articulated position is that neutralization is a prerequisite of object constancy.

For Mahler the evolution of drive energy from its purely instinctual beginning to eventual gradations of neutralization follows a clearer, more fully spelled out course. The infant's activity in the autistic and early symbiotic phases is centered, during his waking life, around the reduction of internally arising tension. The first discrimination between inside and outside (self and non-self) results from the discovery that certain discomforts can only be relieved by ministrations from the symbiotic partner (mother). These ministrations, in which Mahler includes all of the mother's normal caretaking activities, are understood meta-psychologically as a libidinization of endogenously arising aggressive drive forces (see Mahler and Gosliner, 1955). This is the start of the neutralization process. The mother's fondling and cuddling of the infant and the concomitant "affective rapport" between the two lead to neutralization (1952). Neutralization thus follows from a specific interpersonal experience.

The neutralizing function of maternal care extends beyond the symbiotic period. Well into the childhood era, "It is the mother's love and acceptance of the toddler and even of his ambivalence which enable the toddler's ego to cathect his self representation with 'neutralized energy'" (1966, p. 161). This framework is carried intact into Mahler's formulation of the process of child analysis. She states that the therapist's "soothing presence results in a neutralization of the child's aggression, while her libidinal input helps the child to invest his own libido in his body" (1968, p. 216). With these formulations, the traditional drive model view of the relationship between libidinal drive energy and pleasure have been reversed. It is not libidinal discharge that produces the experience of pleasure, but the experience of pleasurable interpersonal relations that gives rise to libido. However, Mahler retains ties to the drive model by arguing that even optimal mothering does not guarantee that adequate neutralization will occur. An infant burdened with an overwhelming amount of unpleasurable internally arising stimuli (the example Mahler most frequently gives is of infants who suffer from painful chronic illnesses, but the formulation can be extended to include those constitutionally burdened with a much greater than average aggressive drive energy) may, even in the presence of an adequately comforting symbiotic partner, fail to neutralize sufficient aggression (1958).

Mahler's strategy of theory construction entails major (if at times implicit) modifications of the drive concept to accommodate a gradually expanded emphasis on the role of early object relations. She frees the "object" from its function as a libidinal target; she expands "narcissism" from a purely energic concept to a formulation that is simultaneously cognitive and energic; she *derives* both the capacity for delay of drive discharge and neutralization from interpersonal experiences. Through these devices she finds a place for her innovations within the framework of the drive model. At the same time, much is lost by these changes, including a conceptual clarity in key areas that serve as seams in her efforts to blend a relational developmental theory with the drive/structure model. For example, an important benefit of the drive-oriented definition of the object is that it distinguishes the role played by certain "things" in the environment from that played by other "things." The "objects" of classical psychoanalysis have a far more specified function in the psychic economy than do the "objects" of Piaget (1937). When Mahler uses the libidinal object (the id aspect) interchangeably with the impinging object (the ego aspect), she loses this specificity. Despite her claims that she follows Hartmann's definition, Mahler's use of the term blurs the distinction between libidinal objects, Piaget's "things," and even percepts. This confusion results from her attempt to encompass phenomena not considered by her predecessors within the drive model, while at the same time retaining the model's underlying assumptions.

Mahler's discussion of the requirements for healthy ego development illustrates this kind of unclarity. What are the crucial determinants of an adequate outcome? For Hartmann there are many: constitutional strength of drive, innate ego capacities, the vicissitudes of libido and aggression, object relations, and the interactions among any and all of these. He is particularly at pains to warn against overestimating the role of object relations vis-à-vis the other factors. As he puts it, "ego development and object relationships are correlated in more complex ways than some recent works let us believe . . . We do not know much about corrections of very early unsatisfactory situations through later maturational processes" (1952, p. 163). But what are "satisfactory" object relationships? How critical are they in fostering healthy ego growth?

When Hartmann talks about "satisfactory" object relationships he means "satisfying" relationships, those that are gratifying from the perspective of drive tension. He equates "the problem of the child's interaction with his objects" with "his indulgences and frustrations" (1952, p. 162). Early in her career Mahler seems to accept this theoretical formulation although from the beginning of her writings she also notices broader aspects of the mother-child interaction. In one of her earliest English-language papers she observed that "The interrelation between the unconscious of the mother and the reception of stimulation of the sense organs of the baby is the prototype for a way of communication between child and adult" (Mahler [Schoenberger], 1942, p. 150). This mode of communication allows for the transmission of signals, for the establishment of a relationship between mother and child that transcends the frustration/gratification sequence. Mahler specifies aspects of this relationship in her early writing on tic disorders of childhood, in which she points out that parental attitudes toward the child's developing locomotor functioning (not only the explicit gratification or frustration of the child's growing abilities, but unconscious attitudes as well) have a direct effect on the child's ability to develop this ego capacity (Mahler, Luke, and Daltroff, 1945; Mahler, 1949).

Another important aspect of the mother-child relationship is the parent's anxiety. Mahler states that "contagion" by the anxious, dissatisfied mother can, independent of provision for vegetative needs, disturb her symbiotic relationship with the child (Mahler and Rabinovitch, 1956).* In a summary statement describing the earliest weeks and months of life, she notes that: "whereas the development from normal autism to normal symbiosis occurs within the matrix of the oral gratification-frustration sequences of the normal nursing situation, it is dependent upon, and synonymous with, need satisfaction only in a very broad sense. This development involves much more than the satisfaction of oral and other vegetative needs" (1961, p. 334). Later in the same paper she suggests that the infant in the autistic state who is handled in a purely vegetative fashion will be unable to develop signals to indicate his needs. Vegetative satisfaction will then become dissociated from "affect hunger," and the infant will fail to learn the connection between satisfaction of needs and its affective concomitants.

Mahler construes the effect of object relationships more broadly than in terms of Hartmann's frustrations and gratifications, at least on the level of observation. She has brought into the picture conscious and unconscious parental attitudes, affective reactions, and responses to the emotional needs of the child. Her "satisfactory" object relations are more multifaceted than Hartmann's, involving as they do a range of aspects of the personalities of both mother and child. But, as with many of her contributions, we must question the extent to which she has integrated her observations into the explanatory framework of drive theory. Here she is up against a difficult problem: the drive model, with its developmental map organized around modes of experiencing pleasure, *requires* the equation of "satisfactory" and "satisfying." An object relationship can be evaluated only with reference to the underlying drive that has cathected the object representation. Thus, despite her assertions of the multidimensional aspects of the earliest mother-child interaction, Mahler concludes that "all happenings in the symbiotic phase are dominated by orality" (Mahler and Gosliner, 1955, p. 200). This is difficult to reconcile with the idea that a great deal more than frustration and gratification of oral needs is critical in the earliest weeks and months of life.

* Although Freud rejected "contagion" as a fundamental explanatory principle, Mahler's formulation is akin to those of Sullivan's interpersonal psychiatry. The concept of "contagion" by the anxious mother is similar in all relevant respects to Sullivan's (1953) statement: "The child empathizes with the anxiety of the mother."

Phrases such as "dominated by orality" and "within the matrix of the oral gratification-frustration sequence" (1961) pay homage more to the theoretical tradition of the drive model than to Mahler's observations. She has noticed in the earliest relationship of the infant with his mother that specific survival needs are being met, that tenderness is being provided, that anxiety reduction through the presence of a calm "auxiliary ego" is made possible, that a shield against overwhelming external stimuli is offered, and that a sequence of gratification and frustration of oral needs is experienced. Selecting one or another of these facets of the mother-child relationship as the "dominating" one, the "matrix" within which the others occur, can only be an a priori and somewhat arbitrary choice; it cannot be deduced from the data. Fairbairn (1952) encompasses the same phenomena under the organizing principle of absolute dependence, an interpersonal or object relational concept divorced from biological/libidinal trends. This choice is no less arbitrary than Mahler's; it is simply different. Mahler knows that from a purely descriptive point of view there is a great deal more to "satisfactory" object relationships than the satisfaction of drive-derived needs; her theoretical and political loyalties, however, make it impossible for her to broaden the underlying explanatory framework. Mahler's work thus retains a blurred focus as well as an unresolved tension between increasingly relational concepts and a recurrent return to drive model principles.

A further cost of Mahler's strategy of accommodation must be measured in terms of the consequences of her revisions for the concept of drive itself. In her account the drives and subsequent modifications of them are in large measure environmentally determined. The child's early relationship with his mother has aspects that are satisfying, or good (relative to the broad range of needs that characterizes his early total dependency), and aspects that are frustrating, or bad. These are organized by the rudimentary psychic apparatus into "good" and "bad" representations of the self and the other. Good images tend to bring self and object into a close, satisfying relationship, while bad images tend to separate the two people involved, placing the child in a lonely, dangerous, and frightening situation. A subsequent preponderance of good experiences works in favor of the amelioration of bad, frightening experiences, allowing the development of a sense of the self as good and effective alongside a sense of "basic trust" in the object and in other people generally. Mahler addresses the energic aspect of this sequence by accepting Jacobson's hypothesis of an initial state of undifferentiated energy which bifurcates into aggression and libido partly by becoming attracted to groupings of good and bad self-object configurations (Jacobson, 1954a, 1964).

Does this formulation preserve the essential sensibility and tone of the drive/structure model? Freud addressed the issue of swings between closeness and separateness with his broadest biological hypothesis—the theory of the life and death instincts. It is the alternating ascendance of Eros, the binding force, and the death instinct, which pulls people apart, that explains this critical dimension of human relatedness (Freud, 1920a). Thus, within the drive model the goodness and badness of relationships is fully determined by the nature of the drive quantity with which they are cathected. The child's experience of parental care as good or pleasurable is understood simply and unequivocally: stroking, fondling, warmth, and so on are good precisely because they gratify *already existing* libidinal part instincts (Freud, 1905a). Mahler's attempts to tie her theoretical formulations to the tradition of the drive model have led her to modify substantially one of the model's fundamental premises. In the framework she proposes, pleasure originates in a particular mode of object relationship, which is subsequently internalized as a libidinal drive; the original concept of the pleasure principle holds that pleasure is a lowering of the tension of innate drive, actualized autoerotically or in a serendipitously achieved object relationship. If libido is derived from specific interactions between the child and his mother, if it is the mother's care that libidinizes undifferentiated energy or even the energy of the aggressive drives, then libido must be built upon internalized fantasies of pleasing mother-child interactions. Mahler's libido is, in the final analysis, social rather than biological; this is one of her major steps on the road to theoretical accommodation.

In a footnote to one of his last published papers, Hartmann (1955) tentatively suggested that in addition to the energy of sexual and aggressive drives and the various grades of neutralization of each, there may be a "primary ego energy" which is "noninstinctual," since it is derived from neither of the two basic drives. He did not develop this idea, nor is it integrated into his metapsychological framework. Mahler, however, does take the concept a step further. In one of her late papers she argues that "the normal infant is endowed with an innate given that prompts him at a certain point of his autonomous maturation to separate from mother—to further his own individuation" (1974, p. 158). A year later she further specified the concept by stating that "We know now that the drive is not toward separation per se, but *the innate given is the drive toward individuation*" (Mahler, Pine, and Bergman, 1975, p. 9n; italics ours). Within the terms of Mahler's theory, this drive provides the infant with a "reason" for moving away from the sense of omnipotence which is presumed to characterize the symbiotic phase.

In her most recent work Mahler is equivocal about whether the impulsion toward autonomy is truly instinctual: her formulation appears to rely more on forces derived from the maturation of autonomous ego functions and thus elaborates Hartmann's structural rather than energic hypotheses (Mahler and McDevitt, 1982). Although this would represent a return to a more conservative theoretical posture, it nonetheless constitutes a major revision of Freud's approach to the problem. In *Beyond the Pleasure Principle* he considered and rejected a concept of a "drive toward mastery," which is a close approximation to a drive toward individuation. This decision represents a crucial choice in theory-building, and it prescribes an interpretive thrust. For Freud, motivation must be understood as ultimately derived from either sexual or aggressive impulses which are themselves manifestations of Eros or the death instinct. The urge to move away from the mother is encompassed explicitly under the characteristics of the death instinct (and its derivative, aggression), as he describes it.

The existence of an innate impulsion toward individuation and the expression of individuality as a primary force is not unknown in psychoanalytic theory. It is suggested most clearly in Kohut's concept of "healthy assertiveness" and of the tendency toward self-cohesion, and in Winnicott's idea of the "true self" which will flourish in the absence of environmental interference. A drive toward individuation is *not*, however, an independent force within the terms of the drive/structure model, nor can it easily be integrated with the hermeneutics of the classical approach.

Mahler as a Transitional Theorist

Much of the history of theoretical accommodation within the drive model is best understood in terms of attempts to integrate peoples' experience of their relations with others, particularly early experience, into a developmental theory predicated on the transformation of drive energy into enduring psychic structure. This entails a movement away from an emphasis on mental mechanisms, the aspect of Freud's theory that was most fully embraced by authors such as Hartmann and Rapaport. Before Mahler the drive model approach to object relations acquired a fullness, a vividness, only with the onset of the oedipal period. Preoedipal interpersonal experience was integrated into Freud's early theory only insofar as it was reflected in the sequence of gratification and frustration of drive demand. Freud's later theory added to this the sequence of specific danger situations, again from the perspective of their impact on drive tension (1926a). Anna Freud's (1936) concepts of identification with the aggressor and defense against external situations somewhat deepened the appreciation of the role of early interpersonal experience, but again the application was limited to its role in instigating specific defense mechanisms. Hartmann's theory of early development described the importance of early reality relationships, including object relationships, but explicitly and intentionally focused on the mechanisms of psychic growth and development rather than on the interpersonal conditions that promoted it.

A major contribution of the body of Mahler's writings is the stress they place on the environmental (object relational) conditions of the preoedipal years and on the interpersonal experience that develops from it. The dyadic aspects of both symbiosis and separation-individuation push the theory toward an appreciation of a broad range of transactions in the earliest era of life and toward the importance of the mental representations to which these transactions give rise. Mahler makes it clear at several points that she is extending the concept of psychic experience back in time to the first months and even weeks of life. Thus, she says, "I believe it is from the symbiotic phase of the mother-infant dual unity that those experiential precursors of individual beginnings are derived which, together with inborn constitutional factors, determine every human individual's unique somatic and psychological makeup" (1963, p. 307).

In offering this perspective, Mahler provides the critical transitional link between the ego psychology of Hartmann and a diverse group of contemporary theorists including Kernberg (1976), Kohut (1971, 1977), George Klein (1976), and Loewald (1980), each of whom has attempted to create a psychoanalytic theory that stays closer to peoples' experience of their lives (Greenberg, 1981). And, as George Klein states explicitly, the new emphasis on experience brings object relations closer to the theoretical core (1976). Through her emphasis on the experiential (representational) residues of early dyadic exchanges, Mahler paved the way for others to shift the delicate balance of the drive model even more dramatically. For example, in equating the appearance of a differentiated ego with "confident expectation" of the appearance of the nurturant mother, she came close to the equation of experience and mechanism which is a central aspect of Klein's theoretical innovation.

There is, however, a critical distinction between Mahler's approach to the relationship of interpersonal experience and psychic mechanism and that of subsequent authors. Even though she dates interpersonal experience to an earlier developmental epoch than had her drive model predecessors, and even though she emphasizes the sequelae of these experiences and of the underlying object relationships, her ultimate explanatory recourse is always balanced by considerations drawn from Hartmann's framework. Her work constitutes a technical adjustment of the drive model—pushing the beginnings of interpersonal experiences and of the residues of object relations back to an earlier phase of development—rather than a change in its fundamental philosophical premises.

Mahler's work is transitional as well in a related area of psychoanalytic controversy—the theoretical status of the concept of the self. The self is a critical aspect of theories of object relations because it is, from one point of view, the logical counterpart of the "other" with whom one is in a relationship. In the early metapsychological formulations of the drive model, the nature of both parties in an object relationship was narrowly construed: the subject from the point of view of his biologically derived impulses; the object from the point of view of his responses to those impulses. With the advent of the structural model and its elaboration by the American ego psychologists, new aspects of object relations were brought under scrutiny. Not only was there a reciprocity of impulse and frustration/gratification between the individuals involved, but ego interests, defensive operations, security needs, superego demands, and so on were involved. These required an elaboration of the nature of the object, as well as of the psychic activity of the subject.

The concept of the self was introduced into the drive model by Hartmann (1950a) in his redefinition of narcissism. His "self" is a representation, an internal image, identical in all theoretical respects to the representations which are formed of objects. While this innovation did introduce the idea of a "whole person" (the counterpart of the "whole," or "constant" object), it stopped short of the use of the concept of the self as it appears in the work of relational theorists such as Sullivan, Winnicott, and Guntrip. Hartmann's self is the *object* of experience; in the work of others the self is the *subject* of experience. This is clear in concepts such as Sullivan's "self-system" and Winnicott's "true" and "false" selves, each of which performs functions which the drive model attributes to the structures id, ego, and superego. (The contrast in these two approaches lies behind the preference of many drive model theorists for the term "identity" rather than "self," since the former has experiential rather than structural/functional connotations.)

Hartmann's approach to the idea of the self is much more conservative and sketchy. Not only does the self lack a role in the psychic economy (except as a target of drive energies), it does not even have a fully developed history. Like object representations, the self-representation appears as a function of ego maturation and developmental experiences, none of which is carefully articulated. Hartmann's self seems to hang in midair, without history or function.

An adequate conceptualization of object relations requires a concept of the self. As Mahler puts it, "to try to speak of self-development separately from the development of object relations imposes an impossible strain on the data" (Mahler and McDevitt, 1982, p. 837). The construct of the self, however, is not easy to integrate into the tripartite psychic apparatus of the drive model. Mahler's strategy of theoretical accommodation is an important contribution to this problem. For her the self is less a functional unit than a critical developmental achievement. The self is, essentially as it was for Hartmann, a self-representation, but its stable establishment, alongside the establishment of stable object representations, is the benchmark of successful emotional growth and is dependent upon specific interpersonal as well as maturational experiences. Mahler's entire concept of separation and individuation is an aspect of this development. What becomes separate and individuated as the result of the process is a whole person, a self, and what results is a coherent sense of identity. In postulating a developmental view of the self, Mahler rejects the recent research of neonatologists who stress the infant's competency and separateness at birth (Stern, 1976; Brazelton, 1981). This perspective allows her to preserve the drive model by minimizing the structural role of the self. Although she defines the self as having "both experiential and structural aspects," her emphasis is principally on the former. She states that "we recognize the largely descriptive, experiential nature of the 'sense of self,' and a metapsychological conceptualization of 'self' is not implied" (Mahler and McDevitt, 1982, pp. 845, 829). The organizing, synthesizing, and integrating functions which give rise to the self are carried out, as they were for Hartmann, by the structure ego.

Adequate separation and individuation is one of two crucial phases of identity formation; the other concerns the resolution of bisexual identity (Mahler, 1958a). This second phase, leading to a stable sense of one's own gender, is described by Mahler in a way that again demonstrates her strategy of accommodation. Three conditions are necessary for this to evolve successfully: there must be an adequate integration of pregenital phases; there must be successful identification with the same sex parent; and the child's ego must be able to organize memories, ideas, and feelings about the self into a hierarchically stratified, firmly cathected organization of self-representations (Mahler, 1958a, 1958b). Aspects of this formulation, particularly the importance attributed to parental reactions to the child's gender and sexuality, are reminiscent of

Sullivan's view of the development of gender identity and of the role of reflected appraisals in self-formation generally. Yet Mahler remains firmly anchored in drive model thinking, reminding us that parental attitudes toward the child take place in the context of a maturationally determined-shifting of libidinal position. For example, the onset of the phallic phase will bring about a concentration of libido in the sexual parts of the body image; "This process occurs regardless of what environmental influences there are" (1958a, p. 81).

Once again we find Mahler occupying a crucial transitional role in the evolution of psychoanalytic thought. By equating the self with the self-representation, and by denying it a functional role as part of the psychic apparatus, she maintains the framework of the drive model. By emphasizing its importance as a developmental achievement and detailing the events necessary for its firm establishment—including not only maturational factors but also interpersonal transactions involving parental reactions to the separation-individuation process as well as reflected appraisals generally—her work assimilates important insights of the relational model. Moreover, her depiction of the conditions necessary for the evolution of a self without function makes it possible for subsequent theorists to develop an account of the evolution of a self with function.

Conclusion: A Fundamental Ambiguity

Mahler's account of the autistic, symbiotic, and separation-individuation phases draws a developmental map from the perspective of object relations. This brings into the drive model a body of observations—innovatively elaborated by Mahler—which is essentially relational in content; it is an act of theoretical accommodation. To accomplish this she has had to build upon, but also to revise and even distort, a broad range of drive model concepts: psychic energy, libido, the object, object relations, adaptation, the average expectable environment, narcissism, and so on. We are left with a final question: has Mahler left the interpretive thrust of the drive model intact or has she introduced a fundamentally new vision of human growth and development?

Late in her career Mahler turns to an explicit concern with this question. Having suggested throughout her writings that difficulties with separation and individuation are at the core of psychotic disorders, she suggests that borderline pathology as well has its roots in this early process (1972). Two years later she returns to the same issue, arguing that disturbances in separation-individuation are the cause of nonpsychotic psychopathology. In the same paper she suggests that the earliest experience with the symbiotic partner is a critical determinant of subsequent personality, both pathological *and* normal. This stands in striking contrast to traditional drive model thinking (especially as presented in the Freud/Abraham developmental map), in which personality, especially its neurotic aspects, is derived from the unfolding of libidinal stages of development and from their culmination in the Oedipus complex. Mahler confronts this issue directly in a late paper:

> Much of the empirical data available to us reveals that, while the concept of infantile neurosis derives from the prototypic source of intrapsychic conflict at its most complex state—the Oedipus complex—there is much in the neurotic development we see daily that derives as well from the prephallic, preoedipal periods, during which crucial forms of psychic organization and reorganization are structured.
>
> As I see it, much of our understanding may depend on developmental aspects in which most important are the qualitative assessment of residues of the symbiotic as well as the separation-individuation periods . . . we today possess *instruments* which, if used to amplify the libido theory, might bring us further in our understanding of the widening scope of neurotic symptoms in childhood as well as during the entire life cycle . . .
>
> We easily forget the fact that the apex of the libido theory which holds the key to neurosis, the Oedipus complex itself, is not only a drive theory but, equally importantly, an object relations theory . . .
>
> A number of problems remain unsettled because of a tendency to underestimate the potentiality of the ego and superego precursors at early levels of development to create intrapsychic conflicts. (Mahler, 1975, p. 190; italics in original)

We have quoted this statement at some length because it demonstrates the extent to which Mahler is committed to integrating a perspective that emphasizes the unfolding of changing modes of object relationship into the drive model. It illustrates her commitment to extend the role of object related conflicts away from their influence on psychopathological conditions that had been of minor interest within the drive model (such as, tics, child psychoses, and borderline states) and toward neurotic conditions, to the very heart of drive model concerns. This statement leads to a subtle but inescapable shift in emphasis away from libido theory toward a perspective drawing on the relational model. Her suggestion of the need to "amplify the libido theory" may amount to a suggestion to abandon it, or at least to minimize its central metapsychological position.

But Mahler raises questions about the drive model in an even broader way. In a moving summary statement about man's difficulties in living she states:

> in the rapprochement subphase, we feel is the mainspring of man's eternal struggle against both fusion and isolation.
>
> One could regard the entire life cycle as constituting a more or less successful process of distancing from and introjection of the lost symbiotic mother, an eternal longing for the actual or fantasied "ideal state of self," with the latter standing for a symbiotic fusion with the "all good" symbiotic mother, who was at one time part of the self in a blissful state of well-being. (1972b, p. 338)

From the point of view of the pleasure sequence, the organizing principle of the Freud/Abraham developmental map, the resolution of the Oedipus complex constitutes the point of separation and individuation. The Oedipus myth, as well as the complex to which it has given its name, tells of man propelled by destiny to seek "a blissful state of well-being" with his archaic objects, even at the greatest cost to himself. Life's tragedy, and also its opportunity, derives from the need for (and the possibility of) renunciation of the archaic objects in favor of new, more realistic ones.

With the full evolution of her theoretical perspective, Mahler no longer sees problems with symbiosis, separation, and individuation simply as etiological factors in previously uncharted psychopathological states, or even in the much-explored waters of neurosis. She sees the need to cope with these changing object relational possibilities as the key to the human dilemma, supplanting the need for renunciation of the oedipal objects. From one point of view, this is mild and cautious change; the theme of attachment and renunciation, like the emphasis on object relationships themselves, is moved back in time from the oedipal period to the subphases of separation-individuation, especially the rapprochement subphase. From another perspective, it is radical change because it constitutes a rejection of the organizing principle of the Freud/Abraham map. Seen in this way, Mahler has redefined the nature of human attachment: what is at stake is not drive gratification but rather a totality of tenderness, security, and pleasure that is experienced in a full relationship with another person.

The Spanish scholar Ortega y Gasset puts it that the man of anti-quity, before he did anything, took a step backwards, like the bull-fighter who leaps back to deliver a mortal thrust. He searched the past for a pattern into which he might slip as into a diving-bell, and being thus at once disguised and protected might rush upon his present problem. —THOMAS MANN, "Freud and the Future"

10 Edith Jacobson and Otto Kernberg

Of Freud's metapsychological points of view, the economic is both the most problematic and the most resistant to change. Acceptance of the idea of drives which set the activity of the psychic apparatus in motion and serve as the crucial bridge between mind and body has become the litmus test for the "orthodox" psychoanalyst. One must not only accept the principle of a psychic energy derived from the instinctual drives as the fundamental motivational force in human life, one must also accept a series of propositions regarding the nature and properties of psychic energy (see Schafer, 1976), and of the principles which govern its vicissitudes. From the early dissents of Jung and Adler, through the heterodoxy of Fairbairn and Sullivan, to the current controversy over Kohut's "psychology of the self," a theorist's attitude toward the drives determines his place in psychoanalytic circles. All relational/structure model theorists have found limitations in the ability of drive theory to account adequately for the complexity of human motivation, and all have subsequently been rejected by the classical psychoanalytic establishment.

Heinz Hartmann and Margaret Mahler attempted to respond to criticisms of drive theory by elaborating the psychology of the ego. Hart-mann's concepts of adaptedness and of processes of adaptation pointed toward an inherent relatedness between the individual and his environment; these concepts implied an enhanced view of the structure ego and suggested that direct environmental influence exerted its own dynamic force independent of the activity of the drives. Mahler's stress on the conditions existing in the child's "average expectable environment" pointed even more specifically to the power of early interpersonal relations. Her concern with separation and individuation spoke to a previously underemphasized aspect of early ego development. The contributions of Hartmann and Mahler enhanced our appreciation of the direction-giving function of the ego, of its role in the coordination and shaping of our daily experience, of its function in the determination of relations with others, and of the impact of early object relationships on the development of our particular, individual ego. But they did not (despite Hartmann's extensive discussion of neutralization and his postulate of noninstinctual energy, and despite Mahler's tentative suggestion of an autonomous "drive toward separation") systematically reconsider the economic point of view per se.

The ego and the id, although each is classed as a psychic "structure," are very different kinds of structures indeed. The ego thinks, feels, tests, considers, judges, and acts; in short it guides. The id, on the contrary, can only drive. Hartmann and Mahler made of the ego a more sophisticated, more capable guidance system and, within limits, assigned it certain driving powers. But these modifications, although clinically compelling, leave psychoanalytic theory in a rather anomalous position. Man's enhanced "guidance system" sits uncomfortably on top of a primitive energy source. It is as if one attempted to power a space capsule, including its elaborate information processing systems, with a steam engine. Even allowing for transformations of the energy produced by the engine (for example, from thermodynamic to electrical, a functional parallel to the idea of neutralization), steam is not up to the task. The conditions in which the machine must operate are too varied, the tasks it must accomplish too multifaceted, the types of power required too differentiated to rest on such an unsophisticated device. Advances in navigation, communication, aerodynamics, and ballistics (parallel to the elaboration of ego psychology) would serve us poorly without corresponding developments in the science of propulsion.

Of all the drive/structure model theorists after Freud, Edith Jacobson has been the most willing to extend her probing to the heart of psychoanalytic metapsychology. Her purpose throughout her writings is to align the economic point of view with the phenomenology of human experience, because it is this experience that highlights the role of relations with others. She has chosen two complementary theoretical strategies for achieving this goal. First, she focuses attention on man's experience of himself in his environment, on what Sandler and Rosenblatt (1962) have termed the "representational world."

Developmentally derived from psychobiological givens, and therefore maintaining ties with her drive/structure model predecessors, Jacobson's "representational world" has a lawfulness of its own, which explains in the fullest psychoanalytic sense both normal and pathological phenomena. The title of her major work, *The Self and the Object World* (1954a, 1964), in seeming conscious parallel with Hartmann's *Ego Psychology and the Problem of Adaptation*, points to Jacobson's emphasis on phenomenological theorizing and to her attempt to merge relational with classical metapsychological explanation.

Jacobson's second theoretical approach is to scrutinize the economic principles themselves. This leads her ultimately to a far-reaching revision of these principles. Whether considering the need to broaden the concept of orality, to modify what is meant by tension and discharge, or to revise the definition of the pleasure principle, she consistently reaches the conclusion that the energy theory must be brought into greater synchrony with the vicissitudes of object relations.

As a result of her willingness to challenge all the essentials of psychoanalytic theory, Jacobson's work overall constitutes what we consider the most satisfying drive/structure model theory after Freud's. But, like all good theory, including Freud's, her work provides not final answers but direction for future thought. Jacobson is the theoretical forebearer of both the complex mix of interpersonal and classical thinking of Otto Kernberg, who acknowledges her influence, and of the anti-metapsychological clinical theory of George Klein, who makes no such acknowledgment.

Jacobson's interest in examining and recasting long-standing psychoanalytic hypotheses, combined with her loyalty to the drive/structure model, was not without its price. In her more abstract theoretical writings (1953, 1954a, 1964, 1971) her prose is dense, almost impenetrable. There are apparent (and sometimes actual) internal contradictions; the papers take on the flavor of a series of conundrums from which the reader must, in concert with the author, extricate himself. The prose lends itself to misreading, even nonreading. Hairs are split and resplit until the flow of Jacobson's argument almost disappears.

The quality of Jacobson's theoretical writing reflects her vacillation between the preservation and revision of critical drive/structure model principles. This is strikingly clear when one turns to her more clinical papers (see Jacobson, 1943, 1946a, 1946b, 1949, 1959, 1967). They are lucid, poignant, colorful, often dramatic, and infused with the concern and warmth of an unusually patient and emphatic clinician. People come alive in them, and Jacobson's thinking is always clear. This contrast suggests that the difficulty of the theoretical works lies in their content.

Jacobson is most difficult to follow when she is most ambivalent, and she is most ambivalent when she is nearest to the core of crucial drive/structure model principles.

The "Self" and the "Object World"

In a prototypical situation to which psychoanalytic theorists have addressed themselves over and over again, a baby, feeling the pangs of hunger, begins to cry. Ideally, the mother hears the cry and brings food to satisfy his need. The baby sucks at the breast and relaxes in a state of pleasant quiescence. The mother may, however, be unavailable either physically or emotionally, and the baby's tension will continue to build—until help arrives or until he is able to employ some internal mechanism to bring about a temporary respite. In yet a third case, the mother may respond but, for her own reasons, respond inadequately (angrily, anxiously, by changing the diaper rather than feeding, and so on). The baby's hunger may or may not be satisfied in this case, and his behavioral response will depend on the specifics of the situation and on a variety of constitutional and developmental factors.

In addressing this behavioral sequence Freud consistently emphasizes the need, its underlying drive, and the vicissitudes of that drive. Gratification leads to a cessation of tension, to the experience of pleasure. Repeated experiences of gratification contribute to development by paving the way to an eventual anaclitic object choice. Frustration, despite inducing feelings of unpleasure, plays an equally important developmental role. It leads to the institution of the reality principle, to the substitution of thinking and purposive action in place of hallucinatory wish fulfillment, and to the development of the structure ego. The crucial element in the situation, from Freud's perspective, is the drive tension and its satisfaction or exacerbation. The *quality* of the maternal response is considered only from that point of view.

An alternative understanding is presented by Sullivan (1953), who points out two parallel but fundamentally unrelated aspects of the situation. First, the infant's biological (in Sullivan's terminology, "zonal") need is or is not being satisfied. This is of no psychological relevance. What is crucial psychologically is that the infant's need brings about a relationship of a particular quality between himself and his mother. Thus, the emotional tone of the mother's response (especially the presence or absence of anxiety, but also anger, kindness, and so on) rather than the extent to which the biological need is satisfied contributes decisively to personality formation. The infant's reaction to this emotional tone forms the basis of the earliest "personifications," first of the breast, eventually of the "whole mother." These personifications are essential in the organization of the "self system" and of personality in general.

The earliest relationship between an infant and its mother is thus simultaneously biological and social. As Hartmann (1939a) implied and Schafer (1976) clarified, the biological and the social are not distinct "parts" of the relationship, but alternative perspectives for viewing the entire situation. Which perspective a theorist chooses is an important aspect of his choice of psychoanalytic model.

In Jacobson's view the baby's experience of pleasure or unpleasure (gratification or frustration) is the core of his relationship with his mother. In this sense her position is well within the drive/structure model. However, she goes further in suggesting that the pleasure/unpleasure experiences lead to specific, developmentally crucial reactions to the object (mother). As experiences of satisfaction and dissatisfaction accrue, images are formed of the gratifying (good) and frustrating (bad) mother. These images, with their attendant emotional attitudes, constitute the beginnings of internal object relations. From early on, the object-related attitudes acquire their own motivational power, independent of the search for drive gratification. In this sense Jacobson's views accord well with those of relational/structure model theorists.

The mother who does not respond adequately to her infant's need both frustrates and disappoints him. Frustration refers to drive demand; disappointment refers to the quality of the nascent object relationship. Disappointment leads to devaluation of the object because it results in the unleashing of aggressive drive energies in frustrating situations (Jacobson, 1946a). Disappointment, with the ensuing devaluation, is thus related but not identical to frustration. Devaluation has a physiological forerunner in the reaction of disgust to unpalatable food. Like disgust, it leads to the desire to expel, to get away from, to be separate from the noxious object.

Experiences of pleasure, like experiences of unpleasure, give rise to specific attitudes toward the object. They lead to an increased valuation of it, and to the desire to possess the powerful source of pleasure, to merge with it (Jacobson, 1954a, 1964). Thus, the inevitable sequence of gratification and frustration gives rise to derivative sequences of attitudes toward the object. Moreover, it gives rise to a sequence of object-directed aims (merging with and separating from) that acquire a dynamic life of their own, relatively independent of the drive demands on which they are genetically based.

To the extent that these sequences are understood in terms of the frustration and gratification of drive, they represent transactions between an organism and its environment in Hartmann's (1939a) sense. To the extent that they are understood in terms of altering attitudes and aims directed toward the caretaking person, they are transactions between the "self" and the "object world."

Jacobson's postulate of two related but nonidentical sequences bears directly on the theoretical status of her concept of the self. The recent history of psychoanalysis is, to a large extent, organized around differing approaches to this issue (see Richards, 1982; Blum, 1982). Is the self a *system* within the psychic apparatus, supplementing the classical tripartite structure, or is it a *content* of the mind, an image comparable to the images formed of objects? Within the drive/structure model the definition of the self as an image is the less radical stance, since this usage leaves intact the explanatory priority of Freud's structural theory.

In her explicit definition of the self Jacobson appears to take a conservative stance. In her first published use of the term, she follows Hartmann's (1950a) distinction between the ego, a mental system, and the self, which refers to a representation within the ego (1954a, p. 85). Jacobson maintains this usage in her later work, reiterating that "the 'self' is an auxiliary *descriptive* term, which points to the person as a subject in distinction from the surrounding world of objects" (1964, p. 6n; italics ours).

In spite of these statements, Jacobson uses her concepts of the self and the object world to carry more theoretical weight than their definitions suggest. The vicissitudes of the self, the object, and their mutual relations not only depend on the actions of the ego but also exert their own influence on ego development. Even before Hartmann's introduction of the "self" into the drive/structure model, Jacobson's (1946a) distinction between frustration and disappointment had implied that the particular qualities of object relations has a profound effect on psychic structure formation. Eight years later, with her adoption of Hartmann's usage, Jacobson went further, stating that "the establishment of the system ego sets in with the discovery and growing distinction of the self and the object world" (1954a, p. 85). (This statement, along with the idea that the self-representations arise and exist *within* the system ego, is an example of the type of conundrum to which we have referred. It is especially confusing in light of Jacobson's admitted failure at times to distinguish the self from its representations.)

Ten years later, referring to a more advanced developmental stage, Jacobson suggests that "the ego cannot acquire a realistic likeness to the love object unless admired traits of this object become enduringly introjected into the child's wishful self images" (1964, p. 51). These statements make it clear that the ego, on the one hand (also the superego), and the self and object images, on the other, exert a reciprocal influence on each other's development. In crucial respects (although not exclusively), maturing means becoming like one's parents. One cannot become like one's parents unless one first experiences them (or aspects of them) as admirable, and additionally is able to have a sense of oneself as potentially like them. The "self and the object world" are thus the medium through which relations with others are assimilated and become usable for structural change.

The causative, functional significance which Jacobson attributes to relations with others is evident in her discussion of severe psychopathology. The characteristic pathology of affective disorders, borderline states, and overt psychoses is derived from disturbances in self and object representations (Jacobson, 1954a; 1959; 1964). The distinction among various types of depression, between depression as a primary illness and depression in schizophrenic conditions, and among other psychotic syndromes is likewise diagnosed on the basis of specific constellations of self and object representations (1954c; 1954d; 1971).

Both normal and pathological development are based on the evolution of images of the self and others. In Jacobson's view fixations refer not to modes of gratification but to modes of object relatedness; what is crucial is how solid, stable, realistic, separate, and articulated concepts of the self and of the object are at the time of developmentally critical disappointments. In one of her early papers, she discusses the little girl's reaction to the discovery that she lacks a penis. Jacobson argues that "though she meets with what must appear to be a real defect, her reaction depends largely on the severity of her disillusionment in the mother" (1946a, p. 133). For Freud (1925a, 1931) the girl's disappointment in not having a penis brings the early positive ties to her mother to an end, thus paving the way to the Oedipus complex. For Jacobson, the severity of the disillusionment, although based on the "real defect," depends ultimately on the quality of the earlier relationship between mother and daughter.

If disappointments are harsh and early, occurring before the consolidation, differentiation, and instinctual investment of the self and object representation, the aggressive devaluation of the object will include a corresponding devaluation of the as yet undifferentiated self. The result will be a merger of idealized self and object images into a wished-for but unattainable goal, with progressive devaluation of other, merged, hated self and object representations (1954a, 1964). To the extent that the idealized images are established as a kind of precocious ego ideal, a forerunner of the superego, the superego itself will be comprised of archaic self and object representation and will ultimately be unduly harsh and punitive. These developments can give rise to depressive or other psychotic psychopathology.

These considerations underscore the functional importance of the self, the object, and object relations in Jacobson's theory. The vicissitudes of self and object representations and the vicissitudes of ego and superego development are mutually influential. Development is conceptualized not only in terms of instinctual states and ego maturation but also in terms (reminiscent of and complementary to Mahler's framework) of stages of object relations.

Jacobson's concept of disappointment in the object is not identical to the concept of maternal failure as conceptualized by some relational/structure model theorists (Fairbairn, 1952; and especially Guntrip, 1967, 1971). Disappointment is always relative to a specific, drive-determined demand rather than to a more global striving for contact or engagement. Thus, from the observer's point of view, the disappointing mother is by no means an inadequate mother. In this sense one can read Jacobson's account of early development as an extrapolation backwards in time from the drive/structure model account of the oedipal period. As with the oedipal period, constitutional drive strength and constitutional ego capacities are critical in determining the point at which the mother will be experienced as disappointing. At the same time, however, Jacobson emphasizes the fact that these early conflicts are based on actual experience; she criticizes Melanie Klein on the grounds that Klein "loses sight of the realistic conflict history throughout later infantile phases" (1946a, p. 145).

From Narcissism to Identity Formation

Since Freud's (1914a) hypothesis of an initial libidinal cathexis of the ego and a corresponding lack of cathexis of the "outside," every drive/structure model theorist has felt it necessary to postulate that man at birth is, from the instinctual point of view, not related to his environment. This is consistent with Freud's underlying assumption that the process of becoming human is a matter of taming and socializing inherently antisocial instinctual drives. It is equally important that no relational/structure model theorist postulates an initial state of unrelatedness. From Melanie Klein's (1959) concept of the object as an inherent component of drive, to Fairbairn's (1952) statement that an objectless ego is (from the very beginning) a contradiction in terms, to Sullivan's (1953) hypothesis of "communal existence" in both biological and social terms, these authors have implicitly and sometimes explicitly argued that man is in effect a "social animal." Disagreement concerning this fundamental aspect of human nature is at the heart of the divergence between the two major psychoanalytic models, and the concept of primary narcissism constitutes a major forum in which this disagreement has been engaged. Because observational data concerning the earliest days or weeks of life is filtered through subjective interpretation, we consider the approach taken to the issue of primary narcissism to be philosophical and a priori rather than empirical.

Even within the terms of the drive/structure model, however, Freud's original formulation of primary narcissism presents formidable conceptual difficulties. Because he never reworked the concept in light of his introduction of the structural model, the richness of the original implication that at the outset of life all psychic energy is invested in the self was lost, since the ego was redefined as only one among the three psychic structures. Moreover, with the advent of the second dual-instinct theory, Freud hypothesized an original aggressive drive which followed a maturational course parallel to that of libido. This would suggest that unmodulated aggression originally is directed toward the self, that a primary masochism must exist alongside of primary narcissism (Freud, 1924a). Jacobson, however, noted that discharge of aggression onto the self prior to the advent of capacities to neutralize and fuse drives implies a self-destructive tendency in the infant that does not accord well with observational data. A further difficulty was caused by the fact that no theorist had coordinated the energic aspects of primary narcissism with considerations of cognitive development, particularly with the possibility that the differentiation of ego from object might be a developmental achievement occurring later than the hypothesized era of primary narcissism. Hartmann and Mahler each refined the concept somewhat, but these refinements brought their own complications.

It was Jacobson who most fully grappled with all of the difficulties posed by this central theoretical premise of the drive model, originally proposing the elimination of both the terms "primary narcissism" and "primary masochism" (1954a). In her later formulation, however, she called for a reinstatement of the former term, but with a drastically altered meaning. Primary narcissism should refer to "the earliest infantile period, preceding the development of self and object images, the stage during which the infant is as yet unaware of anything but his own experiences of tension and relief, of frustration and gratification" (1964, p. 15). This definition eliminates all of the difficulties of Freud's original formulation. It incorporates Hartmann's redefinition of narcissism as a cathexis of the self rather than of the ego, and avoids the problem of aggression by freeing the concept of narcissism from any energic connotation. This last aspect is the most radical. In Jacobson's work, primary narcissism is no longer an instinctual vicissitude; it is a concept drawn directly from the infant's (presumed) state of object-relatedness. This is in line with the first of Jacobson's two theoretical strategies: a recasting of traditional drive/structure model concepts in experiential and relational rather than classical metapsychological terms.

Even in the light of this revision, a problem remains in the classical vision of the earliest mental state. What *is* the original target of the aggressive drive, and how can the infant avoid destroying himself? To this problem Jacobson applies her second theoretical strategy, the modification of the energic hypotheses. She postulates an initial state of undifferentiated energy, which acquires libidinal or aggressive qualities, "under the influence of external stimulations, of psychic growth and the opening up and increasing maturation of pathways for outside discharge" (1964, p. 13). This hypothesis, which represents a radical theoretical shift, is parallel to Hartmann's concept of an undifferentiated matrix from which the structures ego and id emerge. It is, however, a more theoretically radical concept than Hartmann's because it points to direct environmental influence on the most basic qualities of instinctual drive. Jacobson states that "libidinal and aggressive cathectic gathering poles are formed around nuclei of as yet unorganized and disconnected *memory traces*" (1964, p. 52; italics ours).

If libido and aggression are brought into being by good and bad experiences respectively, in what sense do they remain "instinctual" quantities? And, if they are not instinctual, in what way does Jacobson's perspective differ from that of various relational/structure model theorists who argue that motivation is based on the earliest good and bad object relationships? Jacobson walks an uncomfortable tightrope on this issue. She argues that although her idea "may be reminiscent of the frustration-aggression theory, it should be noted that the transformation of undifferentiated psychophysiological energy into two qualitatively different kinds of psychic drives is here regarded as psychobiologically predetermined and as promoted by internal maturational factors as well as by external stimuli" (1964, p. 14). This disclaimer, from our vantage point, emphasizes rather than minimizes the extent of her revision of the classical economic theory.

Having posited the initial state of undifferentiation, Jacobson undertakes to depict the developmental processes leading to the establishment of a stable sense of identity, with the concomitant building up of psychic structure. Throughout, she is aware of the dual connotation of the concept of identity, its reference both to sameness and to difference (Greenacre, 1958; Mahler, 1968). Her vision as it unfolds is one of an exciting, dynamic tension; the reader becomes immersed in the growing child's struggle to carve an identity out of his earliest enmeshment with his caretakers. In this sense her developmental story parallels Mahler's, but in Jacobson we get a feeling for the child's experience that is lacking in Mahler's more detached view.

Jacobson discusses at great length the earliest transactions between mother and infant. She is sensitive to the nuances of this period, to the constant interplay between the mother's affective experience and that of her child, to the evocation in the mother of archaic conscious and unconscious images and fantasies. She is fully aware of the manifold, simultaneous effects which the mother's attention has on the child: "The mothering attitudes and activities which provide the infant with libidinal stimulation, gratifications, and restrictions, and thus pave the way to his emotional attachments, concomitantly turn the mother into his external ego and secure his survival. But, in addition, these very same attitudes and activities directly stimulate and promote his physical growth and the mental growth of his ego and very soon begin to convey to the child the reality principle and the first moral codes" (1964, p. 36).

To the nonpsychoanalytic reader, these observations may seem obvious. Of course the early involvement of mother and infant is rich and meaningful, but has not this been noticed by every devoted mother? This response is tempered in the psychoanalyst, who is aware that the earliest developmental era received scant attention from Freud and even from Hartmann. Jacobson is describing the early oral phase, and drive/structure model conceptualizations of this phase are organized unidimensionally around the vicissitudes of orality; all that is considered is the gratification of frustration of basic biological needs. How can we encompass what Jacobson has described within the explanatory framework of drive theory?

It is Jacobson's strength that she remains aware of both sides of the problem. She argues for the need to broaden the drive/structure concept of orality to include all aspects of the mother-infant relationship. Repeated satisfactions and frustrations of oral drive demands form the core of the child's earliest experiences of pleasure and unpleasure, and these in turn "constitute the first and most significant bridge to the mother" (1964, p. 35). These earliest experiences of the self as orally gratified or deprived become the central element of the first self images, attracting to themselves images from the manifold exchanges between the child and his mother.

Jacobson's view of orality has three aspects. First, she includes within its scope virtually all stimulation, gratification, and frustration that occur during the first months of life. Second, in line with Freud's view that

Eros operates in the service of combining simple into more complex organizations, she interprets the child's oral needs as creating a bond with a mother who is disposed to meet them. Third, and most crucial, she recasts the concept of drive so that it becomes a kind of organizing principle through which the infant can order the entire range of his earliest experiences with his caretakers. Orality, as Jacobson presents it, is a mode of experience, a continuum along which a broad spectrum of pleasurable and unpleasurable sensations can be arrayed. From these early experiences, organized by the infant in terms of their pleasure-unpleasure value, representations of himself and his mother gradually emerge, accompanied by object-directed aims. Experiences of gratification give rise to fantasies of merger; experiences of frustration lead to the wish to expel, to separate. Merger fantasies, which involve ideas of "total incorporation," of becoming the object, are the foundation of all subsequent object relations.

The early, largely fantasized transactions with his mother are carried out by the child through processes of introjection and projection. These terms, which have quite specific meanings within Jacobson's framework, "refer to psychic processes, as a result of which self images assume characteristics of object images and vice versa" (1964, p. 46). That is, they are processes which take place within the representational world, the world of inner objects.

These considerations illuminate the complex structure of Jacobson's theory. With maturation, the ego becomes able to integrate early pleasure-unpleasure experiences into partial, still primitive images of the self and of the object. Subsequent events in reality are experienced as gratifying or frustrating. These experiences in turn determine the nature of transactions within the representational world. They are also influenced by the level of ego development. The more mature ego will resist the merger fantasies that follow realistic gratification (or, at times, severe realistic frustration). However, the events within the representational world reciprocally exert an influence on the structure ego; Jacobson argues that periods of refusion are accompanied by a weakening of perception and reality testing and by a return to an earlier, less differentiated ego state. Thus, one can see clearly the complex interplay of forces derived from instinctual drive, from reality, from the structure ego, and from the inner world of objects.

At the beginning of the second year of life, two ego capacities, mostly maturationally determined, emerge that exert a decisive influence on the child's movement toward identity formation These are the gradually evolving ability to distinguish specific features of the love object and the appearance of an awareness of the time category of the

future. Each makes possible the concept of being like the admired object, rather than becoming the object, which was characteristic of fantasies of complete merger.

With the ability to discern different aspects of the loved object, ambivalence develops along with competitive strivings. The release of aggression in these feeling states promotes processes of (intrapsychic)
separation. Parental, especially maternal, attitudes are crucial at this
time, because an excess of either gratification or frustration can lead to
regressive merger fantasies. Under favorable conditions, however, the
idea of being like the object (Jacobson terms this "selective identification") supplements and gradually comes to replace the tendency toward
refusion. In a further development, the child becomes able to
distinguish between his own realistic and wishful self-images, a distinction which is reinforced by rivalrous competition with peers and
especially with the father. Such competition fosters the desire for
likeness with the powerful rivals and, at the same time, throws the child
back on his own growing resources. Similarly, the child's discovery of the
anatomical difference between the sexes contributes to identity formation by setting limits on what is possible and by driving home the idea of
membership in a gender group.

These processes pave the way to the establishment of stable ego identifications as well as to the establishment of an ego ideal. For Freud
(1914a) the ego ideal served as a refuge for the lost narcissism of early
childhood, as a place where the child's belief in his own perfection (or
perfectability) could be preserved. Jacobson updates the ego ideal concept in accord with her recasting of the concept of narcissism: the ideal
serves as an arena in which fusion between ideal self and ideal object images can take place, thus compensating in part for the lost fantasies of
merger. Formation of the ego ideal contributes to the developing sense
of identity by bringing about a desire for likeness not only with others
but also with one's own internal standards. Following these developments, the emergence of the superego as a cohesive psychic structure is
seen as a three-tiered process. The superego is composed first of archaic,
sadistic images formed early on the basis of introjective and projective
processes; next of the fused ideal self and ideal object images that com-
prise the ego ideal; and finally of realistic, internalized parental
demands, prohibitions, values, and standards.

Jacobson's depiction of the self and the object world remains tied to
the drive/structure model by virtue of the idea that they are shaped by
(are products of) the system ego and acquire their quality via cathexis by
libidinal and aggressive instinctual energies. However, self and object
images are codetermined by reality experiences (by interpersonal rela-

tions) and themselves contribute decisively to structural development. In reading Jacobson an appreciation of emphasis is crucial. A comparison of her account of early development with the schematic formulations of Hartmann highlights the distance she has moved the drive/structure model toward a fuller integration of the impact of the experience and meaning of relations with others.

Affects, Pleasure, and the Psychoeconomic Laws

In two papers on the psychoanalytic theory of affect (1953 and its revision in 1971) Jacobson presented some of her most critical thinking about essential drive/structure model hypotheses, especially of the economic point of view. These papers are dense and difficult, the argument often indirect, the conclusions at times ambiguous. Nevertheless, we will discuss them at length because they illustrate with great clarity the two-pronged theoretical strategy which we have stressed. Because they contain Jacobson's most powerful criticism of the economic laws, they are the theoretical precursors of the even more radical revisions of psychoanalytic theory in the work of Otto Kernberg and George Klein.

Over the course of his career Freud offered three distinct affect theories. First, affect, equated with the quantity of psychic energy, became dammed up in psychoneurotic disorders and was discharged in therapeutic cathartic experiences (1894; Breuer and Freud, 1895). Second, with the advent of the topographic model and the theory of instinctual drive, affect was understood as the nonideational component of the mental representation of drive forces (1915a, 1915b). In his final reworking of affect theory, with the introduction of the structural model Freud located the anxiety affect, and affect in general, within the system ego. The ego was credited with the ability to use anxiety as a signal in dangerous situations, which were instigated by external events but ultimately explained by the potential build-up of instinctual tension (1926a). Ambiguities remained in this third approach because Freud never entirely discarded the second, "toxic" theory of anxiety, nor did he make clear just how far he wished to generalize the signal function of anxiety to include other affects.

Discarding Freud's earliest approach, Jacobson begins by questioning the extent to which affect corresponds to instinctual or ego processes. Dissatisfied with an either/or solution, she suggests a classification in which some affects arise from intrasystemic tensions and some from intersystemic tensions. Thus, affects such as sexual excitement and rage stem directly from the id; fear of reality, object love, and hate arise from the ego; shame and disgust emerge from tensions between the ego and the id; guilt and aspects of depression are the result of ego-superego tensions.

Immediately after suggesting this schema, however, Jacobson points out that its usefulness is severely limited, arguing that: "the final affective expression, in the mature, highly differentiated psychic organization, may develop from a series of inter- and intrasystemic tensions, which are interrelated, which condition one another, and which arise simultaneously or sequentially at various sites in the psychic apparatus. It can be understood only from the study of the associated conscious and unconscious ideational processes" (1953, p. 47). The affects for which her schema cannot account, she notes, include among others "kindness and heartlessness, sympathy and cruelty, loving and hostility, sadness, grief and happiness, depression and elation" (1953, p. 47n).

Interestingly, despite this cogent critique of her own proposed schema, Jacobson repeats both the schema and the critique in her otherwise highly modified 1971 version of the same paper. Why has she chosen to present her views in this way? We suggest that Jacobson is attempting to demonstrate the serious limitations of any metapsychological (structural, dynamic, or economic) conceptualization of affect. The dynamic range and subtlety of affective experience, she argues, is metapsychologically inexplicable in fact and probably in principle. What can be offered in place of metapsychological formulations? Here Jacobson's statement that affects can be understood only from "the study of the associated conscious and unconscious ideational processes" is crucial. Affects are experiences and must be understood in experiential terms. They cannot be derived from underlying quasi-biological processes.

The changing relationship between affect and instinctual drive was a crucial element of Freud's development of the drive/structure model. To the extent that affect is a derivative of instinctual drive, the interpersonal context in which the affects arise loses theoretical importance. When affect is understood as more independent of drive, as it was in Freud's first and third formulations, the role of relational considerations is correspondingly heightened. It is precisely this path which Jacobson follows in her recasting of the affect theory.

Jacobson turns next to the relationship of affects to phenomena associated with drive tensions and with drive discharge. Are affects to be considered manifestations of discharge, tension, or both? This brings into focus considerations about the nature of pleasure, because affects have clear pleasure-unpleasure values and because the psychoanalytic pleasure principle relates pleasure to discharge and unpleasure to tension. Yet here we run into an important empirical difficulty. Some affects associated with a building of tension are clearly pleasant—sexual excitement, pleasurable anticipation, and so on. And some affects associated with discharge—those that accompany crying, for example—are clearly unpleasant. Thus, the relationship between affect, tension, and pleasure is more complex than would be indicated by the metapsychological principles of the drive/structure model. Although Freud's (1924a) revision of the pleasure principle postulated a rhythm in the rise and fall of tension rather than discharge per se as productive of pleasure experience, neither Freud nor any of his followers before Jacobson had integrated this perspective into the broad theoretical framework.

On the basis of these considerations, Jacobson offered a remarkable suggestion: tension and discharge are not to be considered opposites. Taking sexual intercourse culminating in orgasm as an example, she argues that the discharge process itself consists in a dynamic process of flux, only ultimately leading to a drop of tension. She offers the model of a bathtub with the drain open and the faucet running; water is constantly running in and draining out, with the overall level determined by relative quantities and forces. In real life, she notes, we often actively seek tension. Prolonged relaxation, though initially pleasant, will eventually lead us to seek a more stimulating (tension-building) situation which will lead to a different kind of discharge. Therefore, tension and discharge are separable but not necessarily opposing aspects of the flow of human existence.

Jacobson's perspective accords well with our observations about how people live their lives, and her formulation seems reasonably conjunctive with Freud's reformulation of the pleasure principle, but we must not underestimate how far behind we have left drive/structure model metapsychology. As in her discussion of affects and structure, this theoretical tack substitutes subtleties for dichotomies, shadings for polarities. Once again, we are pointed toward a level of theorizing in which the importance of the interpersonal context in which pleasure is experienced will be stressed.

This emphasis becomes even clearer when Jacobson turns her discussion first to a redefinition of the pleasure principle and then to a fresh consideration of the relationship between the pleasure principle and the economic laws. The pleasure principle, in her view, no longer aims at a simple lowering of drive quantity. Instead, "the psychic organization may show a striving for cycles of pleasure alternating between excitement and relief, which correspond to biological swings of tension around a medium tension level . . . The pleasure principle would not have the function to bring about relief of tension . . . [It] would only direct the course of the biological swings around a middle axis of tensions . . . Pleasure qualities would be attached to the swings of the tension pendulum to either side" (1953, p. 58). Given this position, which again leads us away from the metapsychological emphasis on quantity and toward a more gradated, qualitative perspective, what is the relationship between the pleasure principle and the economic point of view? On this point Jacobson can be confusing, perhaps because she is aware of how close she is to drastic revisionism.

In her 1953 paper she states: "My conclusions . . . preclude using 'pleasure-unpleasure' as mere referents to the economical situation . . . In my presentation these terms refer to the *qualities of the felt experience* (p. 56n; italics ours). In her 1971 revision of the original paper, she states that "the pleasure-unpleasure principles cannot be considered economical principles." However, she continues, "the assumption that the pleasure-unpleasure principles work independently of . . . the psychoeconomic laws is not tenable" (pp. 20, 28).*

What is meant by the juxtaposition of these two statements? By way of explanation, let us turn to a parallel example. Within the sphere of biology there are anatomical and physiological laws which govern the use of voluntary muscles. Within the sphere of psychology there are laws governing the manifestations of hysterical conversion reaction, which may also affect the use of those muscles. The laws of conversion are not anatomical or physiological laws, but they are not independent of such laws. No conversion symptom can occur which is anatomically or physiologically impossible, although anatomy and physiology do not sufficiently explain conversion phenomena. The relationship Jacobson seems to postulate between the pleasure principle and the economic laws is similar: the pleasure principle operates within the boundaries set by the economic laws, but it is not reducible to them.

If this is so, where does it leave drive/structure model theory? Freud, and Hartmann after him, each decreed that once a phenomenon was analyzed from the dynamic, structural, and economic points of view, a full psychoanalytic explanation was achieved. The metapsychological

---

*Six pages later, Jacobson states: "in certain situations the pleasure principle can make itself independent [of economic laws] and . . . these two laws can then be in opposition to each other" (1971, p. 34). This evident contradiction appears to result from the thin theoretical line she is attempting to walk. The difficulty in following her argument is clear in the work of George Klein (1976). In a paragraph beginning with the statement that his use of the pleasure principle refers to "pleasure and unpleasure *experiences* — qualities of awareness," Klein cites Jacobson's 1953 paper as standing in opposition to his view (1976, p. 210). He is more impressed by Jacobson's frequent declarations of loyalty to the classical metapsychology than by the substance of her theory.

points of view are both necessary and sufficient explanatory principles. In positing a pleasure principle that operates according to "the qualities of felt experience," however, Jacobson is suggesting that there is a *lawfulness* to experience, that psychoanalysis needs *phenomenological* (and therefore relational) explanatory principles. These may rest on classical metapsychology, as conversion hysteria rests on anatomy and physiology, but they account for dimensions of human experience not previously accounted for, in the same way that anatomy and physiology cannot in and of themselves explain glove anesthesia.

We can thus see that the redefined pleasure principle stands in the same relation to metapsychology (and especially to the economic point of view) as the "self" and the "object world" stand to the classical model (and especially to the dynamic and structural points of view). We have once again encountered, in perhaps its most dramatic manifestation, Jacobson's first theoretical strategy.

Where we encounter this first strategy in Jacobson's writings, we invariably also find the second: the reevaluation and recasting of the economic principles. Thus, Jacobson revises the concept of the constancy principle itself. Rather than operating in the service of keeping the level of tension as low as possible, it is the function of the constancy principle as redefined, "to establish and maintain a constant axis of tension and a certain margin for the biological vacillations around it" (1953, p. 59). The pleasure principle and the constancy law may thus oppose each other, because the pleasure principle controls the swings around the axis of tension, while the constancy principle endeavors to return the level of tension to that axis.

How are conflicts between the pleasure and constancy principles resolved? Here Jacobson is able to use her theoretical modifications to very good advantage. Conflict between the two principles may often be resolved by the reality principle. Specifically, the reality principle may enforce attenuated, unpleasurable discharge as a means of preserving the psychoeconomic balance. Moreover, Jacobson reinterprets the reality principle by "interpersonalizing" it vis-à-vis earlier constructions. She holds that it represents mainly the internalization of parental requirements (1953, p. 64). Thus, the sequelae of early object relations exert a decisive influence both on the experientially oriented pleasure principle and on the psychoeconomic constancy law. We are thus left with a motivational theory that derives as much from specific constellations of self and object representation as it does from the operation of the classical "hydraulic" mechanisms.

Jacobson's affect theory, although difficult, constitutes an important extension of drive/structure model thinking. It is rich and, like all her contributions, of the greatest clinical utility. However, a close reading reveals that it violates classical metapsychological and methodological principles, and that much of the obscurity in Jacobson's writing tends to hide the extensiveness of her theoretical heterodoxy.

The Elusive "Third Drive" of the Ego Psychologists

Every drive/structure model theorist since Freud who has sought to develop a comprehensive framework has alluded to the possibility of a third drive. Hartmann (1955, p. 240n) speculated that there may be a "non-instinctual" energy source fueling the ego apparatus of primary autonomy. Mahler advanced the hypothesis of an autonomous drive toward individuation (Mahler, Pine, and Bergman, 1975) which supplements the dual-instinct theory. Jacobson's theory contains a similar suggestion, although it is implied rather than explicitly formulated.

Jacobson postulates an initial state of energic undifferentiation which, under the influence of developmental and maturational forces, bifurcates into aggressive and libidinal drives. This formulation represents the economic parallel to Hartmann's undifferentiated matrix of ego and id which, in the course of normal development, remains undifferentiated for only a given period of time. The relation of Jacobson's economic schema to Hartmann's structural concept is implicit in her statement that energic regression involves not only deneutralization and defusion but possibly further transformation into primary undifferentiated energy.

This relatively straightforward emendation of the dual-instinct theory becomes more complex when Jacobson suggests that her formulations would: "permit us to include once more physiological tension, such as hunger, in the framework of psychoanalytic theory. This has no place at present in our conception of *only two drives*—libidinal and aggressive. Hunger, once designated by Freud as an ego drive, would then be the expression of such primitive, undifferentiated, psychophysiological drive tensions" (1964, pp. 16–17; italics ours). The inclusion of hunger among the manifestations of undifferentiated drive energies is puzzling, since it suggests that not all of the energy undergoes the bifurcation process and that there is a continuous generation of undifferentiated energy throughout life. Clearly the regular occurrence of hunger could not represent a periodic profound regression. Thus, without announcing it, Jacobson appears to have suggested the possibility of a third drive. However, like Hartmann and Mahler, she never followed through the implication of this hypothesis. She thus joins other drive/structure model theorists in raising the possibility of a third drive and then assigning it a limited role, if any, in the psychic economy. Like her theoretical predecessors, Jacobson did not attempt to integrate the third drive with aggressive and libidinal energies, or to suggest that it has its own independent vicissitudes.

The reason for this suggestive avoidance is inherent in the fundamental premises of the drive/structure model. Freud's determinedly dualistic theory requires that *all* motivation be derived from originally untamed, unmodulated sexual and aggressive energies. This interpretive stricture has seemed confining to many subsequent theorists; hence the idea of a third drive is attractive. Yet the explanatory domain of the "third drive" must always remain vague. To postulate phenomena which require the third drive is to suggest that the dual-instinct theory is not comprehensive enough. This has long been the argument of relational/structure model theorists, but it has no comfortable place within classical theory. The third drive appears to be each theorist's response to a perceived motivational "missing link," but none has been quite willing to make that gap explicit or to tell us just how the third drive might fill it. Despite her commitment to a thorough reexamination of the energic laws, in this respect Jacobson is no more successful than her predecessors.

Approach to Psychoanalytic Technique

Jacobson rarely discussed technical issues explicitly, although she did produce a number of beautifully written case histories. When she did address her technical methods, it was in the context of work with severely disturbed patients: depressives, borderlines, and occasionally overt schizophrenics. In these works Jacobson's personal warmth and sensitivity come through. Commenting on her treatment of a severely depressed patient (1943, 1946a, 1971), her long-term friend George Gero states: "one cannot help but admire Jacobson's courage, determination, and conviction that she could help this patient. I believe that the ultimate success of the therapy was as much dependent upon this quality of Jacobson's personality as it was upon her profound understanding of the pathological process" (1981, p. 76).

With the severely disturbed patients whom Jacobson treated so effectively, she calls for certain modifications of psychoanalytic technique. Having noticed that "depressives try to recover their own lost ability to love and to function through magic love from their love object" (1954b, p. 597), she proceeds to describe in a particular case a lengthy idealizing transference. Her treatment of this is particularly interesting in light of Kohut's (1971) "discovery" seventeen years later of the therapeutic value of such transferences. Jacobson made no attempt to analyze this idealization, instead using it both to carry the treatment and to allow the patient, at least temporarily, to reconstitute some of his self-esteem around it. She makes no therapeutic claims for the technique of not analyzing the transference ("permitting" the idealization) at this time, nor does she fail to recognize the severe ambivalence which such transferences may mask. Rather, her response comes across as simple and humane, stemming from an empathic understanding of what the patient needed at the time.

At a late stage in treatment, Jacobson's spring vacation led to the same patient's feeling abandoned, which led him into a severe depression. He responded by deciding to write a book (the patient was a successful scientist, and was aware of Jacobson's own psychoanalytic publications). Jacobson's interpretation of the ensuing phase of the analysis and her handling of it are illuminating. She states that "The book period represents a definite, narcissistic withdrawal from me and the world in general. He has indeed tried to replace the analyst by a book, a book of which he has robbed her." Of her own response, Jacobson writes: "At this point the analyst's deliberate, supportive counterattitude helps him over the most critical stage. I show a very active interest in his book, as far as my vague familiarity with the subject permits; in other words, I share the book with him and win him back by allowing a temporary situation of participation" (1945b, pp. 601, 602).

The therapeutic action of psychoanalysis, in Jacobson's view, ultimately resides in the analyst's interpretive activity. She addresses many of the questions to which Kohut (1971, 1977) turned his attention years later, such as whether the deepest pregenital fantasy material of severely disturbed patients can be and needs to be interpreted if the outcome is to be successful. Some of her technical procedures in fact sound remarkably like Kohut's. Describing the treatment of one patient, Jacobson reports that "During the initial period and, later on, during times of severe emotional crises, I permitted this patient to 'use' me in the ways and roles that he needed" (1967, p. 57). This constitutes a clear statement of the handling of what Kohut would call a self-object transference. Jacobson, however, does not see these technical procedures as curative per se. It is interpretation that brings about analytic change, and she believes that with adequate preparation and tactful timing, even very severely disturbed patients are capable of hearing and using deep id interpretations (1954b).

Jacobson's failure to link her technical modifications (in Gero's terms, her personal qualities) to the therapeutic improvement of her patients reflects her loyalty to drive/structure model perspectives. Her failure to generalize her findings into a technical theory applicable to a broad range of psychoanalytic patients is likewise understandable. One's impression of her as a clinician, however, remains colored by her sensitive understanding of the nuances of the patient-analyst relationship. In this sense she has contributed greatly if implicitly to contemporary approaches to problems of technique.

Jacobson and Her Followers

One attempts a brief summary of Jacobson's contribution to psychoanalysis at one's own peril. She was a theorist of such scope and such subtlety as to elude synopsis. Her descriptions of the phenomenology of development and of severe psychopathology, her revisions of classical metapsychology, and her clinical work have infiltrated the work of all contemporary analysts in one way or another. Yet she has never achieved the "popularity" that other, less significant theorists have attained.

Jacobson's theory consists of a complex mix of experiential and metapsychological concepts. Although she insists that experiential concepts—pleasure as she has redefined it, the "self," and the "object world"—are derived from innate, biologically given drives, her emphasis is on the phenomenological, and therefore relational side of things. Even when discussing the tripartite structural model, Jacobson justifies this particular way of dividing up the psychic apparatus on the fact by arguing that it is "based on significant inner experiences" (1964, p. 123). Adding to this her emphasis on disappointment as opposed to frustration, her recasting of the pleasure principle, and her revision of the theory of psychic energy, it is clear that she has significantly shifted the focus of drive/structure model thinking.

In important respects, however, Jacobson remains a drive/structure model theorist. She maintains this tie in two ways. The first is by fiat. Even in the midst of her broadening of the concept of orality, Jacobson notes that "the mother's influence on the infantile growth of the ego cannot be conceptualized better than in terms of our drive theory" (1964, p. 37). Jacobson showed a quite remarkable aptitude for scathing criticism of those who had explicitly turned away from drive theory, as her review of Sullivan's work (1955) and her critique of Bowlby (1964) show.

Jacobson's second tie to the drive/structure model is more theoretical. The self and the object world, while exercising a reciprocal influence on the tripartite structures, are products of the structures, and Jacobson insists that the bifurcation of drive energy into libido and aggression is biologically preordained and maturationally achieved. These principles place her firmly within the classical tradition and allow her to assign to the relational patterns which she so carefully and incisively delineates a derivative, secondary status. Thus, her theory remains firmly anchored to the classical approach.

The overall impact of Jacobson's work is, however, more revisionist than she or most commentators acknowledge. Her revisionism becomes quite apparent within the context of the classical psychoanalytic distinction between description and explanation (Hartmann, 1927, 1939a). Within the theoretical guidelines of the drive model, phenomenology and metapsychology are different universes of discourse. Yet, Jacobson's contributions draw heavily on descriptive, phenomenological formulations. This emphasis, combined with and supplemented by Mahler's observations of child development, creates a dilemma for subsequent drive/structure model theorists, a dilemma which has been dealt with in three different ways. One strategy has involved the attempt further to integrate the two levels of theorymaking, recasting essential drive/structure model concepts in experiential terms. This results in a metapsychology even further removed from biological givens, a metapsychology suggesting a less organismic, more social view of man. This is the theoretical strategy of Otto Kernberg. A second strategy has been to acknowledge the power of the phenomenological concepts and also the limitation of the metapsychological base. This leads to a theory in which experiential laws, stressing the critical role of relations with others, are deemed both necessary and sufficient; metapsychology is discarded or relegated to a level of discourse that is biological rather than psychoanalytic. This is the strategy of those contemporary theorists who propose a strictly "clinical" explanatory framework: George Klein, Merton Gill, and others. A third strategy is to acknowledge that both the metapsychological and the phenomological approaches have explanatory value, while holding that the attempt to derive one from the other (as Jacobson does) is theoretically problematic. The solution is to establish parallel, independent systems, one deriving from biologically given drives, the other from relational experiences. This is the "mixed model" approach which characterizes the theory of Heinz Kohut.

Edith Jacobson is thus the theoretical forebear of every contemporary theorist who retains ties of any kind to the drive/structure model. In this sense, the difficulties of her theoretical superstructure are as seminal and provocative as her insights are satisfying.

Otto Kernberg

In a series of books and papers written since the 1960s Otto Kernberg developed a clinical and theoretical framework that has attracted much attention and generated considerable controversy among psychoanalytic theorists. Kernberg has devoted a great deal of effort to positioning himself within the evolving tradition of the drive/structure model. He presents his theoretical base as deriving from and extending Jacobson's integration of the phenomenology of interpersonal relations with classical metapsychology, and he acknowledges the influence of Jacobson (1979) and of Mahler's developmental framework (1980). At the same time, he attempts to blend the perspective of the drive model with sensibilities originating within the relational model. He is the first American theorist who declares himself a Freudian, but who also announces explicitly that he draws from the writings of relational model authors.

Throughout his writings Kernberg retains the language of the drive model. He talks of instincts and of their action within a psychic apparatus divided into the classical tripartite structures ego, id, and superego. Until his recent work (1982), when he discussed the self, he carefully adopted Hartmann's usage: the self was treated as an image, a representation within the ego. Kernberg's careful choice of words has obscured the fundamental thrust of his theory, which as it has evolved reflects merely a political tie to the classical model. His work, unlike that of Jacobson, does not preserve essential drive model principles but only its vocabulary. He is included in our consideration of the drive/structure model on the basis of his declared loyalty and because his work illustrates how the strategy of theoretical accommodation can be pushed to the point of violation of a model's fundamental premises.

Kernberg is the only American psychoanalyst to characterize his own work as an "object relations theory," but in doing so he carefully circumscribes the meaning of the term. He rejects the claim (by theorists like Fairbairn and Guntrip) that object relations theory constitutes a general theory of mind, alternative to classical metapsychology. Rather, he limits his usage to: "a more restricted approach within psychoanalytic metapsychology stressing the buildup of dyadic or bipolar intrapsychic representations (self- and object-images) as reflections of the original infant-mother relationship and its later development into dyadic, triangular, and multiple internal and external interpersonal relationships . . . [W]hat is important is the essentially dyadic or bipolar nature of the internalization within which each unit of self- and object-image is established in a particular affective context" (1976, p. 57).

By limiting the definition of object relations theory, Kernberg declares loyalty to fundamental principles of classical metapsychology. He thus attempts to divorce himself from the relational/structure theories of Sullivan, Fairbairn, and Guntrip, despite the fact that the structure of his theory and its philosophical implications are often close to theirs. For example, he is able to claim that within the context of a circumscribed object relations theory the object "should more properly be 'human object'" (1976, p. 58). Klein and Tribich (1981) point out that this radically changes the meaning of the object, as Freud used the term, and therefore alters the basic implications of drive theory. We agree with this assessment, but throughout this book we have attempted to show that the meaning of the object concept had undergone a gradual but inexorable evolution—from Freud's original usage, through Hartmann's "average expectable environment," to Mahler's "ordinary devoted mother," and Jacobson's "object world." In this sense, in contradistinction to Klein and Tribich, we see Kernberg as attaching himself to an already evolving tradition of theoretical accommodation, a tradition which has been moving drive theory toward a more "social" view of man and of the forces motivating him. In common with Klein and Tribich, however, we believe that Kernberg's theory is a very different theory indeed from Freud's.

Kernberg begins with a clinical data base derived from the psychoanalytic psychotherapy of severely disturbed patients, especially of what he calls "low level character disorders," including narcissistic and borderline personalities. Like Kohut, he derives most of his inferences from the transference reactions characteristically manifested by these patients. These are people, Kernberg observes, who typically become involved in early, intensively experienced, chaotic transferences in which they demonstrate dramatically contradictory attitudes toward the therapist. In rapid succession, the therapist is seen as all good and all bad, strong and weak, loving and hating, and so on. Each of these attitudes is accompanied by a corresponding, equally rapidly fluctuating image of the patient's own self. In contradistinction to neurotic patients, in whom the most intense transferences are evoked only by lengthy analytic work, with more seriously disturbed people they may emerge within the first weeks—or days—of treatment.

The rapid alternation in transference paradigms, which is echoed by what Kernberg calls a "selective impulsivity" in their daily lives, reflects the predominance of primitive defense mechanisms, especially splitting. He ties his concept of splitting to Freud's (1927, 1938), but his actual application has more in common with that of Melanie Klein. As Kernberg defines splitting, "there is a complete, simultaneous awareness of an impulse and its ideational representation in the ego. What are completely separated from each other are complex psychic manifestations, involving affect, ideational content, subjective and behavioral manifestations" (1976, p. 20). The mutually contradictory states of mind are acknowledged by the patient, but their implications are blandly denied. Related to splitting, and occurring along with it, are other early defenses such as primitive idealization and devaluation, projection, and especially projective identification. Each of these is indicative of the fluid qualities of self and object representation (see Jacobson, 1964), and of the emergence of early configurations of self-object relations.

The ease with which these transference paradigms emerge suggests that the early configurations on which they are based continue to exist within the psychic apparatus on what Kernberg calls a "non-metabolized" basis. Metabolization of early object relations refers to the same phenomenon described by the terms "transmuting internalization" (Kohut), "depersonification" (Jacobson), and even, although with a slightly different emphasis, "internalization" in Hartmann's sense. Each suggests that early relations with the environment give rise to enduring psychological patterns (structures) which reflect their influence. In normal developmental situations the early relationships lose their specific early qualities and become assimilated into a smoothly functioning psychic system. In this sense, the process is very much like the digestion and use of food (Bion used "digestion" to describe the same phenomenon), and the concept of metabolization suggests that "We are what we eat" or, more specifically, "We are what we experience."

Unlike actual metabolism, however, the psychological process is, even under optimal circumstances, reversible. Thus, in the course of the analysis of neurotic patients, superego demands and prohibitions that the patient initially experiences only as his own can be experienced as specific parental attitudes, expressed in the context of particular interactions between patient and parent. It is precisely the capacity for this kind of structural demetabolization (the aspect of analytic regression that emerges most clearly in the context of the transference) that makes analysis possible. With neurotic patients, those who in the terms of drive model theory present a firmly consolidated tripartite structure, demetabolization necessarily takes a great deal of time, work, and willingness to regress on the part of the patient.

With the severely disturbed patients treated by Kernberg, however, the emergence of early, unmodulated relationships in the transference occurs quickly because adequate metabolization has never taken place. It is as if food had never been digested properly, so that a simple examination of the contents of the intestine could reveal one's entire nutritional history. Precisely because adequate structure had not been developed, the availability of this information proves to be of no use to the patients; they can only act out and reexperience the chaotic, contradictory self-object configurations. Analytic interpretations with these patients must address the splitting operations and the existence of contradictory states of mind. This, in Kernberg's view, allows the patient to begin to integrate split-off images into a more unified vision of himself and of others.

Kernberg applied the developmental theory provided by Jacobson (and, to a lesser extent, by Mahler) to these observations, concluding that his seriously disturbed patients are pathologically fixated at an early stage of psychic structure formation. The very early ego, he suggests, is too weak—cognitively undeveloped—to integrate very different kinds of early experience. Organization of experience by the primitive ego proceeds according to the affective coloring which accompanies it, that is, whether it is "good" or "bad." Ego weakness keeps these good and bad experiences separated.

A further clinical observation led Kernberg to elaborate the consequences of this early situation. When he pointed out the existence of contradictory ego states to his severely disturbed patients, they would become highly anxious. This anxiety suggests the presence of intense conflict, not merely the incapacity of the ego to contain different types of experience. From this Kernberg concluded that the original ego weakness could later be employed for defensive purposes. It is this continuation of an early, cognitively determined state of affairs that he terms defensive splitting. Defensive splitting is normal in very early childhood, but it can also be pathologically fixated and continue into the adult years of severely ill people.

What is the content of the early experiences that are originally unintegrated and later defensively split, the experiences which optimally would be metabolized into psychic structure? As Kernberg's definition of object relations theory suggests, they are relational configurations, specifically reflecting the interaction of the infant with his "human object," the mother. These configurations consist of three component parts: an image of the object; an image of the self; and an affective coloring determined by the drive derivative active at the time of the interaction (1976, p. 26). Together, these three components compose what Kernberg calls an "internalization system"; they are the "stuff" of which experience and eventually psychic structure are constituted. (Unfortunately, Kernberg's books consist largely of his papers,

which were published over the course of a decade. His views, especially on the nature of drive, change from chapter to chapter. This formulation constitutes an early approach to the relation of drive to affective coloring.)

Internalization systems are of three kinds, each reflecting the normal situation at a particular developmental stage. Kernberg labels these with terms drawn from previous drive model formulations, although each is drastically redefined. The earliest, most primitive form of internalization he calls "introjection." It represents the internalization of the least organized, least differentiated self and object images in the context of the most violent, least modulated affective coloration. Introjection may be used defensively, or it may proceed under the influence of the conflict-free sphere of the ego, the apparatus of primary autonomy, most especially perception and memory. Thus, introjection is not simply a derivative of oral libidinal or aggressive impulses. Neither is it simply a matter of learning; Kernberg holds that introjection leads to "linking 'external' perception with the perception of primitive affect states representing drive derivatives" (1976, p. 29). The next level of internalization, "identification," occurs when the child is able to appreciate the role played by himself and by the object in significant interactions. The components of this system consist of an image of the object in a specific role; an image of the self, perhaps in a complementary role; and an affective coloring determined by an already somewhat modulated drive derivative. The most mature level of internalization, termed "ego identity" after Erikson (1956), refers to "the overall organization of identifications and introjections under the guiding principle of the synthetic function of the ego" (1976, p. 32). The components here are a consistent conception of the object world, a consolidating sense of the self as an ongoing organization, and a mutual recognition of this consistency on the part of the child and his caretakers. This level constitutes an organization and integration of the more primitive internalization processes.

With this formulation Kernberg has built upon the basic framework of Jacobson. However, he has changed several of the terms, reshuffled the dividing lines, and, perhaps most critically, more fully opened the interaction between relationships with others and the nature of instinctual drive.

Kernberg argues that the affective coloring of the internalized interaction constitutes its active valence, especially with regard to the developmentally early introjections. The similarities among valences of different introjections account eventually for their fusion, for the earliest

organization of experience. To this extent, there is a clear correspondence between Kernberg's framework and the developmental schemas of Sullivan and Fairbairn. Sullivan's "personifications" and Fairbairn's early splitting of the ego and of the object both depend on the quality of the interpersonal exchange between mother and infant. Kernberg's partial attribution of internalization phenomena to the operation of primarily autonomous ego functions underscores this similarity with relational model formulations. He departs from the perspective of Jacobson, who sees the earliest "total identifications" (roughly parallel to Kernberg's "introjections") as motivated by drive-derived needs.

What is the role of drive in Kernberg's formulation? At this point in the evolution of his theory, drive derivatives provide the affective coloring of the internalized interactions. They account for the internal experience which is linked with the perceptually determined outer experience, and in this sense the theory retains some tie to the drive model. The drives play a less central *motivational* role for Kernberg than they do for Jacobson, but they do serve a critical *organizational* function. Even in light of their modified function, however, at this point in the theory the drives are conceptually the drives of classical psychoanalytic metapsychology. Accordingly, Kernberg criticizes Fairbairn for neglecting drives and especially the aggressive drive. His own definition of aggression could be that of any classical drive theorist: "The term 'aggression' . . . is restricted to the direct instinctual drive derivatives, as typically related to early, primitive rage reactions; it refers to aggression as opposed to libido" (1976, p. 30n). Moreover, in his subsequent consideration of factors predisposing people to the development of borderline psychopathology, Kernberg points to the presence of a preponderance of negative introjections which can stem either from severe early frustrations or from a constitutional intensity of the aggressive drive.

Over time, maturational and developmental forces acting upon the ego make it difficult or impossible for splitting operations to continue. This leads to a combination of opposite valence self and object images into "good *and* bad" self and "good *and* bad" object representations. This in turn leads to the appearance of ambivalence (Melanie Klein's depressive position, although appearing at a later period of life) and of more mature, object-directed affects such as concern, guilt, and mourning. Along with this, ideal self and ideal object representations develop, so that interpersonal exchanges involve experientially four components: a real and an ideal self and a real and an ideal object. This paves the way for the eventual establishment of the ego ideal.

These processes, vicissitudes of the representational world, facilitate

the consolidation of an integrated ego. (Like Jacobson, Kernberg hypothesizes the reciprocal influence of psychic structure and the representational world.) The consolidation of the ego makes possible, for the first time, repression and the higher level defensive operations organized around repression, which characterize the defensive styles of normal and neurotic people. The emergence of repression in turn leads to the appearance of a "dynamic unconscious" composed of rejected self-object-affect configurations, of internalization units that are unacceptable to the newly strengthened ego.

The synthesis of internalization systems with contradictory affect valences promotes drive neutralization which, in agreement with Hartmann, Kernberg sees as providing the most important energy source for repression. Thus, the developmental relationship between splitting and repression is reflected in their metapsychological relationship: splitting keeps opposite valence introjections apart, which prevents neutralization, thereby depriving repression of the continuously flowing energy source which it requires. This leads to a weakened ego, which falls back on more primitive splitting defenses. The formulation is elegant and compelling, but it is at a greater remove from Hartmann's approach than Kernberg suggests. Kernberg explicitly derives an instinctual vicissitude (neutralization) from the vicissitudes of object relationships. Hartmann frequently and explicitly rejected this type of approach; in fact he asserted the dependence of object relations themselves on instinctual (and structural) factors.

The final stage in structure formation is the establishment and consolidation of the superego. Here, Kernberg follows Jacobson quite closely in postulating a three-level schema derived from different developmental stages of object relations. The superego consists of layers that are precipitates, first, of early, hostile object images reflecting the child's projective processes; second, of an ego ideal composed of fused ideal self and ideal object representations; third, of the integration of realistic parental images, including their values, prohibitions, and demands.

Experience, Relationship, and Psychic Structure

Kernberg suggests that the ego as a structure comes into being with the use of introjection for defensive purposes (1976, p. 35). This is a fascinating idea. Since object images are derived from external experience, from the actual (albeit distorted) interpersonal exchanges in which the infant participates, he implies that *experience precedes the structuralization of the ego.* (Since perception is itself a function of the ego, the concept of "experience" requires that these capacities be present, and Kernberg characterizes these primarily autonomous functions as "forerunners of the ego.") In this view of the origins of the ego, Kernberg has positioned himself *between* the relational and drive model traditions. For Sullivan, human life begins with interpersonal experience. The earliest configuration of "nipple in lips" represents the very beginning of man's psychological existence. For Melanie Klein, although she casts the issue in entirely different terms, there is no drive without an inherent object, no impulse without an associated fantasy, no human life without at least the foreshadowings of relational experience. Moreover, for both Sullivan and Klein, these earliest experiences become the substance of later psychic structure. For Sullivan the personifications evolve into the self-system; for Klein the early fantasies become the later patterns of relationship with real objects. These ideas are in stark contrast to classical drive model formulations, in which the maturation and development of the structure ego by far precedes the most crucial experiences of object relations. Although Kernberg does not go as far as relational model theorists in building social relations into the fabric of the earliest era of life, he has attempted to integrate sensibilities derived from this approach into his own theoretical framework.

Kernberg holds that the dynamic unconscious is composed of rejected introjection and identification systems, and that it comes into being with the consolidation of the ego's repressive capabilities. The idea that the id is composed of self-images, object images, and their associated affective charges is highly reminiscent of Fairbairn's idea that the unconscious is made up of rejected internal object relations. Fairbairn's approach has clearly influenced Kernberg, but their views at this point in the development of the latter's thought are not identical. In his early formulation (chapter 1 of Kernberg, 1976, which was actually written in 1966), Kernberg says only that the "repressed" portion of the id begins with ego consolidation and is comprised of internalization systems. This leaves open the status of the nonrepressed portion of the id, the id aspect of the original undifferentiated matrix, which might be supposed to be the site of drives in their conventional sense. Kernberg does not, however, develop any theoretical place for this more classical aspect of the id, and one is left with the impression that he retains it more out of homage to the drive model than as an integral theoretical construct.

In a later version of this aspect of development (chapter 2 of Kernberg, 1976, written in 1971) he goes beyond the earlier view. Here he holds that the id as a psychic structure comes into being with the establishment of repression. The id *"integrates* functions which previously existed 'separately' or, rather, as part of early, mutually dissociated or split systems of internalized object relations" (1976, p. 69; italics ours). The primary process characteristics of id functioning, he adds, operate as they do because the cognitively primitive nature of the self and object representations, as well as the primitive nature of the underlying drives derivatives, lend themselves well to operations such as condensation and displacement.

With this later formulation Kernberg has made a fundamental break with the drive model that not even his impressive powers of explanation can conceal. We remember: the ego as a structure comes into being with the defensive use of introjection; now, the id as a structure comes into being with the establishment of repression. Therefore, *the appearance of the structure ego precedes the appearance of the structure id.* Taken in combination with the assertion that the id is composed of internalization units and that it exercises an organizing function, we see that Kernberg's version of the tripartite psychic structures bears nothing but a terminological relationship to Freud's or to that of any theorist operating within the drive model. His structures are more like Fairbairn's; they represent and integrate aspects of interpersonal relationships rather than representing varying aspects of man's biological endowment. In this sense we might see Kernberg's formulation as an extension of Jacobson's (1964, p. 129) explanation of the relationship of the psychic structures to our experience of them, but it must be kept in mind that Jacobson is describing the phenomenological overlay of a biologically determined system. Kernberg builds relational experience into the very heart of his psychological model.

Similar considerations apply to Kernberg's recent use of the concept of the self—an area in which his fundamental rejection of drive model premises becomes quite clear. He states: "I propose . . . to reserve the term 'self' for the sum total of self-representations in intimate connection with the sum total of object representations. In other words, I propose defining the self as an intrapsychic structure that originates from the ego and is clearly embedded in the ego" (1982, p. 900). This definition, with its emphasis on the interactive nature of the self, is designed to bring relational factors to the core of the psychic apparatus. In defining the self as a representation, Kernberg appears to follow Hartmann, and the first part of his definition reads a great deal like Jacobson's. When he switches to referring to the self as a structure, however, he violates the crucial distinction between representation and structure followed by all drive model theorists, a distinction which is central to the difference in theoretical style of the two major psychoanalytic models.

That Kernberg means to construe the self as a psychic structure rather than as a representation is made clear in two further statements. He says that the self is "an ego function and structure that evolves gradually . . . into a supraordinate structure that incorporates other ego functions—such as memory and cognitive structures." Again, the "normal self is the supraordinate organizer of key ego functions such as reality testing, ego synthesis, and, above all, a consistent and integrated concept of the self and of significant others" (1982, pp. 905, 914). Here the ambiguity surrounding the functional role of the self has disappeared. The self is a representation only in a genetic sense; once formed, it has the same theoretical status as the id, ego, and superego. Kernberg's theory of psychic structure, therefore, is incompatible with the tripartite model of drive theory.

Experience, Relationship, and Instinctual Drive

Throughout the history of the drive/structure model and within the works of any individual theorist, structural hypotheses are more easily modified than are energic hypotheses. Kernberg's work is no exception, and it was some years after proposing his structural modifications that he turned his attention to drive theory (chapter 3 of Kernberg, 1976, written in 1973).

In earlier presentations Kernberg had used the classical construction of the drive concept. Even then, however, his structural modifications raise questions about his usage, and he had changed the functional role of drive within the framework of his theory. Thus, he states that "the original penetration of the psychic apparatus with drive derivatives is achieved through . . . internalization processes" (1976, p. 31). This depiction no longer presents drive as the prime mover of the psychic apparatus which it was in Freud's (1905a, 1915a) definition of drive as "a demand made upon the mind for work." Rather, drive appears to manifest itself only in the context of the internalization of interpersonal experience. However, at this point Kernberg has left himself a way out. In the passage quoted, and throughout his early discussion, he refers to "drive derivatives," which are not pure drives but the result of drive as filtered through experience. Kernberg does not mention the "pure" drives at this point, in the same way that he does not use any concept of the unrepressed portion of the id, and one is left with a sense that he is dissatisfied with the idea of drive as it stands.

This view is confirmed by the next phase in Kernberg's theoretical development. He describes early, undifferentiated, physiologically determined pleasurable affects evolving into specific pleasure experiences on the basis of four factors: oral satiation; excitement of the erotogenic zones; gratification of exploratory behavior; and, above all, interpersonal experiences (1976, p. 63). A parallel process is understood to underlie the evolution of unpleasure. Here Kernberg has adopted a clear mixing of drive and relational model approaches to the issue of pleasure. The first two factors are part of the classical view; the third integrates considerations derived from the study of early ego development and draws on the work of both Mahler (1966) and Jacobson (1953). The fourth factor, interpersonal experience, is based on but goes a step beyond Jacobson's formulations. For Jacobson, orality is the organizing principle which provided the continuum upon which pleasurable and unpleasurable interpersonal experiences are arrayed in the developing child's mind. For Kernberg, orality is but one among four aspects of the process, and the role of interpersonal experience is promoted to an autonomous position in which it is the most significant single element.

Kernberg argues that "good" and "bad" self and object representations become invested respectively with libido and aggression, suggesting that goodness and badness in relational experience *precedes* drive cathexis. He notes that "From a clinical viewpoint, one might say that the evolving affect states and affect dispositions actualize, respectively, libidinal and aggressive drive derivatives" (1976, p. 64), implying again that it is the affect as a primary quality, and not the instinctual investment, that determines the valence of self and object representations. This stands in sharp contradistinction to the usual drive model approach, in which drive alone, as a biological given, determines the nature of interpersonal experience. With this formulation Kernberg has reversed the direction begun by Freud when he abandoned the original defense model in favor of his drive/structure theory.

It was not, however, until 1973 that Kernberg proposed a full-scale reexamination of the drive concept itself. Employing a general systems theory framework (the hierarchical organization of systems into supraordinate systems), he concludes that "the units of internalized object relations constitute subsystems on the basis of which both drives and the overall psychic structures of ego, superego, and id are organized as integrating systems" (1976, p. 85). Thus, he has extended his claim that object relations constitute the building-blocks of structure to include the view that they constitute as well the building-blocks of the drives themselves. The drives are higher-level systems which organize object relations (including their associated affects, which now constitute the "primary motivational systems") into integrated motivational systems, that is, into libidinal and aggressive aims.

Systems theory is a way for Kernberg to solve for himself the problem of integrating his view that affectively charged relational structures are the basis for development with the classical concept of structure evolving out of transformations of drive, which he wishes to retain. He attempts to do this by suggesting that the relational configurations are merely a subsystem of drive. Good and bad affective experiences accumulate and eventually become the basis of the larger motivational forces of libido and aggression. The accretion of good experiences forms the basis of the libidinal drive; the accretion of bad experiences forms the basis of the aggressive drive. In his reformulation of the drive concept Kernberg draws on contemporary ethology, and he views drives as complex hierarchical organizations evolving out of the interaction between inborn "instinctive components," consisting of neurophysiological reactions and attachment behaviors, with interpersonal experience. He writes: "instincts in the human being develop gradually out of the assembly of these 'building blocks,' so that the series of pleasurable affect-determined units and the series of unpleasurable affect-determined units gradually evolve into the libidinally invested and aggressively invested constellations of psychic drive systems—that is, into libido and aggression, respectively, as the two major psychological drives" (1976, p. 87).

Kernberg likens his concept of drives to Freud's original formulation of instincts forged from their original components. In drawing this parallel, however, he overlooks Freud's understanding of the nature of the building-blocks themselves. For Freud, the blocks are innate, biological givens which emerge sequentially in accord with a phylogenetic pattern; for Kernberg, on the other hand, "the developmental stages of libidinal and aggressive drive derivatives depend upon the vicissitudes of the development of internalized object relations" (1976, pp. 185–186). Thus, by making affectively charged object relations the building-blocks of the "drives," Kernberg has attempted to weld together his own relational theorizing with a preserved drive model. One must determine how good a seam he has provided.

Kernberg makes a crucial conceptual leap between "good" or "bad" constellations of relations with objects, on the one hand, and libido and aggression as drives, on the other. This leap is made plausible by the ambiguous and shifting meanings of "good" and "bad." At first Kernberg uses these terms to designate the child's grouping of his experiences into pleasurable and unpleasurable patterns: "good" and "bad" refer here to organizations and patternings of experience, in much the same fashion as Sullivan spoke of "good" and "bad" nipples, breasts, and so on. Later, Kernberg uses "good" and "bad" to refer to motivational forces originating within the psyche but outside the relations between the self and objects, corresponding to the classical libidinal and aggressive instincts. How this transformation happens is left essentially unexplained; but once it happens, Kernberg is able to attribute to the drives the same properties with which Freud endowed his original concept. Thus, a fundamental discontinuity between the relational and energic meanings of good and bad is covered over by the use of the same term with two very different sets of referents. (This particular semantic ambiguity can be traced historically to Melanie Klein's use of the terms.)

Kernberg derives some support for his approach from Jacobson's concept of an initial undifferentiated energy which, at least partially on the basis of experience, bifurcates into libidinal and aggressive drives. However, Jacobson had argued that the formation of discrete drives is to a large extent based on maturational processes; it is determined not only by experience but also by man's biological nature. For Kernberg it is the affects which are central, and affects (once Jacobson had "freed" them from their presumed instinctual base) are highly responsive to interpersonal experience. Thus, he is able to conclude that "there is no direct relationship between biological pressure and psychic functioning" (1976, p. 114)—which is a far cry indeed from drive as a demand on the mind for work. In Kernberg's final formulation, man is not innately sexual and aggressive; he is innately responsive. The drive model has been left far behind. Kernberg's reintroduction of the classical concept of drive through the device of his systems theory framework obscures the radical nature of his own approach.

The extent of his departure from the classical approach to drive is underscored by a recent formulation. Kernberg holds that "Love and hate . . . become stable intrapsychic structures, in genetic continuity through various developmental stages, and, by that very continuity, *consolidate into libido and aggression*" (1982, p. 908; italics ours). Compare Freud's statement in "Instincts and Their Vicissitudes": "the attitudes of love and hate cannot be made use of for the relations of *instincts* to their objects, but are reserved for the relations of the *total ego* to objects" (1915a, p. 137; italics in original). Freud's perspective, followed by every drive model theorist, indicates that love and hate evolve out of the drives as a consequence of object cathexis. For Kernberg the object-directed affects of love and hate *precede and give rise to* the drives, a position which is compatible with the views of relational model theorists (Fairbairn, for example), but not at all with those of Freud.

Critique

Nobody has ever seen an instinctual drive and nobody ever will. They are not quantities in the body like blood and bones; they are, as Schafer (1968, 1976) points out, theoretical options. We might, therefore, simplify the essential position of the drive model theorist as follows: "I have chosen to think of man as an organism originally motivated by intense, unmodulated sexual and aggressive impulses which are a major part of his biological inheritance and which shape his psychological destiny. These impulses, although not the drives that lie behind them, become modified on the basis of social interactions, and the modifications, in all their shadings, can account for the totality of subsequent behavior. Moreover, the original unmodified state of the drives and the danger which they represent to man's need to live in society provide a useful framework for understanding a wide range of psychopathological phenomena."

Drive theory, like all psychoanalytic theories, is predicated upon philosophical presuppositions concerning the nature of man. It is possible to speak of "drives" in theoretical systems derived from different philosophical presuppositions. For example, one can say that the drives are not essentially sexual and aggressive, but that they represent inherent human strivings for closeness with others and for assertiveness of one's individual potential. This is the position Kohut has taken. Or one can say that early interpersonal experience is crucial to what man becomes and that this experience gives rise to motivational systems which are expressed in sexual and aggressive aims. This is the position which Kernberg has arrived at. *Good* theory can be derived from these premises; *good classical psychoanalytic drive theory* cannot.

Freud was careful to distinguish theoretical premises from observational data. In discussing the derivation of his drive theory he wrote: "Even at the stage of description it is not possible to avoid applying certain abstract ideas to the material in hand, ideas from somewhere or other but certainly not from the new observations alone" (1915a, p. 117). Drives are not a *discovery* of psychoanalysis, they are an a priori statement asserting a particular view of man's basic nature. Changing this assumption necessarily changes the theory; merely asserting that one believes in drives does not make one a drive model theorist.

In evaluating the sum of Kernberg's contribution, he stands in relation to Jacobson (and to earlier drive theorists) somewhat as Guntrip stands in relation to Fairbairn. He presents his work as an extension and application of earlier approaches, but he has dramatically altered the thrust of those approaches.

1. In contradistinction to all other drive/structure model theorists and in common with all relational/structure model theorists, Kernberg sees man as social by nature. He considers that "the condensation of aggression and libido into internalized object relations constitutes the intrapsychic structuring of instinctual needs *in terms of man's social nature*" (1976, p. 115; italics ours).

2. In contrast to all other drive model theorists, Kernberg rejects the concept of primary narcissism (1980, p. 107). His reasoning is that in the earliest state of undifferentiation there is an "external" object present, although its representation is fused with that of the self. This again points to an a priori assumption that man is psychologically object-related from the earliest developmental era.

3. The concept of the "object," critical in any "object relations theory," has been fundamentally changed. Here we refer not only to Klein and Tribich's (1981) point that Kernberg substitutes a specifically human object for Freud's broader concept, but to a more central theoretical issue. We have noted consistently that within the drive model something becomes an "object" as opposed to a percept or a "thing" by virtue of its cathexis with libido or aggression. For Kernberg, however, drives are built from internalization units which include object representations as well as self representations and affect valences. Thus, the object qua object temporally precedes the drive, and Kernberg (like Mahler but more systematically and definitively) divorces the object concept from its roots in drive theory.

4. The psychic structures of the drive model remain in name only. The crucial theoretical distinction between psychic structures and mental representations has been eliminated. Within the structural theory, each sector of the mind is forged *from relational experience*, which it then organizes in characteristic ways. The dynamic id no longer generates an ego as a solution to its conflicts with reality, but is itself created by the ego's repressive capacities. Id contents are no longer biological givens but, in agreement with Fairbairn, are configurations of self and object representations. The self has the status of a psychic structure supraordinate to the ego—thereby undercutting the inclusive nature of the tripartite model of the psychic apparatus.

5. Of the earlier psychoanalytic conception of irreducible, biologically determined drives, *nothing remains but the terms*. Drives are psychological systems that organize early experience and then channel it into future motivational aims. Affects rather than drives are the earliest and primary motivational forces. Libido and aggression develop out of the already object-directed affective states of love and hate.

The Drive/Structure Model in Perspective

In tracing the history of the drive/structure model from its evolution out of Freud's original theory of affect and defense, we have seen that all theorists who embrace this psychoanalytic approach accept certain fundamental premises. These were explicitly stated and elaborated by

Freud, and all subsequent emendations—Freud's own and those of his followers—are built upon them. As they were originally formulated (with the publication of the *Three Essays on the Theory of Sexuality*, before the earliest major defections and before the period of accommodation began), the basic assumptions can be put as follows: The unit of study of psychoanalysis is the individual, the discrete organism which can be conceptualized and studied outside of the environment into which he is born. The human organism enters the world with a phylogenetic endowment consisting of endogenously arising needs (drives) which demand immediate satisfaction. These needs can in principle be classified in a variety of ways, but clinical and theoretical considerations point to their falling into two groups. In Freud's first theory, the two fundamental drives were conceptualized as sexual and self-preservative; in the revised view, which has been accepted by all drive model theorists, they are needs for the expression of sexual and aggressive impulses.

Because the drives constitute the whole of the infant's innate psychological equipment, all of human development and all subsequent behavior grow out of them. The psychic apparatus evolves as a solution to the problem of meeting the innately determined needs, and it operates in accord with a regulatory principle (the constancy or pleasure principle) that is also phylogenetically given and that requires the relief of tension which is caused by the build-up of a quantity of drive. The drives follow their own maturationally determined course, and their state at any particular time decisively determines the nature of the individual's experience. The individual's relationship to the environment into which he is born acquires its psychological value on the basis of its ability to meet his drive-derived needs; these needs thus constitute the foundation of all object relations.

The strategy of theoretical accommodation which we have described in Chapter 4 and throughout Part Three has attempted to stretch the fundamental premises of the drive model to embrace data arising from new clinical experience (psychoanalytic treatment of children, direct observations of normal child development, work with severely disturbed patients, and so on) and to respond to critiques from theorists who reject the drive model itself. Generally accommodation within the drive model has been directed toward broadening its interpretive implications. The actions of the drives are, accordingly, seen as less specific determinants of human behavior, and the specificity which has been lost is replaced by considerations drawn from the study of early relations with others. We can trace three lines in the strategy of accommodation: those that have attempted to rework the concept of drive itself; those that have revised the theory of psychic structure; and those that have modified the classical approach to the nature of the object and to object relations.

The theory of drive. Throughout the history of the model, all human activity has been understood to derive ultimately from the operation of instinctual drive. As applied to this fundamental premise, the strategy of accommodation has taken two forms. First, there has been an attempt to integrate into the theory supplementary concepts which broaden the motivational base, thus avoiding the perceived reductionism inherent in the effort to explain all human experience in terms of the vicissitudes of innate sexual and aggressive impulses. This strategy was first used by Freud in his introduction of the concept of narcissism (1914a). The return of libido to the ego following the loss of a sexual object allows the ego to use the captured energy in pursuit of its own goals, which may oppose the original instinctually determined goals (for example, in the conflict between sexual interest in the oedipal parent and narcissistic interest in avoiding castration). Freud was initially vague in his delineation of the origin of narcissistic aims, but they were elaborated by Hartmann in his concept of adaptation. Because it is an innately given function of the ego, and because it is present and operating from birth, the tendency toward adaptation serves as a motivational force parallel to and independent of that of the drives. Adaptation provides a phylogenetic basis for the force behind the ego's goals, and it pulls the theory away from a monotonic focus on the operation of impulses which originate without regard to the environment.

Hartmann's theory of adaptation and of the "average expectable environment" within which adaptation occurs was broadly sketched; he warned throughout his writings that the "environment" should not be equated with the people who exist within it. For him adaptation is not specifically a force which promoted ties with others. Object relations remain, as they were for Freud, principally determined by instinctual needs. With the work of Margaret Mahler, however, adaptive operations became more "personal." Her theory of symbiosis (which she defined as the first stage of adaptation) and of the process of separation-individuation pointed to aspects of object relations governed by the child's need for caretakers who can support his early helpless dependency and assist him in moving toward eventual self-sufficiency. This dimension of the child's attachment to others operates relatively (although not entirely) outside of the influence of sexual and aggressive impulses. Mahler's vision of the relationship between the infant and his mother is colored by instinctual need; it is also colored by the independent push toward self-development. Her observations were expanded and enriched by Edith Jacobson's theory of the complex transactions between "the self and the object world," transactions which are organized around drive demand but which also embrace a broad range of developmental needs.

The second strategy for modifying the theory of drive has been to suggest change in the nature of drive itself. Although this approach has been used most clearly by Jacobson, it is foreshadowed in the work of Hartmann and even of Freud. Freud's late use of the sublimation concept — in which the term refers to an actual deinstinctualization of drive rather than to a rechanneling of it — suggested for the first time that the very qualities of drive itself were subject to modification on the basis of experience in the world. His idea that the two drives could fuse together with a consequent change in their quality reinforced this perspective. With sublimation and fusion, Freud had a system that was moved not only by the energy of primitive, unmodulated sexual and aggressive impulses. Rather, the psychic apparatus had at its disposal a range of energies which were more or less close to their instinctual source. This trend was developed in Hartmann's work, both through his emphasis on aggression as an equal partner of libido and through his concept of neutralization, which broadened and strengthened Freud's sublimation. Jacobson's idea that all psychic energy begins in an undifferentiated state, bifurcating into libido and aggression partly on the basis of maturation and partly on the basis of interpersonal experience, further stressed the role of reality vis-à-vis innate qualities. Her concept, accepted by Mahler and which continued to inform her developmental observations, works toward diminishing the motivational specificity of the drives, focusing instead on the role of relations with others as partial determinants of the nature of drive itself.

The theory of psychic structure. Accommodation began early in this area and has continued to be the focus of the contribution of many theorists. Freud's first major act of accommodation was his introduction of the reality principle (1911a). Because it placed a limit on the unchecked expression of drive demand, the reality principle called attention to a range of mental functions (perception, judgment, memory, and so on) which were later grouped together under the broad heading of the structure ego. With the structural model, Freud consolidated the ego concept, postulating a developmental history that is drawn at least partially from realistic identifications with the important figures in the individual's early life. The powers of the ego remained weak relative to those of the id, superego, and reality, however. They were expanded by Freud in his revised affect theory, which granted the ego the ability to perceive realistic danger situations and to invoke the anxiety affect in response to them (1926a). Moreover, during the last decade of Freud's life, his followers introduced theoretical concepts that further enhanced the ego's power. Nunberg's (1930) idea of the synthetic function of the ego, Waelder's (1930) principle of multiple function, and Anna Freud's (1936) depiction of the ego's powerful defenses all contributed to a vision of the ego as a powerful force in the psychic economy.

It was principally the work of Hartmann, however, that gave the ego a theoretical status equal to that of the drives. Hartmann's concepts of primarily and secondarily autonomous ego functions, his postulate of the constitutional roots of the ego in the undifferentiated matrix, his stress on the importance of adaptive processes, his idea that the ego is a hierarchically arranged group of functions which may be involved in internal conflict as well as in conflict with the other psychic systems, and his modification of energic hypotheses all were pointed toward the enhancement of the ego's power and of the importance of reality relations. Moreover, Hartmann introduced the concept of the self—the experiential counterpart of the object with whom the individual is involved in a relationship—into the psychoanalytic structural theory. The self in Hartmann's approach, while it is an important aspect of a theory of object relations, is not a mental structure per se. Rather, it is an image, a representation on the same theoretical plane as the representations formed of others. In this sense his view is an alternative to the structural self of relational model theorists (Sullivan, Guntrip, and others), but it does emphasize, for the first time within the drive model, an internal world within which object relations take place.

The concept of an internal world of object relations, and especially of the self, was more fully developed in the work of Mahler and Jacobson. Both of these theorists continued the strategy of accommodation of the structural theory of the drive model by retaining the definition of the self as a representation while giving greater emphasis to its functional importance. For Mahler, achievement of a stable sense of self is a crucial benchmark of successful development: satisfactory experiences in the symbiotic and separation-individuation phases are measured by the firm consolidation of the self, and severe psychopathology is characterized by the failure to achieve this consolidation, with a parallel failure to gain a stable sense of other people. Jacobson followed Mahler in viewing the self as a developmental achievement contingent upon good early object relations. She added a framework within which its firm establishment, along with the establishment of clear boundaries between representations of the self and of others contributed decisively to the formation of a healthy ego. There is a deliberate ambiguity in Jacobson's depiction of the self: although it is not a psychic structure on a theoretical par with the ego, id, and superego (thus allowing Jacobson to remain firmly within the tripartite structural theory of the drive/structure model), it does have crucial functions within the mental economy. Because the self as Jacobson and Mahler (and, by implication, Hartmann) define it is essentially a relational concept, the theoretical emphasis given to its development and vicissitudes becomes a way of integrating the sequelae of early object relations into the framework of the drive/structure model.

The nature and formation of the object. In the terms of Freud's model the object is viewed as a creation of drive demand. A "thing" in the external world (that is, the world external to the psychic apparatus) becomes an object by virtue of its ability to fulfill drive-derived needs. This "thing" may be a part of the individual's own body, it may be another person, or it may be a part of the nonhuman environment — there is no specificity on this point beyond the opportunity which the "thing" presents for discharge. Within the second dual-instinct theory, objects are formed principally out of the demands of the sexual drive, but in some cases (the oedipal rival is probably the clearest example) are in part creations of aggressive impulses as well.

The strategy of accommodation in this area was foreshadowed in Freud's late theory, subsequent to the formulation of the structural model. In some of his writings after 1923 the objects as figures in reality enter the picture in more direct ways than they had earlier, but Freud remained equivocal on the issue, and the balance of his work indicates that the drive itself rather than reality determines the nature of the object. True accommodation begins with Anna Freud's concept of defense against reality situations. The aggressor with whom the child identifies in her model is a realistic figure, although the child's perception of his aggression may be partial and distorted. Hartmann's concept of an "average expectable environment" generalized A. Freud's perspective by adding the idea of a realistic external world which imposes its own requirements on the developing individual independent of defensive operations. The "average expectable environment" is a fact, not a creation, although the specific nature of the objects within the environment remains for Hartmann at least partly determined by drive operations.

The drive model approach to the nature of the object changed decisively in the work of Mahler and Jacobson. For Mahler, Hartmann's average expectable environment is at birth identical with the "ordinary devoted mother" — a person in the real world who must relate to the child in specified ways if development is to proceed unimpaired. The ordinary devoted mother becomes an object for the child during the symbiotic stage of development; without adequate maternal care this first object relationship cannot develop. Thus, the symbiotic object within Mahler's theory is necessarily a person, and a person who behaves toward the child in a highly specified way. This represents a decisive change from earlier drive model formulations, in which it was not necessary for the object to be a person at all. Mahler's attempt to remain within the broad framework of the drive model is contained in her view that symbiotic attachments exist not only in reality but also in fantasy; in the latter sense they are colored decisively by sexual and aggressive vicissitudes. Jacobson, in her depiction of the self and the object world, implicitly relies on Mahler's framework. She undertakes no explicit redefinition of the concept of the object, but it is clear from the complex transactions which she describes that she is referring specifically to people, and that she, too, has abandoned the view of the object as solely a creation of drive.

Throughout our account of the evolution and modification of the drive/structure model we have stressed the issue of its *content*, of what some theorists refer to as its hermeneutic. We have stressed that the model contains within it a particular vision of human growth, development, and experience, and that authors who have adopted the strategy of accommodation have done so because they wish to preserve this vision. Our approach to the major psychoanalytic models is similar to that taken recently by Schafer, who refers to what he calls the "storylines" contained within different theories (1983). In our view, the storyline of the drive model is often deeply embedded in complex, technical, even mechanistic language, but it is there nonetheless and contributes continuity to the model even in the face of the model's ongoing revision.

One major implication of our perspective is that the storyline which a particular theorist adopts determines his relationship to the two major models, irrespective of the language in which he expresses his particular vision. Schafer, for example, in a series of important critiques of classical metapsychology (1976, 1978, 1983), has proposed eliminating most of the major terms which are central to the theoretical exposition of drive model theorists. He rejects energic and structural concepts alike, arguing that they lead to reification and anthropomorphization, thus leading the analyst away from his proper concern with the person as the active agent in both normal and neurotic behavior. His rejection of the language of the drive/structure model appears to place him outside of the classical tradition, and many orthodox analysts view him in this way. As we have defined the models, however, Schafer's approach is well within the orthodox tradition. He states that in his own practice he uses "the storylines that characterize Freudian retellings" (1983, p. 223), and he frequently warns against taking patients' accounts of interpersonal situations within and outside the family too literally, arguing that this may obscure the identifications, projections, and distortions with which the accounts are colored (pp. 151, 258). In summary, he holds that "As analysts we are always concerned to view actions in terms of infantile psychosexual and aggressive conflicts and the variations of these that the analysand has continued to fashion along with a suitable environment in which to enact them" (p. 91).

Schafer's theoretical approach stands in sharp contrast to that of Kernberg, who of the recent major theorists is most insistent on retaining the classical metapsychology and its language. We have shown, however, that beneath Kernberg's linguistic continuity the storyline has been decisively changed. The "infantile psychosexual and aggressive conflicts" which Schafer finds at the core of his patient's difficulties are, in Kernberg's vision, secondary to early object relations which acquire "good" or "bad" affective values. His use of traditional terms obscures the fact that in each case he has changed their original meanings, and that in each case he has used his new definition to bring interpersonal considerations into the core of his theory. Thus, from the hermeneutic perspective, Schafer—despite his overt rejection of the theoretical style of the drive/structure model—emerges as a true accommodator within the classical tradition. Kernberg—despite his attempts to declare loyalty—emerges as a theorist who has moved into the relational model. Only by analysis of an analyst's vision of human experience can his theoretical position be accurately assessed.

Part Four

Implications

Howls the sublime,
and softly sleeps the calm Ideal, in the whispering
chambers of Imagination

—CHARLES DICKENS, *Martin Chuzzlewit*

11 Mixed Model Strategies: Heinz Kohut and Joseph Sandler

With the contributions of Edith Jacobson and Otto Kernberg, the drive/structure model was strained to its limits. Jacobson's description of the complex interchanges between the self and the object world, with their profound and intricate impact on both normal and pathological development, rests uncomfortably on the assumption of a motivational system that is ultimately reducible to sexual and aggressive impulses. Kernberg's attempt to build relational configurations into the concept of drive itself gives rise to a theory which is compelling on its own terms, but which violates many of the fundamental premises of the original framework. As the classical metapsychology underwent the accommodating strategies of authors from Freud to Kernberg, the concept of drive became like the disembodied smile of Lewis Carroll's Cheshire cat—the spirit lingers, but the substance has long since vanished. For those maintaining allegiance to the drive model, the problem remains: what is to be done with the uncomfortable fit between the clinical centrality of object relations and the theoretical centrality of drive?

A current approach which has engendered considerable controversy within orthodox psychoanalytic circles, but which has been embraced enthusiastically by more eclectic psychotherapists, is the attempt to mix theoretical models. Unlike radical revisionists of the relational model, authors employing this strategy do not reject the classical understanding of the nature of drive. Unlike theoretical accommodators who still operate within the drive model, however, they do not simply attempt to integrate relational considerations into a framework ultimately ruled by instinctual activity. Mixed model theorists attempt to juxtapose the fundamental assumptions of the two major models; they believe that a full understanding of man's nature requires a consideration of motivation derived from *both* instinctual and relational considerations, which are treated as more or less independent factors. The difficult task of the analyst who follows this strategy is to find some conceptual glue to join the two models.

Heinz Kohut

Heinz Kohut has been the most important and influential author to pursue this theoretical approach. His writings have gained unrivaled prominence over the past decade within and beyond the psychoanalytic community. In the early years of his career his theory and clinical work were based firmly in the orthodox vision of the drive model. (He was President of the American Psychoanalytic Association in 1964–1965.) As his thinking progressed, however, Kohut began to focus on issues of technique with a group of severely disturbed patients who had been considered inaccessible to the analytic process. *The Analysis of the Self*, published in 1971, delineated "narcissistic personality disorder" as a diagnostic entity with a particular developmental origin. Kohut broke with classical tradition by arguing that these patients could be treated analytically.

The tone and the content of *The Analysis of the Self* stress continuity with the drive model. Kohut suggests some refinements of technique, along with accompanying theoretical formulations for use with a highly specific group of patients, all of which were fully integrable with Hartmann's ego psychology. By 1977, in *The Restoration of the Self*, Kohut suggested that the drive model framework could not contain all the observations which his work with narcissistic patients was generating. Thus, he designated his approach, many features of which had remained implicit in his first book, as the "psychology of the self," and argued that it is not merely an emendation of the classical approach but a novel and comprehensive system.

The vision of human experience which Kohut terms the "psychology of the self" operates on principles derived from the relational/structure model: it is strikingly similar to the approaches developed by Winnicott, Fairbairn, and the interpersonal school. It is a "mixed model" approach, however, because Kohut attempts throughout to preserve the drive concept in its classical sense, arguing that drive theory is not displaced but complemented by his new formulations.

The "Psychology of the Self"

The basic constituent of Kohut's model of the psychic apparatus is the self, "a center of initiative and a recipient of impressions" (1977, p. 99). This formulation attributes functions to the self which in classical drive model theory are ascribed to the structures id, ego, and superego. Thus, the theoretical status of the concept of the self differs from its role in Hartmann's work or even in Jacobson's. The self is no longer a representation, a product of the activity of the ego, but is itself the active agent; it therefore carries more theoretical weight than in the earlier views.

This change is of the utmost theoretical importance: it is the vehicle for Kohut's assimilation of relational model sensibilities. For, if the self has new and more important *functions* in Kohut's system than it did in Jacobson's, it is similar in its *nature* and its *origin*. For Jacobson the self grows out of interpersonal exchanges and throughout life mediates transactions between the individual and the "object world." The same is true in Kohut's "psychology of the self." As Goldberg puts it, "We understand the self as a locus of relationships" (1981, p. 11). The difference between the two views is that, whereas Jacobson employs the concept of the self as representation, thus retaining the functional centrality of the classical structures, Kohut grants the self a functional role, bringing its relational origins right to the theoretical core.

For Kohut, the child is born into an empathic, responsive human milieu; relatedness with others is as essential for his psychological survival as oxygen is for his physical survival. The beginnings of the self emerge at the point where "the baby's innate potentialities and the [parents'] expectations with regard to the baby converge" (1977, p. 99). But the nascent infantile self is weak and amorphous; it has no durable structure or continuity over time, so it cannot stand alone. It requires the participation of others to provide a sense of cohesion, constancy, and resilience. Kohut terms these others, who from the infant's perspective are not yet differentiated from the self, "selfobjects," since they are objectively separate people who serve functions which will later be performed by the individual's own psychic structure. In the child's merger with his selfobjects, there is a subtle yet pervasive participation in the adult's experience, including the adult's experience of the child. In Kohut's words: "The child's rudimentary psyche participates in the selfobject's highly developed psychic organization; the child experiences the feeling states of the selfobject—they are transmitted to the child via touch and tone of voice and perhaps by still other means—as if they were his own" (1977, p. 86). The selfobjects, through their empathic responsiveness to the infant's needs, provide the experiences necessary for the gradual development of the self, and Kohut considers the relations between the infant and his selfobjects the basic constituents of psychic development and structure.

The infant seeks two fundamental types of relationship with his early selfobjects, relationships which Kohut interprets as expressing basic narcissistic needs. First, he needs to display his evolving capabilities and to be admired for them; Kohut considers that this represents his healthy sense of omnipotence and grandiosity. Later, the infant needs to form an idealized image of at least one of his parents, and to experience a sense of merger with an idealized selfobject. In the course of optimal development two relational configurations emerge sequentially: grandiose, exhibitionistic self images become connected to "mirroring" selfobjects ("I am perfect and you admire me"); toned-down images of the self become fused with idealized selfobjects ("You are perfect, and I am part of you").

Under the best circumstances there is a bit-by-bit transformation of self and object images from the more global and archaic to the more complex and resilient, brought about by inevitable, incremental parental failures to mirror the child or to permit idealization. If they occur gradually over time (somewhat on the model of the empathic failures of Winnicott's "good-enough mother"), a slow internalization of the selfobject relations takes place. (We agree with Ernest Wolf that this term is "more euphonious than self-selfobject relations" [1980] and employ it throughout.) This process, which Kohut terms "transmuting internalization," gives rise to the development of a permanent psychic structure, the self, which consists of two "poles" drawn from the early modes of relationship. Either pole can form the core of a healthy and cohesive self. Thus, personality may be organized around a grandiose, exhibitionistic trend, expressed as healthy ambition or assertiveness and derived from the mirroring selfobject, usually the mother. Alternatively, the idealizing selfobject relationship may be the dominant force. Usually derived from the relationship with the father (especially for the boy), this would be expressed in terms of healthy and strongly held ideals and values. The nature of a particular personality is determined both by the content of these poles of the self and by their relation to each other. If there is disturbance at one pole, adequate development of the other can compensate. Failure to develop at least one aspect of the self leads to narcissistic psychopathology, characterized by a defective sense of self and an inability to maintain a steady level of self-esteem.

In his earlier work Kohut characterized the parents' role as selfobjects simply in terms of providing the child with *narcissistic gratification*, a construction that was intended to keep his views embedded in the framework of libido theory. In his later work the role of the parents is broader, encompassing considerably more than simple gratification of drive-derived (even if narcissistic) needs. In his clinical illustrations, although he uses the terms of his original formulations, it is clear that Kohut is speaking of a more inclusive concept of relatedness to parental figures. For example, by 1977 the idea of "mirroring" refers to all of the transactions characterizing the mother-child relationship, including not only reflections of grandiosity but also constancy, nurturance, a general empathy, and respect (1977, pp. 146–147). Writing about the compensatory value of relations with the father, Kohut includes not only idealization, but intimacy, empathy, sharing, and other dimensions of a good relationship. Wolf (1980) extends this description by detailing what he terms "developmental lines" of selfobject relations, including the need for an "antagonist" selfobject at certain points in the process of differentiation. Thus, as developed by Kohut and by his followers, it is apparent that selfobjects serve not only narcissistic functions but also provide more and more complex relational needs and interactions.

Parental deviations from their optimal selfobject functions lead to their being experienced by the child as a "non-empathic attacker of the integrity of his self" (1977, p. 91). Minor or sporadic failure of empathy is not deleterious; periodic lapses facilitate the crucial process of transmuting internalization. The cause of psychopathology, as Kohut sees it, is *chronic* failure in empathy, attributable to parental character pathology, which undermines the healthy development of the child's self. As he puts it, "in the great majority of cases it is the specific pathogenic personality of the parent(s) and specific pathogenic features of the atmosphere in which the child grows up that account for the maldevelopments" (1977, p. 187). Specific traumatic events and memories of them serve as crystalization points for more general disturbances in relations with the parents. Parental seduction, for example, is destructive not in the act itself, but because it reflects the parent's chronic lack of empathy.

Kohut, much in the mode of Fairbairn, holds that manifest drive-related fixations—obsessions with food, anality, or oedipal sexuality, for example—reflect an underlying disorder of the self. These fixations often stem directly from similar drive-related preoccupations in the parents, reflecting *their* underlying disorder of the self. Parents with narcissistic disorders masked and managed by obsessions with food, anality, or hypersexuality are unable to serve as empathic selfobjects; they cannot provide the necessary stimulation for the development of a healthy self. In the face of the parents' failure to respond empathically to the child's emerging self, the child's original search for selfobjects breaks down into sexual and aggressive concerns corresponding to the parents' pathological preoccupations, as the child makes use of whatever selfobject responsiveness is available.

With these formulations Kohut has replaced drive as the basic constituent of mind with factors derived from the earliest relationships between the child and his object world. The child innately needs these relationships. He is not object-seeking in Fairbairn's sense; the selfobject is sought not in itself, but as a vehicle for homeostasis. Nevertheless, the establishment and maintenance of selfobject relations provides the basic motivational energy. Kohut states that "the primary units are *ab initio* the complex experiences and action patterns of a self/selfobject unit" (1977, p. 249). Nondestructive assertiveness and noncompulsive libidinal elements are woven together with and subsumed by the child's early object-seeking. Both infantile sexuality and assertiveness are, when development is proceeding well, components of the larger configurations of relatedness to the empathic selfobject. The appearance of destructive aggression or pure pleasure-seeking in isolation signals that a pathological breakdown has already taken place.

Kohut's depiction of the analytic process is consistent with the relational premises underlying his theoretical position. The analytic situation is defined not in terms of a neutral observer interpreting drive and defense processes within the patient, but in terms of an interpersonal field in which the participation of the analyst is essential. He states that a "fundamental claim of the psychology of the self [is] that the presence of an empathic or introspective observer defines, in principle, the psychological field" (1977, p. 32n). Similarly to Winnicott, disorders of the self in general are understood as environmental deficiency diseases; the caretakers have failed to allow the child to establish and slowly dissolve the requisite narcissistic selfobject configurations which, through transmuting internalization, generate healthy structures within the self. No further psychic growth is possible without these experiences; disorders of the self reflect desperate and necessarily futile attempts to shore up the defective self. In analysis the patient establishes a selfobject transference in either a mirroring or an idealizing mode. This provides a kind of developmental second chance: the transmuting internalization of the transferential relationship can become the core of a compensatory self structure.

It is extremely important, Kohut argues, for the analyst to allow the patient to dwell in and consolidate his relationship with the analyst, which makes possible the recovery of the lost developmental momentum blocked by early selfobject failures. Eventually the patient outgrows the narcissistic features of the transference, a process which is facilitated by the analyst's inevitable empathic failures. The patient thus begins to see both himself and the analyst in more realistic terms. At the same time the patient has gained the capacity to generate his own ambitions and ideals without requiring the analyst as a selfobject providing external mirroring or the opportunity for idealization. (Kohut later suggested that no one fully outgrows the need for selfobjects.)

By 1977 Kohut had extended his views on the mechanism of the therapeutic action of psychoanalysis to include patients suffering from structural neuroses. Characterological change does not take place through interpretation, but through experience, "microinternalizations" of the analyst's functions as a selfobject. He suggests further that much of the therapeutic effect produced by analysts operating out of classical drive theory stems from their intuitive and empathic acceptance of the patient, even though they don't regard these features of the treatment situation as therapeutic in themselves. Although throughout most of his writings Kohut minimizes the significance of interpretation proper, he does regard it as essential that the origins of the structural defects within the patient's self and the pathogenic properties of the parents' character be clarified. He contrasts this with the orthodox view of interpretation on two grounds. First, his reconstructions refer to relational configurations, not to the underlying drives which interpretations within the classical model must always reach. Second, it is not always necessary to make explicit all aspects of the pathogenic experiences. Some may be too highly charged with anxiety to be used effectively by the patient, and Kohut's theory of compensatory structure suggests that some early developmental failures which are not rectified via reconstruction may be adequately ameliorated by satisfactory experiences with the transferential selfobject. For example, it may be too threatening to the patient to acknowledge the depth of his mother's psychopathology and consequent inability to provide adequate mirroring. Gains which accrue from a satisfactory experience with the idealized analyst, however, can lead to a self that is strong enough to render full interpretation of the earliest experience unnecessary (see Kohut, 1977, 1979).

Classical Metapsychology and the Mixed Model Strategy

Kohut has been a theorist in perpetual transition. His positions changed in important respects over the years, and many of these changes reflect a continuing struggle to combine his relational innovations with the tradition of the drive/structure model. In two major volumes Kohut proposed two quite different strategies for mixing psychoanalytic models.

In 1971 he introduced his theoretical and technical innovations *within* the framework of classical drive theory by positing a division of libidinal energy into two separate and independent realms: narcissistic libido and object libido. (Freud believed there is only *one* libido—one finite energy source.) Both types of libido cathect objects, but the objects are vastly different. Object libido cathects "true" objects, experienced as truly separate from the subject. Narcissistic libido cathects selfobjects, in which the object is experienced as an extension of the self, serving the functions of mirroring and idealization. Thus, it is the quality of relatedness, the position of the object vis-à-vis the self, which distinguishes the two kinds of libido. Kohut bifurcated Freud's libido theory into two independent developmental lines, one leading to the development of object love, the other to self love, or healthy narcissism.

Kohut's relational innovations lie within the arena of narcissistic libido, which determines the early selfobject relations. The self grows out of interchanges with parental figures, and these relationships are characterized not by the gratification of impulses but by the establishment and transformation of particular forms of interaction with the parents. "Disorders of the self" represent distortions within the narcissistic libidinal line of development. "Object libido" is preserved as the realm in which impulses, drive-derived wishes, operate. True object relations are developed secondarily, since object-relatedness in Kohut's sense presupposes the formation of a stable self distinct from the objects and hence is a developmental achievement of considerable complexity. The realm of object libido, Kohut argues, has been adequately delineated by classical drive theory; oedipal "structural neuroses" are disorders within the object libidinal line of development. From his 1971 perspective (which Kohut later designates "the psychology of the self in a narrow sense"), oedipal issues and self development stand in sequential relation to each other. The development of a cohesive self is a *prerequisite* to the experience of oedipal struggles as described by classical theory. An appreciation of the importance of the self may enrich our understanding of oedipal issues, but it can be ignored without serious theoretical or clinical consequences. Oedipal issues involve primary sexual and aggressive impulses and defenses against them; the self, already firm, is no longer the central focus.

Here, Kohut preserves drive theory and mixes conceptual models by restricting their applicability to different developmental periods. This strategy has an important history within the drive model tradition. We have seen that Mahler distinguishes between psychopathology centered on early conflicts around separation-individuation (parallel to Kohut's relationships between the self and selfobjects) and later psychopathology centered on conflicts between sexual and aggressive drives and defenses against them (oedipal neuroses). Kernberg goes even further, arguing that the internal representations of early object relations are the building-blocks of the drives themselves, thus generalizing Mahler's schema into a broad principle of normal development. The implication of both positions is that, although early development must be understood in terms of the relations between the self and others, the drive model is applicable once structuralization has been achieved.

In his sequential approach, however, Kohut is much more literal than accommodating drive model theorists. He understands drives and the defenses against them as the critical aspects of late development. The formation of the self, requiring adequate relationships with the selfobjects, is critical only earlier. Unlike Mahler and Kernberg, Kohut does not see the drives as the result of a transformation of the early relationships. Formation of the self is merely a prerequisite and there is a sharper discontinuity between the two developmental periods than there is for other theorists.

Kohut's early attempt at achieving a conceptual mix raises as many questions as it answers. His juxtaposition of relational concepts expressed through the operation of narcissistic libido with drive model concepts expressed in the operation of object libido seems internally inconsistent. On the one hand, he has suggested that the self develops through gradual separation from and internalization of selfobjects from whom it is initially undifferentiated. On the other hand, he suggests that the self from the very beginning (as required by the drive model framework) cathects these same objects with sexual and aggressive impulses, which within his own system implies that the objects are already experienced as distinct and separate. The interplay between narcissistic and object libidinal modes of relatedness is difficult to explain within the confines of Kohut's first formulation. Further, his neat diagnostic distinction between "narcissistic disorders" and "structural neuroses" stemming from instinctual conflicts is politically adroit in that it preserves the drive/structure model for a specific diagnostic realm. This distinction, however, seems fundamentally contradicted by Kohut's formulations concerning the development of the self. If drives are disintegration products reflecting a breakdown of primary relational configurations, how can "structural neuroses" contain at one and the same time no self pathology and conflicts concerning drives, which by definition reflect severe self pathology? Are disorders of the self and "structural neuroses" qualitatively divergent categories of psychopathology, or do both involve disorders of the self in relation to selfobjects, distinguishable mainly quantitatively?

In 1977 Kohut attempted to clarify some of these problems by undertaking a more far-reaching revision of classical metapsychology, based upon a critique of the concept of instinctual drive. He also introduced a second mixing strategy based on what he terms the "principle of complementarity." In common with Fairbairn and Sullivan, he argued that Freud's drive theory embodies an outdated nineteenth-century philosophy of science, predicated upon the possibility of knowing an objective "truth." Applied to psychoanalytic inquiry and to hypotheses derived from it, this reflects an arbitrary split between the observing subject and the observed object. For Kohut, much in the mode of Sullivan, the psychoanalytic situation is characterized by the clinician's participant observation, and psychoanalysis as a science can be defined as the study of human behavior which proceeds on the basis of "introspection and empathy."

Kohut's definition, placed alongside the earlier ones of Freud and Hartmann, is far broader, since it focuses almost purely on methodology, but it serves a specific theoretical purpose. Once we have established an introspective and empathic method, we must ask what can be introspected *about* or empathized *with*. As psychoanalytic observers in Kohut's sense, we can introspect about and empathize with our patients' experience of the events in their lives and the meanings with which they endow those experiences. These considerations led to Kohut's broadest attack on the theoretical structure of the drive model: he argued that because it is essentially mechanistic, it misses the most important level on which human experience operates. (In his final paper, published posthumously, Kohut describes the notion of drive as a "vague and insipid biological concept" [1982, p. 401].) He likens the drive theory approach to trying to understand a great painting by analyzing its pigments; it misses the essential complexity and the crucial scene of the action of the painting as art. Thus, Kohut's emphasis on introspection and empathy goes hand in hand with his shift in conceptual focus from drive to relational issues.

Because of its experience-distant quality, Kohut argues, drive theory and the Freud/Abraham characterology derived from it miss the key issue in all psychopathology, which is not the active libidinal mode but the state of the self. A self that is enfeebled and fragmented will become preoccupied with pure pleasure-seeking aims defensively. The essential meaning of libidinal conflicts is understood only in the context of the issues with which the self is struggling. The drive model has always been concerned with "disintegration products" of faulty self-development. The primary psychological constellations and motivations are composed of the relations of the self to selfobjects. That is, initially the self does not seek tension reduction or instinctual expression but relatedness, attachment, connection to others. If there is a severe injury to the self and its relations, these primary constellations break down and there is a deterioration to pure pleasure-seeking and rage. Thus, classical theory has made the result of severe psychopathology the building-blocks of its developmental psychology.

Kohut designates his more sweeping critique of drive theory the "psychology of the self in the broader sense." Its more radical nature is apparent in his approach to oedipal issues, which differs markedly from his 1971 discussion. Healthy oedipal experiences involve joy, he argues, derived from the exuberant exercise of new capacities and from the selfobjects' sharing of pride over these new capacities. Classical descriptions of the oedipal period as involving intense conflict and murderous competitiveness reflect a secondary consequence of the selfobjects' failure to participate optimally in the child's development. If the parents are truly empathic and not suffering from disturbances of their own, the child's oedipal experience will be essentially joyful and not intensely conflictual. Oedipal crises, therefore, reflect a failure of interpersonal relations, a failure on the part of the selfobjects. Kohut, like other relational model theorists, does not deny the universality of oedipal phenomena, but interprets them in a different context.

In a late essay Kohut goes one step further and suggests that oedipal neurosis *may* reflect a different kind of disorder of the self. Disorders of the self in Freud's day, he argues, were produced by faulty selfobject responses during later childhood, when the parents became stimulated or alarmed by the child's emerging sexuality and acted in a seductive or ragefully competitive fashion. This kind of disorder of the self results in "structural neurosis." Because of the breakdown of the extended family and other social and cultural transformations, Kohut suggests that disorders of the self in our time are produced by faulty selfobject responses much earlier in childhood, resulting in narcissistic personality disorders. He considers replacing the distinction between structural neurosis and narcissistic personality disorder with the distinction between oedipal and preoedipal self pathology respectively, understanding *both* as generated by purely relational issues (1980, pp. 524–525). Such a shift would again highlight the degree to which Kohut's psychology of the self serves as an *alternative* to drive theory, not an emendation of it. He finally decided to avoid such a step, arguing against committing himself "prematurely," and displaying his tendency to make decisions with respect to theoretical options less on their own merits and more in terms of deference to tradition. He states that "I am influenced by a degree of conservatism that . . . leads me to maintain the sense of continuity of our science" (1980, p. 526).

The "psychology of the self in the broader sense" embraces a wide range of developmental phenomena. Unlike the sequential approach, it infiltrates the whole fabric of becoming and being a person. From this perspective the essential meaning of the libidinal conflicts with which people struggle is best understood not in terms of drive demand but in terms of the evolving self in its relations with selfobjects. The self as a theoretical structure is not involved with instinctual expression; rather, it seeks relatedness. The experience of "drivenness" is a defensive and restorative reaction of an already enfeebled self. Far from being primary, innate motivational forces, the drives are manifestations of underlying psychopathology.

Were Kohut to leave his theory at this point it would look much like Fairbairn's. In strikingly similar terms, Fairbairn had described the appearance of unmodulated sexual and aggressive impulses as the result of failures in interpersonal relations. But Kohut's commitment (institutional if not theoretical) to the drive model leads him to reclaim a central role for the drives. He argues that the psychology of the self can be viewed as addressing itself to a different dimension of human experience rather than that addressed by earlier drive model approaches. These two dimensions of experience he terms "tragic man" and "guilty man" respectively. For the guilty man of drive theory, the content of the repressed involves drives and castration anxiety. For the tragic man of the psychology of the self in the broader sense, the content of the repressed involves split-off and fragmented aspects of the self, and the central anxiety revolves around fears of total annihilation. Kohut explains the relationship between the two in terms of his principle of complementarity. The drive model and the self-psychology model tap different dimensions of the complexity of human experience—the struggle with instinctual forces and the struggle for a cohesive and integrated self. Kohut argues that most clinical material can be interpreted both in terms of drive and conflict issues *and* in terms of the psychology of the self.

We have seen a theoretical strategy derived from the principle of complementarity used to good effect within psychoanalysis by Edith Jacobson. Her concept of the independence of the pleasure principle from the classical economic point of view allowed her to introduce relational considerations into the theory of what is experienced as pleasure. She relates the laws governing the experience of pleasure to the psychoeconomic laws in the same way that the laws governing conversion hysteria are related to neurological laws. Psychology and neurology here stand in complementary relation to each other: they are different perspectives on a phenomenon.

Kohut's invocation of the principle of complementarity to integrate relational and drive-derived concepts is more problematic. The dimensions he proposes to integrate are not only *not* truly complementary, they are *mutually exclusive*. Throughout *The Restoration of the Self* Kohut stresses that drives are disintegration products that appear *only* as the result of the frustration of healthy narcissistic needs. Sexual and aggressive impulses are not fundamental human motivations, but distorted, disintegrated fragments. If impulses result from a deterioration of relationship, how can one have impulse and relationship simultaneously and complementarily? A theory that sees relational configurations as primary and drive-derived impulses as secondary breakdown products does not complement a theory that sees impulses as the building-blocks of relational configurations. Kohut uses complementarity to obscure the necessity for choice.

Kohut also argues that most clinical material can be interpreted both in terms of drive and conflict issues and in terms of the psychology of the self. But the fact that interpretations can be drawn both ways does not necessarily mean that it is useful or adds anything to the explanatory power of one's interpretive framework to do so. In this case it merely compounds formulations in an internally inconsistent way. Kohut defends the validity of drive theory, despite his own trenchant criticisms, with an analogy to algebraic equations: the drive theory model can explain structural conflict, even though it leaves out the self, because it leaves out the self on both sides of the conflict so the effect of the omission is equalized and nullified (1977, pp. 96–97). This argument is puzzling. How can one "disregard the participating self" (1977, p. 136) and still essentially understand the phenomena? If drives result from the disintegration of primary relatedness, does not a theory that views drives as primary and psychopathology as consisting of conflicts concerning drive derivatives fundamentally misunderstand the central difficulties? Kohut argues that "The deepest level to be reached is not the drive, but the threat to the organization of the self" (1977, p. 123). To say that leaving out the self on both sides of the conflict is algebraically insignificant does not address the fact that it also omits a focus on what Kohut claims are the fundamental psychological issues.

The "principle of complementarity" seems less designed to integrate two compatible and mutually enriching perspectives than to preserve an older framework that is conceptually incompatible with a newer one. Every psychoanalyst makes a choice whether to place drive or relational forces at the center of his theory. Once he has argued that drive follows relational failure, Kohut has embraced the fundamental premise of the relational model, and his use of the principle of complementarity becomes mere homage to a model which he himself has forsaken.

Kohut's deep concern for theoretical continuity, which underlies and necessitates his strategy of model mixing, is expressed explicitly at several points throughout his work. He describes the view of man dictated by classical psychoanalysis as a "bundle of insecurely tamed drives," a view of human experience which does not inform his own work. Yet, "Self psychology does not deny the validity of this conception of man — how could it? It is not only Freud's conception but also that of such widely divergent viewpoints which jointly shaped the basic convictions of the Western world as Christianity (which teaches sin and redemption) and Darwinian evolutionism and its biological applications (which teaches development from the primitive to the progressively mature)" (1980, pp. 539–540). Traditional theory must be preserved, Kohut suggests, even if it is wrong or misleading. Two footnotes in *The Restoration of the Self* illuminate his control and titration of innovations in theory. In one he praises Schafer's theoretical contributions, but reproaches him for not taking into account "the need for gradualness in theory change if the psychoanalytic 'group self' is to be preserved" (1977, p. 85n). Later he defends his temporary use of Freud's terms "narcissistic libido" and "object libido" in 1971, and his preservation of the terms "exhibitionism" and "voyeurism" in his 1977 volume, even though their meanings for him are very different from their original usage. This is made necessary by the importance of doing "our best to ensure the continuity of psychoanalysis" (p. 172n).

Kohut speculates that Freud's own narcissistic problems contributed to his lack of focus on various issues in the development of the self; he further suggests that training analyses in all previous generations of psychoanalysts have overlooked disorders of the self. This has resulted in unanalyzed "Freud-idealization" (1980, pp. 530–531). Between the lines and in the footnotes Kohut is suggesting that the psychoanalytic "group self" must gradually abandon its original idealized, but no longer fully adequate, conceptual framework as formulated by its original, idealized founding-theorist (selfobject), but that too abrupt a deidealization would disrupt and endanger our group cohesion. Kohut solves the problem of integrating the old with the new by steering a course between what he regards as the Scylla of orthodox dogmatism and its limited vision and the Charybdis of hereticism and its disruption of continuity, by placing the psychoanalytic community on the metaphorical couch and deciding just how much disillusionment is optimal at any given time.

Contributions and Limitations

Kohut has emphasized several issues and perspectives that enrich the theorizing of other relational model theorists. His emphasis on the crucial importance of the cohesiveness, continuity, and integrity of the subjective experience of self has been original and extremely useful clinically. In contrast to other relational model authors, Kohut continually emphasizes (drawing on his theoretical heritage in classical ego psychology) not the relationship per se, but the manner in which the relationship affects the self-experience. His analysis focuses on the threats that unmodulated archaic grandiosity and idealization pose to the organization and coherence of the self. He depicts these repressed residues of infantile experience as accompanied by an intense excitement which undermines psychic equilibrium; their reemergence carries the threat of a repetition of the trauma of original selfobject failure. He sees much of psychopathology involving disorders of the self as attempts to control that excitement, while avoiding self-depletion and collapse, through various splitting and displacing operations. He has added to our understanding of the psychoanalytic situation by demonstrating that the difficulty analysts have in allowing grandiosity and idealization to emerge and develop in the transference often stems from a countertransferential anxiety concerning their own split-off grandiosity and wish to be idealized. Because the self develops around these narcissistic core configurations, Kohut suggests that we all struggle with these issues.

Kohut's placing of the "subjective self" at the center of psychodynamic theorizing, although not an advance in theory per se, has served as a balance against other authors, particularly those influenced by the Kleinian tradition, who use psychodynamic language rife with reified structural concepts and processes. Kohut has emphasized the importance of "immersion" in the patient's subjective experience and the use of theoretical concepts which are as "experience-near" as possible. What is crucial, he stresses, is listening *from the patient's frame of reference*. His use of this phenomenologically based descriptive mode has lent a simplicity and incisiveness to his writing style (since 1977, when he began writing of the psychology of the self as an independent theoretical system) which contributes greatly to its impact and readibility.

Kohut has called attention to the importance of the parents' role in the reflection of infantile grandiosity and the provision of opportunities for idealization. Neither grandiosity nor idealization has gone unnoticed by previous theorists (see Winnicott on infantile omnipotence, and Klein on the function of idealization in early object relations). But Kohut's approach is particularly useful in its stress on the normal developmental significance of these experiences and their place in the development of creativity, his focus on the actual behaviors of the parents, and in the depiction he provides, through his concept of transmuting internalization, of the manner in which parental functions gradually become internalized into inner resources. (See Kernberg, 1975, for a critique of Kohut's claim that infantile grandiosity and idealization are normal developmental stages.)

Kohut's writings on technique have contributed to a shift in emphasis within the relational model from interpretation per se to the provision by the analyst of crucial missing developmental experiences. Through his stress on empathic reflection, Kohut has contributed a great deal to our understanding of the importance of the manner, delivery, and timing of interpretations, in addition to their content. In his formulations concerning infantile grandiosity and idealization he has introduced a novel approach to the handling of the emergence of these phenomena in the transference, in which they are seen as developmentally normal phenomena to be encouraged (passively) rather than as regressive and defensive operations to be resolved quickly through interpretation.

Several problematic features of Kohut's relational model must also be noted. The first concerns his recurring exaggerated claims to uniqueness and originality. The theoretical model he has developed often strikingly resembles the work of other relational model theorists. These similarities are never openly addressed or considered by Kohut, who presents himself as if he were working in a vacuum, continually breaking new ground. At times he has admitted that parallels exist but has left comparison and integration to the future "scholarly studies" of others (1977, p. xii). His tendency to pursue his own line of theory construction unfettered by the demands of attribution to the work of others would be fair enough, if the claims which he and his collaborators make to uniqueness were not so great. In fact, in his last writings Kohut compares his contributions to the invention of the machine, suggesting that they constitute mankind's greatest hope for survival (1980, pp. 463–465).

Many features of Kohut's depiction of the earliest relations between the infant and caretakers echo Sullivan's formulations. There is a great similarity between Kohut's vision of the psychological field of relations between the self and selfobjects and Sullivan's formulations concerning the interpersonal field and the principle of communal existence, and Kohut, like Sullivan, designates his methodology as "operationalism" (1982, p. 400). The view of the infant's nascent self as an interactional product of the innate potentials of the baby and the selfobject's expectations recalls Sullivan's discussion of the parents' personifications of the child and their impact on early development. Kohut's discussion of the sensitivity of the child to the feeling states of the selfobject strikingly recalls Sullivan's concept of "empathic linkage." His emphasis on parental character pathology and its deleterious impact on the child's development overlaps many features of both psychoanalytic models which we have considered, from the interpersonal tradition to Fairbairn, Winnicott, Guntrip, Mahler, and Jacobson. Kohut's discussion of trauma, for example, as impacting on the child not so much as a discrete event but as a crystallization point for distorted empathy and warped relationships in general recalls Fromm-Reichmann's (1950) discussion of the role of trauma in almost identical terms. His critique of libido theory and the Freud/Abraham characterology and his argument that libidinal modes reflect the underlying state of the self recalls many similar arguments in the work of Horney (1937, 1939) and Fromm (1941, 1947). His view of the analytic process as necessarily interactional and his stress on the function of the empathic observer are very similar to Sullivan's early formulations concerning participant observation. Many of the similarities between Kohut and Sullivan have become clearer as followers of the former have translated his ideas from his original language laden with energic concepts into more straightforward terminology. For example, Stolorow (in Stolorow and Lachmann, 1980) proposes a "functional" definition of narcissism in terms of self-esteem regulation.

Kohut's theorizing is consistent with many features of the British tradition of object relations theory, particularly with the work of Fairbairn and Winnicott. His argument that drives are not primary elements but constitute a deteriorative breakdown of relational configurations is prefigured in Fairbairn's work in almost identical terms. Kohut's extremely important discussion of the role of infantile sexuality and pleasure-seeking as a constituent of larger selfobject relational configurations echoes Fairbairn's depiction of the erogenous zones as channels to the object. Kohut's discussion of the child's absorption of the parents' infantile bodily preoccupations suggests, in different language, Fairbairn's formulations concerning the internalization of and attachment to bad objects. There are also striking similarities between Kohut's depiction of the crucial developmental role of early infantile grandiosity and Winnicott's earlier treatment of the same issues. Both see infantile omnipotence as providing the centerpiece for the development of the self; both stress the necessity for a slow, progressive adaptive failure on the part of the parents, allowing the development of durable internal resources. We note these parallels not to devalue Kohut's contributions —*purely* original theorizing is unknown in the history of psychoanalytic ideas, including even Freud's contributions—but to balance his omission of parallel lines of theory construction.

The most recent expression of Kohut's interest in divorcing his work from that of other theorists has appeared in the claim that the psychology of the self is conceptually unintegrable, despite the "principle of complementarity," with virtually all other psychoanalytic theorizing, including the developmental approaches of Mahler, Winnicott, and all other authors writing from within the traditions of ego psychology and the British object relations school. On what grounds does Kohut make this statement?

All other psychoanalytic developmental theories, he argues, and "all schools of child observation that are not guided by the self psychological point of view," base their theorizing on a common assumption: "that man's life from childhood to adulthood is a move forward from a position of helplessness, dependence, and shameful clinging to a position of power, independence, and proud autonomy . . . [taking] . . . for granted that the undesirable features of adulthood, the flaws in the adult's psychic organization, must be conceptualized as manifestations of a psychological infantilism." This common assumption is in opposition, Kohut holds, to his own view, in which he stresses the need for selfobjects throughout the entire lifespan. He thus rejects any formulation suggesting that the infant is symbiotic, unintegrated, or dependent. The infant "is not dependent, clinging or weak, but independent, assertive, strong — it is psychologically complete so long as it breathes the psychological oxygen provided by contact with empathically responsive selfobjects and, in this respect, it is no different from the adult who is complete, independent, and strong only as long as he feels responded to" (1980, pp. 480, 481).

Kohut regards relational configurations and experiences described by other theorists — such as the anxiety vis-à-vis strangers described by Spitz, the reaching for substitutes for the unresponsive mother noted by Winnicott, or the ebbs and flows of anxiety during separation-individuation described by Mahler — to be secondary phenomena due to disturbances in the self-selfobject unit. Adults need selfobjects even at the highest levels of psychological functioning, he argues, pointing to the reliance on selfobjects by O'Neill, Nietzsche, and even Freud, particularly during periods of intense creative activity. An appreciation of this phenomenon, Kohut suggests, calls for a reevaluation of our standards of psychological health and a reconsideration of the emphasis we place on autonomy. His psychology of the self, by emphasizing the enduring need for selfobject relations throughout life and by stressing that infantile demands are not only a source of disease but a "wellspring of health and productivity" (1980, p. 496), avoids the covert "developmental morality" inherent in all other psychodynamic theories.

We regard this argument as a misrepresentation of Kohut's own theory and of the theories of the authors whose work he dismisses. Kohut has presented the development of the self as a fundamentally linear progression. To say that there is a continuous need for selfobject relations throughout life says nothing about change *within* those relations, and all of Kohut's formulations concerning development suggest a progression in health from "archaic," "infantile" forms of selfobject relations to more mature, differentiated, resiliant forms. The key process of transmuting internalization facilitates the movement from relations with others in which selfobjects are needed desperately to shore up defects within the self, to the internalization of resources *within* the self, imparting a self-generated sense of continuity and coherence. In depicting these processes Kohut has portrayed development as a move from addictive dependence to greater resilience and independence. His close collaborator, Ernest Wolf, describes the "developmental *line*" (italics ours) of selfobject relations into maturity as follows: "substitution of persons, depersonal diffusion, and symbolization create for the adult a whole matrix of selfobject relations that take over much of the function of the originally highly personal, concrete, and focused relation to the archaic selfobjects of childhood" (1980, p. 130). Thus, while the need for others remains throughout, the quality of the need changes.

Kohut's definition of psychopathology is couched in terms of defects in the self and the consequent archaic and infantile nature of object relations. Unless he is arguing that it is no better to be free of self pathology than to be riddled with it (which would make psychoanalysis a particularly pointless enterprise), Kohut's claim to have achieved a value-free developmental psychology is misleading. This does not belie the value of his reflections on artistic creativity; creative people often seem to draw intensity from troubled areas within their personalities. (Rilke, for one, avoided psychoanalysis for precisely this reason.) However, the maintenance of infantile modes of relationship, despite their contributions to the creative process, are often troublesome and, as Kohut himself has shown, impediments to the maintenance of a cohesive sense of self and a stable sense of self-esteem.

What of other developmental theories which Kohut dismisses as simply linear in direction, regarding all residues of infantile experience as unquestionably deleterious and morally suspect? This claim has some validity in pointing to an overemphasis on autonomy and separation in the work of authors representing both major psychoanalytic models — Hartmann, Mahler, Fromm, and Horney, for example. However, Kohut overlooks the extent to which some theorists stress, as he does, the importance of infantile experience as a resource for and precondition of adult passion and creativity. Harold Searles has frequently stressed the value in analysis and in everyday life of experiences of merger with other people (see his critique of Jacobson's emphasis on separation in Searles, 1965). Martin Bergmann (1971) has demonstrated the importance of a recreation of symbiosis in the adult capacity to love; Klein and her disciples continually refer to the generative and restorative function of good internal object relations as an underpinning for adult functioning; Winnicott stresses the primacy of subjective and transitional objects in all truly creative processes; Fairbairn felt that continued interdependence with others was so central in maturity that he terms psychological health the stage of "mature dependence."

Kohut writes as if these authors saw psychological maturity as a desolate and schizoid state of total self-sufficiency, where any kind of need for others is held as a moral defect of the most heinous sort. He states: "We need mirroring acceptance, the merger with ideals, the sustaining presence of others like us, throughout our lives . . . one can never be completely autonomous and independent . . . the self can live only in a matrix of selfobjects . . . it is not immature and contemptible to search for them and to elicit their empathic support" (1980, pp. 494–495). Certainly the authors of the theories Kohut dismisses as incompatible with his own (including those against whom the charge of holding a "developmental morality" carries some weight) would wholeheartedly endorse such a statement.

Other problematic features of Kohut's relational model involve internal aspects of the system itself. He establishes a vision of mental health which is ideal in nature, linked with a depiction of good parenting which is likewise unattainable. Reflecting a utopian strain similar to that observed in Guntrip's writings, Kohut envisions the possibility of an essentially conflict-free existence, in which healthy exhibitionism and healthy voyeurism serve as the basis for a spontaneous, joyful, and creative self. There would be little narcissistic vulnerability, since the self is cohesive and resilient, and severe conflicts (the product of a breakdown in self cohesion) would be unknown. Kohut's depiction of the healthy oedipal period highlights this vision of mental health. If the parents provide the necessary experience, none of the phenomena so prevalent in the descriptions of other theorists—such as dependency strivings, greed, envy, conflicts over separation, loyalty struggles with respect to the parents, stranger anxiety, and so on—would appear. Normal, expectable selfobject failures would not produce these phenomena, Kohut argues, since incremental failures of perfect responsiveness are necessary and actually facilitate structure-building.

Kohut believes that the kinds of struggles depicted by other theorists are already the product of a severe breakdown of self-organization, itself the product of self-pathology in the parents which seriously contaminates their role as selfobjects. This standard seems to us to have limited usefulness in the face of reality. Neither of us has known anyone who is entirely free of dependency strivings, greed, envy, separation conflicts, divided loyalties and identifications, and so on, and we question Kohut's vision of healthy development. Are these problematic phenomena deterioration products or are they an inevitable part of life? It seems to us more economical conceptually to acknowledge that life, both for the child and for adults, is fraught with struggles and conflicts, no matter how ideal the parenting. In moving away from drive theory by designating "drivenness" as a deterioration product, Kohut has given secondary status to everything in life apart from joyful exuberance.

A final weakness of Kohut's psychology of the self is the narrowness of its interpretive focus. The origins of Kohut's innovative concepts in his formulations concerning "narcissistic libido" skewed his depiction of relational configurations and development always in the direction of "narcissistic" issues, defined in terms of mirroring and idealization. The complexities of the child's wishes and feelings concerning his parents are uniformly arranged in two categories: the desire for empathic mirroring and the opportunity to idealize the parent. As a consequence, developmentally significant persons often appear in Kohut's case descriptions as somewhat schematic and shadowy figures, important principally in terms of their role as narcissistic gratifiers or frustrators. For example, most of the case material points to gross defects in the parents' personalities, including depressions, withdrawal, emotional shallowness, violent mood swings, and mechanical relatedness to the child. One might question whether the salient dimension here is the break in idealization and the failure to reflect infantile grandiosity, or the lack of any real emotional contact. Likewise, Kohut maintains his 1971 formulation that the structures of the self grow, both in childhood and in analysis, wholly out of narcissistic fusions and gradual, incremental disappointments. *There is never any actual engagement* between the parent and the child, any encounter between real as opposed to inflated and idealized people. One might question whether the very lack of contact between parent and child is not at the bottom of the disturbances Kohut reports. His universe of interpretive options often seems limited to either classical oedipal or narcissistic themes.

In an effort to move beyond Freud's depiction of neurotic psychopathology based on conflict involving object libido, Kohut has stretched the concept of narcissism past the point of usefulness, setting it apart from other features of interpersonal relations. This has led to a blurring of crucial distinctions between mirroring of grandiosity and realistic caring and recognition, and between idealization and respectful commitment. First narcissism is set apart from object love (the realm of classical structural neurosis); then everything is understood to derive from disturbances within narcissism. The birth of Kohut's psychology of the self in the classical concept of narcissism skews his interpretive framework away from other distinct, although always interdependent dimensions of relations between self and others, those which play a more prominent role in other relational model theories.

Joseph Sandler's Mixing of Models

Despite several different attempts, Kohut and his collaborators have been unsuccessful in their efforts to juxtapose and convincingly combine the drive/structure model with the relational/structure model. Did Kohut simply go about mixing theories in the wrong way, or do his difficulties call into doubt the feasibility of mixing psychoanalytic models altogether? Some light is shed on this difficult question by a brief consideration of the intriguing evolution of theorymaking in the work of Joseph Sandler.

Over the past twenty years Sandler and his collaborators have been gradually developing a theory of motivation and psychopathology that has drawn increasingly upon the relational model for its premises and general thrust. (Because it would be cumbersome and distracting to delineate the contributions of his numerous collaborators, we use Sandler's name to represent both himself and his co-workers.) Yet, Sandler, who presents himself explicitly as a codifier and preserver of theoretical models, has neither explicitly broken with drive theory metapsychology nor attempted to amend and stretch drive concepts to contain his contributions. Rather, he has attempted to leave the drive model essentially intact and to add relational model premises to it. His efforts highlight some of the difficulties inherent in model mixing, even if one goes about the task with a serious effort at integration. A balance between the two models is very difficult to obtain, and even more difficult to maintain. Tracing Sandler's work chronologically, we find a gradual shift in the balance of his mixed models. In his early papers relational model concepts are simply tacked on to the original drive theory foundation, like a new facade on a durable but weathered edifice. At midpoint in his work Sandler places relational model premises alongside the original drive model formulations, as if he now has two sturdy bearing beams, one old, one new, equally sharing the weight of the theory. This would amount to a genuine mixing of models. In his latest papers, however, this symmetry has shifted once again, as Sandler gives more and more weight to relational model formulations, and the older drive theory concepts serve the purpose of adornment rather than structural support, like the placing of old barn beams in a modern house for aesthetic and nostalgic purposes.

Sandler's early efforts at integration were based on an elaboration of Hartmann's concept of "object representation" into a series of formulations concerning the "representational world." Although Stolorow and Atwood (1979) have developed this concept into a phenomenologically based alternative to drive theory metapsychology, Sandler himself does not use the concept of the representational world in this way. When it was introduced in 1962, Sandler was operating fully within the drive model, and his concept of self and object representations originally helped clarify the important, yet always secondary position of objects within classical theory. The concept of the representational world was developed by Sandler and Rosenblatt as part of a more general project, the Hampstead Index Studies, aimed at clarifying and distinguishing from each other basic, yet variably used, psychoanalytic concepts such as "superego," "identification," "introjection," and so on. The variability in the usage of these terms was partially the result of the influx of Kleinian theory into the psychoanalytic literature, with its vast array of internal objects and processes. By clarifying the use of these concepts, and by employing the construct of the "representational world," Sandler managed to contain within drive model terms the increasing emphasis in the literature on internal objects.

As the child gets to know himself and the world in which he lives, Sandler suggests, he develops relatively stable ways of representing his experience to himself. These are not simply perceptions, which are fleeting and imply no enduring impression. Nor are they simply memories of discrete experiences. Representations are organized compilations of past experiences, relatively enduring impressions, constellations of perceptions and images, which the child culls from his various experiences and which in turn provide for the child a kind of cognitive map, a subjective landscape within which he can locate and evoke the cast of characters and events within the drama of his experience. It would be impossible even to begin to speak of the *internalization* of objects, Sandler suggests, without the establishment of representations of objects. The parents cannot be "taken in" in any respect until after they are grasped, perceived, and subjectively maintained. It is not only objects, however, which are maintained as representations. The child develops, Sandler argues, all sorts of representations, including representations of himself in various respects, his body, and his experience of drive pressure and affects. Thus, self and object representations, culled from a multitude of impressions, constitute a network of concepts and enduring images, a "representational world" which provides the basic organizational framework for the child's experience.

At first Sandler used the concept of the representational world generally within the framework of Freud's structural model. Although the concept granted increasingly greater prominence to object relations, they remain throughout the derivative of drives. The construction of the representational world, Sandler suggests, is the product of ego functions. The representational world itself is not active; it has no motivational properties. Self and object representations are drawn by the ego out of experience, and in turn are used by the ego as a "set of indications which guides the ego to appropriate adaptive or defensive activity" (Sandler and Rosenblatt, 1962, p. 136). The self representation is an organization within the representational world. Id impulses become associated with self and object representations, through experience. Impulses make themselves known through wishes, and wishes become associated, through gratifying experiences, with various self and object images. *All* wishes, Sandler argues, involve self and object representations, as well as some anticipated interaction between self and object. (The influence of Klein and Fairbairn is apparent here.) One never sees a drive aim simply seeking gratification. All drive aims seek gratification through wishes, and all wishes involve fantasies of self and other in a "wished for interaction." Object relations serve the function of drive gratification; what is gratified is not simply a bodily tension, but a wish consisting of images of self and other involved in specific, fantasied relational configurations. Thus, drive gratification, in Sandler's system, is inherently object-related. The search for objects in general and the search for need-satisfying objects can be regarded as essentially the same.

In 1978 Sandler departed sharply from this approach, arguing that the drives cannot be considered to be the sole source of human motivation and that object relations cannot be considered simply derivatives of drive processes. He suggested that the classical approach to object relations, defined as the energic investment (libidinal or aggressive) of an object, is inadequate and overly simplistic. Drawing on the work of Mahler, Winnicott, and other developmental and child-observational psychoanalytic authors, he argued that the primacy, pervasiveness, and multifaceted functions of object relations makes any attempt to understand their meaning in terms of drive cathexis unpersuasive.

Human beings are motivated by wishes, Sandler argues, but wishes are not all derived from instinctual impulses. Drive-based wishes, entailing the pursuit of gratification, are a subgroup of the broader motivational category of wishes in general. Sandler states that "Many wishes arise within the mind as responses to motivating forces which are not instinctual" (Sandler and Sandler, 1978, p. 286). While drive-based wishes are precipitated by *internal* stimuli, many other kinds of wishes are precipitated by events within the world of other people or by internal stimuli involving processes other than drives. Thus, Sandler employs the concept of "wish" as an indeterminate array of desires in much the same way that Freud used the term prior to his development of the drive/structure model.

Sandler provides a developmental history of object relations not reducible to the vicissitudes of drive which echoes the formulations of Jacobson as well as of authors within the British school. The child is oriented toward objects from the start, reflecting "a given, inborn basis for the child's early responses to external objects [consisting of] . . . inborn organized perceptual and response tendencies related to *potential* object representations" (Sandler and Sandler, 1978, p. 293; italics in original). Sandler emphasizes the word "potential" presumably to distinguish his point of view from that of Klein; the child possesses no inherent knowledge of others, but an orientation toward them, a set of preprogrammed responses. The first distinction in life is that which the child gradually makes between two broad, global affective states—pleasurable and unpleasurable. Although he doesn't spell this out, it is clear that Sandler is not defining these states in terms of drive gratification or frustration, but in terms of more general and global conditions between the child and his objects, much in the way Winnicott and Sullivan describe the earliest interactions between baby and mother. It is out of these two global experiences, initially entailing no differentiation between self and other, that the first objects are formed, which Sandler designates as "primary objects." Initially, this process entails an undifferentiated "division into pleasure and unpleasure per se as objects" (Sandler and Sandler, 1978, p. 292), but gradually more defined and separate self and object representations, and "wished for interactions" emerge. Among the earliest motivational tendencies in the child are attempts to maintain the relationship to the good primary object and to make the relationship to the bad primary object disappear. These relations to primary objects serve as the prototype for various kinds of wishes involving all subsequent object relations.

Sandler describes the repetitive attempt to reestablish early object relations. This repetition he understands in terms of a "need for actualization," a making real of the wished for relational configuration (1981). The wish to reexperience satisfying aspects of past relations is constant, he argues, so there is a continual attempt to structure one's present interactions according to these configurations, to induce others to play the complementary role necessary if the wish is to be fulfilled. The process of object choice involves a testing out of the "role-responsiveness" of the other person: if I act in such-and-such a fashion, will they respond in sought after ways, re-creating the original satisfying interaction (Sandler, 1976). Thus, we continually choose and are chosen by other people on the basis of mutual role-responsiveness, and continually attempt to induce others to play the necessary parts. This process forms the basis for the establishment of the transference in the psychoanalytic situation, and for an understanding of various pulls in the countertransference as well, as the analyst becomes the vehicle for reenactments and role-evocations.

Sandler suggests that a pervasive attempt to reexperience earlier satisfying object relationships underlies much of human behavior and experience, including dreams, in which wish-fulfillment concerns not only drive gratification but also the establishment of the "identity of perception" (see Freud, 1900) which signals the successful actualization of earlier experience. He comes increasingly to emphasize the importance of the study of actual interpersonal relations as the arena for the actualization of early self and object representations and of early object relations. We need to take "into account the various hidden ways in which people attempt to actualize their conscious and unconscious wishes and the object relationships inherent in the individual's wishful fantasies" (Sandler and Sandler, 1978, p. 291).

At this point in his work Sandler can be considered a genuine mixed model theorist. He has challenged the notion that drives serve as the exclusive motivational source for human experience and behavior, and he has established relational needs and desires as having a motivational primacy and a developmental history of their own. The press of drive is now a subcategory of the more general phenomenon of "wishes," some of which derive from drives, some from object-seeking and object-maintaining, apart from drive gratification. In this approach Sandler has introduced a framework in which drive model premises and relational model premises appear to bear equal weight. Yet even at this point his delicate symmetry betrays signs of instability, in that his approach to relational issues seems to grant them an ultimate priority over drive-derived processes.

In Sandler's view, object relations provide the individual with a basic sense of connectedness with the interpersonal world around him, which is necessary for a feeling of emotional equanimity and security. Sandler establishes this basic need for relational security as the *superordinate motivational principle* of mental life. The need for safety constitutes the primary regulatory principle within the mental apparatus, surpassing and preempting all other concerns, including the pursuit of pleasure. The regulation of feeling states which maintain a sense of security and safety is the most important goal of mental processes. This basic need for security, constituted by the establishment of object relations separate and distinct from drive gratification, manifests itself in a need for "affirmation": "The individual is constantly obtaining a special form of gratification through his interaction with his environment and with his own self, constantly providing himself with a sort of nutriment or aliment . . . the need for this 'nourishment,' for affirmation and reassurance, has to be satisfied constantly in order to yield a background of safety" (1978, p. 286). The need for affirmation, Sandler suggests, takes on important motivational properties, particularly for persons who live with chronic anxiety and insecurity in their relations with others. In such situations, where present relationships do not provide the necessary affirmation, there is an attempt to reestablish aspects of earlier object relationships, often in disguised form, resulting in much of what we regard as compulsive and symptomatic patterns of behavior.

In granting the need for safety and self-esteem a primary regulatory function, Sandler has toppled the delicate balance he attempted to create by establishing drive-derived wishes and relational wishes on an equal motivational footing. Relational needs cannot be independent of drive-related needs and at the same time operate with a peremptory primacy in the interests of security, since security, Sandler points out, is a constant human concern. In his recent work he expresses this shift in the direction of the relational model much more explicitly: "The need to maintain or sustain such feelings is an over-riding one in mental functioning, and the urge to obtain direct erotic gratification may have to be sacrificed in the interest of preserving safety or well-being. A psychoanalytic psychology of motivation related to the control of feeling states should, I believe, replace a psychology based on the idea of instinctual drive discharge" (1981, p. 188).* Thus, Sandler appears to be abandoning his efforts to rest psychoanalytic concepts on the twin pillars of drive model and relational model premises. Although he has not yet explicitly rejected drive model language and concepts, the center of gravity of his approach has shifted, and the weight of his theoretical constructs is fully supported by relational model premises.

---

*Merton Gill notes the way in which Sandler's emphasis on affects operates as a bridge between drives and relational theories. In the classical model, affect is a representation of drive. If affect is approached in terms of subjective state, it can be understood as a representation of the state of the self in relation to others (personal communication).

Joseph Sandler has been one of the most subtle and comprehensive synthesizers within the history of psychoanalytic ideas. The version of the relational model which he has developed represents a clear and compelling integration of many of the developments in theory and practice which we have traced throughout this volume. Like British school theorists, he emphasizes the inborn and primary significance of relations with others; like Fairbairn, he depicts self and object representations joined in wished-for interactions; like Sullivan, he emphasizes the importance of actual events and transactions between people, and the induction of others to play desired roles. Whereas Klein and Fairbairn worked mostly with fantasy, and whereas Sullivan stayed mostly with description of what was actually taking place, Sandler combines an account of actual transactions with hypotheses concerning unconscious fantasy and the repetition of early object relations.

Yet, despite his skill as a synthesizer, Sandler's efforts at integrating these various relational formulations into a conceptual parity with earlier drive model premises were short-lived and unstable. His efforts at a genuine mixed model, like those of Kohut, apparently have failed. These failures suggest an intrinsic incompatibility between the drive/structure and relational/structure models, one which can be neither overcome nor circumvented.

For *the beginning is assuredly*
the end — since we know nothing, pure
and simple, beyond
our own complexities.

— WILLIAM CARLOS WILLIAMS, *Paterson*

12 Diagnosis and Technique: A Deeper Divergence

We began this book with the observation that psychoanalysis today is characterized by a proliferation of theoretical approaches, each with its own formulations, language, and perspective. From the unified and integral system of the original architect of psychoanalytic theory have sprung a multitude of competing models, ideologies, and conceptualizations apparently bearing, at best, a complex and ambiguous relationship to each other. Adherents of each tradition focus on their own school, dismissing the value of alternative points of view. This threatens to dissolve psychoanalysis into cultish islands of devotional fealty.

Beneath this confusion there is a deeper convergence of interest and understanding. Despite their differences, all contemporary theorists are concerned with a common problem: how to account for the preeminent importance in all clinical work of relations with other people. Finding a role in theory for object relations has been the central conceptual problem throughout the history of psychoanalysis because Freud's original drive theory takes the discharge of psychic energy as its fundamental conceptual building-block, assigning to relations with others a status which is neither central nor immediately apparent. Every major psychoanalytic theorist has had to address himself to this problem.

There have been two major strategies for reconciling the clinical primacy of object relations with the theoretical primacy of drive. The *strategy of accommodation* attempts to stretch the original drive model, assigning more weight to the role of early relations with others, while re-

379

taining drive in its central motivational position. The *strategy of radical alternative* places relationships with others at the center of theory, building a model which derives all motivation, including sexual and aggressive urges, from the vicissitudes of relationship-seeking and relationship-maintenance. In this model the drive concept is abandoned entirely.

Each theorist declares his allegiance, explicitly or implicitly, to either the drive/structure model or the relational/structure model. This allegiance determines his theoretical strategy. Adherents of the drive model become concerned with accommodating its premises to clinical data which always involve people, real or fantasied, in relationships with each other. Adherents of the relational model become concerned with fashioning coherent alternatives to the long-standing premises of the drive model. A third approach, the strategy of "model mixing," is an attempt to circumvent this choice by juxtaposing relational theorizing alongside the classical system. Drive model principles are neither abandoned nor stretched, but preserved and mixed with relational model observations and formulations. This solution is unstable, at times contrived. Theory construction apparently gravitates toward one model or the other, and a choice is eventually made.

We propose an approach that operates as a map for orienting oneself within and making one's way through many of the complexities of contemporary psychoanalytic theories, a kind of reader's guide through major dimensions of the history of psychoanalytic ideas. The value of all guides depends on their utility; ours rests upon its effectiveness in highlighting both the similarity of concern among all theorists we have considered and the extent to which their differences in focus, sensibility, and language derive from their allegiance to one or the other of the models. We have shown that Freud moved from an early approach which has a great deal in common with later relational principles to the establishment of the drive model itself. Many of his later concepts—the reality principle, sublimation, narcissism, and the revised anxiety theory—represent his efforts to preserve the drive concept at the theoretical center, while granting an increasing role to early relations with others.

Much of the work of Hartmann, Mahler, Jacobson, and Kernberg has been toward the same goal. Hartmann's elaboration of the workings of the ego, the structure which mediates our relations with the external world and is in some measure derived from early object relations, enhanced our appreciation of the role of the environment in the psychic economy. His concept of adaptation introduced a motivational force which supplements the impact of the drives, while modifying the drive concept as little as possible. Mahler's theory of a developmental movement from symbiotic merger with the mother through various stages of separation and individuation specified the "average expectable environment" which Hartmann had broadly sketched; it also spelled out the developmental tasks inherent in adapted living. Mahler's framework presents a view of development couched in terms of shifts in the relational configurations of self and object, but these shifts are ultimately determined by the changing vicissitudes of drive demand. Jacobson, in her compelling picture of the self in interaction with its object world, added theoretical depth to Mahler's observational material. Her work added to the classical approach a level of phenomenological theorymaking which allowed her to integrate her own and Mahler's innovative relational principles into the framework of drive theory. Finally, Kernberg's blending of Mahler's and Jacobson's ideas with those of Melanie Klein and Fairbairn led him to a perspective in which affects rather than drives represent the fundamental source of human motivation. As actualized in relationships with others, affects become the building-blocks of the drives themselves, although once formed the drives operate much as they do in the classical model. Kernberg's theory retains the language of the drive/structure model, but its sensibilities are closely related both to Freud's earliest views and to the fundamental principles of the relational model.

Our approach has made it possible to explore different versions of the second tradition, the strategy of radical alternative. We considered the transitional nature of the work of Melanie Klein, with its increasingly relational premises, discovering that many of the difficult and problematic features of her contributions result from her attempt to develop relational concepts, while retaining the drive model premise that the salient features of emotional life evolve from within. Thus, her allegiance leads her to postulate a priori knowledge of objects, and very early and sophisticated cognitive capacities. In contrast, Sullivan and Fairbairn broke with the drive model more completely, although with different sensibilities and from different philosophical and linguistic traditions. Much of Sullivan's work involves a reinterpretation of Freud's clinical observations in a purely relational context. Similarly, Fairbairn proposes a model of mental functioning in which Freud's pleasure principle and repetition compulsion are understood as a means to a more basic end: the establishment and maintenance of object ties. Winnicott as well developed a purely relational/structure theory, although it was not presented explicitly as such. His manner of juxtaposing his innovations with prior theory become understandable only within the framework of his allegiances, a loyalty to the classical tradition not strong enough to affect the basic structure of his thought, but sufficient to proclaim a continuity which is not there. A similar split in loyalties underlies Balint's retreat from the logic of his version of the relational model. The concept of models has also made it possible to set Kohut's work in a larger context: to see the striking similarity between many of his formulations and those of the relational theorists, to see the unique features of his fundamentally relational model, and to understand some of the more perplexing features of his writings as deriving from his preoccupation with model mixing. Finally, we have provided a frame of reference for tracing the shifts in Sandler's formulations over time, as he moved the center of gravity of his theorizing from the drive/structure to the relational/structure model.

We have shown that there is a fundamental agreement across all psychoanalytic models which leads us to suggest a definition for the elusive term "psychoanalysis." Each of the theorists discussed embraces a dynamic view of the process of human living, considering our lives determined by the complex interplay of a variety of motivational forces which may operate concordantly or conflictually. Each believes in a concept of the unconscious (although Sullivan is somewhat hesitant about the term), endorsing the idea that many or most of the motives that move us function outside of our normal awareness. Each believes that the most effective way of studying man is through the kind of intense, collaborative inquiry that defines the psychoanalytic situation.

These, then, are the defining characteristics of a psychoanalytic vision. The models within psychoanalysis differ with respect to the *content* each attributes to the operative dynamic forces, especially to those which are most commonly a part of the repressed unconscious. For the drive/structure model theorist the repressed unconscious consists of the derivatives of phylogenetically determined sexual and aggressive impulses which have for one reason or another been deemed "unacceptable" within the structure of society. For the relational/structure model theorist the unconscious consists of particular images of the self and others which have been similarly rejected. Each of these formulations contains within it a particular vision of the role of relations with others. The convergence and divergence of theories throughout the history of psychoanalytic ideas is best understood in terms of underlying strategies for positioning observations and formulations concerning object relations vis-à-vis the traditional concept of drive.

To speak of "strategies" and "positioning" risks suggesting a deliberateness and conscious contrivance which we by no means presume. All psychoanalytic theorists operate out of a model, a "metaphysical commitment" of one sort or another. For the adherent of the drive model the strategy of accommodation comes naturally; for the relational model theorist the strategy of radical alternative comes naturally. Both think in terms of a set of premises presumed to be fundamental and true and attempt to reconcile old and new ideas, old and new data, in terms of what they already believe. Why has the divergence between adherents of these two models been of such long duration? Why has one not simply proved to be the "truest," or the closest to what is true?

The Models and Psychodiagnosis

Why are psychoanalytic theories not simply tested against the available data? The drive model and the relational model point to different issues as determining psychopathological difficulties in living. Is it not possible just to collect descriptions of the kinds of patients practicing clinicians encounter, arrange them according to diagnostic categories, and decide which model accounts for the psychopathology of most patients? Unfortunately, it is not so easy. It is extremely difficult, perhaps impossible, to separate clinical data from theory. The way a psychoanalytic observer views a patient, the way he describes the patient's struggles, the kinds of diagnostic categories into which he places the patient—these are all themselves contingent upon the observer's prior theoretical assumptions concerning the basic constitutents of human experience, that is, his commitment to a theoretical model.

Consider the following example. Within the drive model, before the advent of the emendations of the ego psychologists, psychopathology was understood in terms of impairment of sexual functioning. This perspective, which follows naturally from the view that transformations of sexual energy are at the root of all human behavior, has its origin in Freud's early comment that "neuroses are the negative of perversions" (1905a). Thus, Fenichel (1945) argued that the neurotic must *by definition* be sexually impaired. Furthermore, he *observed* that no neurotic was capable of full genital orgasm: there must be some disturbance in the ability to find an appropriate heterosexual partner, in potency, in ability to reach a climax, or in the capacity to enjoy the experience fully. For Karen Horney sexual fantasies are not necessarily the principal content of the unconscious, and neuroses are neither necessarily nor usually the result of sexual disturbance. She *observed* (1937) that many neurotics are capable of full orgiastic enjoyment, a point on which she takes direct issue with Fenichel. Here are two astute and experienced clinicians, each following the dictates of his own theory, unable to agree on what to the naive observer would appear to be a clearcut fact.

To understand psychoanalytic diagnosis we must understand psychoanalytic theory. Freud's psychoanalysis originated as a treatment designed to alleviate neurotic symptoms. He saw patients who suffered from seemingly meaningless, inexplicable symptoms: obsessional thoughts, compulsive rituals, conversion reactions, and hysterical fugue states. As a result of his encounters with them Freud came to the conclusion that the basic difficulty underlying these manifest symptoms is invariably intense, drive-related conflict. Drive, experienced as wishful impulse, comes into conflict with the demands of reality as mediated by the ego and the superego. Conflict occurs between opposing drives (libidinal and aggressive), experienced as ambivalent impulses toward another person or among the opposing demands of the three psychic structures. Conflict gives rise to "compromise formations," manifesting themselves as symptoms or as repetitive, self-defeating character traits. Neurotic psychopathology in adults is understood to be a derivative of an infantile neurosis based on the conflicts of the oedipal period. These conflicts presuppose at least a minimally stable, integrated ego; the patient possesses a sense of himself as a cohesive and enduring individual in interaction with others experienced as possessing the same qualities. Patients who have not achieved this level of self and object consistency, those suffering from more severe psychopathology, were considered untreatable by the method of psychoanalysis. Psychoanalysis as a treatment approach, therefore, was predicated on a patient whose difficulties originated in conflict instigated by drive-derived impulse.

Many of the modifications of the theory of psychoanalysis, including those which have led to the emergence of the relational model, have come from analysts whose clinical experience drew heavily on work with patients considered more disturbed than those thought to be treatable by classical psychoanalytic methods. These patients, whether diagnosed as schizophrenic (Sullivan), schizoid (Fairbairn), borderline (Kernberg), or narcissistic (Kohut), have been understood to have in common a developmental deficit that has left them incapable of the consistent experience of themselves and others that is assumed of the classical, conflict-ridden oedipal neurotic. Analysts working with such patients have looked beyond the conflicts of the oedipal period and focused on the very early disturbances in the relations of the patient and others that give rise to the failure to relate (even conflictually) as a whole self to a whole other. Thus, consistent with the growing emphasis on object relations, there is fairly general agreement among psychoanalysts today that a psychopathology predicated on disturbances in the early relations of the individual and other people is needed at least as a supplement to a psychopathology based on drive and ensuing conflict. The *manner* in which this generally shared emphasis has been developed by various theorists, however, depends to a large extent on the theorist's position vis-à-vis the models. One crucial way in which theory dictates thinking about diagnosis is in the terms chosen to designate the more severe psychopathology.

Consider the popularity of the nosological category of "narcissism" within the work of some American analysts in contrast to the popularity of the category of "schizoid personality disorder" within the British school. It is rare to find in the works of American clinicians any reference to schizoid psychopathology, and British authors rarely mention narcissistic disorders. Nevertheless, the clinical examples of "schizoids" presented by British authors such as Guntrip bear a striking resemblance to the clinical examples of "narcissistic personality disorders" discussed by American authors such as Kohut.

This terminological distinction is based less on clinical description and phenomenology than on differing allegiances to the drive model. "Narcissism," despite its drastic revision in recent years (Jacobson, 1964; Kernberg, 1975), connotes a particular vicissitude of drive. Narcissism as a diagnostic label recalls libido theory. "Schizoid," on the other hand, refers to splitting. It is the ego or the self that is split, in a particular constellation of early object relations. "Schizoid" as a diagnostic label connotes primitive defenses within early object relations and avoids any necessary reference to drive. The term "narcissism" tends to be employed diagnostically by those proclaiming loyalty to the drive model (Kernberg) and mixed model theorists (Kohut), who are interested in preserving a tie to drive theory. "Schizoid" tends to be employed diagnostically by adherents of relational models (Fairbairn, Guntrip), who are interested in articulating their break with drive theory. Formulations of narcissistic disorders recall a particular stage of libidinal development which is etiologically important (even when, as with Kernberg, a stage of primary narcissism is no longer part of the developmental schema). Formulations of schizoid difficulties stress object relationships as pathogenic factors which transcend the impact of drives. These two differing diagnoses and accompanying formulations are applied to patients who are essentially similar, by theorists who start with very different conceptual premises and ideological affiliations.

A second area of diagnostic controversy whose solution is contingent upon the position of the author in relation to the broad dialectic between the two models is the very existence of a group of patients usefully understood as "oedipal neurotics." For Fairbairn oedipal neurotics do not exist, a stance clearly consistent with his position as a proponent of the purest expression of the relational model. Within his theory *all* neurotic and psychotic problems originate in the matrix of relatedness of the child and his caretakers. Schizoid phenomena are therefore at the core of all psychopathology, with apparent conflict based on drive and defense (oedipal neurosis) expressing the more fundamental underlying relational difficulties. The interpretive leverage of psychoanalytic treatment, therefore, resides not in the working through of drive-derived conflict but in the repair of faulty conceptualizations and experiences of the self and others. Oedipal neuroses disappear as a distinct nosological entity in Fairbairn's work.

Theorists who maintain an allegiance to the drive model necessarily retain a concept of the oedipal neuroses explained as a function of conflict. This is perhaps clearest in the work of Kohut (1977), where these conditions are specifically postulated as a distinct diagnostic entity to be explained by the classical concepts of drive and structure. They are contrasted with the "narcissistic" disorders, which require a new explanatory system (the psychology of the self) derived from the relational model. For Kohut, in contrast to Fairbairn, the two categories and the two theories never meet. They exist side by side, allowing the author both to preserve his ties to the original model and to introduce relational model formulations with respect to presumably more severe psychopathology. Just how theory-bound this is is evident in a recent paper by Rangell, which is devoted to an intense critique of Kohut's theory of the self and to a defense of drive model metapsychology. Rangell states that Freud's "early division of psychopathology into transference versus narcissistic neuroses was the one clinical observation he made which did not stand the test of time. As clinical experience has amassed, there is no transference neurosis without narcissistic conflicts and no patient with 'narcissistic neurosis' who does not form a transference" (1982, p. 866). Rangell's argument attempts to undercut Kohut's theory at its very data base, and his comment illustrates the way in which theoretical predispositions influence diagnostic judgment.

A quite different attempt at integrating the two views of psychopathology is evident in the work of Kernberg. In distinguishing between "higher level" and "lower level" character disorders, Kernberg preserves the oedipal concept, while integrating insights derived from the relational model theorists. The "higher level" disorders, corresponding to the classical oedipal neuroses, are defined by the individual's reliance on repression as the primary defensive operation. The ability to repress presupposes the existence of an integrated ego and of a whole, consistent self relating to whole, consistent others. Kernberg's "lower level" disorders are characterized by primary reliance on defensive techniques organized around splitting of self and object representations.

A consistent self in relation to consistent others has not developed in these individuals, and analysis is directed toward the repair of the defect that has given rise to this developmental failure. It is directed, that is, to the amelioration not of conflict but of difficulties in the very ability to experience oneself in interaction with other people. Like Kohut, Kernberg does not replace the diagnostic category of oedipal neuroses (and the underlying conflict theory) with a category derived from difficulties in early object relations; his "lower level" disorders supplement rather than displace the earlier framework.

The very same patient, in the eyes of theorists of different persuasions, is a very different creature. Freud looks at the patient and sees someone struggling with underlying conflicts over sexual and aggressive impulses, giving rise to bizarre symptoms. Fairbairn sees the same patient as struggling with universal, underlying conflicts over attachments and allegiances to early significant others, giving rise to the same symptoms. Kohut sees the patient as does Freud, but in a different context, not as manifesting a universal form of psychopathology but as an embodiment of one of two great classes of human struggles. Kernberg sees the same patient as does Freud, but with a different psychological life history, as having arrived at his current oedipal struggles through the transformation and consolidation of early object relations.

Diagnosis does not and cannot stand prior to and independent of theoretical commitment. Let us examine a recent attempt to use diagnosis to validate theory, again by Leo Rangell. In the 1982 article just cited, Rangell quotes his own earlier response (1954) to a statement by Fromm-Reichmann (1954) asserting that oedipal conflicts are rare. Rangell answers that "the technique employed determined the depth of the intrapsychic pathology which could be reached . . . Psychotherapy or even analysis directed to outer layers could not then claim with authority that oedipal conflicts were the exception" (1982, p. 865). He claims that the "deepest" data are discovered only by the use of a specific technique, and that the validity of the technique is proved by its ability to uncover these particular data! Moreover, both the utility of the technique and the "depth" of the data are derivatives of a particular theoretical perspective! No relational model analyst would agree that oedipal issues represent the psychological "depths"; yet Rangell is able to dismiss their argument because the argument itself *proves* that the theorist has used an inadequate technical procedure. His position is tautological, unassailable, and theory-bound. Differences and controversies concerning diagnosis are fully understandable only in the context of the larger tension between the two major psychoanalytic models.

The Models and Psychoanalytic Technique

What of the clinical process of psychoanalytic therapy? Is it not possible to evaluate the two models in terms of their efficacy in explaining the analytic process, in accounting for what happens in the psychoanalytic setting and for the manner in which patients change? As Rangell's argument shows, technique is by no means independent of theoretical allegiance. We have been charting formal theory construction, the manner in which the major theorists establish basic premises and from them construct an explanatory framework. The choices made have a profound effect on the way clinicians *conceptualize* what they do. (There is also a relationship, more intricate, between conceptual models and what analysts *actually* do.) The manner in which one understands the basic nature of human experience and the fundamental motives of human behavior inform one's understanding of the nature of the psychoanalytic situation and analytic process. The drive model and the relational model embody fundamentally different visions of human nature, and the theories of technique which have developed from them are similarly divergent in their basic premises.

For the drive model analyst the patient comes into treatment with self-contained, encapsulated pathogenic conflicts. It is the purpose of the analysis to elucidate those conflicts, to make the unconscious conscious. The analyst's position vis-à-vis the patient is similar to the position, within the drive model, of an individual's objects. As the object is external to drive-derived aims, so the analyst is external to the neurotic process. Freud's "blank screen" and "reflecting mirror" are designed to underscore this understanding of the psychoanalytic situation (1912d).

Theorists operating within the drive model understand virtually all of the patient's relationship to the analyst in terms of displacements from the past (transference). Transference is predetermined solely by the patient's developmental history; its content is a function of demands made upon early objects and defenses against those demands. Given minimal interference by the analyst, and an analyzable patient, these early issues will unfold, at first piecemeal but eventually crystallizing into the transference neurosis. Interruptions of the associative process are conceptualized as resistance, stemming from the anxiety which the conflict-laden impulses generate. A desire "not to know" opposes the work of the treatment.

Countertransference—the analyst's intense feelings toward the patient—is understood in a manner paralleling the understanding of the patient's transference. It arises edogenously and signals unresolved neurotic conflicts in the analyst. The only role that the particular characteristics of the patient have in affecting countertransference is as a trigger—the influence is felt only insofar as it touches material in the repressed unconscious of the analyst (a role similar to that of the day residue in the formation of a dream). Any expression or acting out of countertransferential feelings by the analyst will impede treatment, because it will interfere with the unfolding of the transference. Counter-transference, like transference, is simply a sign that more analysis is needed.

For the relational model analyst the psychoanalytic situation is inherently dyadic; events within the analysis are not understood as preset and unfolding from within the dynamic structures of the patient's neurosis. Rather, they are created in the interaction between the patient and the analyst. As in the drive model, the analyst is cast into a series of roles derived from the patient's old relationships. He sometimes plays the part of old objects, sometimes of aspects of the patient's self. This construction differs from that of the drive model, however, because the analyst can never function entirely "outside" the transference. As a particular person the analyst not only participates in these various patterns, but precipitates them as well. Whatever the analyst does shapes the transference paradigm, whether he responds to the patient or fails to respond. The analyst's participation exerts a pull on the patient, and the analyst serves as a co-creator of the transference. Similarly, the patient's experience of and behavior toward the analyst exert pulls on the analyst, who can usefully employ his awareness of these pulls in the service of understanding the patient's *relational* patterns. Thus, countertransference provides the crucial clues to the predominant transferential configurations, since transference and countertransference reciprocally generate and interpenetrate each other. Countertransference is an inevitable product of the interaction between the patient and the analyst rather than a simple interference stemming from the analyst's own infantile drive-related conflicts.

In addition to the repetition of old, often self-defeating patterns, something else happens in the patient's experience of his relationship with the analyst. A "genuine emotional contact" (Fairbairn, 1940, p. 16) develops, with an intimacy and a freedom unknown in the patient's interpersonal history. This allows the patient to transcend the old perimeters of relationship, maintained because of anxiety (Sullivan) or attachments to bad objects (Fairbairn). Within the relational model approach to technique, "resistance" is not a rejection of awareness of mental content within the mind of the patient, but a response to the person of the analyst. It is a relational process involving wary and sabotaging patterns of relationship with another person who is perceived as threatening. The task of the analyst is not to remain outside of a process which is unfolding from within the mind of the patient, because this is theoretically impossible in the terms of the model's basic premises, but to engage the patient, to intervene, to participate in, and to transform pathogenic patterns of relationship.

A fundamentally different understanding of human development directs the two models toward equally incompatible approaches to the therapeutic action of psychoanalysis. Within the drive/structure model, development is conceptualized in terms of the integration of infantile impulses (the component drives) into structured, unitary aims. These aims are then brought under the control of the ego, which can exert a decisive role in organizing, channeling, delaying, or gratifying particular needs. Pathogenic conflicts arise because for one reason or another the drives have not been brought adequately under the ego's domination. Psychoanalytic treatment can facilitate this attenuated development by making the unconscious conscious, thus strengthening the ego's impact vis-à-vis infantile drive demands. Thus, both the goal of analysis and its therapeutic action remain, as they were for Freud, enhancing the power of the ego by increasing its knowledge and its hegemony over the drives.

Because the goal of analysis is knowledge, the role of the analyst is to interpret the patient's defenses and the underlying impulses which have given rise to them. This allows conflicts to be played out on the field of consciousness, under the watchful eye of the ego. Conscious choice replaces unconscious defense. By knowing himself better, a knowledge which includes awareness of and respect for previously disavowed aspects of his personality, the patient will be more able to renounce old, impossible, and frustrating aims and to embrace new ones which are attainable and true to himself.

The therapeutic role of transference in the drive/structure model follows naturally from the emphasis on increased knowledge. Transference, especially given the analyst's nonparticipation, is a recreation in the present of old conflicts which, by virtue of their recreation, are made accessible to interpretation. Interpretation leads to insight, and insight alone is curative. Although the patient may experience the analysis as beneficial in other ways, as cathartic or supportive, for example, these are not a part of analytic change. True analytic change comes only from knowledge, because only knowledge can reinstate the developmental process which was interrupted by pathogenic defenses.

For relational model analysts, no less than for those of the drive model, the therapeutic action of psychoanalysis is built upon the ability of the analysis to remediate developmental failures. However, since it is the quality of early relationships that are seen as developmentally crucial within this model, it is the quality of the analytic relationship that is seen as fundamentally therapeutic. The patient is viewed as having lived in a closed world of archaic object relationships which lead to neurotic self-fulfilling prophecies. Through his new interaction with the patient, the therapist is able to enter that previously closed world and to open the patient to new relational possibilities. Although the analyst may interpret, may communicate information, it is not the information alone that is understood as producing change. The nature of the relationship that develops around this communication (for example, awareness that the analyst understands without judging, cares without impinging, is affected without being overwhelmed or retaliating) is essential to cure.

Within the relational model different theorists construe the impact of the analytic relationship differently. Fairbairn stresses the importance of the analyst's becoming a "good object" as a prerequisite to the patient's relinquishing his ties to a bad object (although he does not spell out the precise mechanisms through which this good object relationship is developed). Authors in the Kleinian tradition tend to stress the manner in which the act of interpretation itself transforms the relationship between patient and analyst. James Strachey, whose early work (1934) provided a key transition from the classical theory of technique to later relational models, sees transference interpretations as "mutative." By forcing the patient to see that his intense feelings toward the analyst are displacements from the past, these interpretations make it possible for the patient to see the analyst as someone real and different, someone new. The patient is able to accept and express previously repressed material only because he experiences the analyst as an object different from the stereotyped characters methodically projected from his harsh superego. The sine qua non for effective interpretation is the internalization of the analyst as a real, benign figure.

Racker (1968) similarly stresses the relationship-transforming power of interpretation. The patient experiences the analyst in the context of his internal object relations, which he projects onto the analytic situation. The analyst comes to understand these projections of self and object images through trial identifications with them, and he subsequently interprets these projections to the patient. In interpreting the transference, the analyst is saying, implicitly and sometimes explicitly: I am not the same as your bad internal objects or rejected parts of yourself; I am trying to understand you, to enable us to reach each other in a more meaningful way. For Racker the interpretation is an act of engagement and caring that transforms the relationship.

Relational authors within the interpersonal tradition tend to deemphasize interpretation per se. Sullivan stresses the importance of the analyst's establishing himself as different from earlier people in the patient's life, a technique which Havens (1976) has designated "counterprojective" and elaborated into a systematic approach to treatment. Levenson (1972) argues that the analyst is transformed by the patient's "system" of interpersonal integrations. The analyst becomes the patient's anticipation of him, heard and experienced by the patient in nonproductive although accurate ways. The analyst, he suggests, by becoming aware of his reactions and his participation in the patient's system, engages the patient in elucidating this mutual participation in the perpetuation of the patient's difficulties. This engagement is effected through the analyst's attempt to understand, with the patient, what has happened to the two of them. This understanding enables the analyst, then the patient, to "resist transformation" and to allow a new relationship to develop. Kohut, whose technical recommendations stem from the more relational aspects of his mixed model theory, sees specific *behaviors* of the analyst as compensating for old developmental failures. It is the patient's *experience* of the analyst's mirroring and allowing himself to be idealized which are crucial. This view, although derived specifically from Kohut's developmental theory, shares in common with other relational model approaches a conviction that it is the actual interpersonal experience with the analyst (which may or may not enhance self-knowledge per se) that carries the treatment's therapeutic action.

The manner in which any theorist or clinician **understands** the therapeutic action of psychoanalysis is greatly determined by his theory. When an analyst makes an interpretation, he is simultaneously engaging in an interpersonal exchange with the patient. As Friedman puts it: "Telling a patient what he is doing is a response of the object. As such it will contribute to a concept of the object (the analyst) and of the patient's action, and of the patient's nature. But it does not do that by sheer exposition . . . the significance of an interpretation is always the significance of a reaction from someone perceived as a certain kind of person" (1978a, pp. 561–562).

Thus, the interpretive event has at least two major dimensions: information is conveyed; and, in the act of conveying that information, the relationship between the patient and the analyst is deepened or altered. A correct interpretation implies a deep and empathic form of relatedness. A deep and empathic engagement of the patient by the analyst communicates information — about the patient, about the analyst, or about their interaction. There is no imaginable referent within the analytic process for concepts like "contentless empathy" or "unempathic understanding." Meaningful interpretation and deep relationship imply each other. Which dimension of analytic activity is emphasized within any particular theory of technique? This is an a priori choice informed by the more fundamental premises of one's theoretical model. Drive model theorists, even those who have stretched the model through the strategy of accommodation, tend to stress the information aspect of the interpretive event. Relational model theorists, by contrast, tend to stress the relationship-transforming aspects of the interpretive event. The debate between different constructions of the analytic process echoes the deeper divergence between theoretical models.

As differences between the major psychoanalytic models have bred attempts at theoretical integration, so they have bred attempts to mix constructions of the analytic process. These efforts, which have achieved a great deal of popularity in recent years, strive to preserve the drive model theory of treatment virtually intact, while adding many of the contributions derived from the relational model. Two basic strategies have been employed in effecting this mixture: the bifurcation of psychoanalysis into two essentially different forms of treatment, and the introduction of relational processes as a prerequisite of insight-oriented interpretation.

The first strategy is based on the argument that there are two different kinds of analytic treatment: one in which insight is central, and the other in which relationship is central. This distinction is predicated upon the kind of diagnostic split just discussed. Some patients are understandable within the context of the theory of drives and conflict as developed by Freud; they require insight arrived at through interpretation. Other, more disturbed, patients suffer from deficiencies in early relations with others, leading to fundamental deficits in the structure of the self; these require the participation of the analyst in specific interactions, which produces a healing of the developmental omissions and distortions.

Through this strategy Freud's understanding of neurosis and the analytic process is left unchallenged within its original metapsychological framework, while important and innovative contributions are introduced in connection with severe pathology. Kohut used it when diagnosing "narcissistic personality disorders," which he distinguished from classical transference neuroses. For the latter, suffering from structural conflict, classical technique, with its emphasis on the interpretation of the transference leading to insight, is appropriate. Patients with "narcissistic personality disorders," however, suffer from deficiencies *within* psychic structuralization itself, as a result of disturbances in early relationships with parental figures. Such patients require not just interpretation, but specific experiences in the relationship to the analyst to make up for early relational deficiencies. Thus, cure for patients with transference neuroses entails insight and memory; cure for patients with narcissistic personality disorders entails the establishment and transformation of certain types of relationship. The latter may be effective even in the absence of full recall and working through of repressed material.

Stolorow and Lachmann likewise separate patients into two groups. They hold that it is "necessary to distinguish between psychopathology that is the product of intrapsychic conflicts and psychopathology that is the remnant of developmental voids, deficiencies and arrests." For the former, less severely disturbed group, the classical model of psychoanalytic treatment is suitable which calls for "interpretations of sexual and aggressive wishes and defenses against them" (1980, pp. 171, 175). For the latter, more severely disturbed group, the patient establishes a primitive selfobject relationship with the analyst in a reparative effort to provide for himself what was denied him in infancy through parental psychopathology. Here, the relationship to the analyst is crucial and must be preserved and protected with minimum interpretation, to allow missing developmental experiences to take place. Stolorow and Lachmann hold that "the maintenance of this primitive state is necessary for the gradual differentiation, integration, and consolidation of self and object representations." With even more severely disturbed patients, with great developmental deficits and profound impairment of self and object differentiation and synthesis, the analyst must do more than provide and protect the formation of primitive selfobject relations. He must "provide a model for the defective discriminitive and integrative functions by articulating for the patient these usually silent processes" (pp. 174, 175). Thus, the primary function of the analyst with patients suffering from structural conflict is as an interpreter; the patient grows by developing insight into his conflicts. The primary function of the analyst with more severely disturbed patients is to provide a relationship. "By accepting his role as a selfobject, the analyst is in a position to make a contribution to the patient's capacity for self-observation through the eventual internalization of the empathic bond which becomes established" (p. 182).

In this first strategy of mixing treatment models, diagnostic distinctions concerning the severity of psychopathology allow the preservation of the classical model and the introduction of a relational model for more disturbed patients. Diagnoses of borderline and narcissistic disorders have been used in this fashion. Many important contributions to the understanding of object relations and their implication for the analytic relationship have been introduced by being tied to a diagnostic entity of greater severity. An interesting feature of this strategy is that, once the new approach is introduced, a diagnostic spread develops: more and more patients are then viewed as borderline, narcissistic, pregenital, schizoid, and so on.

The second strategy for preserving the classical theory of technique while introducing relational contributions has been based on the argument that the relationship between the patient and the analyst is crucial to the analytic process, but as a *prerequisite* to insight-producing interpretations, which are preserved as the essential therapeutic agent. Greenson's concept of the "working alliance" has been the most elaborate development of this approach. He begins by distinguishing between two major dimensions of the ongoing relationship between the patient and the analyst—the transference and the working alliance.* The transference is constituted by a displacement onto the analyst of the patient's early object relations, motivated by a search for instinctual satisfaction. Greenson holds that "instinctual frustration and the search for gratification are the basic motives for transference phenomena" (1967, p. 177). The working alliance, by contrast, is constituted by the development of a *new* object relation, based on collaboration between the patient's "reasonable ego" and the analyst's "analyzing ego."

Greenson posits an essentially classical model of treatment, in which the therapeutic action lies in the interpretation of the transference resulting in insight and memory. However, he suggests that *in order to interpret*, a working alliance must exist, and he describes the kind of analytic demeanor which makes the development of this new object relation possible. He emphasizes the importance of the analyst's warmth and responsiveness, humanness and compassion, the experience of his therapeutic intent, and a sympathetic explanation of the procedures and processes of the treatment. Thus, many of the factors which in the relational model are seen as curative are emphasized by Greenson, but as prerequisites to the interpretive function of the analyst. Two dimensions of the relationship between patient and analyst have been neatly separated: transference and transference interpretation providing insight constitute one dimension; a preliminary working alliance resulting in a new relationship constitutes the other.

However, this neat bifurcation, like many of the strategies for mixed

*Greenson also speaks of the "real relationship" between patient and analyst, consisting of realistic perceptions of the analyst's particular qualities and limitations. In 1967 he sees the real relationship as playing a minor role in treatment, important only at the very beginning and again at the very end. In later papers (Greenson and Wexler, 1969; Greenson, 1971) he gives more prominence to the real relationship, locating it variably at the "core" of the working alliance and as the result of the resolution of the transference.

model theorizing, does not hold up under close scrutiny. *How* does the working alliance come about? After suggesting that it seems to evolve spontaneously in less severely disturbed patients after three to six months of treatment, Greenson states more specifically that the working alliance actually derives from transference interpretation itself: "Only after some effective piece of transference resistance analysis does it seem that the patient is able to develop a partial working alliance" (p. 204). With more severely disturbed patients, intense transference reactions involving the destruction of real conversation and meaning interferes with the development of the working alliance. The analyst attempts actively to reach the patient and establish the alliance by clarifying these distortions. What has happened here? The kind of relatedness that Greenson has characterized as the working alliance is established as a product of the interpretation of the transference. That which was supposed to be a prerequisite has become a consequence! Greenson establishes transferierence and the working alliance as two independent dimensions of the analytic process, a division which allows him to preserve the classical model based on interpretation and insight, while introducing relational issues as a prerequisite. However, as he himself clearly demonstrates, the alliance is *not* independent of transference; it is created through the interpretation of transference. Thus, the interpretation of transference transforms the relationship between the patient and the analyst, which allows for further interpretation. Insight and relationship interpenetrate in ways more complex than Greenson suggests. Simply to introduce relational concerns as prerequisite to interpretive activity obscures the central function which Greenson actually grants them in the analytic process.

Although Greenson's attempt to integrate the working alliance into the classical model of psychoanalytic technique led him into internal inconsistency, his work does reflect a growing trend within the drive model to take account of relational and specifically nontransferential aspects of the patient-analyst interaction. Loewald (1960) reconceptualizes the therapeutic action of psychoanalysis, including "classical" analysis of neurotic patients, in terms of the relational dimensions of the analyst's interpretive activity. People grow, he suggests, by internalizing interactions between themselves and others in their environment. The mother provides certain organizing and regulating functions; the child's identification with these functions becomes the basis for the child's own developing capacities. Similarly, the analyst's interpretations provide an "integrative experience" for the patient, mediating between the infantile systems of meaning and higher order cognitive processes. The patient internalizes these integrative experiences with the analyst; the change produced is thus based on the "internalization of an interaction process" (p. 30). Loewald makes it clear, however, that his formulation does *not* constitute a new technical procedure; rather, it stems from a new perspective on the interpretive process. Gill (1980, 1982) emphasizes the importance of contemporary and accurate aspects of the patient's reaction to the analyst in contrast to a preoccupation with the genetic roots of the transference, similarly pointing to the novel and therapeutic features of the psychoanalytic relationship. Schafer (1983) and Spence (1982) have understood the collaboration between patient and analyst in creating an account of the patient's life history. Both believe that the therapeutic action of psychoanalysis resides ultimately in the analyst's interpretive activity. However, each in his own way rejects the orthodox model of the analyst as a strict interpreter of the patient's endogenously unfolding psychic productions. Each argues that the patient's productions are a product of *both* the patient and a *particular* analyst and become meaningful only in the exchange between the two.

The two psychoanalytic models provide different ways of understanding the analytic process. Do they also imply different suggestions as to what the analyst should *do*? Here the problem is more difficult, because the privacy of the clinical setting and the ambiguity of technical concepts make it almost impossible for any analyst to know very much about how another analyst works. The drive model demands neutrality, but how neutral is neutral? The relational model demands participation, but how participatory is participation, and what form should it take? A wide range of factors—the analyst's personality, his experience with his own analyst and supervisors (including his transferential interpretation of that experience), and his idiosyncratic clinical judgment—all contribute decisively to his decisions about what to do. Further, there is often (perhaps always) a considerable gap between the way any given analyst thinks about what he does and how he actually operates. Recent reports by Freud's patients of their experience with him (Kardiner, 1977; Blanton, 1971) as well as Freud's own case studies (1909b, 1918b) make it clear that he was an active participant in the analytic process. Freud hid neither his wide-ranging personal interests nor his strongly held opinions from his patients, and his relationships with them encompassed not only his position as analyst but as friend, teacher, and host. On the other hand, Guntrip's (1975) account of his analysis with Fairbairn indicates that, despite his emphasis on the analyst as a new object, Fairbairn was a rather remote, austere authority figure who operated in the analysis largely as a detached interpreter of Guntrip's disavowed desires.

Nevertheless, despite ambiguities, we can point to specific technical injunctions generated by the two models. The drive model, with its stress on the independence of the patient's conflicts from external influence, emphasizes the analyst's creation of an atmosphere of noninterference and respect for the patient's autonomy. To the extent that this is integrated into one's technical procedure, it encourages silence, careful listening, and a disinclination to interrupt the patient's productions with any quick response. By focusing on the neurotic aspect of countertransference phenomena, the model urges on the analyst an awareness of the ways in which his own difficulties can attenuate a complete analytic inquiry. The relational model, with its emphasis on the inevitability of the analyst's participation, urges on the clinician an attentiveness to ways in which he and the patient are mutually influencing each other. This increases his ability to use countertransference as an empathic tool. Analysts operating under the premises of this model can develop a greater freedom to use the entire range of their feelings and experiences to promote the patient's growth. If the drive model stresses respect for autonomy, the relational model stresses respect for the intricacy of human relationships and for the impact which everything the analyst does (or does not do) inevitably has on his patient.

These subtle differences in emphasis by no means preclude each other. The analytic process obviously cannot be used as a basis for choice between theoretical models. The very nature of the analytic situation and the manner in which it is established are products of the analyst's theoretical allegiance. Depending upon his theoretical model, he is likely to operate differently, thus constituting a particular kind of analytic situation, and he is certain to understand what is happening differently from an analyst of a different persuasion. Like the process of diagnosis, the analytic process is contingent on theoretical commitment.

The Models: A Deeper Divergence

Why has the split between psychoanalytic models been so deep and of such long duration? Adherents of the drive model are as committed to it today as Freud was when he fashioned the strategy of accommodation. Adherents of relational models are as committed as was Sullivan when he fashioned the first comprehensive strategy of radical alternative. Why has this split been so entrenched?

One might argue that the divergence in theory is simply a function of political style, a contrast between conservatives and radicals, between those who believe that institutions and traditions represent the wisdom of the ages and should be tinkered with only when absolutely necessary and only at great risk, and those who regard institutions and traditions as constrictive influences on free thought. Edmund Burke, the most eloquent of political conservatives, described the British constitution as follows: "Our constitution stands on a nice equipoise, with steep precipices and deep waters up on all sides of it. In removing it from a dangerous leaning towards one side, there may be a risk of oversetting it on the other. Every project of material change in a government so complicated as ours is a matter full of difficulties; in which a considerate man will not be too ready to decide, a prudent man too ready to undertake, or an honest man too ready to promise" (1770, p. 416).

By substituting "metapsychology" for "constitution," Burke's warning might serve as a motto for adherents of the drive model, who are deeply concerned about the dangers of losing the thrust of Freud's great contributions and upsetting the delicate and complex balance which constitutes classical psychoanalytic theory. Karl Marx expressed a different view: "The tradition of all the dead generations weighs like a nightmare on the brain of the living" (1852, p. 15). His anguish might serve as a motto for adherents of relational models, who feel that classical theory is a dead weight that impedes the development of imaginative and constructive solutions to problems in clinical practice and theorymaking. Surely this difference in political style has some bearing on allegiances to models within the psychoanalytic community.

One might further argue, turning psychoanalytic interpretation back upon psychoanalytic theorists, that allegiance to models—and political style as well, for that matter—is psychodynamically determined. Freud is the "father" of psychoanalysis; all subsequent psychoanalysts must have a relationship to him, and that relationship is determined by one's oedipal dynamics. Such an argument can be (and has been) employed in two ways, depending upon one's position. Those who reject Freud's theory are acting out murderous wishes toward the father; defenders of Freud's theory are acting out an idealizing submission to the father. This sort of explanation, like the analysis of political styles, has some obvious relevance to the durability of the models throughout the history of psychoanalysis. Its explanatory power is limited, however, because one's estimation of the salient psychodynamic issues (neurotic defiance or neurotic submission) is a direct consequence of one's own position or values.

Transference to Freud is not the only transference affecting psychoanalytic commitments. Psychoanalysis is not simply an intellectual or academic discipline. To learn the theory and to enter the community of practioners, one undergoes a training analysis conducted by a training analyst of a particular political persuasion, an adherent of a theoretical model and strategy. Each analysand's ultimate understanding of himself is shaped at least partially by the training analyst's world view. The training analyst's premises concerning man's fundamental struggles are apt to become the basis for the analysand's grasp of his own experience, history, and motives—and thus of the fledgling analyst's approach to his patients as well. The initiate psychoanalyst turns to problems of theory construction and to technical issues with a deep identification with his own analyst's world view and a deep personal stake in that identification. The tenacity of theoretical commitments within psychoanalysis and the durability of lines of influence are partially a result of these mediating identifications. Yet, psychoanalysts *do* change their points of view: this explanation too seems inadequate to account fully for the continuity of the models.

The human condition embraces a fundamental paradox. On the one hand, man lives an individual existence. Each person is born, is caught in time, and dies. Each individual has his own idiosyncratic experience of life, woven out of his constitutional equipment and potential and out of the serendipity of his fate. Each of us lives in his own subjective world, pursuing personal pleasures and private fantasies, constructing a lifeline which, when his time is over, will vanish. On the other hand, people live necessarily and unavoidably within a human community. The human infant cannot survive without parental care. Much of the process of child development is constituted by the internalization of interactions with others. Although there may have been feral children, living briefly outside a human community, their status as fully human is questionable; there are no feral men or women. The most reclusive hermit thinks in language learned from others, experiences the world in categories influenced by early social relations. The human community and culture transcend the individual life span; in some sense the community creates the individual life, giving it substance and meaning.

Man is an essentially individual animal; man is an essentially social animal. The history of Western social and political philosophy has revolved around the tension between these two views of the nature of human experience. One school of thought, finding its fullest expression in British eighteenth-century philosophy (which formed the basis for the political institutions of the United States), takes as its premise that human satisfactions and goals are fundamentally personal and individual. Human beings pursue their own separate aims, argue Hobbes and Locke, and these atomistic, discordant pursuits are likely to interfere with each other. As Hobbes states, "I put for a general inclination of all mankind, a perpetual and restless desire of power after power, that ceaseth only in death" (1651, p. 64). Each man builds his own world, pursues his own pleasures, seeks his own gratifications. The "state of nature" created by "natural" man seeking personal satisfactions is one of great chaos, the state of war. Each man tries to broaden his acquisitions, to maximize his pleasures, and, in this self-expansion, tramples the boundaries of his neighbor's holdings. In this process the claims and satisfactions of all men are put into jeopardy. The function of the state is to insure personal property and private satisfactions. This entails a certain loss of freedom for each citizen; in subscribing to a social contract, he curtails his own options, limits his range of actions. Nevertheless, this sacrifice is essential to preserve his life, his pleasures, and his property—all of which are at perpetual peril in a natural state of war. Locke says: "to avoid this State of War . . . is one great *reason of men's putting themselves into Society*, and quitting the State of Nature" (1690, p. 323; italics in original).

In his classic essay "Two Concepts of Liberty," Isaiah Berlin characterizes the principle upon which British political philosophy rests as the concept of "negative liberty." Meaning in human life resides in individual fulfillment. The essential function of the state, whether an absolute monarchy a la Hobbes or a democracy a la Locke, is to preserve the possibility of that personal fulfillment. Thus, the state does not provide anything positive; society cannot add anything essential to individual fulfillment as such. The state prevents something negative, the interference with individual satisfactions, and in so doing guarantees the meaningfulness of human existence. "We must preserve a minimum area of personal freedom if we are not to 'degrade or deny our nature' " (Berlin, 1958, p. 11). The manner in which one conceptualizes the function of society and the state is contingent upon one's view of human nature. Within the negative liberty tradition, each man is viewed as seeking personal satisfactions which are by no means compatible or integratable with those of his neighbors. This approach is based on the premise assigned more narrowly to Toryism, the theory "that government must save human nature from itself" (Bredvold, 1962, p. 145).

A second school of political philosophy, with roots going back to Aristotle, developing through the work of Rousseau, Hegel, and other continental philosophers and culminating in Marx's vision of human history, takes as its premise that human satisfactions and goals are realizable only within a community. Man is intrinsically social; he cannot be said to exist meaningfully apart from others. Human nature is completely realized only in relationship, interaction, participation with others. The state of nature within this approach is quite different from that envisioned by the British philosophers. Individual aims are not viewed as inimical to each other, leading inevitably to a state of war. Human nature is felt to contain feelings of natural affiliation and mutual concern. Social participation opens up a new and higher form of existence, where "men can mutually perfect and enlighten one another" (Rousseau, 1755, p. 119). Through the social contract, the individual transcends his private, isolated existence to become part of something broader and more meaningful, "a larger whole, from which he in a sense draws life and being" (Rousseau, 1762, p. 58). It is only in recognition by and participation with his fellows that man becomes fully human. Berlin characterizes the principle upon which this continental tradition of political philosophy rests as the concept of "positive liberty." Meaning in human life is possible only through social fulfillment. The individual by himself cannot create a fully human life. The state provides an indispensable "positive" function by offering its citizens that which they cannot provide for themselves in isolation. Berlin argues that traditions in political philosophy rest upon different visions of "what constitutes a self, a person, a man" (p. 19). For positive liberty theorists, individual man is, by himself, incomplete. The state, according to Hegel, grants to the individual the very "feeling of selfhood" (1952, p. 37). Man apart from the state is less than human, a stunted product of an interference with his fully human potentials. "The human essence," argues Marx almost a century before Sullivan developed interpersonal psychoanalysis, "is no abstraction inherent in each single individual. In its reality it is the ensemble of the social relations" (1845, p. 244).

The drive/structure model and the relational/structure model embody these two major traditions within Western philosophy in the relatively recently developing intellectual arena of psychoanalytic ideas. The drive model of the mind, like the negative liberty model of the state, takes as its fundamental premise that the individual mind, the psychic apparatus, is the most meaningful and useful unit for the study of mental functioning. That individual unit, for Freud as for Hobbes, is dominated by desires for personal pleasures and power, for private gratification. In the pessimism of his later years (1930), Freud becomes most fully Hobbesian. Man cannot live in an uncivilized state without suffering from continual threat and peril from his similarly self-seeking neighbors. Social organization is essential for survival, yet it is purchased at the price of massive instinctual renunciation. Man cannot live outside society, but society is in a fundamental sense inimical to his very nature and precludes the possibilities for his deepest, fullest satisfactions. Social man is safe but resigned, and he gains his satisfactions within the limited arena society allows and safeguards. In the drive/structure model of the mind and the negative liberty model of the state, human fulfillment is sought on an individual level, in the satisfaction of personal desire.

The relational/structure model of the mind, like the positive liberty model of the state, takes as its fundamental premise the principle that human existence cannot be meaningfully understood on individual terms, that, as Sullivan puts it, man is not capable of "definitive description in isolation" (1950a, p. 220). For Sullivan and Fairbairn, as for Rousseau and Marx, the very nature of being human draws the individual into relations with others, and it is only in these relations that man becomes anything like what we regard as human. Individual man is inconceivable; there is no human nature outside society. Within the relational/structure model of the mind and the positive liberty model of the state, human fulfillment is sought in the establishment and maintenance of relationships with others.

Placing the divergence of psychoanalytic models which we have traced throughout this volume within the larger context of the divergence of theories about human nature throughout the Western philosophical tradition sheds light both on the durability of the models within psychoanalysis and on the difficulties encountered by those who have tried to combine them. The persistence and tenacity of the drive model and the relational model derive from that fact that they draw on two of the most fundamental and compelling approaches to human experience, approaches which have dominated our civilization and entered into the thinking of each of us. We began this discussion with the observation that human life reflects a paradox—we are inescapably individual creatures; we are inescapably social creatures. Psychoanalytic theorists, like political philosophers, have built models on one or another side of this paradox. Why not both? Kohut and Sandler, in different ways, attempted just that in their development of a mixed model approach, and we explored the difficulties they encountered. Model mixing is unstable because the underlying premises upon which the two models are based are fundamentally incompatible. Psychoanalytic models, like political philosophies, are based on a "vision by which we are consciously or unconsciously guided of what constitutes a fulfilled human life" (Berlin, 1958, p. 55). The drive model and the relational model rest on different visions, and each is a complete account. Berlin points to the futility of mixing models within political philosophy: "These are not two different interpretations of a single concept, but two profoundly divergent and irreconcilable attitudes to the ends of life. It is well to recognize this, even if in practice it is often necessary to strike a compromise between them. *For each of them makes absolute claims.* These claims cannot both be fully satisfied . . . the satisfaction that each of them seeks is an ultimate value which, both historically and morally, has an equal right to be classed among the deepest interests of mankind" (1952, pp. 51–52; italics ours). Psychoanalytic models rest upon similarly irreconcilable claims concerning the human condition.

It is neither useful nor appropriate to question whether either psychoanalytic model is "right" or "wrong." Each is complex, elegant, and resilient enough to account for all phenomena. The drive model establishes individual pleasure seeking and drive discharge as the bedrock of human existence; the rest of human behavior and experience, including social needs and activities, is derived from the operation of drive and its vicissitudes. The relational model establishes relational configurations as the bedrock of existence; all other human behavior and experiences, including compulsive and impulsive sexuality and aggression, are relational derivatives. Each model establishes a different natural order; each can explain everything. Each model swallows up the other. The models, to use Kuhn's term, are "incommensurable"; they rest on fundamentally different a priori premises. Any dialogue between their adherents, although useful in forcing a fuller articulation of the two models, ultimately falls short of meaningful resolution.

Proponents of the relational model believe that, although Freud's depiction of the passionate conflicts that exist beneath the veneer of consciousness opened the door to a deep and profound understanding of human experience, he was wrong about the underlying *content* of these conflicts. For the relational theorist, all people struggle to establish and maintain relationships with other people, from their earliest efforts to reach their parents to their current efforts to consolidate safe and meaningful intimate relationships in their adult lives. Clinical work is filled with other people, these analysts argue: parents who are unavailable, who have to be shared with siblings, who can never provide the attention desired. Parents are simultaneously loved and hated, and they love and hate in return. The child fears alienating his parents, who themselves seem burdened with life's struggles. He wants to help, to save them; he fantasizes about having parents more wonderful than he has known in reality. Fragments of experience with other adults, images of oneself in relation to others, fantasies of ideal others, grand fantasies of oneself, internal voices derived from real and imagined experience—these become the very stuff of the self. Contradictory demands set up excruciatingly divided loyalties, unresolvably incompatible allegiances. For theorists of this persuasion the pervasive presence of others, real and imaginary, past and present, in every moment of our lives, demands a relational model theory and can never be adequately encompassed by a theory in which object relations are a function of primitive instinctual drives. People need contact with other people not for pleasure and tension-reduction but simply *as contact*. Often the contact is sought not through pleasure but in pain. It is the engagement that is crucial, not the pleasure seeking. For clinicians and theorists who think in relational/structure terms, to say that pleasure seeking is at the root of all relations with others is to skew the data—it is simply too reductionistic.

For the drive model theorist it is precisely the concept of drive that explains the intense attachment of each of us to other people. Why is the child so passionately involved with his parents? Why is it so hard to share them? Why are the demands so intense, the hatred so deep? The drives represent fundamental human passions; they give rise to the deepest and most intense feelings we have. It is the instinctual satisfactions which we have achieved with family members that embroil us in our lifelong struggles with them. The very need to relinquish these early channels to satisfaction makes the establishment of later relationships so problematic. Any theory must posit some basic motivational force, whether it is Freud's sexual and aggressive passions, Sullivan's anxiety avoidance, or Bowlby's attachment. Such specification, when viewed from another perspective, is necessarily reductionistic. What matters is that the fundamental force be close to our human nature and elastic enough to explain a range of phenomena. For the drive model theorist no force serves this theoretical purpose as well as the drives. They not only draw on our biological inheritance but also explain the clinical preponderance of impersonal sexual and aggressive impulses which seem to be directed toward indifferent objects.

Pure pleasure seeking and pure rage are encompassed within the relational model not as primary forces which are modulated and acquire objects secondarily but as reactions to object-related failures. When the search for contact and rich emotional exchange with others is available, sexual pleasures become one among many forms of interchange. When object-seeking is severely thwarted, impulsiveness and aggression result. The child (and later the adult) attempts to reach others through perverse and compulsive sexuality, through power and dominance. The sex is merely a vehicle for the desperate attempt to reach another person; more basic interpersonal needs have become sexualized. In cynical despair about ever having emotional intimacy with anyone, fleeting pleasure (or even pain) with anyone will do, as long as there is some contact, some recognition. Moreover, for the relational model adherent the hedonistic vision of drive theory is contradicted by the facts of human behavior. People are notoriously inept at finding pleasure; they repeatedly engineer situations which make them unhappy. Only a fundamental need for human contact at any cost accounts for the perpetuation of unpleasure in the lives of so many people.

For drive model theorists the repetition of painful experiences is more meaningfully understood in terms of instinctual conflict and subsequent anxiety and guilt. The earliest objects of the drives are desired so intensely and fear of retaliation for desiring forbidden gratification carries so much weight that reaching out for any kind of pleasure brings with it an archaic anxiety that can be paralyzing. These infantile fears and the perpetuation of infantile danger situations are the cause of the repetitive neurotic misery of which patients complain. The fact that retaliation is feared, even by the child who grew up in an objectively benign atmosphere, suggests that such fears are based on *projected* aggression. The problem is inside the child, in his struggles with powerful and conflictual instinctual needs, not only or even principally in environmental deprivation and failures. Drive theory is uniquely suited to account for the generalized ways in which children distort their interpersonal world. Because the objects are created from drive-derived wishes, they reflect what is desired more than what actually existed.

The relational model accounts for the child's distortions of his objects by pointing to the inherent difficulty in the search for relatedness. The human condition can be frightening and overwhelming, especially for the small child. Whatever is provided in terms of parental attention is ultimately not enough. What is missing is made up for through fantasy, splitting, and distortion. What is important is not only what others have been for the child but what the child wanted them to be. Early cognition is filled with distortions. Piaget and other cognitive theorists have demonstrated that the development of the capacity for consensually valid perception and thought is long and complex. Although cognitive development is not independent of affective factors and psychodynamic struggles, early primitive forms of cognition are unavoidable and universal. Children perceive themselves and their parents in fragmented, moment-to-moment, larger-than-life terms. Early forms of perception and cognition, lacking a sense of time, space, and object constancy, contribute to the painful intensity of the struggles within early object relations. For the relational model theorist one need not fall back on drives to account for distortions of interpersonal reality.

The drive model and the relational model are complete and comprehensive accounts of the human experience. The premises upon which they rest constitute two incompatible visions of life, of the basic nature of human experience. Although these premises are not subject to empirical verification, they can be evaluated according to many kinds of standards. Kuhn establishes five criteria on the basis of which theories can be judged: accuracy, consistency, scope, simplicity, and fruitfulness. However, it is unlikely that a consensus will be reached concerning the overall preferability of the two basic models. As Kuhn points out, the evaluation of criteria like scope, simplicity, and fruitfulness cannot be determined in any science universally or with pure objectivity. One's estimation of where a theory stands depends at least partially on one's subjective judgments, on the evaluator's own values and presuppositions.

Apart from Kuhn's criteria, and perhaps superordinate to them, the evaluation of psychoanalytic theories is a matter of personal choice. The theory stands or falls on how compelling it appears to be, on its underlying vision of human life. Does the theory speak to you? Does it seem to account for your deepest needs, longings, fears? In your clinical work does it provide a convincing account of your patients which corresponds with your own experience of them? Many subjective factors contribute to personal response: one's own life history and training, the kinds of patients one has worked with, the life history and training of one's training analyst and supervisors, and so on. Because the values underlying commitment to theory depend on complex subjective factors does not mean that they are arbitrary. However, the complexity of the subjective factors underlying theory choice in psychoanalysis does render communication among adherents of different models difficult. Kuhn argues that this is so in all disciplines: "communication between proponents of different theories is inevitably partial . . . what each takes to be facts depends in part on the theory he espouses, and . . . an individual's transfer of allegiance from theory to theory is often better described as conversion than as choice" (1977, p. 338).

It is difficult to predict the future direction of a discipline as complex as psychoanalysis. It may be that the drive/structure model will prove compelling and resilient enough to incorporate within its boundaries all the data and concepts generated by the study of object relations. In that case the relational/structure models will wither away, having served a useful purpose in prodding and provoking an expansion of the earlier approach. On the other hand, relational models may prove to be more and more compelling, expanding and combining to provide a more encompassing and enticing framework for theory and practice. If so, the drive model will slowly lose adherents, becoming an important, elegant, but no longer functional antique.

We suspect that neither of these two scenarios will come to pass. The paradox of man's dual nature as a highly individual yet social being runs too deep and is too entrenched within our civilization to be capable of simple resolution in one direction or the other. It seems more likely that both the drive model and the relational model will persist, undergoing continual revision and transformation, and that the rich interplay between these two visions of human experience will generate creative dialogue. We hope that our efforts will contribute to making more meaningful dialogue possible.

References

Abraham, K. 1908. The psychosexual differences between hysteria and dementia praecox. In *Selected papers of Karl Abraham*. London: Hogarth Press, 1968.

_____ 1919. A particular form of neurotic resistance against the psycho-analytic method. In *The evolution of psychoanalytic technique*, ed. M. Bergmann and F. Hartman. New York: Basic Books, 1976.

_____ 1924. The influence of oral erotism on character-formation. In *Selected papers of Karl Abraham*. London: Hogarth Press, 1968.

Ansbacher, H., and R. Ansbacher. 1956. *The individual psychology of Alfred Adler: A systematic presentation in selections from his writings*. New York: Basic Books.

Arlow, J., and C. Brenner. 1964. *Psychoanalytic concepts and the structural theory*. New York: International Universities Press.

BALINT, M. Unless otherwise noted, all references can be found in *Primary love and psycho-analytic technique*. New York: Liveright, 1965. *(PLPT)*

_____ 1935. Pregenital organization of the libido. *PLPT*.

_____ 1937. Early developmental states of the ego. *PLPT*.

_____ 1948. Sandor Ferenczi, obit. In *Problems of human pleasure and behavior*. New York: Liveright, 1956.

_____ 1951. On love and hate. *PLPT*.

_____ 1952. The paranoid and depressive syndromes. *PLPT*.

_____ 1956. Pleasure, object and libido. In *Problems of human pleasure and behavior*. New York: Liveright, 1956.

_____ 1968. *The basic fault*. London: Tavistock.

Barnett, J. 1980. Interpersonal processes, cognition and the analysis of character. *Contemporary Psychoanalysis* 16: 397–416.

Benjamin, J. 1966. The contribution of Heinz Hartmann. In *Psychoanalysis: a general psychology*, ed. R. M. Loewenstein. New York: International Universities Press.

Bergmann, M. 1971. Psychoanalytic observations on the capacity to love. In *Separation-*

individuation: essays in honor of Margaret S. Mahler, ed. J. McDevitt and C. Settlage. New York: International Universities Press.

Berlin, I. 1958. *Two concepts of liberty*. Oxford: Clarendon Press.

Bettelheim, B. 1982. *Freud and man's soul*. New York: Alfred A. Knopf.

Bibring, E. 1936. The development and problems of the theory of the instincts. *International Journal of Psychoanalysis* 22: 102-131, 1941.

———— 1947. The so-called English School of psycho-analysis. *Psychoanalytic Quarterly* 16: 69–93.

Bion, W. R. 1957. Differentiation of the psychotic from the nonpsychotic personalities. In *Second thoughts*. New York: Jason Aronson, 1967.

Blanck, G. and R. Blanck. 1974. *Ego psychology: theory and practice*. New York: Columbia University Press.

Blanton, S. 1971. *Diary of my analysis with Sigmund Freud*. New York: Hawthorn Books.

Bleuler, E. 1912. *Dementia praecox or the group of schizophrenias*. New York: International Universities Press, 1950.

Bloom, H. 1973. *The anxiety of influence*. New York: Oxford University Press.

Blum, H. 1982. Theories of the self and psychoanalytic concepts: discussion. *Journal of the American Psychoanalytic Association* 30: 959–978.

Bowlby, J. 1958. The nature of the child's tie to his mother. *International Journal of Psychoanalysis* 39: 350–373.

———— 1960. Grief and mourning in infancy and early childhood. *Psychoanalytic Study of the Child* 15: 9–52.

———— 1969. *Attachment*. Volume one of *Attachment and loss*. New York: Basic Books.

———— 1973. *Separation: anxiety and anger*. Volume two of *Attachment and loss*. New York: Basic Books.

———— 1980. *Loss: sadness and depression*. Volume three of *Attachment and loss*. New York: Basic books.

Brazelton, T. B. 1981. Neonatal assessment. In *The course of life: psychoanalytic contributions toward understanding human development*, volume 1, ed. S. I. Greenspan and G. H. Pollock. Washington, D.C.: U.S. Government Printing Office.

Bredvold, L. 1962. *The intellectual milieu of John Dryden*. Ann Arbor: University of Michigan Press.

Brenner, C. 1976. *Psychoanalytic technique and psychic conflict*. New York: International Universities Press.

———— 1978. The components of psychic conflict and its consequences in mental life. Delivered as the 28th Freud Anniversary Lecture, New York Psychoanalytic Institute, April 11, 1978.

Brentano, F. 1924. *Psychologie vom empirischen standpunkt*, ed. O. Kraus. Leipzig.

Breuer, J., and S. Freud. 1895. *Studies on hysteria*. In *The standard edition of the complete psychological works of Sigmund Freud*, volume 2. London: Hogarth Press.

Bridgeman, P. W. 1927. *The logic of modern physics*. New York: Macmillan.

Burke, E. 1770. Thoughts on the cause of the present discontents. Quoted in *Encyclopedia Britannica*, volume 4, 1959, p. 416.

Chapman, A. H. 1976. *Harry Stack Sullivan: the man and his work*. New York: G. P. Putnam's Sons.

Eissler, R., and K. Eissler. 1966. Heinz Hartmann: a biographical sketch. In *Psychoanalysis: a general psychology*, ed. R. M. Loewenstein. New York: International Universities Press.

Erikson, E. 1950. *Childhood and society.* New York: Norton.

———— 1962. Reality and actuality. *Journal of the American Psychoanalytic Association* 10: 451–474.

FAIRBAIRN, W. R. D. Unless otherwise noted, all references can be found in *An object-relations theory of the personality.* New York: Basic Books. 1952. (*ORTP*)

———— 1939. Is aggression an irreducible factor? *British Journal of Medical Psychology* 18: 163–170.

———— 1940. Schizoid factors in the personality. *ORTP.*

———— 1941. A revised psychopathology of the psychoses and psychoneuroses. *ORTP.*

———— 1943a. Repression and the return of bad objects (with special reference to the "war neuroses"). *ORTP.*

———— 1943b. The war neuroses—their nature and significance. *ORTP.*

———— 1944. Endopsychic structure considered in terms of object-relationships. *ORTP.*

———— 1946. Object-relationships and dynamic structure. *ORTP.*

———— 1949. Steps in the development of an object-relations theory of the personality. *ORTP.*

———— 1951. Addendum to endopsychic structure considered in terms of object-relationships. *ORTP.*

———— 1952. *ORTP.*

———— 1954. Observations on the nature of hysterical states. *British Journal of Medical Psychology* 27: 105–125.

Fenichel, O. 1945. *The psychoanalytic theory of neurosis.* New York: Norton.

Ferenczi, S. 1921. Psycho-analytic observations on tic. In *Further contributions to the theory and technique of psycho-analysis,* 3rd edition. London: Hogarth Press, 1969.

Freud, A. 1927. Four lectures on child analysis. In *The writings of Anna Freud,* volume 1. New York: International Universities Press, 1974.

———— 1936. *The ego and the mechanisms of defense.* New York: International Universities Press.

———— 1960. Discussion of "Grief and mourning in infancy and early childhood" by J. Bowlby. *Psychoanalytic Study of the Child* 15: 53–62.

———— 1965. *Normality and pathology in childhood.* New York: International Universities Press.

———— 1966. Heinz Hartmann's influence on my work. In *Psychoanalysis: a general psychology,* ed. R. M. Loewenstein. New York: International Universities Press.

FREUD, S. All references are to *The standard edition of the complete psychological works of Sigmund Freud,* volumes 1–24. London: Hogarth Press, 1953–1974. (*SE*)

———— 1894. The neuro-psychoses of defense. *SE,* 3: 43–61.

———— 1895a. Project for a scientific psychology. *SE,* 1: 283–387.

———— 1895b. On the grounds for detaching a particular syndrome from neurasthenia under the description "anxiety neurosis." *SE,* 3: 85–117.

———— 1895c. A reply to criticisms of my paper on anxiety neurosis. *SE,* 3: 119–139.

———— 1896a. Further remarks on the neuro-psychoses of defense. *SE,* 3: 159–185.

———— 1896b. The aetiology of hysteria. *SE,* 3: 187–221.

———— 1896c. Heredity and the aetiology of neuroses. *SE,* 3: 141–156.

———— 1898. Sexuality in the aetiology of the neuroses. *SE,* 3: 259–285.

———— 1900. *The interpretation of dreams. SE,* 4 and 5.

———— 1905a. *Three essays on the theory of sexuality. SE,* 7: 125–245.

———— 1905b. Fragment of an analysis of a case of hysteria. *SE,* 7: 1–122.

———— 1905c. *Jokes and their relation to the unconscious. SE,* 8.

_____ 1906. My views on the part played by sexuality in the aetiology of the neuroses. *SE*, 7: 269–279.

_____ 1909a. Analysis of a phobia in a five-year-old boy. *SE*, 10: 1–149.

_____ 1909b. Notes upon a case of obsessional neurosis. *SE*, 10: 151–318.

_____ 1910a. The psychoanalytic view of psychogenic disturbance of vision. *SE*, 11: 209–218.

_____ 1910b. A special type of choice of object made by men. *SE*, 11: 163–175.

_____ 1910c. *Leonardo da Vinci and a memory of his childhood*. *SE*, 11: 57–137.

_____ 1910d. Five lectures on psycho-analysis. *SE*, 11: 7–55.

_____ 1911a. Formulations on the two principles of mental functioning. *SE*, 12: 218–226.

_____ 1911b. Psycho-analytic notes on an autobiographical account of a case of paranoia (dementia paranoides). *SE*, 12: 1–82.

_____ 1912a. A note on the unconscious in psycho-analysis. *SE*, 12: 255–266.

_____ 1912b. On the universal tendency to debasement in the sphere of love. *SE*, 11: 177–190.

_____ 1912c. Types of onset of neurosis. *SE*, 12: 227–238.

_____ 1912d. Recommendations to physicians practicing psycho-analysis. *SE*, 12: 109–120.

_____ 1912–1913. *Totem and taboo*. *SE*, 13: 1–162.

_____ 1913. The disposition to obsessional neuroses: a contribution to the problem of choice of neurosis. *SE*, 12: 311–326.

_____ 1914a. On narcissism: an introduction. *SE*, 14: 67–102.

_____ 1914b. On the history of the psycho-analytic movement. *SE*, 14: 1–66.

_____ 1915a. Instincts and their vicissitudes. *SE*, 14: 117–140.

_____ 1915b. Repression. *SE*, 14: 141–158.

_____ 1915c. The unconscious. *SE*, 14: 159–215.

_____ 1917a. Mourning and melancholia. *SE*, 14: 237–258.

_____ 1917b. A metapsychological supplement to the theory of dreams. *SE*, 14: 217–235.

_____ 1917c. On transformations of instinct as exemplified in anal erotism. *SE*, 17: 125–133.

_____ 1918a. The taboo of virginity. *SE*, 11: 191–208.

_____ 1918b. From the history of an infantile neurosis. *SE*, 17: 3–122.

_____ 1920a. *Beyond the pleasure principle*. *SE,* 18: 3–64.

_____ 1920b. The psychogenesis of a case of homosexuality in a woman. *SE*, 18: 145–172.

_____ 1921. *Group psychology and the analysis of the ego*. *SE*, 18: 65–143.

_____ 1923a. *The ego and the id*. *SE*, 19, 1–66.

_____ 1923b. The infantile genital organization of the libido: an interpolation into the theory of sexuality. *SE*, 19: 139–145.

_____ 1924a. The economic problem of masochism. *SE*, 19: 155–170.

_____ 1924b. Neurosis and psychosis. *SE*, 19: 147–153.

_____ 1924c. The loss of reality in neurosis and psychosis. *SE*, 19: 181–187.

_____ 1924d. The dissolution of the Oedipus complex. *SE*, 19: 171–179.

_____ 1925a. Some psychical consequences of the anatomical distinction between the sexes. *SE*, 19: 241–258.

_____ 1925b. Negation. *SE*, 19: 233–239.

_____ 1926a. *Inhibitions, symptoms and anxiety*. *SE*, 20: 75–175.

_____ 1926b. The question of lay analysis: conversations with an impartial person. *SE*,

20: 177–258.

_____ 1926c. Psycho-analysis. *SE*. 20: 259–270.

_____ 1927. Fetishism. *SE*, 21: 147–157.

_____ 1930. *Civilization and its discontents*. *SE*, 21: 59–145.

_____ 1931. Female sexuality. *SE*, 21: 221–243 .

_____ 1933. *New introductory lectures on psycho-analysis*. *SE*, 22: 1–182.

_____ 1937. Analysis terminable and interminable. 23: 209–253.

_____ 1937–1939. *Moses and monotheism*. *SE*, 23: 1–137.

_____ 1938. Splitting of the ego in the process of defense. *SE*, 23: 275–278.

_____ 1940. *An outline of psycho-analysis*. *SE*, 23: 139–207.

_____ 1950. Extracts from the Fliess Papers. *SE*, 1: 173–280.

Friedman, L. 1978a. Trends in the psychoanalytic theory of treatment. *Psychoanalytic Quarterly* 47: 524–567.

_____ 1978b. Piaget and psychotherapy. *Journal of the American Academy of Psychoanalysis* 6: 175–192.

Fromm, E. 1941. *Escape from freedom*. New York: Avon.

_____ 1947. *Man for himself*. Greenwich, Conn.: Fawcett.

_____ 1955. *The sane society*. Greenwich, Conn.: Fawcett.

_____ 1962. *Beyond the chains of illusion*. New York: Simon and Schuster.

_____ 1970. *The crisis of psychoanalysis*. Greenwich, Conn.: Fawcett.

Fromm-Reichmann, F. 1950. *Principles of intensive psychotherapy*. Chicago: University of Chicago Press.

_____ 1954. Psychoanalytic and general dynamic conceptions of theory and therapy: differences and similarities. *Journal of the American Psychoanalytic Association* 2: 711–721.

Gedo, J. 1979. *Beyond interpretation: toward a revised theory for psychoanalysis*. New York: International Universities Press.

_____ and A. Goldberg. 1973. *Models of the mind: a psychoanalytic theory*. Chicago: University of Chicago Press.

Gero, G. 1981. Edith Jacobson's work on depression in historical perspective. In *Object and self: a developmental approach*. *Essays in honor of Edith Jacobson*, ed. S. Tuttman, C. Kaye, and M. Zimmerman. New York: International Universities Press.

Gill, M. 1976. Metapsychology is not psychology. In *Psychology versus metapsychology: psychoanalytic essays in memory of George S. Klein*, ed. M. Gill and P. Holzman. *Psychological Issues*, Monograph 36. New York: International Universities Press.

_____ 1982. *Analysis of transference*, volume 1. New York: International Universities Press.

_____ 1983. The point of view of psychoanalysis: energy discharge or person. *Psychoanalysis and Contemporary Thought* 6: in press.

Glover, E. 1961. Some recent trends in psychoanalytic theory. *Psychoanalytic Quarterly* 30: 86–107.

Goldberg, A. 1980. Introductory remarks. In *Advances in self psychology*, ed. A. Goldberg. New York: International Universities Press.

_____ 1981. One theory or more. *Contemporary Psychoanalysis* 17: 626–638.

Greenacre, P. 1957. The childhood of the artist: libidinal phase development and giftedness. *Psychoanalytic Study of the Child* 12: 27–72.

_____ 1958. Early physical determinants in the development of the sense of identity. *Journal of the American Psychoanalytic Association* 6: 612–627.

Greenberg, J. 1981. Prescription or description: the therapeutic action of psychoanalysis. *Contemporary Psychoanalysis* 17: 239–257.

Greenson, R. 1967. *The technique and practice of psychoanalysis*, volume 1. New York: International Universities Press.

———— 1971. The "real" relationship between the patient and the psychoanalyst. In *Explorations in Psychoanalysis*. New York: International Universities Press, 1978.

———— and M. Wexler. 1969. The nontransference relationship in the psychoanalytic situation. In *Explorations in Psychoanalysis*. New York: International Universities Press, 1978.

Guntrip, H. 1961. *Personality structure and human interaction: the developing synthesis of psychodynamic theory.* New York: International Universities Press.

———— 1969. *Schizoid phenomena, object relations and the self.* New York: International Universities Press.

———— 1971. *Psychoanalytic theory, therapy and the self.* New York: Basic Books.

———— 1975. My experience of analysis with Fairbairn and Winnicott. *International Review of Psychoanalysis* 2: 145–156.

HARTMANN, H. Unless otherwise noted, references are from *Essays on ego psychology.* New York: International Universities Press, 1964. (*EEP*); or from *Papers on psychoanalytic psychology. Psychological Issues*, Monograph 14. New York: International Universities Press, 1964. (*PPP*)

———— 1927. Understanding and explanation. *EEP*.

———— 1927 [1964]. Concept formation in psychoanalysis. *Psychoanalytic Study of the Child* 19: 11–47.

———— 1933. An experimental contribution to the psychology of obsessive-compulsive neurosis. *EEP*.

———— 1934–35. Psychiatric studies of twins. *EEP*.

———— 1939a. *Ego psychology and the problem of adaptation.* New York: International Universities Press.

———— 1939b. Psychoanalysis and the concept of health. *EEP*.

———— 1944. Psychoanalysis and sociology. *EEP*.

———— 1947. On rational and irrational action. *EEP*.

———— 1948. Comments on the psychoanalytic theory of instinctual drives. *EEP*.

———— 1950a. Comments on the psychoanalytic theory of the ego. *EEP*.

———— 1950b. Psychoanalysis and developmental psychology. *EEP*.

———— 1950c. The application of psychoanalytic concepts to social science. *EEP*.

———— 1951. Technical implications of ego psychology. *EEP*.

———— 1952. The mutual influences in the development of ego and id. *EEP*.

———— 1953. Contribution to the metapsychology of schizophrenia. *EEP*.

———— 1955. Notes on the theory of sublimation. *EEP*.

———— 1956a. Notes on the reality principle. *EEP*.

———— 1956b. The development of the ego concept in Freud's work. *EEP*.

———— 1958. Comments on the scientific aspects of psychoanalysis. *EEP*.

———— 1959. Psychoanalysis as a scientific theory. *EEP*.

———— 1960. *Psychoanalysis and moral values.* New York: International Universities Press.

———— and E. Kris. 1945. The genetic approach in psychoanalysis. *PPP*.

———— E. Kris, and R. Loewenstein. 1946. Comments on the formation of psychic structure. *PPP*.

———— 1949. Notes on the theory of aggression. *PPP*.

———— 1951. Some psychoanalytic comments on "culture and personality." *PPP*.

———— 1953. The function of theory in psychoanalysis. *PPP*.

_____ and R. Loewenstein. 1962. Notes on the superego. *PPP*.

Havens, L. 1976. *Participant observation*. New York: Jason Aronson.

_____ and J. Frank, Jr. 1971. Review of P. Mullahy, *Psychoanalysis and interpersonal psychiatry*. *American Journal of Psychiatry* 127: 1704–1705.

Hegel, G. 1821. *Hegel's philosophy of right*, trans. T. M. Knox. Oxford: Clarendon. 1952.

Heimann, P. 1952a. Certain functions of introjection and projection in early infancy. In *Developments in psycho-analysis*, ed. M. Klein, P. Heimann, and J. Riviere. London: Hogarth Press.

_____ 1952b. Notes on the theory of the life and death instincts. In *Developments in psycho-analysis*, ed. M. Klein, P. Heimann, and J. Riviere. London: Hogarth Press.

Hobbes, T. 1651. *Leviathan*. Oxford: Basil Blackwell. N.d.

Holt, R. 1976. Drive or wish? A reconsideration of the psychoanalytic theory of motivation. In *Psychology versus metapsychology: psychoanalytic essays in memory of George S. Klein*, ed. M. Gill and P. Holzman. *Psychological Issues*, Monograph 36. New York: International Universities Press.

Horney, K. 1937. *The neurotic personality of our time*. New York: Norton.

_____ 1939. *New ways in psychoanalysis*. New York: Norton.

Isaacs, S. 1943. The nature and function of phantasy. In M. Klein, P. Heimann, S. Isaacs, and J. Riviere, *Developments in psycho-analysis*. London: Hogarth Press, 1952.

Jacobson, E. 1943. Depression: the Oedipus conflict in the development of depressive mechanisms. *Psychoanalytic Quarterly* 12: 541–560.

_____ 1946a. The effect of disappointment on ego and super-ego formation in normal and depressive development. *Psychoanalytic Review* 33: 129–147.

_____ 1946b. A case of sterility. *Psychoanalytic Quarterly* 15: 330–350.

_____ 1949. Observations on the psychological effect of imprisonment on female political prisoners. In *Searchlight on delinquency*, ed. K. R. Eissler. New York: International Universities Press.

_____ 1953. The affects and their pleasure-unpleasure qualities in relation to the psychic discharge process. In *Drives, affects, behavior*, ed. R. M. Loewenstein. New York: International Universities Press.

_____ 1954a. The self and the object world. *Psychoanalytic Study of the Child* 9: 75–127.

_____ 1954b. Transference problems in the psychoanalytic treatment of severely depressed patients. *Journal of the American Psychoanalytic Association* 2: 595–606.

_____ 1954c. Contribution to the metapsychology of psychotic identifications. *Journal of the American Psychoanalytic Association* 2: 239–262.

_____ 1954d. On psychotic identifications. *International Journal of Psycho-Analysis* 35: 102–108.

_____ 1955. Review of Sullivan's *Interpersonal theory of psychiatry*. *Journal of the American Psychoanalytic Association* 3: 149–156.

_____ 1959. Depersonalization. *Journal of the American Psychoanalytic Association* 7: 581–610.

_____ 1964. *The self and the object world*. New York: International Universities Press.

_____ 1967. *Psychotic conflict and reality*. New York: International Universities Press.

_____ 1971. *Depression: comparitive studies of normal, neurotic and psychotic conditions*. New York: International Universities Press.

Jung, C. G. 1913. *The theory of psychoanalysis*. In C. G. Jung, *Critique of psychoanalysis*. Princeton, N.J.: Princeton University Press, 1975.

Kardiner, A. 1977. *My analysis with Freud: reminiscences*. New York: Norton.

Kernberg, O. 1975. *Borderline conditions and pathological narcissism*. New York: Jason Aronson.

———— 1976. *Object relations theory and clinical psychoanalysis*. New York: Jason Aronson.

———— 1979. An overview of Edith Jacobson's contributions. *Journal of the American Psychoanalytic Association* 27: 793–819.

———— 1980. *Internal world and external reality*. New York: Jason Aronson.

———— 1982. Self, ego, affects, and drives. *Journal of the American Psychoanalytic Association* 30: 893–917.

Khan, M. 1975. Introduction to D.W. Winnicott, *Through paediatrics to psycho-analysis*. London: Hogarth Press.

Klein, G. 1976. *Psychoanalytic theory: an exploration of essentials*. New York: International Universities Press.

KLEIN, M. Unless otherwise noted, references are from *Contributions to psychoanalysis, 1921–1945*. New York: McGraw-Hill, 1964. (*CP*)
    or from *Envy and gratitude and other works, 1946–1963*. New York: Delacorte Press, 1975. (*EG*)

———— 1923. The role of the school in the libidinal development of the child. *CP*.

———— 1925. A contribution to the psychogenesis of tics. *CP*.

———— 1928. Early stages of the Oedipus conflict. *CP*.

———— 1929. Infantile anxiety-situations reflected in a work of art and in the creative impulse. *CP*.

———— 1930. The importance of symbol-formation in the development of the ego. *CP*.

———— 1931. A contribution to the theory of intellectual inhibitions. *CP*.

———— 1932. *The psycho-analysis of children*. London: Hogarth Press.

———— 1933. The early development of conscience in the child. *CP*.

———— 1935. A contribution to the psychogenesis of manic-depressive states. *CP*.

———— 1936. The psychotherapy of the psychoses. *CP*.

———— 1940. Mourning and its relation to manic-depressive states. *CP*.

———— 1945. The Oedipus complex in light of early anxieties. *CP*.

———— 1946. Notes on some schizoid mechanisms. *EG*.

———— 1948. On the theory of anxiety and guilt. *EG*.

———— 1952a. The mutual influences in the development of ego and id. *EG*.

———— 1952b. The origins of transference. *EG*.

———— 1952c. Some theoretical conclusions regarding the emotional life of the infant. *EG*.

———— 1952d. On observing the behavior of young infants. *EG*.

———— 1957. *Envy and gratitude*. *EG*.

———— 1958. On the development of mental functioning. *EG*.

———— 1959. Our adult world and its roots in infancy. *EG*.

———— 1960. A note on depression in the schizophrenic. *EG*.

———— 1964. Love, guilt and reparation. In M. Klein and J. Riviere, *Love, hate and reparation*. New York: W. W. Norton and Co., 1964.

Klein, M. and D. Tribich. 1981. Kernberg's object-relations theory: a critical evaluation. *International Journal of Psychoanalysis* 62: 27–43.

Klenbort, I. 1978. Another look at Sullivan's concept of individuality. *Contemporary Psychoanalysis* 14: 125–135.

Kohut, H. 1971. *The analysis of the self*. New York: International Universities Press.

———— 1977. *The restoration of the self*. New York: International Universities Press.

_____ 1980. Summarizing reflections. In *Advances in self psychology*, ed. A. Goldberg. New York: International Universities Press.

_____ 1982. Introspection, empathy and the semi-circle of mental health. *International Journal of Psycho-Analysis* 63: 395–407.

Konner, M. 1982. *The tangled wing: biological constraints on the human spirit*. New York: Holt, Rinehart and Winston.

Kris, E. 1952. *Psychoanalytic explorations in art*. New York: International Universities Press.

Kuhn, T. 1962. *The structure of scientific revolutions*, 2nd edition. Chicago: University of Chicago Press.

_____ 1977. *The essential tension*. Chicago: University of Chicago Press.

Laing, R. and A. Esterson. 1964. *Sanity, madness and the family*. London: Tavistock.

Lampl-de Groot, J. 1928. The evolution of the Oedipus complex in women. *International Journal of Psychoanalysis* 9: 332–345.

Levenson, E. 1972. *The fallacy of understanding*. New York: Basic Books.

Lichtenberg, J. 1979. Factors in the development of the sense of the object. *Journal of the American Psychoanalytic Association* 27: 375–386.

Lichtenstein, H. 1977. *The dilemma of human identity*. New York: Jason Aronson.

Lifton, R. 1976. From analysis to formation: toward a shift in psychoanalytic paradigm. *Journal of the American Academy of Psychoanalysis* 4: 65–94.

Locke, J. 1690. *Two treatises of government*. New York: Mentor, 1947.

Loewald, H. 1960. On the therapeutic action of psychoanalysis. *International Journal of Psychoanalysis* 58: 463–472.

Loewenstein, R. 1966. Heinz Hartmann: psychology of the ego. In *Psychoanalytic pioneers*, ed. F. Alexander et al. New York: Basic Books.

Maccoby, M. 1972. Developments in Erich Fromm's approach to psychoanalysis. Address delivered to the William Alanson White Psychoanalytic Society, New York, December 6, 1972.

Mahler [Schoenberger], M. 1941. Discussion of Dr. Silberpfennig's paper: Mother types encountered in child guidance clinics. *American Journal of Orthopsychiatry* 11: 484.

_____ 1942. Pseudoimbicility: a magic cap of invisibility. *Psychoanalytic Quarterly* 11: 149–164.

Mahler, M. 1946. Ego psychology applied to behavior problems. In *Modern trends in child psychiatry*, ed. N. D. C. Lewis and B. L. Pacella. New York: International Universities Press.

_____ 1949. A psychoanalytic evaluation of tic in psychopathology of children: symptomatic tic and tic syndrome. *Psychoanalytic Study of the Child* 3–4: 279–310.

_____ 1952. On child psychosis and schizophrenia: autistic and symbiotic infantile psychoses. *Psychoanalytic Study of the Child* 7: 286–305.

_____ 1958a. Autism and symbiosis: two extreme disturbances of identity. *International Journal of Psychoanalysis* 39: 77–83.

_____ 1958b. On two crucial phases of integration of the sense of identity: separation-individuation and bisexual identity. *Journal of the American Psychoanalytic Association* 6: 136–139.

_____ 1960. Symposium on psychotic object-relationship: III. Perceptual de-differentiation and psychotic "object relationship." *International Journal of Psychoanalysis* 41: 548–553.

_____ 1961. On sadness and grief in infancy and childhood: loss and restoration of the symbiotic love object. *Psychoanalytic Study of the Child* 16: 332–351.

_____ 1963. Thoughts about development and individuation. *Psychoanalytic Study of the Child* 18: 307–324.

_____ 1965. On the significance of the normal separation-individuation phase: with reference to research in symbiotic child psychosis. In *Drives, affects, behavior*, volume 2, ed. M. Schur. New York: International Universities Press.

_____ 1966. Notes on the development of basic moods: the depressive affect. In *Psychoanalysis—a general psychology: essays in honor of Heinz Hartmann*, ed. R. Loewenstein, L. Newman, M. Schur, and A. Solnit. New York: International Universities Press.

_____ 1967. On human symbiosis and the vicissitudes of individuation. *Journal of the American Psychoanalytic Association* 15: 740–763.

_____ 1968. *On human symbiosis and the vicissitudes of individuation*, volume 1, *Infantile psychosis*. New York: International Universities Press.

_____ 1971. A study of the separation-individuation process and its possible application to borderline phenomena in the psychoanalytic situation. *Psychoanalytic Study of the Child* 26: 403–424.

_____ 1972a. Rapprochement subphase of the separation-individuation process. *Psychoanalytic Quarterly* 41: 487–506.

_____ 1972b. On the first three subphases of the separation-individuation process. *International Journal of Psychoanalysis* 53: 333–338.

_____ 1974. Symbiosis and individuation: the psychological birth of the human infant. In *The selected papers of Margaret S. Mahler*, volume 2. New York: Jason Aronson.

_____ 1975. On the current status of the infantile neurosis. In *The selected papers of Margaret S. Mahler*, volume 2. New York: Jason Aronson.

_____ and M. Furer. 1963. Certain aspects of the separation-individuation phase. *Psychoanalytic Quarterly* 32: 1–14.

_____ M. Furer, and C. Settlage. 1959. Severe emotional disturbances in childhood psychosis. In *American Handbook of Psychiatry*, volume 1, ed. S. Arieti. New York: Basic Books.

_____ and B. Gosliner. 1955. On symbiotic child psychosis: genetic, dynamic and restitutive aspects. *Psychoanalytic Study of the Child* 10: 195–212.

_____ J. Luke, and W. Daltroff. 1945. Clinical and follow-up study of tic syndrome in children. *American Journal of Orthopsychiatry* 15: 631–647.

_____ and J. McDevitt. 1968. Observations on adaptation and defense in statu nascendi: developmental precursors in the first two years of life. *Psychoanalytic Quarterly* 37: 1–21.

_____ 1982. Thoughts on the emergence of the sense of self, with particular emphasis on the body self. *Journal of the American Psychoanalytic Association* 30: 827–848.

_____ F. Pine, and A. Bergman. 1975. The psychological birth of the human infant: symbiosis and individuation. New York: Basic Books.

_____ and R. Rabinovitch. 1956. The effects of marital conflict on child development. In *Neurotic interaction in marriage*, ed. V. W. Eisenstein. New York: Basic Books.

_____ J. Ross, and Z. DeFries. 1949. Clinical studies in benign and malignant cases of childhood psychosis (schizophrenia-like). *American Journal of Orthopsychiatry* 19: 292–305.

Marcuse, H. 1955. *Eros and Civilization*. Boston: Beacon Press.

Marx, K. 1845. Theses on Feuerbach. In *Basic writings on politics and philosophy: Karl Marx and Friedrich Engels*, ed. L. Feuer. Garden City, N.Y.: Anchor, 1959.

_____ 1852. *The eighteenth brumaire of Louis Bonaparte*. New York: International

Publishers, 1963.

Masterman, M. 1970. The nature of a paradigm. In *Criticism and the growth of knowledge*, ed. I. Lakatos and A. Musgrave. Cambridge: Cambridge University Press.

McDevitt, J., and C. Settlage. 1971. Editor's foreword to *Separation-individuation: essays in honor of Margaret S. Mahler*. New York: International Universities Press.

Meissner, W. 1976. A note on internalization as process. *Psychoanalytic Quarterly* 45: 374–393.

_____ 1980. A note on projective identification. *Journal of the American Psychoanalytic Association* 28: 43–68.

Meltzer, D. 1974. Mutism in infantile autism, schizophrenia and manic-depressive states. *International Journal of Psychoanalysis* 55: 397–404.

Mendez, A., and R. Fine. 1976. A short history of the British school of object relations and ego psychology. *Bulletin of the Menninger Clinic* 40: 357–382.

Mitchell, S. 1981. The origin and nature of the "object" in Klein and Fairbairn. *Contemporary Psychoanalysis* 17: 374–398.

Modell, A. 1968. *Object love and reality*. New York: International Universities Press.

Muslin, H. 1979. Transference in the Rat Man case: the transference in transition. *Journal of the American Psychoanalytic Association* 27: 561–578.

_____ and M. Gill. 1978. Transference in the Dora case. *Journal of the American Psychoanalytic Association* 26: 311–328.

Nunberg, H. 1930. The synthetic function of the ego. In *Practice and theory of psychoanalysis*. New York: International Universities Press, 1960.

Ornston, D. 1982. Strachey's influence: a preliminary report. *International Journal of Psycho-Analysis* 63: 409–426.

Perry, H. S. 1964. Introduction to H. S. Sullivan, *The fusion of psychiatry and social science*. New York: Norton.

_____ 1982. *Psychiatrist of America: the life of Harry Stack Sullivan*. Cambridge, Mass.: Harvard University Press.

Piaget, J. 1937. *The construction of reality in the child*. New York: Basic Books, 1954.

Racker, H. 1968. *Transference and countertransference*. New York: International Universities Press.

Rangell, L. 1954. Similarities and differences between psychoanalysis and dynamic psychotherapy. *Journal of the American Psychoanalytic Association* 2: 734–744.

_____ 1965. The scope of Heinz Hartmann. *International Journal of Psychoanalysis* 46: 5–30.

_____ 1982. The self in psychoanalytic theory. *Journal of the American Psychoanalytic Society* 30: 863–891.

Rank, O. 1929. *The trauma of birth*. New York: Harper and Row, 1973.

RAPAPORT, D. Unless otherwise noted, all references are from *The collected papers of David Rapaport*, ed. M. Gill. New York: Basic Books, 1967. (CPDR)

_____ 1951a. The autonomy of the ego. *CPDR*.

_____ 1951b. The conceptual model of psychoanalysis. *CPDR*.

_____ 1957. A theoretical analysis of the superego concept. *CPDR*.

_____ 1958. A historical survey of psychoanalytic ego psychology. *CPDR*.

_____ and M. Gill. 1959. The points of view and assumptions of metapsychology. *CPDR*.

Richards, A. 1982. The superordinate self in psychoanalytic theory and in the self psychologies. *Journal of the American Psychoanalytic Association* 30: 939–957.

Ricoeur, P. 1970. *Freud and philosophy: an essay on interpretation*. New Haven: Yale

University Press.

Riviere, J. 1936a. On the genesis of psychical conflict in early infancy. *International Journal of Psychoanalysis* 55: 397–404.

———— 1936b. A contribution to the analysis of the negative therapeutic reaction. *International Journal of Psychoanalysis* 17: 304–320.

Rosenfeld, H. 1965. *Psychotic states: a psychoanalytic approach*. New York: International Universities Press.

Ross, N. 1970. The primacy of genitality in the light of ego psychology. *Journal of the American Psychoanalytic Association* 18: 267–284.

Rousseau, J. 1755. *Discourse on the origin and foundations of inequality*. In *The first and second discourses*. New York: St. Martin's, 1964.

———— 1762. *The social contract*. Chicago: Gateway, 1954.

Sandler, J. 1976. Countertransference and role-responsiveness. *International Review of Psycho-Analysis* 3: 43–47.

———— 1981. Unconscious wishes and human relationships. *Contemporary Psychoanalysis* 17: 180–196.

———— and B. Rosenblatt. 1962. The concept of the representational world. *Psychoanalytic Study of the Child* 17: 128–145.

———— and A. Sandler. 1978. On the development of object relationships and affects. *International Journal of Psychoanalysis* 59: 285–296.

Schachtel, E. 1959. *Metamorphosis*. New York: Basic Books.

Schafer, R. 1968. *Aspects of internalization*. New York: International Universities Press.

———— 1972. Internationalization: process or fantasy? *Psychoanalytic Study of the Child* 27: 411–436.

———— 1976. *A new language for psychoanalysis*. New Haven: Yale University Press.

———— 1978. *Language and insight*. New Haven: Yale University Press.

———— 1979. On becoming an analyst of one persuasion or another. *Contemporary Psychoanalysis* 15: 345–368.

———— 1983. *The analytic attitude*. New York: Basic Books.

Searles, H. 1965. Identity development in Edith Jacobson's *The self and the object world*. *International Journal of Psychoanalysis* 46: 529–532.

Segal, H. 1964. *Introduction to the work of Melanie Klein*. New York: Basic Books.

———— 1979. *Klein*. Glasgow: Fontana/Collins.

———— 1981. *The work of Hanna Segal*. New York: Jason Aronson.

Shapiro, D. 1981. *Autonomy and rigid character*. New York: Basic Books.

Spence, D. 1982. *Narrative truth and historical truth: meaning and interpretation in psychoanalysis*. New York: Norton.

Spitz, R. 1945. Hospitalism: an inquiry into the genesis of psychiatric conditions in early childhood. *Psychoanalytic Study of the Child* 1: 53–73.

———— 1946. Anaclitic depression: an inquiry into the genesis of psychiatric conditions in early childhood, II. *Psychoanalytic Study of the Child* 2: 313–342.

———— 1965. *The first year of life*. New York: International Universities Press.

Stern, D. 1974. The goal and structure of mother-infant play. *Journal of the American Academy of Child Psychiatry* 22: 268–278.

———— 1977. *The first relationship: mother and infant*. Cambridge, Mass.: Harvard University Press.

Stierlin, H. 1970. The functions of inner objects. *International Journal of Psychoanalysis* 51: 321–329.

Stolorow, R., and G. Atwood. 1979. *Faces in a cloud: subjectivity in personality theory*.

New York: Jason Aronson

Stolorow, R., and F. Lachmann. 1980. *Psychoanalysis of developmental arrests*. New York: International Press.

Strachey, J. 1934. The nature of the therapeutic action of psychoanalysis. *International Journal of Psychoanalysis* 15: 127–159.

———— 1966. Notes on some technical terms whose translation calls for comment. In *The standard edition of the complete psychological works of Sigmund Freud*, volume 1. London: Hogarth Press.

Sugarman, A. 1977. Object-relations theory: a reconciliation of phenomenology and ego psychology. *Bulletin of the Menninger Clinic* 41: 113–130.

SULLIVAN, H. S. Unless otherwise noted, references are from *Schizophrenia as a human process*. New York: Norton, 1962. (*SHP*)
or from *The fusion of psychiatry and social science*. New York: Norton, 1964. (*FPSS*)

———— 1924. Schizophrenia: its conservative and malignant features. *SHP*.

———— 1925a. Peculiarity of thought in schizophrenia. *SHP*.

———— 1925b. The oral complex. *Psychoanalytic Review* 12: 31–38.

———— 1927. Tentative criteria of malignancy in schizophrenia. *SHP*.

———— 1929. Archaic sexual culture and schizophrenia. *SHP*.

———— 1930. Socio-psychiatric research. *SHP*.

———— 1931. The modified psychoanalytic treatment of schizophrenia. *SHP*

———— 1934. Psychiatric training as a prerequisite to psychoanalytic practice. *SHP*.

———— 1936. A note on the implications of psychiatry on the study of interpersonal relations for investigators in the social sciences. *FPSS*.

———— 1938a. The data of psychiatry. *FPSS*.

———— 1938b. Anti-semitism. *FPSS*.

———— 1940. *Conceptions of modern psychiatry*. New York: Norton.

———— 1948. Beliefs versus a rational psychiatry. *FPSS*.

———— 1950a. The illusion of personal individuality. *FPSS*.

———— 1950b. Tensions interpersonal and international: a psychiatrist's view. *FPSS*.

———— 1953. *The interpersonal theory of psychiatry*. New York: Norton.

———— 1956. *Clinical studies in psychiatry*. New York: Norton.

———— 1972. *Personal psychopathology*. New York: Norton.

Sulloway, F. 1979. *Freud: biologist of the mind*. New York: Basic Books.

Suppe, F. 1977. *The structure of scientific theories*, 2nd edition. Chicago: University of Illinois Press.

Thomas, A., and S. Chess. 1980. *The dynamics of psychological development*. New York: Brunner-Mazel.

Thompson, C. 1964. *Interpersonal Psychoanalysis*, ed. M. Green. New York: Basic Books.

Waelder, R. 1930. The principle of multiple function. *Psychoanalytic Quarterly* 15: 45–62, 1936.

WINNICOTT, D. W. Unless otherwise noted, references are from the *Through paediatrics to psycho-analysis*. London: Hogarth Press, 1958. (*TPP*)
or from *The maturational process and the facilitating environment*. New York: International Universities Press, 1965. (*MPFE*)

———— 1936. Appetite and emotional development. *TPP*.

———— 1941. The observation of infants in a set situation. *TPP*.

———— 1945. Primitive emotional development. *TPP*.

———— 1947. Hate in the countertransference. *TPP*.

———— 1948a. Paediatrics and psychiatry. *TPP*.

———— 1948b. Reparation in respect of mother's organized defense against depression. *TPP*.

———— 1949a. Mind and its relation to the psyche-soma. *TPP*

———— 1949b. Birth memories, birth trauma, and anxiety. *TPP*.

———— 1950. Aggression in relation to emotional development. *TPP*.

———— 1951. Transitional objects and transitional phenomena. *TPP*.

———— 1952a. Anxiety associated with insecurity. *TPP*.

———— 1952b. Psychoses and child care. *TPP*.

———— 1954a. Metapsychological and clinical aspects of regression within the psychoanalytical setup. *TPP*.

———— 1954b. The depressive position in normal emotional development. *TPP*.

———— 1956a. Primary maternal preoccupation. *TPP*.

———— 1956b. The antisocial tendency. *TPP*.

———— 1956c. Paediatrics and childhood neurosis. *TPP*.

———— 1958a. The sense of guilt. *MPFE*.

———— 1958b. The capacity to be alone. *MPFE*.

———— 1959. Classification: is there a psycho-analytic contribution to psychiatric classification? *MPFE*

———— 1960a. The theory of the parent-infant relationship. *MPFE*.

———— 1960b. Ego distortion in terms of true and false self. *MPFE*.

———— 1962a. Ego integration in child development. *MPFE*.

———— 1962b. A personal view of the Kleinian contribution. *MPFE*.

———— 1963. Communicating and not communicating leading to a study of certain opposites. *MPFE*.

———— 1965a. *MPFE*.

———— 1965b. *The family and individual development*. London: Tavistock.

———— 1971. *Playing and reality*. Middlesex, England: Penguin.

———— and M. Khan. 1953. A review of Fairbairn's *Psychoanalytic studies of the personality*. *International Journal of Psychoanalysis* 34: 329–333.

Witenberg, E. 1979. Are object relations as much fun as interpersonal relations? Or vice versa? Address delivered to the William Alanson White Psychoanalytic Society, New York.

Wolf, E. 1980. On the developmental line of selfobject relations. In *Advances in self psychology*, ed. A. Goldberg. New York: International Universities Press.

Wolstein, B. 1971. Interpersonal relations without individuality. *Contemporary Psychoanalysis* 8: 75–80.

Index

Abraham, Karl, 119, 120, 157

Accommodation, strategy of, 37, 50-78, 233-348, 379-380, 382, 393, 398

Action, 19, 226, 239, 245. *See also* Reality

Activity, 19, 48-49, 91; ego, 70, 122, 244; phantasied, 131; distinction between, and energy, 155; and aggression, 206. *See also* Autonomy

Actualization, 375-376

Adaptation: and psychological development, 194, 236; parental failures in, 199-200, 201; and ego, 242, 246; and motivation, 243, 263, 267, 380; and action, 245; modes of, 247, 250, 268; and reality, 251, 265, 266; and equilibrium, 257, 267-269; and art, 268-269; to human environment, 272, 282-284, 304; infant's capacity for, 284; and theoretical accommodation, 301. *See also* Hartmann, Heinz; Symbiosis

Adler, Alfred, 2, 25, 50-51, 52, 53, 79

Adolescence, 112, 186, 223

Affect, 64-67, 317-319, 344; and drives, 25-27, 52, 318, 331, 336, 337, 339, 341, 377n, 381; early expression of, 273, 294; and splitting, 329, 332-333

Affirmation, 377

Agency, 70-71, 106, 109, 154, 155

Aggression: in relational theory, 32, 183, 404; and drives, 62n, 64, 251, 261, 292, 308, 313; Freud's view of, 74, 123-124, 142, 213, 312; and culture, 106, 107; focus on, in Kleinian theory, 120, 123, 125, 126, 131, 132, 135, 138-139, 140, 142, 144, 145, 146-147, 175-176, 202, 205, 220, 224; and envy, 128-130; and Fairbairn's theory of motivation, 159, 169-170, 171; Winnicott's view of, 205, 206; and parental attitudes, 254, 316, 355-356; and energy, 257, 313; and ego, 258, 259; and neutralization, 258-259, 292, 312; Kernberg's definition of, 332; and bad selfobject representation, 337, 338, 340; and object-seeking, 405; projected, 406. *See also* Hate

Aims, instinctual: and libido, 37, 64; origin of, 61-62; diversion of, 63; and object relations, 68, 72, 141, 337, 374; of children, 74; and tension, 138, 140; and bodily functions, 140-141; and social reality, 167; and development, 390

Aloneness, 108-109, 110, 111, 112

Ambivalence: in Sullivan's theory, 112; and depressive dynamics, 171-172, 332; in Freudian theory, 207; in